SIR PHILIP SIDNEY AS A LITERARY CRAFTSMAN

By

KENNETH MYRICK

A BISON BOOK

UNIVERSITY OF NEBRASKA PRESS · LINCOLN

To

MY MOTHER

PREFACE TO THE SECOND EDITION

IN this edition no changes have been made in the text, except for the correction of a few misprints and the revision of a few passages translated from Friedrich Brie's study of Sidney's *Arcadia*. When other changes have seemed necessary, I have supplied them in notes at the end of the book, beginning on page 350. The notes are signalled in the text by an asterisk.

The extraordinarily involved plot of the *Arcadia* and the plethora of characters (numbering well over a hundred) present formidable obstacles even to the most conscientious reader. He is therefore provided in the Appendix with a summary of the plot and a list identifying all the characters of any significance.

I take pleasure in acknowledging the aid and encouragement I have received from others. To Dr. Thomas J. Wilson, Director of the Harvard University Press, I am indebted for permission to have this book republished by another university press. To Professor John C. Wells, of the Tufts Department of German, I give my warm thanks for aid in revising the translations from German.

My special debt is to a young friend and gifted scholar, Professor William Leigh Godshalk, of the College of William and Mary, a former colleague in the Tufts Department of English, and a special student of Sidney. The fully annotated Bibliography of Sidney Studies since 1935 is entirely his work.

My deepest obligation is to my wife for her assistance and quiet encouragement.

K. M.

Tufts University
Medford, Massachusetts
July 18, 1965

PREFACE

THIS book is addressed chiefly to the reader who has more than a passing acquaintance with the writings of Sir Philip Sidney. The scholar, however, will find few items of information that he cannot easily find elsewhere. What I have attempted is a new synthesis of facts which for the most part are already well known. In the urbane quality which Castiglione called *sprezzatura* I have sought a key alike to Sidney's character and to his artistic temper. That this approach does not give the whole truth need hardly be said while studies like Miss Denkinger's and Mr. Goldman's are being made from year to year. Certain aspects of Sidney's work, moreover, I have deliberately omitted or have touched only lightly.

So far as it goes, this essay at reinterpretation would not have been possible without the labors of many scholars during the past generation. To the writings of Mr. Spingarn and the late Mr. Greenlaw, and to M. Feuillerat's definitive edition of Sidney's works, I owe much more than can be acknowledged in footnotes or a preface. It is a pleasure to thank Mr. Bennett M. Hollowell for permission to quote from his doctoral dissertation. In interpreting several passages from Latin or Italian I have had generous help from my colleagues, Professors William K. Denison and George H. Gifford of Tufts College, and from my old teacher, Professor E. K. Rand of Harvard; although for the translations as they stand the responsibility is my own. At an early period of my study I had valuable criticism from a number of friends. My special gratitude is due to four Harvard teachers. To Mr. Lowes, Mr. Rand, and the late Irving Babbitt I am indebted for courses which have been indispensable in this study, for wise counsel, and for unfailing kindness. Finally, to Mr. Rollins, who has patiently gone over every part of the work, I owe invaluable assistance in all that makes the scholar's craft a science and a fine art.

K. O. M.

MEDFORD, MASSACHUSETTS
April 26, 1935

CONTENTS

SIR PHILIP SIDNEY AS A
LITERARY CRAFTSMAN

An asterisk following a word in the text indicates that a note appears in the section beginning on page 350.

CHAPTER I

Humanist, Courtier, and Poet

ACCORDING to the opinion prevailing among scholars, Sidney regarded his literary work as "never more than a pleasant pastime." [1] This view has been challenged, to be sure, by the late Edwin Greenlaw,[2] by Herr Friedrich Brie,[3] and by one or two other scholars. And yet it remains a dogma of criticism. It is restated, though with modifications, by a recent student of the *Arcadia*,[4] and has not been quite discarded by one of the latest and best of Sidney's biographers.[5]

The view has much to recommend it, for it appears to be authorized by Sidney's own words, and it seems to explain certain puzzling contradictions which nearly every modern reader feels on first examining the *Arcadia*, the *Defence of Poesie*, and *Astrophel and Stella*. As a man, Sir Philip Sidney has a perennial fascination for all who belong to the English tradition. In his lifetime he seemed to draw all men to him, and in the three and a half centuries since he died his story has become one of the legends of his race. How could this able man of action have taken seriously a work like the *Arcadia*? For most of us today, as for Haz-

1. H. R. Fox Bourne, *Sir Philip Sidney*, 1891, p. 255.
2. "Sidney's *Arcadia* as an Example of Elizabethan Allegory," *Kittredge Anniversary Papers*, 1913, pp. 327–337; "The Captivity Episode in Sidney's *Arcadia*," *Manly Anniversary Studies*, 1923, pp. 54–63.
3. *Sidneys Arcadia, Eine Studie zur Englischen Renaissance, Quellen und Forschungen*, CXXIV (1918).
4. R. W. Zandvoort, *Sidney's Arcadia, A Comparison between the Two Versions*, 1929, pp. 120–135.
5. Mona Wilson, *Sir Philip Sidney*, 1931, pp. 142–143.

litt, it is "one of the greatest monuments of the abuse of
intellectual power upon record." [1] And it seems at variance
not only with Sidney's character, but with his other works.
"This man of tact, this clever critic, this admirable poet,"
says Jusserand, "has left samples of such refined bad taste
that the most perverse imagination could scarcely invent
worse." [2]   The contradictions disappear if we suppose
Sidney to have looked on his literary work, or at least
the *Arcadia*, as merely "a pleasant pastime." Moreover, his
friend and first biographer, Fulke Greville, declares that
Sidney's books "were scribled rather as pamphlets, for
entertainment of time, and friends, than any accompt of
himself to the world." [3]   And finally, Sidney himself refers
to the *Defence of Poesie* as an "inck-wasting toy"; [4] and in
his famous letter to the Countess of Pembroke, prefaced
to the printed editions of the *Arcadia*, he calls this work
also "a trifle, and that triflinglie handled." [5]

The evidence is impressive.   And yet it is not conclusive.
It depends in part upon our personal impressions of Sidney's works, and impressions are notoriously unreliable.
If we moderns are bored or exasperated by the *Arcadia*,
the Elizabethans admired it and distinguished it not as the
worst but the best of the author's writings.   Greville mentions no other, and though he thinks it gives a very imperfect "accompt" of his friend "to the world," yet he
bestows upon it six pages of glowing praise. [6]   There is
therefore only one strong support for the view that Sidney
did not regard his literary work seriously: namely, his own
disparaging references to it, and particularly his letter to
the Countess of Pembroke.

1. Hazlitt, *Collected Works*, ed. Waller and Glover, V (1902), 320.
2. *A Literary History of the English People*, 2nd ed., II (1926), 535.
3. *Life of Sir Philip Sidney*, ed. Nowell Smith, 1907, p. 17.
4. *Complete Works*, ed. Feuillerat, Cambridge English Classics, 1912–1926,
III, 45.
5. I, 3.
6. Greville, pp. 11–17.

Now to this letter a new interpretation has been attached ever since the late Bertram Dobell discovered the original version of the *Arcadia*.[1] In the partly revised version known to generations of readers, the romance falls into two disconnected fragments. In the original draft, however, it is an unbroken and unified whole. Because in the letter to his sister the author refers to the *Arcadia* as though he was at last done with it, all scholars agree that he is speaking of the first draft, the only one that he ever brought to completion. Hence even if Sidney intended his modest words to be regarded seriously, we need not apply them to the more mature revised version. And why, after all, must we take his self-disparagement with solemn literalness?

"It was a point of honor among gentlemen writers in that age," Greenlaw observes, "to affect contempt for their literary works." [2]

Sidney, be it noted, speaks slightingly not only of the original *Arcadia*, but of the *Defence of Poesie*, which no one else has ever called an "ink-wasting toy." Quite possibly, then, his references to the romance also are not to be taken exactly at their face value. The problem challenges more careful investigation than it has yet received.

The purpose of the present study, therefore, is to discover in what spirit this typical courtier of the English Renaissance composed his works of literary art. Sidney's theories are well known. My concern is rather with the habits of his mind, and with the sense of values which prompted his instinctive actions. Thanks to recent scholarly labors, such a study is not out of the question. The *Defence of Poesie* has been shown to be related to the Italian criticism of the sixteenth century. The sources of the *Arcadia* have been ferreted out, and have thrown into high relief the elaborate structure of the revised version.

1. See *The Quarterly Review*, CCXI (July, 1909), 74–100.
2. "Sidney's *Arcadia* as Elizabethan Allegory," p. 329.

The autobiographical elements in the sonnets have been debated for a generation, if without conclusive results.[1] These studies of separate writings suggest the need for a new synthesis. How could the same man produce three works of such contradictory mood, and at the same time be the trusted friend of Walsingham and William the Silent?

Astrophel and Stella, though pertinent to this study, raises so many controversial questions that I shall omit it almost entirely from the discussion. In later chapters I shall take up the supposed contradictions between the *Arcadia* and the *Defence of Poesie*, and shall show a close relation between the two works; for contrary to the prevailing view, the one illustrates the theories of the other, and both reveal the same quality of deliberate art, guided by critical law. In the present chapter I shall try to explain why Sidney, like other "courtly makers," speaks so slightingly of his literary achievement.

Rightly to understand the poet in Sidney, we must understand the humanist, the courtier, and the man of action. We must view him in his own age, when the medieval world was being so swiftly transformed. At home, feudalism was yielding to modern statecraft, Catholic to Protestant Christianity, scholasticism to the New Learning. Abroad, the encroaching power of Spain was about to be checked, and the foundations of the British Empire were soon to be laid. And in all these changes the strength of the English middle classes was beginning to be manifest. For the moment, however, the world seemed made for the aristocrats, and Sidney was one of them. Their ideals had been changing with the new age. For several generations the most powerful men had been not the military leaders, but statesmen like Wolsey, Walsingham, and Burghley. Politics and learning, hardly less than arms, were becom-

1. For a recent (but unconvincing) study of the question, see James M. Purcell, *Sidney's Stella*, 1934.

ing the profession of the gentleman. Chivalry was still
a force, but the knight had become a courtier.

The monk had been replaced by the humanist. These
two new types, the humanist and the courtier, could not
always see eye to eye. Yet in the multifarious and warring
tendencies of the age we may find in them one ideal that is
clearly articulated and for Sidney, I think, more influential
than any other. It is the ideal of the harmonious life.

From Plato, Aristotle, and Cicero, down through Castiglione, Roger Ascham, and John Milton, this conception
has been central in the tradition of humanism. For all
these writers the true aristocrat, though distinguished first
of all by personal integrity and devotion to the public wel-
fare, will seek to develop every faculty which can add
beauty or dignity to life. In adopting this ancient ideal,
the Elizabethan gentleman made certain modifications
which are typical of his age or race. Political changes and
national dangers made him as ardent a patriot as Regulus
or Cicero; the Reformation made him a Protestant; the
voyagers and discoverers stimulated his imagination with
strange tales from the New World; while the new opportunities that opened out to the individual and the startling
uncertainty of life filled him with a gambler's hope and a
gambler's energy — no less often with a gambler's dis-
illusionment. And so in the infinite complexity of the English Renaissance, one man would grasp the Greek ideal
chiefly on the side of its moral seriousness and practicality,
another on the side of its abounding energy, and few
achieved that superbly harmonious and yet vigorous development of all the faculties which has always been the
goal of humanistic training.

Highly significant for our study is the type of culture
developed at St. John's College, Cambridge, under the
leadership of Sir John Cheke. Men who had witnessed
revolutions in the church and the state were preoccupied
with religion and politics. Ascham, with all his love of

beauty and learning for their own sake, writes his *Schole-master* for the youth "that should becum hereafter, either a good minister in Religion, or a Ciuill Ientleman in ser-uice of his Prince and contrie." [1] England and the Refor-mation are the causes which command the deepest loyalty of earnest men in the reign of Queen Elizabeth. The con-tact is close between scholars and men of affairs, and in fact the distinction often breaks down altogether. Sir John Cheke himself was the brother-in-law of Cecil and a mem-ber of the Privy Council. Ascham, who was Queen Eliza-beth's tutor, enjoyed the respect of her counselors. Thomas Wilson and Sir Thomas Smith rose high in the public service. Ashton, the great master of Shrewsbury School, was the trusted agent of Leicester, Essex, Burghley, and Sidney's own father.[2] Sir Nicholas Bacon, like his more illustrious son, was famous for his learning. Sound scholar-ship, if we may trust Ascham, was one of the most vigor-ous interests of the men who formed Elizabeth's Privy Council in 1563. Cecil, he says, "though his head be neuer so full of most weightie affaires of the Realme, yet, at diner time he doth seeme to lay them alwaies aside: and findeth euer fitte occasion to taulke pleasantlie of other matters, but most gladlie of some matter of learning." [3]

Now although some of the men I have just named are not associated with St. John's, they are not distinguishable from the rest. The men of St. John's, then, are representa-tive of English humanism in the generation immediately before Sidney. Their ideal is still the all-round man. The scholar is a statesman, and the statesman is a scholar. But neither of them is Aristotle's "high-minded man." In the humanism of Ascham and Cheke there is no adequate place for beauty.

1. *The Scholemaster, English Works*, ed. Wright, Cambridge English Classics, 1904, p. 287.
2. G. W. Fisher, *Annals of Shrewsbury School*, 1899, pp. 25 ff.
3. Page 175.

Before them, Sir Thomas Elyot had likewise failed to
see the place of art in the harmonious life. After Æsop's
Fables and Lucian, or Aristophanes, he would have the child
hasten to Homer and Virgil. In Homer "be contained,
and moste perfectly expressed, nat only the documentes
marciall and discipline of armes, but also incomparable
wisedomes, and instructions for politike gouernaunce of
people; with the worthy commendation and laude of
noble princis: where with the reders shall be so all in-
flamed, that they most feruently shall desire and coueite,
by the imitation of their vertues, to acquire sem-
blable glorie."[1] In his enthusiasm for poetry and his high
opinion of its moral and educational value, Elyot reminds
us of the author of the *Defence*. And like Sidney, too, he
admits pleasure, as well as profit, as a legitimate end of
poetry. Whether the child delights in hunting,[2] in athletic
games,[3] in listening to minstrels,[3] or in hearing "thinges
marueilous and exquisite, whiche hath in it a visage of
some thinges incredible,"[4] he is certain to take pleasure in
Virgil. The governor should be able to play musical in-
struments,[5] paint,[6] carve,[6] and dance.[7] And in all these
arts, Elyot admits the twofold function of pleasure and
profit.

Nevertheless Elyot's failure as a critic is patent. He
assigns poetry to the early years of the child's education,
and after the age of thirteen, "in which time childhode de-
clineth, and reason waxeth rype,"[8] he would have the
future gentleman pass to logic,[9] rhetoric,[9] cosmography,[10]
history,[11] and moral philosophy.[12] Of the growth of a child's
mind Elyot may know something, but obviously in the
qualities of the mature man he exalts judgment at the
expense of imagination.

1. Sir Thomas Elyot, *The Boke Named the Gouernour*, ed. Croft, 1883, I,
58–59.   2. Page 63.   3. Page 64.   4. Page 65.
   5. Pages 38 ff.   6. Pages 43 ff.   7. Pages 203 ff.
   8. Page 70.   9. Pages 72 ff.   10. Pages 76 ff.
11. Pages 81 ff.   12. Pages 91 ff.

The same emphasis appears in the humanists of St. John's College. "Labour and intent study," by which Milton hoped to "leave something so written to after-times, as they should not willingly let it die," [1] are regarded by Ascham as the lot of the statesman or orator, but not of the poet. Quick wits, he believes, are "soone hote and desirous of this and that: as colde and sone wery of the same againe. . . . Soch wittes delite them selues in easie and pleasant studies, and neuer passe farre forward in hie and hard sciences. And therfore the quickest wittes commonlie may proue the best Poetes, but not the wisest Orators; readie of tonge to speake boldlie, not deepe of iudgement, either for good counsell or wise writing." [2] The distrust of imagination is significant. Rhetoric, not poetry, is for the men of St. John's the queen of the arts.

Ascham reports Sir John Cheke as saying many times:

I would haue a good student passe and iorney through all Authors both *Greke* and *Latin*: but he that will dwell in these few bookes onelie: first, in Gods holie Bible, and than ioyne with it, *Tullie* in *Latin*, *Plato*, *Aristotle*: *Xenophon*: *Isocrates*: and *Demosthenes* in *Greke*: must nedes proue an excellent man.[3]

The orators are in good company, but we look in vain for the poets. It is no accident that Cheke's associates left treatises on rhetoric, logic, and education, but no systematic literary criticism.

The preoccupation with prose style appears to be a compromise between the artistic instincts of the humanists and their extreme emphasis upon religion and politics. They could not live in the Renaissance without loving beauty. "A faire stone," says Ascham, "requireth to be sette in the finest gold, with the best workmanshyp, or else it leseth moch of the Grace and price." [4] And so Ascham's

---

1. "The Reason of Church-government," *Works*, ed. Patterson and others, 1931, III, 236.
2. *The Scholemaster*, pp. 188–189.   3. Page 275.   4. Page 194.

artistic no less than his practical instincts are satisfied in the ancient masters of prose, where he finds "alwayes, wisdome and eloquence, good matter and good vtterance, neuer or seldom a sonder." [1]

Thus the scholars and statesmen in the generation of Sidney's father show certain definite views which constitute a body of conservative opinion with which any gentleman would have to reckon. They lay great stress upon morality, religion, and politics. They have a zeal for broad and thorough learning, not primarily as an end in itself, but as a means of preparing for a life of action. They feel the lure of beauty, and they love poetry, but though recognizing all the arts, they give first place to rhetoric, as the most practical.

Most significant of all, they fear and distrust the imagination. They appear to associate it with the dangerous excesses of the age. "Newfangleness," whether in language, dress, manners, or morals, meets with fierce scorn. But this very fact shows that the English type of humanism was only one influence in the turbulent days of Queen Elizabeth. Other forces were at work to fire men's passions, nerve them to heroic adventure, and show them almost unguessed regions of the human spirit no less than of the wide world. The tidal forces of an epoch were not to be tamed by St. John's. It was to be an age of imagination and poetry; an age not of good sense, but of daring energy. Milton, reinterpreting in the next century the ancient ideal of the cultivated man, was to call "a compleat and generous Education that which fits a man to perform justly, skilfully and magnanimously all the offices both private and publick of Peace and War." [2] If we have here classic decorum and completeness, we have also the abounding vigor of the Renaissance.

The thesis I propose to defend is that Sidney stands for a deeper, richer, and more imaginative humanism than his

1. Page 265.   2. *Works*, IV, 280.

predecessors in the English tradition. Personal integrity, lofty patriotism, and religious reverence are still the strongest traits of his character, as they are of every true humanist, but his preoccupation with these interests seems to me less exclusive than his biographers before Miss Wilson would lead us to think.

Their evidence, however, is not to be ignored. The most conservative and hard-headed statesmen-scholars of the age speak of him with the deepest respect. Burghley, Walsingham, Du Plessis Mornay, Languet, William of Orange, Henry of Navarre, and Sir Henry Sidney are only a few of the practical men of affairs who recognized his statesmanlike qualities. William of Orange told Fulke Greville that "her Majesty had one of the ripest, and greatest Counsellors of Estate in Sir *Philip Sidney*, that at this day lived in *Europe*." [1] Greville's own statements are explicit: "Above all," he writes, "he made the Religion he professed, the firm Basis of his life"; [2] and this first biographer of Sidney gives nearly exclusive attention to his hero's political activities. It is almost as if Greville were deliberately trying to emphasize the essential sobriety of Sidney's temperament, to correct a prevailing popular opinion of his devotion to the arts. "Though I lived with him, and knew him from a child, yet I never knew him other than a man," [3] he tells us. The substantial truth of Greville's interpretation is supported by overwhelming evidence. The earnest, forthright character of Sir Henry Sidney is reflected in the son. The admirable letter which he wrote to Philip when the boy was at Shrewsbury closes with the words, "Your mother and I send you our blessings, and Almighty God grant you His, nourish you with His fear, govern you with His grace, and make you a good servant to your prince and country!" [4] The home influences toward religion and

1. Greville, p. 27.   2. Page 35.
3. Page 6.
4. Malcolm W. Wallace, *Life of Sir Philip Sidney*, 1915, p. 69.

patriotism must have been deepened at Shrewsbury by Thomas Ashton,[1] a humanist, a man of affairs, and the writer of religious plays; at Oxford by Puritan tutors;[2] in France by the massacre of St. Bartholomew's, which Sidney witnessed; on the grand tour by the Huguenot diplomat and humanist, Languet; and throughout his short lifetime by the constant danger to English liberty and to Protestantism from Catholic Spain.

The judgment of Greville and of William the Silent is confirmed by what we know of Sidney's mature life. "To what purpose should our thoughts be directed to various kinds of knowledge," he asks in a letter to Languet, "unless room be afforded for putting it into practice, so that public advantage may be the result, which in a corrupt age we cannot hope for?"[3] Clearly he was discontented with the restraints and vanity of court life. His early diplomatic mission to the German princes and the Emperor Rudolph, his attempt against the queen's wishes to join Drake in attacking the West Indies, his bold opposition to Elizabeth's marriage to a son of Catherine de' Medici, the energy and capacity for leadership which he displayed in the otherwise dismal campaign in the Low Countries, all reveal Sidney as a soldier and statesman, and all show his passionate loyalty to England and to Protestantism. Indeed, "his chief ends" were "not Friends, Wife, Children, or himself; but above all things the honour of his Maker, and service of his Prince, or Country."[4]

All this, however, does not show us Sidney's attitude toward poetry, nor does it reveal much of the man's temper.

1. Cf. Wallace, pp. 37–38, and Fisher, pp. 17–18.
2. Cf. Wallace, p. 103.
3. *Correspondence of Sidney and Languet*, ed. and trans. Pears, 1845, p. 143. Cf. *Works*, III, 119.
4. Greville, p. 40.

Shelley speaks of

> Sidney, as he fought
> And as he fell and as he lived and loved
> Sublimely mild, a Spirit without spot.[1]

This is a curiously pale picture of a vigorous man of action, one which is neither accurate nor perhaps altogether flattering. Far truer, it seems to me, is the glimpse we get of Sidney in his relations with Drake. Tired of the idleness of court life and of Elizabeth's Fabian policy toward Spain, Sidney, unknown to her and even to his father-in-law, determined to join Drake in an attack on the Spanish power in America. While the affair "past unknown, he knew it would pass without interruption; and when it was done, presumed the success would put envy and all her agents to silence." [2] Sidney left court on a pretense of meeting Don Antonio, the Portuguese pretender, and joined Drake, not to Drake's entire satisfaction, as Fulke Greville thought.

Neverthelesse that ingenuous spirit of Sir *Philip's*, though apt to give me credit, yet not apt to discredit others, made him suspend his own, & labor to change, or qualifie my judgement; Till within some few daies after, finding the shippes neither ready according to promise, nor possibly to be made ready in many daies; and withall observing some sparcks of false fire, breaking out unawares from his yoke-fellow daily; It pleased him (in the freedom of our friendship) to return me my own stock, with interest. . . .

It may be the leaden feet, and nimble thoughts of Sir *Francis* wrought in the day, and unwrought by night; while he watched an opportunity to discover us, without being discovered.

For within a few daies after a post steales up to the Court, upon whose arrivall an Alarum is presently taken: messengers sent away to stay us, or if we refused, to stay the whole Fleet. Notwithstanding this first *Mercury*, his errand being partly advertised to Sir *Philip* beforehand, was intercepted upon the

---

1. "Adonais," ll. 401–404.   2. Greville, p. 71.

way; his letters taken from him by two resolute souldiers in
Marriners apparell; brought instantly to Sir *Philip*, opened, and
read. The contents as welcome as Bulls of excommunication to
the superstitious Romanist. . . .

The next was a more Imperiall Mandate, carefully conveyed,
and delivered to himself by a Peer of this Realm; carrying with
it in the one hand grace, the other thunder.[1]

Sidney obeyed. With characteristic generosity, he
"saves Sir *Francis Drake* from blastings of Court," and on
leaving his forces delivers an address, promising his own
support and encouraging them to hope for the queen's
hearty sympathy.[2]

Sidney appears here not as a spirit "sublimely mild,"
but superbly virile. With stunning audacity he brushes
aside every obstacle that impedes his purpose. Candid and
generous by nature, he is not blind to the men around him,
sees through Drake's duplicity, outwits him, and when
finally beaten by the royal authority, shows himself a
sportsman and bears not a trace of rancor. Throughout
he acts with perfect dignity. I do not find in Sidney any
suggestion of what Professor Babbitt called the Rousseau-
istic opposition between the head and the heart. Adven-
turous though he is, he has no mere boyish irresponsibility.
When he acts, his whole mind seems to approve, and he
has no suspicion that he has placed himself in a ludicrous
position. "After mature deliberation being once resolved,
he never brought any question of change to afflict himself
with." [3]

This singleness of heart often appears in the incidents
of Sidney's life, and explains, I think, the audacity which
characterizes him. He ventures to give the Emperor
Rudolph advice about how to treat his Protestant subjects.
He boldly argues with Queen Elizabeth against her marriage with the Duc d'Alençon. He cuts her favorite the

1. Pages 74–76.   2. Page 76.   3. Page 28.

Earl of Ormonde for his treachery to Sir Henry Sidney, and refuses on one memorable occasion to apologize to another favorite, the Earl of Oxford, even at Elizabeth's personal request. "Certaynly, Sir," we find him writing to Sir Christopher Hatton, "howe soever I mighte have forgeven hym, I should never have forgeven my self, yf I had layne under so proude an injurye, as he would have laide uppon me, neither can any thinge under the sunne make me re-pente yt, nor any miserye make me goo one half worde back frome yt." [1] Proud, sensitive of his own honor, con-scious of the rectitude of his purposes, Sidney reminds us sometimes of Milton's firm and ardent nature. Like Mil-ton the pamphleteer, he sometimes gives way to passion. "Mr. Mollineax," he writes to his father's faithful secre-tary, ". . . I assure yow before God, that if ever I know yow do so muche as reede any lettre I wryte to my Father, without his commandement, or my consente, I will thruste my Dagger into yow." [2]

And yet Sidney shows even here something more than impulsiveness. He shows also, as in his effort to join Drake and in his bold yet courteous letter to Queen Elizabeth, an instinct for direct action joined with firm self-assurance. "After mature deliberation being once resolved," he is ready to go the limit. In this case his ripe-ness of judgment is wanting, and yet his native temper is the same as in the campaign in the Low Countries, in which he won a reputation for discretion no less than for valor.

Sidney's political judgment is hard to estimate. Per-haps Elizabeth's Fabian policy was wiser than his eager desire to beard the Spanish lion in his den, but he possesses at least the statesman's breadth of view. His foreign policy, which Greville discusses at length,[3] shows a thor-ough knowledge of the political situation in Europe. In

1. *Works*, III, 128.   2. Page 124.
3. *Life of Sir Philip Sidney*, pp. 78–120.

1585 he doubted the wisdom of the expedition to the Low
Countries, preferring a direct attack on the Spanish coast
or the Spanish power in America. Whether in 1585 the
time was ripe for his bold plan it is not easy to say, but
certainly he was observant and farsighted. As a matter of
fact, the expedition under Leicester failed, and England
later adopted the policy of Sir Philip. In his own part in
the campaign he showed himself prudent and skilful, as well
as bold. And in the foreign policy which Greville ascribes
to him, he reveals a quality of imagination which might in
time have made him not only an able but a great statesman. His mind runs easily through the maze of European
politics, tracing in every country the possible effect of an
English attack on Spain. In his youthful enthusiasm, he
even hopes that Catholic countries [1] and possibly the pope [2]
himself will find it to their interest to check the power of
the greatest Catholic kingdom. The world-wide sweep of
his imagination places Sidney in the high days of Drake,
of Raleigh, and of Marlowe. He includes, but transcends,
the elder English humanism.

With all his exuberance, Sidney is more than a mere
adventurer. In fact, it is the breadth of his nature which
seems to me his most striking characteristic.

Indeed he was a true modell of Worth; A man fit for Con-
quest, Plantation, Reformation, or what Action soever is
greatest, and hardest amongst men: Withall, such a lover of
Mankind, and Goodnesse, that whosoever had any reall parts,
in him found comfort, participation, and protection to the uttermost of his power. . . . The Universities abroad, and at home,
accompted him a generall *Maecenas* of Learning; Dedicated their
Books to him; and communicated every Invention, or Improvement of Knowledge with him. Souldiers honoured him, and
were so honoured by him, as no man thought he marched under
the true Banner of *Mars*, that had not obtained Sir *Philip
Sidney's* approbation. Men of Affairs in most parts of Christen-

---

1. Page 96.   2. Page 105.

dome, entertained correspondency with him. But what speak I of these, with whom his own waies, and ends did concur? since (to descend) his heart, and capacity were so large, that there was not a cunning Painter, a skilfull Engenier, an excellent Musician, or anyother Artificer of extraordinary fame, that made not himself known to this famous Spirit, and found him his true friend without hire; and the common *Rende-vous* of Worth in his time.[1]

Allowing for the exaggeration of eulogy, I feel that Fulke Greville's estimate is confirmed by all the evidence about Sidney which later biographers have collected. His human sympathies and intellectual interests alike are generous and varied. His letters, usually brief and matter-of-fact, are filled with promises of aid to worthy suitors, or with appeals in their behalf to influential men. In his will he left legacies to a long list of relatives, friends, and servants. More important for us than his genius for friendship, and also more difficult to establish, is the breadth of his intellectual sympathies. His zeal for learning, as we have seen, he shares with the scholars and statesmen of his day who were his friends and patterns. No one without a taste for dialectics and analysis would have translated Du Plessis Mornay's treatise, *Of the Trewnes of Christian Religion*. There are hints here and there in Sidney's life of a restless curiosity. He seems willing to consider that outer fringe of oddities who lie beyond the pale of conventional scholarship. He visited the astrologer, Dr. John Dee,[2] appointed a Ramist,[3] William Temple, as his private secretary, visited in Prague the Catholic enthusiast Campion,[4] and was the first Englishman to show kindness to Giordano Bruno,[5] whom the universities in England were treating as a heretic. Sidney may not have taken all these men too seriously. But when we remember how he was stirred by the

1. Pages 33-34.   2. Wallace, p. 173.
3. Page 334.   4. Pages 177-178.
5. Bourne, pp. 292-293; cf. also Wallace, pp. 299 ff.

discoveries of Frobisher and Drake, and how in his acts he seems to move all together, with his mind, imagination, and feelings directed to one object, can we doubt that here in more purely intellectual realms he responded whole-heartedly to the strange and the novel? I agree with Mr. Wallace [1] that A. S. Cook [2] fails to prove any direct influence of Bruno upon Sidney, but I do find evidence in their relations of a keen curiosity and catholic tastes. In spite of his own ardent convictions, Sidney is singularly free from bigotry, and his alert mind responds to a touch.

The humanist is a conservative, and Sidney is a humanist. There is no denying that "regarding the social structure of English society, as far as we can know, he had no misgivings." [3] Yet when Mr. Wallace goes on to declare, "It is scarcely possible that he had been seriously touched by the philosophic and scientific stirrings of the time. His religious beliefs were as simple as those of a little child," [3] one wonders if there is evidence for so sweeping a generalization. Original, subtle, or "daring speculations" like Bruno's do not seem to have come naturally to Sidney. His is rather a teachable mind, responsive to "the best that has been thought and said," but there is nothing "strangely simple in [his] attitude toward most of life's problems." [3] Greenlaw is nearer the truth, when, after a careful analysis of Pamela's reply to Cecropia's atheism, he says:

His chapter is remarkable for its recognition of the chief points in the Lucretian philosophy and for its direct reply to the atomic theory. It is this last point that is the most interesting. The doctrine of "substances" was not so easily grasped by men of Sidney's circle as the more general implications of the philosophy. That Sidney recognized its importance is another proof of his intellectual curiosity, and helps us to understand why a man

---

1. *Life of Sir Philip Sidney*, p. 301.
2. *The Defense of Poesy*, ed. Cook, 1890, pp. xiii–xiv.
3. Wallace, p. 401.

like Bruno, himself deeply interested in the problem of the
origin of the universe and deeply versed in Lucretius, should
have dedicated to the young Englishman a number of his
philosophical treatises.[1]

What, then, shall we say are the essential traits of Sidney's mind? What except energy and gravity? On the
one hand he enters with fiery zeal into an adventure with
Drake, a war with Spain, or a quarrel with the Earl of
Oxford; his imagination leaps at the thought of the pope's
joining against Spain, and no less does he respond to the
novel ideas of Bruno and Campion or the strange discoveries of Frobisher. He lives in his ardent imagination. But
he keeps his head; his foreign policy is based on accurate
knowledge of a complex situation; in dealing with a man
like Drake, he is generous, alert, self-possessed; and though
stimulated by philosophic speculation, he holds firmly to
his religious convictions. In the very torrent, tempest, and
whirlwind of passion, he acquires and begets a temperance
that gives it smoothness.

In this eager yet seasoned temper, there is, furthermore,
a large receptiveness blended with a fine poise. Sidney
warms to a new friend or a new idea or a new adventure,
but he remains himself. The courtesy and personal charm
which so won his contemporaries bespeak an indefinable
tact, the *je ne sais quoi* that the Frenchman of the seventeenth century saw in poetry and wished to have in his life.
To all his virile energy and high determination, Sidney
unites an instinctive and exquisite sense of fitness, concealed in an air of easy nonchalance. Something of this
dash there is in his reckless effort to join Drake; still more
in his spontaneous generosity before the battle at Zutphen,
where seeing a friend without cuisses he removed his own
and made possible the fatal wound in his thigh. "If it be
now," says Hamlet with the noble indifference that was

1. "The Captivity Episode," p. 63.

Sidney's, "if it be now, 'tis not to come; if it be not to come, it will be now; if it be not now, yet it will come; the readiness is all."

The exuberant and finely tempered vitality of such a man, with the easy grace that covered a vigorous purpose, might conceivably have given, if joined with ripe experience and a great intellect, a great statesman such as Sidney aspired to be. But such intellectual strength as Bacon's does not appear to have been his; and he died young. Essentially his temper is that of a soldier and man of action. No less essentially it is that of a poet. And if the statement appears to be a paradox, we need only remember that Matthew Arnold declared poetry to be one of the chief glories of the race which has built the British Empire.

And so we come to the core of our problem: what was Sidney's attitude toward art and poetry? In the traditions of English humanism, as we have seen, poetry is subordinated to rhetoric, and the imagination to judgment. In Sidney's temperament, however, the strongest traits are imagination and poise. May we not expect in him a larger and richer humanism than in the men of St. John's?

Those who hold that literature was for Sidney little more than a recreation base their opinion chiefly on his own modest references to his works, and on the supposed contrast between them and his real interests. His ambitions, to be sure, were largely for a life of action, and his deepest enthusiasm was for his country and his religion. This objection, however, is beside the point. Every humanist, indeed every man of common sense, gives first place to these loyalties. The essential question is: what emphasis did Sidney give to art? He may have given it a very high place, even if he put other things first. More important evidence is his habitual disparagement of his writings. It appears in passages of the *Defence of Poesie*, in the letter to the Countess of Pembroke, and in the fact that on his deathbed Sidney asked to have the *Arcadia* destroyed. On the other hand, the man was by temperament a poet; his literary achievement is probably with the exception of Spenser's the most noteworthy in English from the death of Chaucer to his own time; perhaps his most successful work is actually a *Defence of Poesie*; and among his contemporaries his fame as a poet was high. How seriously, in view of these facts, can we take his disparaging references to his writings, especially since "it was a point of honor among gentlemen writers in that age to affect contempt for their literary works" ? [1]

The reason for their attitude is not far to seek. The conservative opinion of the age was, as we have seen, somewhat over-practical. Even a Greek scholar like Ascham, with all his love of chaste beauty, subordinates poetry to refined prose. And after all the glories of Elizabethan drama and lyric, which might have been expected to dispel this prejudice, John Selden could say:

Tis ridiculous for a Lord to print verses, 'tis well enough to make them to please himself but to make them publick is foolish. If a man in a private Chamber twirles his Band string, or playes with a Rush to please himselfe 'tis well enough, but if hee should goe into Fleet streete & sett upon a stall & twirle his bandstring or play with a Rush, then all the boyes in the streete would laugh att him.[2]

We may indeed take a hard-headed man like Bacon to be sincere when he begins his essay "Of Masques and Triumphs" with the words, "These Things are but Toyes, to come amongst such Serious Observations." [3] But in view of the scornful attitude of the sober-minded, and in view of Sidney's political ambitions and the consequent necessity of keeping the respect of men like Burghley and Walsingham, must we not discount heavily his slighting allu-

1. Greenlaw, "Sidney's *Arcadia* as Elizabethan Allegory," p. 329.
2. *Table Talk*, ed. Pollock, 1927, p. 96.
3. *Essays*, ed. Wright, 1887, p. 156.

sions to his poetry? May we not be skeptical when a poet speaks of "I know not by what mischance in these my not old yeares and idlest times, having slipt into the title of a Poet"?[1]

We have here, then, if I am not mistaken, what Jonson called a "diligent kind of negligence."[2] Universal in the Renaissance is the idea that the highest beauty is in an art that seems no art. Webbe, in 1586, translates from George Fabricius the maxim: "So to hyde ones cunning, that nothing should seeme to bee laborsome or exquisite, when, notwithstanding, euery part is pollished with care and studie, is a speciall gyft which *Aristotle* calleth κρύψιν [*sic*]."[3] "Oftimes," writes E. K. in his preface to the *Shepheardes Calender*, "we . . . take great pleasure in that disorderly order."[4] Spenser is conscious of this principle when he describes the Bower of Bliss:

> And that which all faire workes doth most aggrace,
> The art, which all that wrought, appeared in no place.[5]

Milton, perhaps echoing his master, writes of

> Flours worthy of Paradise which not nice Art
> In Beds and curious Knots, but Nature boon
> Powrd forth profuse.[6]

And Herrick gives the idea perhaps its most graceful expression:

> A sweet disorder in the dresse
> Kindles in cloathes a wantonnesse:
> A Lawne about the shoulders thrown
> Into a fine distraction: . . .

---

1. *Defence of Poesie, Works,* III, 3.
2. *Timber, or Discoveries, Critical Essays of the Seventeenth Century,* ed. Spingarn, I (1908), 47.
3. *Elizabethan Critical Essays,* ed. G. Gregory Smith, 1904, I, 301.
4. Spenser, *Poetical Works,* Cambridge edition, 1908, p. 5.
5. Page 320.
6. *Paradise Lost,* IV. 241-243 (II, 115).

> A carelesse shooe-string, in whose tye
> I see a wilde civility:
> Doe more bewitch me, then when Art
> Is too precise in every part.[1]

How often do the Elizabethan lyricists, as Lodge, for example, in the songs of *Rosalind*, achieve an art which seems no art, and unite an exquisite finish with the illusion of perfect spontaneity.

This classic quality has always been fostered, of course, by the study of Horace and Ovid. In the English Renaissance it is closely related to what Professor Rand has called "the long tradition of assumed Christian simplicity," to which the apologetic envoys of Lydgate belong. Ascham frequently refers to his *Scholemaster* as a "litle poore booke," [2] and carefully apologizes for quoting his poem on the death of one John Whitney, "which . . . fell forth, more by chance, than either by skill or vse, into this kinde of misorderlie meter." [3] If he really thought the verses so bad, why did he make them public? He has himself given the answer, when to those busybodies who scoff at his choosing "to spend soch tyme in writyng of trifles, as the schole of shoting, the Cockpitte, and this booke of the first Principles of Grammer," he retorts:

> Let them read that wise Poet *Horace* in his *Arte Poetica*, who willeth wisemen to beware, of hie and loftie Titles. For, great shippes, require costlie tackling, and also afterward dangerous gouernment: Small boates, be neither verie chargeable in makyng, nor verie oft in great ieoperdie: and yet they cary many tymes, as good and costlie ware, as greater vessels do.[4]

In other words, a modest bearing will help to disarm criticism.

Another case in point is the author of the *Arte of English*

1. "Delight in Disorder," *Poetical Works*, ed. Moorman, 1915, p. 28.
2. *The Scholemaster*, p. 268.
3. Page 241.   4. Page 217.

Poesie. He labors to exalt the dignity of poetry, urges gentlemen who have written prose or poetry of "rare inuention" not to "be any whit squeimish to let it be publisht vnder their names,"[1] and defends even anagrams against the practical-minded. "As I can not denie but these conceits of mine be trifles, no lesse in very deede be all the most serious studies of man, if we shall measure grauitie and lightnesse by the wise mans ballance, who ... cryed out, ... *Vanitas vanitatum & omnia vanitas.*"[2] And yet the author concludes his analysis of the divine art of poetry with an apology to the queen for having held her "eares so long annoyed with a tedious trifle,"[3] which "was but the studie of [his] yonger yeares, in which vanitie raigned."[4] Plainly, he is insincere either in his exaltation of poetry or in his apology for his interest in it. A courtier, the author reminds us, conceals his real feelings.

When Sidney, therefore, speaks of himself as a "paperblurrer"[5] and of the *Defence of Poesie* as an "inck-wasting toy,"[6] he may well be using merely the language of the time, and deliberately cultivating an air of amateurishness. The existence of a convention does not prove, of course, that Sidney happens to be following it. But to show that he actually was not following it requires further evidence, which is not forthcoming. We are more true to his spirit, I believe, if we interpret such phrases as a bit of light irony directed at himself.

We are certainly more true to the courtly fashions of the day. Few books in the Renaissance were more representative or more influential than Castiglione's *Courtier*. Of first importance, therefore, is his making the highest perfection of the courtier's art a certain dash and easy grace which conceals the seriousness of his purposes. *Sprezzatura* is his name for this quality. Above everything, the gentleman

1. *Elizabethan Critical Essays*, II, 23–24.
2. Page 116.   3. Page 192.   4. Page 193.
5. *Works*, III, 36.   6. Page 45.

must eschew affectation and exaggerated seriousness, and "use in every thyng a certain Reckelesness,[1] to cover art withall, and seeme whatsoever he doth and sayeth to do it wythout pain, and (as it were) not myndyng it. . . . Therfore that may be said to be a very art that appeereth not to be art, neyther ought a man to put more diligence in any thing then in covering it: for in case it be open, it loseth credit cleane." [2] On the other hand, this engaging air of nonchalance does not prevent a man from secretly cherishing ardent purposes. "Let him set all his delite and dylygence to wade in everye thyng a litle farther then other menne, so that he maye bee knowen among al menne for one that is excellente. As it is reade of Alcibiades, that he excelled all other nations wheresoever he came, and everye manne in the thynge he hadde moste skyll in." [3] Castiglione later specifies skill in language [4] as one of the courtier's necessary accomplishments.

Sidney is a thorough disciple of Castiglione. In his character, as I have tried to show, we find exactly this union of deliberate purpose with an appearance of easy nonchalance. Not only in such comparatively external things as fine horsemanship [5] or in so obvious a matter as a sensitive personal honor,[6] does he personify the courtier of Castiglione. Nor is it merely that in his devotion to soldiery [6] and tournaments or in his plain speech [7] to Queen Elizabeth, he gives, like his master, the chief place in his thoughts to war and statecraft. More than this, he has caught the very temper of Castiglione. Both men represent the most worthy traits of the courtier. Sidney has much of that quality of temperance which, says the Italian, pours into the mind "a vehement persuasion that may incline him to honestie, maketh him quiet and full of rest, in

---

1. The Elizabethan translation of *sprezzatura*.

2. Castiglione, *The Book of the Courtier*, trans. Hoby, Tudor Translations, 1900, p. 59.

3. Page 54.

4. Pages 62–75.

5. Cf. *The Courtier*, p. 54.

6. Cf. p. 48.

7. Cf. p. 297.

everie part equall and of good proportion: and on everie side framed of a certein agreement with him self, that filleth him with such a cleare caulmenesse, that he is never out of pacience." [1] To be sure, Sidney can lose his temper with his father's secretary, or resent an affront from the Earl of Oxford. But seldom does he act without the calm of the man who is sure of himself. By his love of intellectual activity, too, he resembles the speculative author of the *Courtier*. In short, his humanism is much nearer Castiglione's than Ascham's. And the Italian, be it noted, has a greater artistic power, and gives a higher place to beauty, than does Sidney's more practical-minded countryman.

Since Sidney, therefore, is so closely akin to Castiglione, and since in uniting an ardent purpose with an air of graceful negligence he reveals in life and action the rare quality which the Italian writer calls *sprezzatura*, may we not expect to find him turning also to literature, as his master advises, with an eager ambition to surpass the poets in their own art? The very ease of manner which has deceived his biographers is evidence of his debt to Castiglione, and we may accordingly suppose him to desire, like the Italian courtier, to excel "every man in the thing he had most skill in."

The burden of proof, at least, is plainly on those who think Sidney's enthusiasm for letters was comparatively superficial; for, without evidence to the contrary, a poet may be assumed to be devoted to his art! Sidney's disparaging references to his "ink-wasting toy" can be explained by the prejudices of English men of affairs and even scholars against too great an interest in literature, and by the Renaissance principle of concealing art, which not only had become associated with a well-defined literary convention of assumed simplicity, but also was the special ideal of the courtier.

Of what significance, then, is Sidney's famous letter to

1. Page 308.

the Countess of Pembroke? The question has been largely answered, and yet it invites further analysis. Sidney is no isolated phenomenon. He is one of many literary courtiers in the age of the Tudors. To understand him we must know something of the conventions which he inherited.

If a courtier, as Castiglione holds, is normally "a Gentleman borne and of a good house," [1] in England he may be said to be the son or heir of a knight or a lord. By this definition, the more important courtiers who achieved fame as poets before Sidney are Wyatt, Surrey, Lord Vaux, Sackville, and the Earl of Oxford. Others whose work has perished or cannot now be identified are George Boleyn, Lord Rochford; Edmund Sheffield, first Baron Sheffield; and Sir Francis Bryan; besides Henry Parker, Lord Morley, who was also a voluminous prose writer. Other prose writers are John Bourchier, Lord Berners; Sir Thomas More; Sir Thomas Elyot; John, Lord Lumley; and Sir Thomas North. Of these fourteen men, the most significant for the present study are Wyatt, Surrey, Sackville, Elyot, and North.

The careers of all form instructive parallels to the career of Sidney. Most of them were products of the New Learning. Of Sheffield's education, indeed, I have learned nothing, and Rochford, though he must have been a master of French, confesses he could "nether wright latin nor italian well." [2] Surrey, Elyot, and perhaps Sackville were not university men, but were well educated. And the other nine men probably attended Oxford or Cambridge for at least a year. Only four, however,— More, Elyot, Morley, and North — may be described as learned. The typical courtier is a well-educated man of the world, not a scholar. Of the group we are considering, all except Sheffield traveled

---

1. Page 44. The definition is too narrow, but it centers attention on the writers of Sidney's own social class.

2. Edmond Bapst, *Deux Gentilshommes-Poètes de la Cour de Henry VIII*, 1891, p. 10, n. 1.

abroad. All except Sheffield and Oxford accompanied embassies, and ten were actually ambassadors. Many were soldiers. Most of them occupied civil posts in the government. In rank, education, and the externals of their careers, these men are Sidney's predecessors. Son to the lord president of Wales and lord deputy of Ireland, heir to the Earls of Warwick and Leicester, educated at Oxford, trained in the ways of the world by foreign travel, the queen's ambassador at twenty-two, second in command of the English forces in the Low Countries, — a soldier, a statesman, and something of a scholar, Sidney is the ripe product of a tradition.

How notable was the literary achievement of the courtiers before him? How ambitious were they of a poet's honor? How often did they attain it? Above all, why, if they were interested in their art, did they shrink from publishing their verses? If to some of these questions our answers are but tentative, we shall still find on the whole strong evidence to corroborate our conclusions about the seriousness of Sidney's devotion to poetry.

In his literary work, no less than in his career, Sidney reminds us of his predecessors; yet with a difference. Like the courtly poets before him, he wrote love lyrics; like Wyatt and Surrey, he translated some of the Psalms; but he is like no earlier Englishman in writing a sonnet sequence. His translations of Aristotle's *Rhetoric* (now lost) and of Du Plessis Mornay's *Vérité de la Religion Chrestienne* are quite in line with earlier translations or adaptations of works on history, government, moral philosophy, education, and theology. His *Defence of Poesie* and his *Arcadia* strike out new paths. Among the writings of earlier courtiers, literary criticism appears only incidentally in Elyot's discussion of education; fiction appears only in Lord Berners' translations of French and Spanish romances. Creative literature, therefore, receives from Sidney an altogether new emphasis in both the theories of the

Defence and the example of the *Arcadia.* Yet in thus breaking with tradition, Sidney could have been emulating his most gifted predecessors: Wyatt, who domesticated the Petrarchan lyric; Surrey, who rendered two books of the *Æneid* into creditable blank verse; Sackville, who contributed to the *Mirror for Magistrates* the only part of it that has survived, and who collaborated in the first English tragedy. These men stand out from their fellows: they were innovators. Some of their experiments inevitably were failures: Wyatt's apprentice work in decasyllabic verse has only an historic interest, like Sidney's efforts in classical meters. Yet even the failures testify to the eagerness with which the experiments were pursued, and Wyatt, Surrey, and Sackville all achieved a notable success. They suggest that at least the gifted courtiers were ambitious of literary distinction.

Personal renown, moreover, was a goal which every courtier strove to attain. Even the idealistic Castiglione advises him in battle to separate himself from the multitude and undertake his exploits in the presence, and if possible "beefore the very eyes," of his lord.[1]

Now literature did bring fame to Sidney and his predecessors. Interesting evidence of the fact occurs in Wyatt's adaptation of one of Petrarch's canzone. In the Italian version, Love, accused before the tribunal of Reason, closes his defense thus:

> Ancor (e questo è quel che tutto avanza)
> da volar sopra 'l ciel li avea dat' ali
> per le cose mortali,
> che son scala al fattor, chi ben l'estima.[2]

Now Wyatt inserts the idea that the poetic flights inspired by love have brought him earthly glory:

1. *The Courtier*, p. 113.
2. "Le Rime Sparse," ccclx, *Le Rime Sparse e I Trionfi*, ed. Ezio Chiorboli, 1930, p. 267.

> But oon thing there is above all othr:
>   I gave him winges, wherwith for to flye
>   To honor and fame: and if he would farther
>   Then mortall thinges, above the starry sky. [1]

Whether Wyatt is describing the reception accorded his own verses, or whether, as it is safer to assume, he is making use of a well-known commonplace, the passage shows the thought of literary renown to have been perfectly familiar to him and to his courtly audience.

That he did acquire fame by his poetry is seen from Tottel's address to the reader of his *Miscellany*:

> That to haue wel written in verse, yea & in small parcelles, deserueth great praise, the workes of diuers Latines, Italians, and other, doe proue sufficiently. That our tong is able in that kynde to do as praiseworthely as ȳ rest, the honorable stile of the noble earle of Surrey, and the weightinesse of the depewitted sir Thomas Wyat the elders verse, with seuerall graces in sondry good Englishe writers, doe show abundantly. It resteth nowe (gentle reder) that thou thinke it not euill doon, to publish, to the honor of the Englishe tong, and for the profit of the studious of Englishe eloquence, those workes which the vngentle horders vp of such treasure haue heretofore enuied thee. [2]

Unquestionably the "courtly makers" won honor by their achievements. And yet they refused to print their verses. Why?

Now it is significant to note that they did frequently publish their prose works. Obviously the general public opinion set a higher value on prose than on poetry. It is not so clear that the poet himself, or the limited audience where his manuscripts were circulating, shared the prevailing view. But once outside the circle of his friends and the members of his own class, his works were exposed to the most merciless criticism and ridicule.

On this point, the testimony of the prose writers is

1. *Poems*, ed. Foxwell, 1913, I, 75.
2. Ed. Rollins, I (1928), 2.

unmistakable. Long before the Puritans launched their attack upon poetry and the stage, Sir Thomas Elyot encountered a storm of outrageous abuse by publishing treatises on government and medicine. His complaints are bitter. In the preface to the *Image of Gouernance*, for example, he writes:

> Yet am I not ignoraunt that diuerse there be, which do not thankfully esteme my labours, dispraysinge my studies as *vayne and vnprofitable*, sayinge in *derision*, that I haue *nothing wonne* therby, but the name onely of a maker of bokes, and that I sette the trees, but the printer eateth the fruites.[1]

Here is a passage from the "proheme" to the *Castell of Helth*:

> Galene the moste excellent Phisicion feared, that in writing a compendiouse doctrine for the curynge of sickenesse, he shoulde loose all his labour, for as muche as no manne almost dydde endeuour hym selfe to the findyng of truth, but that all men dydde so much esteme riches, possessions, authoritee, and pleasures, that they supposed them, which were studious in any part of Sapience, to be madde or distract of their wittes. . . . Sens this noble writer foũd that lacke in his time, whan there flourished in sundry countreis a great multitude of men excellent in all kindes of lerning, . . . why should I be greued with reproches, wherwith some of my countrei do recompẽce me, for my laboures takẽ without hope of temporall reward, only for the feruent affection, whiche I haue euer borne toward the publike weale of my countrei? a worthy matter saith one, syr Thomas Eliot is become a phisicion, and writeth in phisicke, which beseemeth not a knight, he mought haue beene muche better occupied.[2]

Particularly noteworthy is the idea that to write "in physic . . . beseemeth not a knight." These mocking words are ascribed by the modern editor of Elyot's *Gouernour* to an indignant physician.[3] But the context shows

---

1. 1541, sig. a 2. The italics are mine.
2. 1541, sigs. A1ᵛ–A2.   3. Ed. Croft, I, cxi.

the criticism to have been more general. Even Galen, Elyot observes, found that all men thought "them which were studious in *any part of sapience* to be mad or distract of their wits." Elyot is speaking here of a prejudice against all forms of scholarship, particularly in a knight. Indeed, he goes on to justify the dignity of medicine (which he would not do if his critic were a physician) by showing how "emperors, kinges, and other great princes . . . did not only aduaunce and honour it: with special priuiledges, but also diuers and many of theim were therin right studiouse." [1]

If conservative opinion generally declared that to write books "in physic . . . beseemeth not a knight," the physicians were equally contemptuous of Elyot's other studies: "Some of them herynge me spoken of, haue saide in derision, that although I were pretily seene in histories, yet being not lerned in physicke, I haue put in my booke diuers errours, in presumyng to write of herbes and medicines." [2]

"Histories" are apparently narratives illustrative of an idea, like "the wonderfull history of Titus and Gisippus, and whereby is fully declared the figure of perfet amitie," which Elyot had inserted in his *Boke of the Gouernour*.[3] He seems to have felt keenly the insulting reference, and goes out of his way to prove histories are "not so light of importance as they doe esteme them." [4]

Against the abusive contempt of his critics, Elyot's defense was that his studies were a public service. "God . . . is my wytnes," he declares solemnly, "that to the desire of knowlege, whervnto I haue hither to ben euer of my nature disposed / I haue ioyned a constant intent to profyte therby to [*sic*] my natural countre[i]." [5] And in another

---

1. *Castell of Helth*, sig. A 2.   2. Sig. A 3.
3. II, 132–166.   4. *Castell of Helth*, sig. A 3.
5. *Of the Knowledeg* [sic] *whiche maketh a wise man*, 1533, sig. A 2. The final letter in the passage is illegible.

place, after listing his writings and showing that they are
far from "vain and unprofitable," he concludes, "I trust
vnto god, myn accompt shall of hym be fauorably accepted: all though some ingrate persons with ille reporte or
mockes requite yl my labours." [1]

Unless Elyot is an exception, we may conclude that even
the prose writer exposed himself to "ill report or mocks"
by printing his works. And Elyot is representative. Sir
Thomas More felt himself driven to publish his *Dialogue
Concerning Tyndale*, because, in his words, "me thought
grete parell myght arise, if some of that company (whiche
are confedered & conspired together, in the sowynge &
settyng forth of Luthers pestilent heresies in this realme)
sholde maliciously chaunge my wordes to the worse, and so
put in prynte my boke, framed after their fantasies." [2] Not
only the malignancy of the criticism is significant, but also
the fact that More should need to apologize at all for printing his book. Not every writer was so bold or so disinterested as Elyot, or found publication so difficult to avoid as
did More. Lord Lumley's youthful translation of Erasmus'
Institution of a Christian Prince (1550) has never existed in
any but manuscript form. The same is true of Lord Morley's voluminous works, with only a few trifling exceptions.
One printed during his lifetime was an innocuous work of
devotion, the *Exposition and Declaration of the Psalme
Deus ultionum dominus*. One other, a metrical translation,
the *Tryumphes of Fraunces Petrarcke*, was printed without
date in the reign of Queen Mary, quite possibly after Lord
Morley's death in 1556. Sir Francis Bryan's *Dispraise of
the Life of a Courtier* appeared anonymously in 1548. Even
as late as 1589 so important a work as the *Arte of English
Poesie*, which has recently been ascribed to Lord Lumley,
was printed likewise without the author's name. [3]

1. *Image of Gouernance*, sig. a 3ᵛ.   2. Facsimile reprint, 1927, p. 106.
3. See B. M. Ward, "The Authorship of *The Arte of English Poesie*,"
Review of English Studies, I (July, 1925), 284–308.

The courtier, we may infer, was often unwilling to print his works, even in prose. That one reason was the sort of abuse which Elyot encountered seems certain from the evidence of other Renaissance writers of humbler rank. Robert Braham's preface to Lydgate's *Troy-Book* (1555) is in part a defense against "the malice of suche, as shal happlye accompt my trauayle herein rather rashe presumpcyon then anye vertuouse imitacion of wel doynge." [1] William Turner, in dedicating *A New Herball* to Queen Elizabeth (1568), declared his need of "suche a Patron as had both learning & sufficient autoritie/ioyned therewith to defend my poore labours against their aduersaries," [2] and he longed for "rest and quietnes in my olde age/ and defence from my enemies / whiche haue more then these eight yeares continvallye troubled me verye muche." [3] Gascoigne, publishing Sir Humphrey Gilbert's *New Voyage to Cathaia* without the author's consent (if his words may be credited), defends it against "such as list to cavill at everie commendable enterprise." [4] "Pardon mee, (good Gentlemen)," the printer, Richard Jones, beseeches the readers of *Brittons Bowre of Delights* (1591), "of my presumption, & protect me, I pray you, against those Cauellers and findfaults, that neuer like of any thing that they see printed, though it be neuer so wel compiled." [5]

The sort of criticism a poet might expect in 1577 is thus described by Nicholas Breton, in his *Works of a Young Wit*:

Some wyl say, It is too dry, it wants the sap of Sapience. . . . Some other wyl say, It is too ful of the whay of wantonnesse. . . . Some wyll say, The inuention is prety, but it is yll pend. Some other wyll more commend the pennyng, then the matter. Some wyl say, It is prety Poetrie. Some wyl say, It is meane stuffe. And some (perhaps) wyl say, It is bald ryme, not worth the

---

1. *Prefaces, Dedications, Epistles*, ed. W. C. Hazlitt, 1874, p. 21.
2. Hazlitt, *Prefaces*, p. 25.   3. Page 31.
4. Gascoigne, *Works*, ed. Cunliffe, II (1910), 563.
5. Hazlitt, *Prefaces*, p. 105.

reading: but that is a malicious Lob, for my lyfe. Some wyll say, Tis verse: he speakes his mynd plainly. Some wyl say, Twil passe for Poetrie: let hym passe for & cetera. Some wyl say, It is good enough to reade, when a man hath nothing els to doo: he may reade it (if he can come by it) in such idle tyme. Some (perhaps) wyll prayse it more then it deserues, and geue coyne for it, rather then goe without it.[1]

What knight or nobleman, already possessed of worldly honor, would expose his verses to criticism so merciless? The more he cherished them, the less would he be willing that they be printed. And he often felt much the same reluctance about his prose works.

The prejudice against a courtier's printing verses was, then, a part of the prejudice against anybody's books on any subjects. Just as many men felt it was unbecoming in a knight to write books on medicine, and as physicians were contemptuous of Elyot's pretty "histories," so other critics censured Turner for dedicating to Queen Elizabeth "a booke of wedes or grasses (as some in despite of learninge will call precious herbes)," declaring it "a right vnmete gift for suche a Prince."[2] Nor was it only science and fiction and poetry which were open to attack. Witness the Spanish humanist Guevara:

The greatest griefe that learned menne feele in their writing is, to thinke, that if there be many that view their doings, to take profit therby: they shall perceiue that there are as many moe, which occupy their tonges in the sclaunder and disprayse thereof.[3]

And again,

The authours, and wryters are ofttimes reproued, not of them whiche can translate, and compile workes: but of those whiche can not reade, and yet lesse understande them, to thintent simple folkes shold count them wise, & take their partes

1. Hazlitt, *Prefaces*, pp. 56–57.
2. Page 30.
3. "The Generall Prologue," *Dial of Princes*, trans. North, 1568, sig. * 5ᵛ.

in condemning this worke, and esteme him for a great wyse man.[1]

We are dealing, then, with no isolated phenomenon, but with a general condition marked by proneness to malicious slander and by prejudice against all learning — scientific and humanistic, as well as literary and artistic. The prose works of Elyot which met such fierce criticism were on sober matters like government, education, moral philosophy, practical medicine, the life of a Roman emperor, not to mention his dictionary and his translation of a sermon of St. Cyprian's. Elyot is a humanist. But so, too, is Lord Morley, with his translations from Boccaccio, Petrarch, Seneca, Plutarch, Cicero, Erasmus, and Politian; and where his works are not humanistic they seem to be Catholic. Lord Lumley, translating Erasmus' *Institution of a Christian Prince*, is a humanist, and so is North, putting into his eloquent and idiomatic English Plutarch's *Lives* and the monumental work of Guevara. The courtier's prose works are humanistic studies, not literary toys. Yet he often was reluctant to print them, and when he did, he encountered, at least in Elyot's day, a storm of misinterpretation and derision.

By Sidney's time the general prejudice against learning had grown less formidable. If we may believe the contemporary dialogue *Of Cyvile and Uncyvile Life* (1579) old-fashioned folk were now ready to consider the learned professions as offering both profit and honor to the sons of gentlemen. "But wee gentlemen in the Country, vnlesse our sonnes proceed in the study of the cõmon lawes, Diuinitie, or Phisicke, doo holde them learned ynough if they can write and read English, and congrue (*sic*) Latine."[2] The malice and contempt which Elyot had

1. "The Argument," sig. *** 1. I use here a conventional sign for the signature, since the original cannot conveniently be reproduced.

2. *Inedited Tracts*, ed. W. C. Hazlitt, 1868, p. 21. A later edition of the dialogue (1586) was entitled *The English Courtier, and the Cûtrey-gentleman.*

suffered was apparently not inflicted upon Sir Thomas
North, a generation later. But a complete humanistic culture had not yet won the respect of Sidney's countrymen.

Especially strong, of course, was the opposition to
poetry. The attack was renewed by the Puritans, but we
cannot fairly blame them alone for the prejudice. Long
before Gosson published his *School of Abuse*, it must have
been clearly evident, since even treatises on medicine and
government were regarded as "vain and unprofitable."
Of the four arguments against poetry which Sidney refutes,
only two are based upon morality: "that it is the mother
of lyes," and "that it is the nurse of abuse." One other,
"that Plato banished [the poets] out of his Commonwealth," is the objection of a scholar of narrow sympathies; but the very first argument mentioned by Sidney,
to which his whole *Defence* is a reply, is "that there beeing
manie other more frutefull knowledges, a man might better
spend his time in them, then in this." [1] "He mought haue
beene muche better occupied," [2] hostile critics said of
Elyot, when he published his *Castell of Helth*. In the days
of Sidney the utilitarians have become reconciled to the
practical subjects in the humanistic program — "the
common laws, divinity or physic" — but they still maintain the war against the arts.

No doubt the hue and cry against poetry was led by the
Puritan moralists. But what rendered the position of the
"courtly maker" especially insecure was the traditional
attitude of the English public at large and even, as we
have seen, of the humanists themselves. In defense of his
verses the courtier could not follow Elyot's example and
show an obvious utility. If he proceeded with tact and
discretion, he might, like Wyatt and Surrey, win honor
among the members of his own class. But unless he took
good heed, "ill reports and mocks," peculiarly damaging

1. *Works*, III, 28.
2. *Castell of Helth*, sigs. A1ᵛ–A2.

in the close society of the court, would make his position ludicrous, and would seriously lower his prestige.

Now if personal distinction was the courtier's aim in battle, as we know it was, in peace he would not willingly exchange honor for malicious ridicule. The Earl of Surrey might risk the anger of London citizens, by breaking their windows in a midnight escapade, but it was a very different thing to acquire the contempt of one's fellows. Gabriel Harvey, when some of his verses were published even anonymously by Spenser, calls the action "the very greatist and notabliste discourtesy in good erneste that ever heretofore was offerid me"; [1] and demands, "If peradventure it chaunce to cum once owte whoe I am, . . . howe will my right worshipfull and thrisevenerable masters of Cambridge scorne at the matter?" [2] In an atmosphere of prejudice, with the certainty of facing ridicule or slander, no ambitious courtier would publish verses, however serious an artist he might be.

What could the courtier do to win honor by his verses, instead of ridicule? He could do nothing without an appreciative audience, which obviously he would find not in the general public, but among men and women of his own class. He could refuse to take himself too seriously, concealing any earnest love for his art under a cloak of urbane indifference. He could prove his mettle in the tourney, in diplomatic missions, and in war, and win the favor of his sovereign, as did Rochford and Wyatt, Surrey and Sir Philip Sidney. And once poetry became the fashion, as it was in the courts of Henry and Elizabeth, he could make his skill in verse a means to the personal distinction which he craved. To this end his poetry was peculiarly effective, for it was beyond cavil his own, in no sense dependent on the fortune that ruled in war or at court. If discreet, the courtier could win admiration by his verses. But he would

1. *Works*, ed. Grosart, I (1884), 112.
2. Page 114.

need to bow to prejudice and fashion, and to follow the course that Castiglione recommends for one who is skilful in tennis:

I will have oure Courtier therfore to do this and all the rest beside handlyng his weapon, as a matter that is not his profession: and not seeme to seeke or loke for any praise for it, nor be acknowen that he bestoweth much study or time about it, although he do it excellently well.[1]

Once more, then, we come back to *sprezzatura*, the urbane nonchalance which seems to treat lightly what must be treated seriously if one is to win distinction. It is the perfect defense against ridicule or malice. It seems to give the case away. It meets the charge that poetry is a mere toy, by saying with the suave good humor of Sidney, "I know not by what mischance in these my not old yeares and idlest times [I have] slipt into the title of a Poet." [2] Thus amiably does the courtier seem to mock his works, standing serenely above them and his critics.

But *sprezzatura* is more than a magic armor against mockery and backbiting. Like Socratic irony, it is at once an invulnerable defense and the mark of a more spiritual quality, the quality of urbane poise by which a man is enabled to see himself and his best-loved works as they really are, without self-flattery. The air of nonchalance is therefore not merely an external mannerism. It reveals the fine sense of proportion which has always gone with the ideal of the harmonious life. It implies a scale of values. The courtier does not give the highest place to his literary creations. His chief ends are not even "Friends, Wife, Children, or himself; but above all things the honour of his Maker, and service of his Prince, or Country." [3] The solemnity with which a Wordsworth or a Shelley can view his writings is therefore utterly foreign to the mind of the

1. *The Courtier*, p. 115.
2. *Works*, III, 3.   3. Greville, p. 40.

courtier. But although poetry is not his chief concern, he nevertheless gives it a place in his scale of values, and an honored place.

The happy instinct for what is graceful and fitting is essentially an artistic quality. Is it unnatural that men trained to speak the right word alike in social gatherings and in counsels of state, should sometimes turn out to be poets? In Sir Philip Sidney, moreover, there is a passionate energy for which literary creation could afford a partial outlet. If he turned to art, therefore, would it not be with the same concentration of his powers which he showed as the would-be associate of Drake and as the military governor of Flushing? Sidney has himself given us the key to his attitude, when as a youth of twenty he writes to Languet:

> I readily allow that I am often more serious than either my age or my pursuits demand; yet this I have learned by experience, that I am never less a prey to melancholy than when I am earnestly applying the feeble powers of my mind to some high and difficult object.[1]

One wonders how such a man could merely dabble in literature "to beguile a summer's holiday." [2] His real attitude, I think, may be discovered from a passage in the *Defence of Poesie*: "Now wherein we want desert, were a thank woorthie labour to expresse. But if I knew I should have mended my selfe, but as I never desired the title, so have I neglected the meanes to come by it, onely overmastered by some thoughts, I yeelded an inckie tribute unto them." [3]

Certainly Sidney never desired exclusively the title of a poet. Yet even as he modestly disclaims the ambition, he

1. Pears, *Correspondence*, p. 29. Cf. Sidney, III, 84.
2. H. J. C. Grierson and A. Melville Clark, in *The Year's Work in English Studies*, VIII (1927), 187.
3. *Works*, III, 36.

reveals two of the poet's most familiar traits. The one is a creative energy which drives him to write; he has been "over-mastered by some thoughts." The other is an artistic conscience; he would have mended himself if he had known wherein he wants desert, but like many another zealous craftsman, he finds his best efforts have sometimes failed.

All the evidence, therefore, points to one conclusion: Sidney's devotion to art is real and enthusiastic. He disparaged his works partly to forestall malignant criticism, partly because he was conscious of their defects; but he wrote eagerly, and he wrote as well as he knew how.

What other conclusion can be drawn from his letter to the Countess of Pembroke?

Here now have you (most deare, and most worthy to be most deare Lady) this idle worke of mine: which I fear (like the Spiders webbe) will be thought fitter to be swept away, then worn to any other purpose. For my part, in very trueth (as the cruell fathers among the Greekes, were woont to doo to the babes they would not foster) I could well find in my harte, to cast out in some desert of forgetfulnes this child, which I am loath to father. But you desired me to doo it, and your desire, to my hart is an absolute commandement. Now, it is done onelie for you, onely to you: if you keepe it to your selfe, or to such friendes, who will weigh errors in the ballaunce of good will, I hope, for the fathers sake, it will be pardoned, perchance made much of, though in it selfe it have deformities. For indeede, for severer eyes it is not, being but a trifle, and that triflinglie handled. Your deare selfe can best witnes the maner, being done in loose sheetes of paper, most of it in your presence, the rest, by sheetes, sent unto you, as fast as they were done. In summe, a young head, not so well stayed as I would it were, (and shall be when God will) having many many fancies begotten in it, if it had not ben in some way delivered, would have growen a monster, & more sorie might I be that they came in, then that they gat out. But his chiefe safetie, shalbe the not walking abroad; & his chiefe protection, the bearing the liverye of your name; which (if much much good will do not deceave me) is worthy to be a sāctuary for a greater offender. This say I, because I knowe the vertue so; and this say I, because it may be ever so; or to say better, because it will be ever so. Read it then at your idle tymes, and the follyes your good judgement wil finde in it, blame not, but laugh at. And so, looking for no better stuffe, then, as in an Haberdashers shoppe, glasses, or feathers, you will continue to love the writer, who doth excedinglie love you; and most most hartelie praies you may long live, to be a princi-pall ornament to the familie of the Sidneis.[1]

Does not the letter bear out all we know of Sidney and of the fashions of his class? The great danger he fears is "ill reports and mocks" such as Elyot encountered. The countess must keep the work to herself or "to such friends who will weigh errors in the balance of good will. . . . But his chief safety shall be the not walking abroad." The danger is the greater because the work is full of deformities, due in part to the haste with which it was written. The author is not yet satisfied. Is he not to rewrite the book within a few years? Yet though it is "but a trifle," unfit for severer eyes than his sister's, he has done his best under somewhat adverse circumstances. Like other poets, he has been overmastered by his thoughts, "having many many fancies begotten in" his "young head." It is but an "idle work," though perchance it may be "made much of." What is the letter but an example of *sprezza-tura*, the nonchalance which conceals a real enthusiasm, the poise by which a man is enabled to detach himself from his works, and see them "in an unflattering glasse of reason"?[2]

Sidney was not primarily a poet. But we get the com-plete man only if beside Greville's assertion that his works "were scribled rather as pamphlets, for entertainment of time, and friends, than any accompt of himself to the

<hr>

1. I, 3-4.   2. III, 37.

world," [1] we place Greville's enthusiastic praise of the *Arcadia*, or Ben Jonson's allusion to

> his great birth, where all the Muses met,[2]

or words like those of George Whetstone:

> About his healme, a lawrell wreath is brayde,
> And by his swoorde, a silver penne is layd.[3]

Fulke Greville himself, indeed, offers an instructive parallel to Sidney. After frequently breaking away from the restraints laid on him by the queen, to seek, as Sidney did, a life of action, and after finding under so imperious a mistress as Elizabeth "the specious fires of youth to prove far more scorching, then glorious," Greville decided to contract his thoughts "within the safe limits of duty." [4] "In which retired view," he goes on to say,

> Sir *Philip Sidney*, that exact image of quiet, and action . . . being ever in mine eyes, made me thinke it no small degree of honour to imitate, or tread in the steps of such a Leader. So that to saile by his Compasse, was shortly (as I said) one of the principall reasons I can alleage, which perswaded me to steale minutes of time from my daily services, and employ them in this kind of writing.[5]

In his leisure hours, or even in moments snatched from business, he turns to literature in the same spirit of adventure as he might have turned to a voyage with Drake: "After I had once ventured upon this spreading *Ocean* of Images, my apprehensive youth, for lack of a well touched

1. *Life of Sir Philip Sidney*, p. 17.
2. "To Penshurst," *The Forest*, *Works*, ed. Gifford and Cunningham, 1875, VIII, 244.
3. *Sir Philip Sidney, his Honorable Life, his Valiant Death, and True Virtues: A perfect Myrror for the followers of Mars and Mercury*, sig.A4ᵛ (*Frondes Caducae*, 1816).
4. Page 149.
5. Page 150. I have corrected the misprint of *faile* for *saile*.

compasse, did easily wander beyond proportion." [1] Greville tells how, with the courtier's thirst for unique achievement, he chose to write tragedies rather than works like his
friend's *Arcadia*, "presuming no man that followes can
ever reach, much lesse go beyond that excellent intended
patterne of his"; [2] and how, in exactly the temper of an
eager artist, he reworked his material many times without
satisfying himself,[3] until finally "from these checks a new
counsell rose up in me, to take away all opinion of serious-
nesse from these perplexed pedegrees; and to this end carelessly cast them into that hypocriticall figure *Ironia*,
wherein men commonly (to keep above their workes)
seeme to make toies of the utmost they can doe." [4]

What parallel could better illustrate the spirit in which
Sidney wrote? Like other courtiers, he longs for a life of
action, but like his fellow poets in every age, he is eagerly
in love with his art. In the temper of the Elizabethan voyager, he launches boldly upon his course, only to find himself soon in strange waters, and greatly in need of compass
and chart. In the mood of the patient craftsman, he shapes
and reshapes his material over a long period of experimentation, never resting while he sees a chance to make the
work better. Like Wyatt, Surrey, and Sackville, he is an
innovator. His final achievement is distinctive, and distinctive he must have meant it to be. But "to keep above
his works," he appears "to make toys of the utmost he
can do."

1. Greville, p. 151.   2. Pages 223–224.
3. Pages 150–154.   4. Pages 153–154.

CHAPTER II

The *Defence of Poesie*[1] as a Classical Oration

EVIDENCE has been given for thinking that Sidney's disparaging references to his literary work are an example of *sprezzatura*, the attribute not of a dabbler or dilettante, but of a sophisticated man of the world who has learned the art of concealing his art. If in his life and actions he shows this quality, we may expect to find in the *Defence of Poesie*, the *Arcadia*, and *Astrophel and Stella*, an artistry no less self-conscious, though often concealed here also in an appearance of spontaneity.

Scholars are sharply divided, however, about the extent to which Sidney is a serious craftsman. Their divergence is particularly wide on the relation between the *Defence of Poesie* and the *Arcadia*. On the one hand, Greenlaw holds

1. Sidney's critical treatise, of course, has two equally familiar titles, for each of which there is good authority. I use only the title given in Feuillerat's edition of Sidney's works, because I regularly use that edition in my quotations, and because the editor shows sufficient reason for preferring the text he has chosen. "Two quartos appeared in the year 1595, the one published by Ponsonby under the title of *The Defence of Poesie*, the other published by Olney under the title of *An Apology for Poetry*. That Ponsonby was the originator of the publication is made clear by ... entries in the Register of the Stationers' Company.... Nor can it be doubted that the Ponsonby text is the more authoritative of the two. It contains two passages not to be found in Olney's quarto; and it was preferred by the Countess of Pembroke when the folio of 1598 was prepared for the press." (Sidney, *Complete Works*, ed. Feuillerat, Cambridge English Classics, 1912–1926, III, v–vi, prefatory note.) I may add that the Penshurst manuscript, once owned by Robert Sidney, has the title of *Defence of Poetry*. (Cf. Sidney, *Works*, III, 377.)

that Sidney's romance is really an epic in prose, a "concrete application of the theories of the province of poetry laid down in his *Defense*." [1] On the other, one of the most recent Sidney scholars declares that "Greenlaw really begs the question" "in the first two words of his article — '*By Sidney* and his contemporaries, *Arcadia* was regarded as an heroic poem.' " [2] Though this same writer, in his comparison of the two versions of the *Arcadia*, is like Dr. S. L. Wolff [3] in showing the self-conscious art with which Sidney worked, the relation between the theories of the *Defence* and the practice of the *Arcadia* still remains obscure. Only lately Mr. Mario Praz has asked "why the man who wrote *The Defence of Poesie* should have thought his trifling pastoral such a momentous affair as to summon up an almost incredible skill in reweaving his story upon the loom of Heliodorus, as Dr. S. L. Wolff has shown." [4] Recent criticism, then, has tended to follow Mr. J. E. Spingarn, who, contrasting Sidney with Ben Jonson, declares that only with Jonson did "the study of the art of poetry [become] an inseparable guide to creation; and it is this element of self-conscious art, guided by the rules of criticism, which distinguishes him from his predecessors." [5]

In the thirty-odd years since Mr. Spingarn gave this opinion, other scholars have come to believe that Sidney's art was "self-conscious"; but there is still a wide difference of judgment whether it was "guided by the rules of criticism."

To offer a partial solution of that problem is the general

1. "Sidney's *Arcadia* as an Example of Elizabethan Allegory," *Kittredge Anniversary Papers*, 1913, p. 337.

2. R. W. Zandvoort, *Sidney's Arcadia, A Comparison between the Two Versions*, 1929, p. 123.

3. *The Greek Romances in Elizabethan Prose Fiction*, Columbia University Studies in Comparative Literature, 1912.

4. "Sidney's Original *Arcadia*," *The London Mercury*, XV (March, 1927), 509.

5. *A History of Literary Criticism in the Renaissance*, Columbia University Studies in Comparative Literature, 5th ed., 1925, p. 258.

aim of the present study. Later chapters will compare Sidney's *Arcadia* with his ideal of an heroic poem, and will touch on *Astrophel and Stella*. The present chapter will discuss the *Defence of Poesie*, not as a statement of critical theory, but as itself an example of literary art, guided by rules.

In the useful arts, at least, the close connection between theory and practice was well recognized. Sidney himself wrote emphatically to his brother Robert, in the very letter in which he refers to his *Arcadia*: "At horsemanshipp when yow exercise it reade Grison[,] Claudio, and a booke that is called La gloria del calvallo, withall, that yow may joyne the through contemplation of it with the exercise, and so shall yow profite more in a moneth then others in a yeare."[1] And nine years before Sidney was born, Roger Ascham wrote of archery in almost the same words: "Aptnesse wᵗ Vse may do sumwhat without Knowlege, but not the tenthe parte, if so be they were ioyned with knowlege."[2] That Ascham's view is characteristic of the age is suggested by the innumerable handbooks on etiquette, fencing, hawking, husbandry, politics, warfare, and almost every other conceivable subject, all showing with what a thrill of discovery Elizabethan England learned that theory may be a guide to practice even for the most gifted. Ascham states the ancient commonplace with great precision:

Aptnesse, Knowlege, and Vse, euen as you saye, make all thinges perfecte. Aptnesse is the fyrst and chyefest thinge, without whiche the other two do no good at all. Knowledge doeth encrease al maner of Aptnesse, bothe lesse and more. Vse sayth Cicero, is farre aboue all teaching. And thus they all three muste be had, to do any thinge very well, and yf anye one be awaye, what so euer is done, is done verye meanly. Aptnesse is yᵉ gyfte of nature, Knowlege, is gotten by yᵉ helpe of

1. Correspondence, *Works*, III, 133.
2. *Toxophilus*, *English Works*, ed. Wright, Cambridge English Classics, 1904, p. 60.

other: Vse lyeth in our owne diligence & labour. So that Aptnesse & vse be ours and w⁺in vs, through nature & labour:
Knowledge not ours, but cōmynge by other: and therfore moost
dilligently, of all men to be sought for.[1]

Now this knowledge which is to guide the learner is itself
derived from the practice of the master. Thus "there lieth
hyd in the nature of Shootinge, an Arte, whiche by notynge,
and obseruynge of him, that is exercised in it, yf he be any
thyng learned at al, maye be taught." [2] Yet the rules of
art, which are thus discovered, though indispensable, are
not enough. For beautiful, or "comely," work, the mark
of perfect skill, "may be perceyued well when it is done,
not described wel how it should be done." [3] Hence there
must be good models to imitate. "In shotynge yf a man,
woulde set before hys eyes .v. or .vi. of the fayrest Archers
that euer he saw shoote, and of one learne to stande, of a
nother [*sic*] to drawe, of an other to lowse, and so take of
euery man, what euery man coulde do best, I dare saye he
shoulde come to suche a comlynesse as neuer man came
to yet." [3]

To sum up the Renaissance doctrine, he who would excel
in any art needs natural gifts, diligent practice, and knowledge. That knowledge has three sources: rules, formulated
from the best practice, imitation of the best models, and,
of course, the experience of one's own practice.

These ideas, applied by Ascham to a practical art, reappear in Sidney's discussion of poetry, with a somewhat
altered emphasis:

Marrie they that delight in *Poesie* it selfe, should seek to
know what they do, and how they do: and especially looke
themselves in an unflattering glasse of reason, if they be enclin-
able unto it. For *Poesie* must not be drawne by the eares, it
must be gently led, or rather it must lead, which was partly the
cause that made the auncient learned affirme, it was a divine gift

---

1. Page 58.   2. Pages 60–61.   3. Page 100.

& no humane skil; since all other knowledges lie readie for anie that have strength of wit: A *Poet* no industrie can make, if his owne *Genius* be not carried unto[1] it. And therefore is an old Proverbe, *Orator fit, Poeta nascitur.* Yet confesse I alwaies, that as the fertilest ground must be manured, so must the highest flying wit have a *Dedalus* to guide him. That *Dedalus*, they say both in this and in other, hath three wings[1] to beare it selfe up into the ayre of due commendation: that is Art, Imitation, and Exercise. But these neither Artificiall Rules, nor imitative pat-ernes, we much comber our selves withall. Exercise indeed we do, but that verie fore-backwardly; for where we should exer-cise to know, we exercise as having knowne: and so is our braine delivered of much matter, which never was begotten by knowledge.[2]

It is obvious that Sidney here is in the same all-pervad-ing tradition as Ascham. He lays the same emphasis upon deliberate craftsmanship, the "Dedalus" who must guide even "the highest flying wit." But he puts a new emphasis upon natural aptitude and personal experience. Unlike the archer, "a poet no industry can make, if his own genius be not carried unto it." Again, the art of English poetry is still so undetermined that it needs intelligent experiments: "where we should exercise to know, we exercise as having known." These views make it difficult to classify Sidney as either romantic or neo-classical. On the one hand, the importance that he gives to imagination and experimenta-tion is hardly Augustan. On the other, the value that he attaches to models and rules would be unpleasant to the devotees of original genius.

However this may be, if in his own literary work we find a rich imaginative energy, guided by "artificial rules," "imitative patterns," and actual experimentation, we may describe Sidney as, in a deeper sense than has yet been recognized, a deliberate and conscious artist.

1. Corrected from variant readings, *Works*, III, 384.
2. *Defence of Poesie, Works*, III, 36–37.

One great obstacle to this view is the contrast, which nearly all modern readers feel, between the *Defence of Poesie* and the *Arcadia*, not in ideas alone, but in style. We admire in the one the humor, the eloquence, the skilful integration of parts, the good taste with which rhetorical figures are generally used. In the other we are repelled by the labyrinths of the plot, the intricate sentences, the over ornateness. This contrast in style has helped to stamp the *Defence* as classical, the *Arcadia* as romantic, and to strengthen the impression that the longer work is only a "trifling pastoral," as Mr. Praz [1] calls it. Yet the difference between the two works may be only apparent. Arcadian mannerisms, as A. S. Cook has shown, occur in the essay.[2] And in organic form, too — *style* in the classical sense — the difference, as I hope to show, has been exaggerated. For if we should find that the rules and "imitative patterns" which Sidney followed, while clear for the *Defence of Poesie*, were uncertain for the *Arcadia*, we should then see that the artistic unity of the one, the comparative formlessness of the other, were both inevitable. The romance would then fall into line with the author's theories, as an example of just the sort of experiment that he believed English literature needed in the 1580's.

Our present concern is with the *Defence of Poesie* as a work of literary art: What rules and models was Sidney following? And how did he mould his material into his chosen form?

For the *Defence*, if not for the *Arcadia*, the "artificial rules" and "imitative patterns" lay ready at hand. No man in the Renaissance could avoid either the classical theories or the classical examples of oratory. What particular orations of Cicero Sidney knew best, whether he had read Demosthenes, what handbooks of rhetoric he thumbed most familiarly, or whether he knew Quintilian at first

1. See above, p. 47, and *The London Mercury*, XV (March, 1927), 509.
2. *The Defense of Poesy*, ed. Cook, 1890, pp. xxi–xxviii.

hand — all these questions are beside the point. In any case, Sidney, in school and university, could not have escaped either Ciceronianism or the general influence of Quintilian, both of which pervaded Renaissance education. In the main, therefore, he could have derived his art either from the study of Cicero's orations or from study of the *De Oratore* or the *Institutes*. Almost certainly he derived it from both the classical theory and the classical practice. Yet it is not his indebtedness to this or that rhetorician or orator, but to the whole tradition of rhetoric, which is the fact of prime importance. From the ancient Greek and Roman orators down to the writers and diplomats of the sixteenth century, from the Sophists down through Aristotle, Cicero, Quintilian, and the rest, to humble Thomas Wilson, the practice of oratory had gone hand in hand with the theory. Both formed, together, a single dominating influence in the education of an Elizabethan gentleman. Both taught the same lesson of form, the same general analysis of a public address. Thus whether we measure Sidney's *Defence* by the "imitative patterns" of the classical orators, or by the "artificial rules" of the rhetoricians, the result will be the same. For the sake of simplicity, therefore, I shall compare Sidney's practice only with that taught in certain well-known treatises on rhetoric, particularly Cicero's *De Oratore*, Quintilian's *Institutes*, and Wilson's *Arte of Rhetorique*. The first he quotes [1] and refers [2] to in the *Defence*. General probability and the evidence about to be presented make his acquaintance with the other two almost certain, and in any case they are wholly representative of the tradition of rhetoric.

Sidney's indebtedness to the tradition is not vague or intangible. Not only does his so-called critical essay have a general oratorical flavor, characteristic of so much of the writing of the sixteenth century; it can be classified as a speech of a well-recognized variety. Quintilian, following

1. *Works*, III, 12.   2. Page 43.

the earlier Greek rhetoricians, divides public addresses into three kinds: panegyrical, deliberative, and judicial.[1] The last, which has to do especially with legal trials, may be either an attack or a defense.[2] Now it needs no great analysis to see that the *Defence of Poesie* bears at least a superficial resemblance to a judicial oration in behalf of an accused client. The very title suggests a trial in a regular court. So, occasionally, does the language, as when Sidney proposes to examine poetry first "by his workes, and then by his parts," and hopes that "if in neither of these Anatomies hee be condemnable, . . . we shall obteine a more favourable sentence."[3] But the resemblance goes much deeper.

From beginning to end the essay is planned according to the instructions of the rhetoricians. Every oration, we are told by the Englishman Thomas Wilson,[4] has seven parts: "the Enterance or beginning; the Narration; the Proposition; the Deuision or seuerall parting of things; the confirmation; the confutation; the Conclusion;" or to use the Latin terms, the *exordium, narratio, propositio, partitio, confirmatio, reprehensio,* and *peroratio.* Quintilian finds only five parts in an oration.[5] But, as Cicero[6] points out, whether the main divisions be four, five, six, or seven is of small consequence, for it is merely a question of whether the propositio, partitio, and confutatio (or reprehensio) be parts of the confirmatio, or independent elements. In any case, the normal oration contains them all. And in addition some authorities, says Cicero, "direct you, before you come to the peroration, to make a digression by way of embellishment or amplification, then to sum up and conclude."[6] The digression and the seven other parts are unmistakable in the *Defence of Poesie.*

---

1. *Institutes*, trans. Watson, 1856, III. iv. 12–15 (I, 182–183).
2. III. ix. 1 (I, 240).   3. *Works*, III, 11.
4. *Arte of Rhetorique*, 1560, ed. Mair, 1909, p. 7.
5. III. ix. 1–2 (I, 240).
6. *De Oratore*, trans. Watson, 1860, II. 19 (p. 104).

The exordium contains the anecdote of Pugliano's praise of horsemanship, Sidney's comments upon it, and the transition to the subject of the essay. The narratio, introduced by the connective clause, "and first truly to all them that professing learning envey against Poetrie," [1] describes the civilizing influence of poetry throughout its history, and shows particularly its high reputation among the Romans and Greeks. The propositio is the definition, "*Poesie* therefore, is an Art of *Imitation*," *et cetera*.[2] The partitio, beginning "Now let us goe to a more ordinarie opening of him," [2] contains the propositio within itself, distinguishes three types of poetry, shows that there is disagreement only about the third, and closes with the promise "first to way this latter sort of poetrie by his workes, and then by his parts." [3] The confirmatio follows immediately, comprising the two divisions [4] indicated in the partitio, and a summary [5] at the end. The reprehensio begins with the introductory sentence, "But bicause we have eares aswell as toongs, . . . let us heare, and as well as we can, ponder what objections be made against this Art," [6] and itself includes a clearly marked partitio,[7] and closing summary.[8] There follows a digression,[9] comprising the famous remarks on English literature, which begin with the sentence, "But since I have runne so long a Carrier in this matter, me thinkes before I give my penne a full stoppe, it shall be but a litle more lost time, to enquire why England . . . should be growne so hard a stepmother to *Poets*." [8] Finally, the peroratio, with its inevitable transitional words, "so that since," [10] brings the whole to a close. Thus the seven parts of an oration, plus a digression in the most approved place, are all here. And nothing else is here: the

1. *Works*, III, 4.   2. Page 9.
3. Page 11.
4. Pages 11-22, 22-25.
5. Pages 25-26.   6. Page 26.
7. Page 28.   8. Page 35.
9. Pages 35-45.   10. Page 45.

Defence contains no material that does not fall within the divisions I have described.

For evidence that these divisions are of Sidney's own making, we have first of all the transitional expressions with which each one begins.   These are so plain that some of the sections, particularly the exordium, the reprehensio, and the peroratio, have always been recognized as independent units.   The others, except the digression, have generally been described as belonging to the proof.   The *narratio* has not even been taken as a single part, but as two.[1]   And the relation of each section to the classical model has never been pointed out.   To establish that relation will require a detailed comparison of the *Defence* with the precepts of the rhetoricians.

The aim of an exordium, says Quintilian, is "to prepare the hearer to listen to us more readily in the subsequent parts of our pleading. This object, as is agreed among most authors, is principally effected by three means, by securing his *good will* and *attention*, and by rendering him *desirous of further information*."[2] One good method, according to Thomas Wilson, is, "if time may so serue, . . . to begin with some pleasaunt tale, or take an occasion to iest wittely."[3] Now Sidney's anecdote of Pugliano is just such a "pleasant tale," and his humorous comments are just the sort of witty jesting which Wilson advises, and which obviously serves to win the hearer's "good will and attention," and to render him "desirous of further information." Again, Sidney's modest references to his "having slipt into the title of a poet" in his "not old years and idlest times," and to the likelihood that he will defend his "unelected vocation" "with more good will, than good reasons," are exactly in line with the ancient teaching that the orator should begin modestly. Quintilian, for example, thinks that "it is a sort of tacit commendation to him, if

1. See below, pp. 61 ff.
2. *Institutes*, IV. i. 5 (I, 254).   3. *Arte of Rhetorique*, p. 104.

he represents himself as weak, and inferior in ability to
those acting against him." [1] Cicero declares that there is
no "doubt, but that the beginning of a speech ought very
seldom to be vehement and pugnacious." [2] And Thomas
Wilson suggests that "if the cause be . . . such as will not
be well borne with all, but needeth much helpe and fauour
of the hearers: it shalbe the speakers part priuely to get
fauour, & by humble talk to win their good wils." [3] Sidney's modesty, then, accords with established doctrine, as
old as "that dissembling of the speakers of antiquity to
conceal their eloquence." [4] Far from showing a real indifference to his other works, therefore, his depreciatory
allusions show instead the deliberate and careful art of the
work in hand. Again, the reference to his "unelected vocation" illustrates the ancient rule that the advocate should
appear to plead from "obligations of kindred or friendship," [5] or from other high motives, in order to convey an
impression of integrity. Related to these qualities of apparent ingenuousness and self-depreciation is the air of
easy naturalness which distinguishes the exordium — in
accordance, be it noted, with the advice of Wilson, "that
euermore the beginning be not ouermuch laboured, nor
curiously made, but rather apt to the purpose, seeming
vpon present occasion, euermore to take place, and so to
bee deuised, as though wee speake altogether, without any
great studie." [6]

Not only do the humor, the apparent modesty and sincerity, the prevailing lightness of touch, conform to rhetorical teaching; so, too, does the substance of the exordium.
For the beginning of a speech, says Cicero, ought not to
"be sought from without, or from any thing unconnected
with the subject, but to be derived from the very essence of

1. *Institutes*, IV. i. 8 (I, 255).
2. *De Oratore*, II. 78 (p. 176).
3. *Arte of Rhetorique*, p. 100.   4. *Institutes*, IV. i. 9 (I, 255).
5. IV. i. 7 (I, 254).   6. Page 105.

the cause." [1] Now the heart of Sidney's argument, of course, is that poetry, giving both precept and example, is an eloquent speaking picture, a more effective teacher than philosophy, with its "bare rule," or history, with its mere facts. And the relation between precept and example is skilfully suggested in Sidney's humorous account of his instructor in horsemanship, who, "according to the fertilnes of the Italian wit, did not onely affoord us the demonstration of his practise, but sought to enrich our mindes with the contemplations therein, which he thought most precious." [2] Furthermore, in Pugliano's panegyric upon the horse, Sidney professes to discover evidence that "selfe-love is better then any guilding, to make that seem gorgious wherin our selves be parties." [2] Thus in deriving a conclusion from an example, he illustrates the interrelation between theory and practice which in the first sentence he has mentioned in abstract terms. This highly complex passage, like all good exordia, has "wholly grown out of the cause under consideration," [1] for it expresses the fundamental idea on which the entire argument is to be built.

Sidney's introduction, then, is in both substance and manner a classical exordium. Yet it gives an illusion of perfect spontaneity. The jesting, the self-disparagement, the apparent ingenuousness, the light touch conceal the fact that they are all according to rule, as they veil also the leading idea. The exordium is thus a notable example of art which seems no art.

The section that I have called the narratio offers greater difficulties. Yet close examination will show that, like the exordium, it conforms to ancient precedent.

The Latin term narratio has no exact English equivalent. "Narration" is with us too nearly identical with "story-telling." "Statement of facts," which is Watson's translation, is cumbersome, though accurate. The Latin word includes the ideas of both narrating and expounding.

---

1. *De Oratore*, II. 78 (p. 177).   2. *Works*, III, 3.

In judicial oratory it is the lawyer's "*account of a thing done, or supposed to have been done; which account is adapted to persuade;* or, as Apollodorus defines it, *a narrative to inform the auditor what the matter in question is.*" [1] In a legal trial, of course, it deals largely with specific incidents. What was the defendant doing at the moment the crime charged to him was committed? But it may also include, where pertinent, a description of his life as a whole and of his reputation. "A person accused of bribery" would not "act wrong in stating what sort of parents he had, how he himself has lived," [2] and so forth.

Now when the art of poetry is on trial, there is obviously no question of what the defendant did at a particular time or place. As in a suit for libel, the character of the defendant is the point at issue, and the significant evidence is his past life and his reputation. It is, therefore, with precisely these two subjects that Sidney deals in his narratio.

The part that deals with the antiquity and universality of poetry gives, as it were, the condensed life story of the accused. And the part that discusses the names which the ancients gave the poet shows his high reputation. The first section marshals a long array of facts: that poets were the first writers and the earliest civilizing influence, most notably in Greece, but also in Rome, modern Italy, and England; that the fathers of philosophy and the greatest historians have had to borrow the poet's art in order to teach their lessons to a general audience; that even today, among half-civilized or barbaric peoples, as the Turks, the Irish, the American Indians, and the Welsh, poetry is still the "right popular philosopher"; so that "it is not more notable in the soone beginning, then in long continuing" [3] to be "the first light giver to ignorance." [4] The second part of the narratio discusses the Roman word for "poet," and then the Greek, showing the dignity of each, and its appro-

1. Quintilian, IV. ii. 31 (I, 279).   2. IV. ii. 15 (I, 275).
3. Sidney, *Works*, III, 6.   4. Page 4.

priateness. The Latin *Vates* is a "heavenly" title, suited to "this hart-ravishing knowledge." Its appropriateness appears in the Roman custom of consulting the *Sortes Virgilianæ*; in prophecies of oracles, which "were wholly delivered in verses"; and best of all in the "heavenly poesie" of David's Psalms. The Greek ποιητῆς, equivalent to the English "maker," is a "high and incomparable" title, fitly describing the creative power of the poet. By virtue of this power, not only is he superior to the professors of all other arts, but he is himself in effect "an other nature: in making things either better then nature bringeth foorth, or quite a new";[1] so that of all mankind, formed in the likeness of "the heavenly maker," the poet, in his creative activity, is nearest to that divine origin, and has fullest dominion over the works of nature.

In this whole division of the essay, then, every detail is suited to a narratio. The defendant has had a long life of honorable service, and has enjoyed among the noblest peoples an incomparable reputation. Since there is no specific incident to be described, this is all that in the nature of the case the narratio can contain.

If the substance of this part of the *Defence* is suitable to a classical oration, so also is the style. The three essential qualities of *lucidity, conciseness*, and *credibility*[2] seem too obvious to require elaborate proof. *Magnificence*, a quality which some authorities added to the other three (though Quintilian,[3] with greater discrimination, includes it only where it is appropriate), appears fitly in the eloquent passage that describes the august titles bestowed by the Romans and Greeks upon the poet. Besides attaining all these qualities, Sidney seems to have kept in mind "the following directions . . . [which] are commonly given respecting the statement of facts; that no *digression* is to

1. Page 8.
2. See Quintilian, iv. ii. 31 ff. (I, 279 ff.).
3. iv. ii. 61–62 (I, 285).

be made from it; that we are *to address ourselves constantly
to the judge;* that we are *to speak in no character but our own;*
and that we are to *introduce no argumentation;* and some
even add that we are *not to attempt to excite the feelings.*" [1]
These five precepts, be it noted, have only the qualified
approval of Quintilian: they "are to be in general observed;
. . . unless the nature of our cause obliges us to disregard
them." [1] The last of them he thinks quite wrong as usually
stated. And it is in the critical spirit of Quintilian that
Sidney appears to have regarded them all. Each throws
interesting light upon his literary methods, the last two
most clearly.

His general adherence to the first rule is manifest from
the summary and analysis that have already been made.
He has no long digression, but he has a short one at the
very beginning of the narratio, where, as Cook [2] shrewdly
observes, he is parodying Gosson's euphuism: "And will
you play the Hedgehogge . . . ? Or . . . the Vipers?" [3]
This slight departure from the rule is precisely of the kind
approved by Quintilian, who directs that in the narratio
there be no digression "except such as is short, and of such
a nature that we may seem to be hurried into it, out of our
right course, by the strength of our feelings," [4] an injunc-
tion which emphasizes for us the mock-heroic tone in which
Sidney begins the *Defence.* The second precept, "that we
are to address ourselves constantly to the judge," is violated in this same digression, for Sidney is apostrophizing
his opponents. Yet Quintilian gives his approval to such
a "brief diversion of our speech from" the judge. [5] Moreover, in the main, Sidney obeys the precept scrupulously.
Though he rarely uses the pronoun *you,* he directs his
rhetorical questions at the judge, that is, the reader. That
he had constantly in mind an audience none too favorable

1. *Institutes,* iv. ii. 103 (I, 294).   2. See *The Defense of Poesy,* p. 61.
3. *Works,* III, 4.   4. iv. ii. 104 (I, 294 f.).
5. iv. ii. 106 (I, 295).

to his cause, is suggested by the tact and caution of such a passage as "And may not I presume a little farther, to shewe the reasonablenesse of this word *Vatis* [*sic*], and say that the holy *Davids* Psalms are a divine *Poeme*? . . . But truly now having named him, I feare I seeme to prophane that holy name [*i.e.*, David], applying it to Poetry."[1] The same passage illustrates the third rule, "that we are to speak in no character but our own." In contrast to a passage[2] a few pages later, where Sidney has the historian speak in the first person, the "I" of the narratio always refers to the writer. Sidney's fidelity to even these comparatively minor precepts shows the care with which he was following the best rhetorical doctrine.

The fourth rule, "that we are to introduce no argumentation," he appears at first sight to have ignored. This, at least, is the view of two of his modern editors. Mr. J. Churton Collins divides what I have called the narratio into eight sections, heading the first the "first argument in its [*i.e.*, Poetry's] favour — its antiquity."[3] Cook[4] divides the narratio into the two sections that I have described, but makes them two of nine independent parts of the essay. Neither editor treats it as a single unit with two subdivisions; neither mentions the ancient analysis of the oration; both take the whole division as part of the proof, instead of a preparation for it. In support of this interpretation there is the fact that Sidney himself includes the two subdivisions of the narratio in his summary at the end of the confirmatio,[5] and that they do in fact advance the argument of the whole, since an art that has always been "a light giver to ignorance" and that has received the highest honor among the most civilized nations needs little further defense.

1. Pages 6–7.
2. Pages 12–13.
3. *Sidney's Apologie for Poetrie*, ed. J. Churton Collins, 1907, p. 2.
4. *The Defense of Poesy*, p. xli.
5. *Works*, III, 25–26.

But these facts only mean that the essay is a skilful piece of work. Part of the art lies in so arranging the statement of facts that the favorable verdict shall follow inevitably. If it be "the chief excellence of narration," as Cicero observes, "that it be pleasing and adapted to persuade," [1] then it will seem its own proof. Moreover, Sidney's method, so far as it departs from the rule, has the sanction of Quintilian. "Continued *argumentation*," observes that authority, ". . . we must never use in our statement of facts; though we may introduce a *single argument* occasionally." [2] And after citing the example of Cicero, he continues significantly that "we are not to state things as a witness, but as an advocate." [3] This is precisely what Sidney has done. He has stated the facts of literary history in the most favorable light. He has even introduced "single arguments" in passing: as when he supports with reasons the statements that Solon was a poet; [4] that in Plato's dialogues "the skin as it were and beautie, depended most of Poetrie"; [4] that "*Davids* Psalms are a divine *Poeme*"; [5] or that the phenomenon of poetic inspiration offers "no small arguments . . . of that first accursed fall of *Adam*." [6] Yet all these brief single arguments stand independent one of another. They are brought in to give to statements of fact that quality of credibility, which, all authorities agreed, is essential to a narratio. Here is no "continued argumentation," but narration and exposition turned to the purposes of debate. The procedure is precisely in accord with Quintilian's instructions, and with the practice of Cicero: "What he stated he made credible by giving a reason for it, and made a strong impression, at the same time, on the feelings of his audience." [7]

Sidney, like Cicero, does not hesitate to appeal to the

1. *De Oratore*, II. 80 (p. 179).
2. *Institutes*, IV. ii. 108 (I, 295–296).
3. IV. ii. 108 (I, 296).   4. *Works*, III, 5.
5. Page 6.   6. Page 9.
7. *Institutes*, IV. ii. 110 (I, 296).

feelings, thus disregarding the fifth rule to which Quintilian alludes. Here, as usual, he has the support of that great authority, who insists that "the statement of facts requires . . . to be adorned with all the attractions and grace of which it is susceptible. But it makes a great difference what the nature of the case . . . is." [1] "In the smaller sort," he continues, ". . . the garb of the statement ought to be neat, and, as it were, close-fitting; . . . here every word ought to be expressive; . . . the style should be apparently artless, but as agreeable as possible; there should be no figures borrowed from poetry, . . . but such only as lessen tedium by variety, and relieve attention by change." [2] On the other hand, "when the cause is of greater moment, it will be proper to speak of heinous crimes in a tone of invective, and of mournful occurrences in one of pity." [3] At bottom, then, it is a question of fitness to the occasion, to be decided by the sense and good taste of each speaker, rather than by rules.

If Sidney, then, must determine by his own tact the emotional tone of his speech, perhaps each reader, also, must estimate it for himself, since he best knows the impression on his own feelings. Thus much, however, seems clear: that in the two parts of his narratio the style varies almost exactly as Quintilian would have approved, in the first part being comparatively simple, in the second being adorned with a splendor suitable for describing the poet's lofty titles. In the one there is a humorous allusion to Plato's dialogues, "wherein hee faines many honest Burgesses of *Athens* speak of such matters, that if they had bene set on the Racke, they would never have confessed them." [4] In the other there is no trace of humor, but much enthusiasm and much religious reverence. In language warm with Platonic imagination, Sidney refers to David as "a passionate lover of that unspeakable and everlasting

1. IV. ii. 116 (I, 297). 2. IV. ii. 117–118 (I, 297).
3. IV. ii. 120 (I, 298). 4. *Works*, III, 5.

bewtie, to be seene by the eyes of the mind, onely cleared by fayth."[1] He has in the first part no images so striking as "that high flying libertie of conceit propper to the Poet,"[2] or "freely raunging within the Zodiack of his owne wit";[3] no passage so glowing as the description of the poet's golden world, set forth in rich tapestry, with "pleasaunt rivers, fruitfull trees, sweete smelling flowers, . . . [or] whatsoever els may make the too much loved earth more lovely."[3] To be sure, matter-of-fact passages in the second part and poetic figures in the first emphasize the underlying unity of the whole narratio. The contrast in style is not violent. But it is sufficiently unmistakable to show that Sidney uses poetic imagery to touch the feelings, with exactly that fine sense of fitness prescribed by Quintilian.

Thus in all five of the common rules of style, Sidney conforms to ancient usage, as modified and taught by the great Latin rhetorician. Lucid, concise, persuading belief, everywhere suited to his purpose, Sidney's manner of writing no less than his subject matter proves that he has made a classical narratio.

Scrupulously obedient to precedent, he is free from all taint of servility, so wholly is he guided by his own "learned discretion."[4] Nowhere is this better shown than in the neatness with which he fits the narratio into the general plan of the *Defence*. For just as in the exordium he introduces the fundamental idea of the relation between practice and theory, so here also he brings in numerous hints of what is to follow. The allusion to the use of the poetic art by philosophers and historians paves the way for a later contrast which is to form the corner stone of the confirmatio. The mention of Plato's genius for "feigning" points forward both to the refutation of the charge that Plato was hostile to poets, and to the doctrine, developed

1. *Works*, III, 7.   2. Page 6.
3. Page 8.
4. Page 10.

in the partitio, that the essence of poetry is fiction rather than verse. The argument that "if ever learning come among [the Indians], it must be by having their hard dull wittes softened and sharpened with the sweete delights of Poetrie," [1] foreshadows the emphasis upon the moving power, by virtue of which that art is a better teacher than philosophy. Finally, the Roman *Vates* and the Greek ποιητῆς are examples respectively of the religious and the creative poets defined in the partitio.

Not only is the statement of facts built most skilfully into the whole structure of the oration; it is admirably suited to the court audience of the 1580's. I will not discuss its grace and eloquence, so agreeable to the best taste of the age. Its substance, too, is precisely what the occasion required. For, as Quintilian observes, "there are some causes, and indeed not a few, which are easy to be defended so far as to refute the charge on which the trial bears, but which labour under many grievous enormities of the defendant's former life; and these must first be set aside, in order that the judge may listen favorably to the defence of the point about which the question really is." [2] In the years when the Puritans launched their attack, the cause of poetry was of this kind; it "laboured under many grievous enormities" with which the defendant was not explicitly charged. Courtly "making" began to flourish when startling innovations were filling thoughtful lovers of England with uneasiness and dread. It was practiced by that "devil incarnate," the Italianate Englishman. Inevitably there was a feeling "that before *Poets* began to be in price, our Nation had set their hearts delight uppon action, and not imagination, rather doing things worthie to be written, thē writing things fit to be done." [3] Sidney could produce an elaborate philosophical argument in favor of feigned examples; he could demolish the four

1. Page 5.
2. *Institutes*, IV. ii. 27 (I, 278).   3. Sidney, III, 31.

definite charges of his opponents; but the less articulate, though deeply felt, prejudice against poetry as a new-fangled innovation had first to be set aside. To show its antiquity, therefore, and the honorable names given it by the ancients was to strike at the root of this prejudice. The best argument might only have awakened antago-nism; and so Sidney's method is to give new light, without even mentioning the feeling that he seeks to remove. Then later, when he does allude to it, he can brush it aside with gentle irony, and a glance at his statement of facts: "What that before tyme was, I thinke scarcely *Sphinx* can tell; sith no memory is so auncient that hath the precedence of Poetrie." [1] Of Sidney's narratio we can say what Quintil-ian said of one of Cicero's: that "if the particulars had been stated in other terms, they would have warned the judge . . . to be on his guard against the pleader." [2] It is one of those most excellent preparations, "of which the intention is not apparent." [3]

Thus Sidney's art has the sanction of illustrious teachers. Following with minute fidelity their instructions for writ-ing a narratio, he is yet so true to their inward spirit as to give an impression of unstudied genius.

The rest of the *Defence* may be analyzed more briefly, though the propositio and partitio offer some difficulty.

These must be considered together. Both of them, according to Wilson and those ancients who distinguished seven main divisions in an oration, are independent ele-ments. According to Quintilian, both are parts of the proof. Cicero pays little attention to the propositio, but makes a separate division of the partitio. Sidney, who apparently follows Cicero, has a clearly marked partitio, of which his propositio forms the first element.

1. I follow here the text of Olney, as given by Collins, *Sidney's Apologie*, p. 42. Ponsonby's text, reprinted by Feuillerat, which I ordinarily follow, has a *not* after *hath* in this passage — which seems obviously corrupt. Cf. *Works*, III, 31.

2. *Institutes*, IV. ii. 58 (I, 285).   3. IV. ii. 57 (I, 284).

The propositio, when it occurs, stands normally just after the narratio.[1] It is defined by Wilson as "a pithie sentence comprehended in a small roome, the somme of the whole matter."[2] Now in Sidney we find, in the normal position, the definition of poetry: "*Poesie*, therefore, is an Art of *Imitation* — for so *Aristotle* termeth it in the word μίμησις, that is to say, a representing, counterfeiting, or figuring forth; to speake Metaphorically, a speaking *Picture* — with this end, to teach and delight."[3] It is "pithy." It is "comprehended in a small room", the only parenthesis being an explanation of the technical term *imitation*. It is "the sum of the whole matter"; for if poetry teaches and delights, how can it fairly be attacked? Clearly this definition is a propositio. In the opinion of Quintilian a propositio may be of two kinds: one may be advanced "in stating the principal question," the other "to introduce particular arguments."[4] The one quoted from Sidney is of the first sort. The other may be illustrated by the saying of Aristotle "that Poetrie is φιλοσοφωτερων and σπουδαιοτερον [*sic*], that is to say, it is more Philosophicall and more studiously serious then History."[5] This statement, since with it Sidney begins his comparison of poetry with history, illustrates further Quintilian's dictum that "the commencement of any proof is a *proposition*."[6] But Sidney's general propositio (the definition of poetry) is less a part of a proof than the beginning of the partitio.

Rightly used in a cause, a partitio lights up and clarifies the whole speech. Its parts are two. . . . One part shows in what we agree with our opponents, and what is left in controversy; out of which one point in particular is made fast in the hearer's mind, on which he is to fix his undivided attention. The other

---

1. Cf. Wilson, *Arte of Rhetorique*, p. 111, and Quintilian, IV. iv. 1 (I, 304).
2. Page 7.
3. *Works*, III, 9. The punctuation is mine. Cf. variant readings, p. 379.
4. IV. iv. 1 (I, 304–305).
5. Sidney, III, 16. I emend the text from the variant reading of Olney, as given in Feuillerat's notes, III, 380.   6. IV. iv. 1 (I, 304).

is the part in which an exposition of those subjects on which we are to speak is briefly laid forth in orderly fashion.[1]

Such is Cicero's view, in his early treatise on rhetoric; and the more mature *De Oratore* states the same ideas more briefly and less formally.[2] Quintilian emphasizes the second function of the partitio, "the enumeration, according to their order, of our own propositions, or those of our adversary, or both." [3] Such an enumeration occurs in Sidney's refutation, where he states the four main arguments to which he will reply.[4] Another stands just before his proof, where he proposes "first to way this latter sort of poetrie by his workes, and then by his parts." [5] *Partition* in this limited sense is the act of enunciating propositions, preparatory to proof or refutation. But the partitio as described by Cicero is that division of the speech in which the case is analyzed.

In this sense, the partitio in the *Defence of Poesie* is the passage which begins significantly, "Now let us goe to a more ordinarie opening," [6] and which ends with the promise (in the sentence just quoted) to consider first the works, then the parts, of poetry. Proceeding from the definition of poetry, Sidney distinguishes three kinds: religious, philosophical, and creative. The first, all reverent persons will agree to honor. The second, though grammarians may dispute whether it be truly poetry or no, can at least give no offense to persons of the least judgment. The third only is the occasion of disagreement. It has eight species. Its essential is not verse, but "delightful teaching" by means of fiction. The argument for the defense, therefore, will inquire first if it works this pleasing and useful effect, second if in all its eight kinds there is anything hurtful.

1. Cicero, *Art of Rhetoric*, I. xxii. 31. I translate from "M. Tullii Ciceronis *Artis Rhetoricae*, Libri duo, recensuit Andreas Weidner, Berolini, apud Weidmannos," 1878, pp. 29–30.   2. *De Oratore*, II. 81 (p. 180).

3. *Institutes*, IV. v. 1 (I, 307).   4. *Works*, III, 28.

5. Page 11.   6. Page 9.

Manifestly, the first half of this passage, containing the definition of poetry and the discussion of its three kinds, is that part of the partitio which, in the language of the *De Oratore*, lays down "the matter in question", and settles "what is the point that comes under dispute." [1] The rest of the passage amplifies the point at issue, in particular "making fast in the hearer's mind" the idea that the essential thing is fiction; and closes with the brief "exposition of the subjects on which" Sidney is to speak. The whole, there can be no doubt, is a Ciceronian partitio: an analysis of the case, in which the first step is the defining of poetry; thus it includes the propositio as one of its elements.

Of the four remaining divisions of the *Defence*, two have always been recognized as the refutation and the conclusion. That the other two are the confirmatio and digressio of the ancient oration would be apparent from a very brief analysis. More extended discussion will show Sidney's artistry more clearly.

His affirmative argument, as we have seen, has generally been described as including what I have called the narratio and partitio, as well as the confirmatio. Since the first two have been shown to be independent parts preparatory to the proof, there can be no objection to restricting to the third the term proof, or confirmatio.

In this part of an oration, the laws of rhetoric coincide nearly with the rules of logic. [2] Now "euery single questiõ," says Wilson in his *Rule of Reason* (1553), "is eight waies examined." [3] Among these Sidney has made chief use of the third and fifth. "The thirde question is, when the partes, & euery seuerall kinde is considered, and for this question the diuisiõ and particion dooe muche good. . . .

---

1. *De Oratore*, ii. 81 (p. 180). See the quotation from the *Artis Rhetoricae*, given above, pp. 67–68.
2. Cf. Wilson, *Arte of Rhetorique*, p. 112.
3. Fol. 17.

The fifte question is, when the effecte, the office, or propre woorkyng is examined." [1]   Clearly, these two "questions" correspond to the two broad divisions in Sidney's confirmatio, where we first weigh poetry "by his workes, and then by his parts." [2]

Of Wilson's six other ways of examining a subject, Sidney makes incidental use of three. Already, in the partitio, and particularly in the definition of poetry, he has answered Wilson's second question, "what [the] thing is." [1]   Another he answers in the very beginning of the confirmatio. "The fowerth question is, to aske what are the causes, & especially what is the efficient cause, and what is the final cause, or the ende of any thing." [1]   The efficient cause Sidney omits, but the "finall end [of poetry, as of all learning], is to lead and draw us to as high a perfection, as our degenerate soules . . . can be capable of." [2]   Again, Wilson's eighth question, "what example there is, or aucthoritie to proue it," [3] is answered many times in Sidney's confirmatio. His favorite method of supporting a general statement is by citing illustrative examples. If Sidney has omitted three of the eight questions, he is justified by Quintilian:

Students of eloquence . . . need not search for every topic of argument, and knock as it were, at its door, to know whether it will answer, and serve to prove what they desire. . . . And I know not whether all rules for argument would not be a hindrance to us, unless a certain penetration of mind, engendered in us by nature and exercised by study, conducted us straight to all the considerations suited to any particular cause. [4]

Thus Sidney's native discretion, guided everywhere by the art of logic, governs the progress of his whole proof. This may be illustrated in the part in which he examines poetry by its effect. The final end of all learning, he tells

1. Wilson, *Rule of Reason*, fol. 17.   2. *Works*, III, 11.
3. *Rule of Reason*, fol. 17ᵛ.
4. *Institutes*, v. x. 122–123 (I, 361).

us, is to draw our souls to as high a perfection as possible. The branches of learning fall into two groups: those which, like astronomy, natural science, metaphysics, and mathematics, contribute only indirectly to this end; and those which, teaching the knowledge of a man's self, contribute directly and much more effectually. Among the second sort, moral philosophy teaches by precept, history by example; divinity and law are ruled out of the discussion; and there are no others except poetry. This art teaches more clearly than philosophy, because its speaking picture is more vivid than the abstract precepts of philosophy, and yet often quite as complete. Poetry teaches more truly than history because its examples are more universal, it can give the causes of events better, its feigned incidents are quite as instructive as the true events of history, and it can show much better the reward of virtue and the punishment of vice. Above all, poetry teaches more powerfully than either philosophy or history, because it more strongly moves the mind to the love of virtue, thus leading not alone to the knowledge of it, but to the practice. Of all human sciences, therefore, poetry, "being the most familiar to teach [virtue], and most Princely to move towards it, in the most excellent worke, is the most excellent workeman." [1]

This whole passage illustrates two of the kinds of argument analyzed by Wilson. In all there are four: "a perfeicte Argument, an vnperfeicte Argumente, an inductione, an example." [2] A perfect argument is a formally complete syllogism, an "unperfect" one is a true, but formally incomplete, syllogism; an example includes what we should call comparison, as well as example in the more limited sense of illustration. Sidney does not use induction or "a perfect argument," but rather the incomplete syllogism and the example, in both its kinds.

1. Pages 21–22. I summarize here pp. 11–22.
2. *Rule of Reason*, fol. 23.

His "imperfect arguments" can readily be made perfect, as thus:

The best sciences best teach virtue.
Sciences which study man best teach virtue.
Therefore sciences which study man are the best sciences.

Or again,

A science which teaches virtue better than philosophy and
history is the best science of all.
Poetry is a science which teaches virtue better than philosophy and history.
Therefore poetry is the best science of all.

In these two syllogisms is the sum of Sidney's argument.

Example and comparison, though they are distinguished by Cicero, are treated together by Wilson, as by Quintilian.[1] The first Sidney uses when he supports general statements by illustrative facts and authorities; as when he shows that poetry is more universal than history by citing the authority of Aristotle, and then the examples of "the fained Cyrus," Æneas, Tantalus, Atreus, and Ulysses from poetry, and from history "the true Cyrus," Æneas, Alexander, and Scipio.[2] In fact, he gives this sort of example in support of nearly every generalization, drawing several times from the Bible. The second sort he uses through his whole comparison of poetry with philosophy and history. The argument may be summarized in this form: "If philosophy, with its precepts, and history, with its examples, are both good teachers of virtue, much more so is poetry, which embodies both precepts and examples," — a form precisely parallel to an illustration which Quintilian gives of one type of comparative argument: "If theft is a crime, much more is sacrilege."[3]

Not only does the first part of the confirmatio illustrate two well-recognized kinds of argument. It is equally logi-

1. *Institutes*, v. xi. 2 (I, 362).   2. *Works*, III, 16.
3. v. x. 89 (I, 353).

cal in the arrangement of the ideas. Here Wilson lays down two rules, the first making merely for clear presentation, the second for clear reasoning. "The diuision," he says, "asmoche as maie bee (for it cannot alwaies bee so) ought to bee made with twoo contrarie differences, fully conteinyng in theimself, the whole coumpasse or widenesse of the generall woorde, or that whiche is diuided. . . . Again, the difference [*sic*] whiche diuide the generall woorde, beyng ioigned bothe together, must be equall to thesaid [*sic*] general woorde." [1] Sidney heeds both injunctions. In following the first he makes a division of all learning into "two contrary differences": those subjects which do not study man directly, and those which do. Among those that do, he distinguishes four besides poetry, which he again divides into two groups, containing respectively the subjects that are important, and those that are unimportant, to the present discussion. Hence in each of these two lesser groups, there are again two parts: in the first, philosophy and history; in the second, divinity and law. Thus, though Wilson's first direction is but a convenient rule of thumb, Sidney has adhered to it closely. Inevitably, therefore, he has followed the important principle expressed in the second rule. Each of his pairs of "differences," "being joined together," is equal to "the whole compass . . . of . . . that which is divided." All learning is included in the branches that study man, and those that do not. Among those that do, there can be none except those that are important to the discussion and those that are not. And, as Sidney observes, there are no other sciences "that any way deale in the consideration of mens manners" but the four that comprise these two groups. The analysis has thus the completeness, as it has also the simplicity, prescribed by Wilson.

In the second division of the confirmatio there is an analysis that forms an instructive parallel. It has, to be

1. *Rule of Reason*, fols. 16–16ᵛ.

sure, eight subdivisions instead of the approved two; but since there are eight varieties of poetry to be discussed, the larger number cannot well be avoided; and it is authorized by Wilson's statement that the division into but two differences "cannot always be." Sidney ignores the rule of thumb in order to adhere to the principle of completeness. In his rapid examination of all eight varieties of poetry, he makes no omission which can furnish a watchful adversary with an opportunity. He makes his proof "refutation-tight," to use Carlyle's phrase, and he follows the rules so far as they are applicable to the case in hand.

In this second division of his confirmatio, he uses a method of argument different from that in the first part. There it was deductive. Here it is inductive. He presents evidence from every kind of poetry, and draws the inference that they give no "fast handle to . . . carping disprayse." [1] Thus in the two parts of the proof, taken together, he uses induction, example, and the incomplete syllogism — three of Wilson's four kinds of argument. In his analyses, as also in his ways of examining the question, he follows rules with similar fidelity, yet without slavishness, guided always by his sense of fitness. Throughout his proof, therefore, Sidney shows himself no mean logician.

His art is as skilful as ever. Especially worth noting are two rhetorical qualities in the confirmatio.

One is emphasis. Important things stand out. In the first division Sidney puts the significant idea of the moving power of poetry at the end. In the second division he touches lightly on pastoral, elegiac, iambic, and satiric poetry; discusses the comic, tragic, lyric, and heroic kinds in much more detail; and ends with the eloquent praise of the heroic. Comedy, the most vulnerable variety, he places inconspicuously between those that are wholly innocent. The ancients had discussed the question of order, some placing the strongest arguments in front, some in the

1. *Works*, III, 25.

rear, some "partly in front and partly in the rear, so that, according to Homer's arrangement, the weakest may be in the middle." [1] Sidney appears to have chosen this third arrangement. Each division of the confirmatio ends, and the whole begins, with arguments "that deserve distinction." [2] The space given to each division illustrates the same principle of emphasis. The discussion of the kinds of poetry occupies but four pages. The comparison of poetry with philosophy and history occupies ten.

The second rhetorical quality is what we today call coherence. The significant comparison which begins the proof has partly forestalled three of the four adverse arguments that are to be discussed in the refutation. The first, "that there beeing manie other more frutefull knowledges, a man might better spend his time in them, then in this," [3] has been wholly answered by the demonstration "that no learning is so good, as that which teacheth and moveth to vertue, and that none can both teach and move thereto so much as *Poesie*." [3] The second, "that it is the mother of lyes," [3] Sidney has prepared for most skilfully, not only in his partitio, by emphasizing fiction as the distinguishing trait of poetry, but in his confirmatio, by showing the superiority of feigned examples to the dry rules of philosophy and the mere facts of history. The third, "that it is the nurse of abuse, infecting us with many pestilent desires, with a *Sirens* sweetnesse, drawing the minde to . . . sinfull fansies," [3] he has prepared to answer by showing that this very moving power is what makes poetry so excellent a teacher. The fourth objection to poets — "that *Plato* banished them out of his Commonwealth" — [3] he does not touch on in his proof, though, as we have seen, he has already done so in his narratio. Thus the foreshadowing of what is to follow, which we have noted so often, is conspicuous in the confirmatio.

1. Quintilian, v. xii. 14 (I, 376).
2. Barrett Wendell, *English Composition*, 1891, p. 103.   3. III, 28.

Here is the apparent explanation of the one point in which the *Defence of Poesie* departs from the classical model. "If we are defendants," declares Quintilian, "we have to commence with refutation." [1] Sidney begins with proof. His procedure is apparently dictated by that controlling principle which can set aside every other rule — regard to the nature of the case. For it is not the specific objections to poetry, as we have seen, that are important; it is the inarticulate, unreasoning prejudice against it as something not worthy of notice. To begin with refutation is to rouse the spirit of contention. To begin with establishing the excellence of poetry, even as compared with philosophy and history, is to invoke the spirit of persuasion. Henceforth poetry cannot be treated with contempt, except by those who, opposing all learning, may themselves be dismissed in contempt. The humanistic program which Elyot had defended needed no advocate in Sidney's day. By placing his proof before his refutation, therefore, Sidney is enabled to pour scorn — "if at leaste it be in the goodnesse of that nature to scorne" [2] — upon the quips and scoffs of "all that kind of people who seek a praise, by dispraising others." [3]

The *reprehensio*, thus so skilfully prepared for, begins with a general answer to such trifling objections as "these smiling Raylers" [4] can muster, and a specific answer to their ridicule of "ryming and versing" [4] in particular. Then follows the orderly statement of the four main objections to poetry, an answer to each, and finally a brief summary of both refutation and proof. The first adverse argument — "that a man might better spend his time" [5] than in poetry — merely begs the question. The second — that poets are "the principall lyers" [5] — has no force, be-

1. *Institutes*, v. xiii. 53 (I, 392).
2. Spenser's letter to Gabriel Harvey, October 5, 1579; in Harvey, *Works*, ed. Grosart, I (1884), 8.
3. *Works*, III, 26.
4. Page 27.   5. Page 28.

cause everyone knows that poetry is fiction, and nobody is misled into taking it for fact. The third — that poetry "abuseth mans wit" — shows only that a good thing, being abused, is dangerous; and the absurd notion that England was once more manly than since "*Poets* began to be in price" is in reality "a chain-shot against all learning." [1] Finally, Plato's judgment of poetry, rightly understood, places him not among its adversaries, but at the very head of its patrons.

In the general method of its argument, the reprehensio follows the direction of Quintilian: that "the form of our refutation . . . must be adapted to the interest of our cause; we may sometimes state the arguments of our adversary separately, and sometimes collect them in a body." [2] "We may assail a number at once," as Sidney does the more trifling objections to poetry, "if they are either so weak that they may be borne down in a mass, or so annoying that it is not expedient to engage them in detail." [3] The jests about poetry are of this sort, troublesome if debated seriously, but really weak, and therefore to be brushed aside in contempt. The arguments which, on the other hand, Sidney singles out are of precisely the kind which, Quintilian says, "taken together, have much weight; but if you divide them, and consider them separately, they will be like . . . large rivers, which, if they are divided into rivulets, become fordable in any part." [2] Taking the objections in the mass, Sidney can say, "Truly this is much, if there be much truth in it." [4] But when he considers them separately, their magnitude dwindles, and he can conclude, "what dispraise may set uppon [poetry], is either easily overcome, or transformed into just commendation." [5]

But not only does the general method of the argument

1. Page 31.
2. v. xiii. 13 (I, 382).   3. v. xiii. 11 (I, 382).
4. *Works*, III, 28.   5. Page 35.

accord with the great traditions of oratory. So, too, does
the prevailing tone. The Roman rhetorician tells us that
"an orator . . . should carry confidence in his manner, and
speak as if he had the highest assurance of the success of
his cause. This quality . . . is eminently apparent in
Cicero" [1] — and, we may add, in Sidney. Notably in the
refutation, but more or less also through the whole *Defence*,
he treats his opponents with a sort of kindly scorn. He
thinks some of their objections "deserve . . . no other
answer, but in steed of laughing at the jeast, to laugh at
the jeaster." [2] The more important imputations he answers carefully, yet without apparent labor. On nearly
every page he has a touch of playfulness.

The *Poet* never maketh any Circles about your imaginatiō,
to conjure you to beleeve for true, what he writeth.[3] . . . Even
some of my maisters the *Philosophers* spent a good deale of their
Lampoyle in setting foorth the excellencie of [love].[4] . . . The
lesse they could overthrow [the poets], the more they hated
them. For indeed they found for *Homer*, seven Cities strave who
should have him for their Cittizen, where many Cities banished
Philosophers, as not fit members to live among them.[5] . . . Even
. . . Socrates . . . is said to have spent part of his olde time in
putting *Esopes* Fables into verses. And therefore full evill
should it become his scholler *Plato*, to put such words in his
maisters mouth against *Poets*.[6]

Nowhere does Sidney's urbane humor show to better
advantage. Need we call it *sprezzatura*, or cite Cicero and
Quintilian to demonstrate its classical quality? Surely
temper and method alike show the force of ancient
teaching.

Sidney closes his reprehensio, as he has closed his confirmatio, with a brief recapitulation — sanctioned, of

1. *Institutes*, v. xiii. 51–52 (I, 392).
2. *Works*, III, 26.
3. Page 29.   4. Page 30.
5. Page 33.   6. Pages 34–35.

course, by Quintilian, "even in other parts of a pleading [than the very end], if the cause be complex and require to be supported by numerous arguments." [1] The summary emphasizes the break between what has gone before and what is to follow. The formal demonstration is now complete. The defense can rest its case.

But before concluding, Sidney pauses "to enquire why England . . . should be growne so hard a stepmother to *Poets*." [2] The inquiry is technically a digression. The very first sentence marks it as something added after the rest seems complete: "it shall be but litle more lost time" to make the inquiry. The place where the passage comes is just the place most approved; for, as Cicero observes, some authorities "direct you, before you come to the peroration, to make a digression by way of embellishment or amplification." [3] Yet this passage, though a digression, is intimately related to the whole argument. The confirmatio has presented excellent reasoning in defense of poetry. The refutation has overthrown the specific charges against it. Yet the English poetry that was actually being produced, a cynical reader could have observed, seemed little to deserve the high praise that Sidney lavished upon the art at its best. Sidney must bring his principles to the test of experience. Thus the criticism of the national literature, though strictly speaking the refutation is over, is in a broad sense the last step in the refutation; for it shows that if English makers deserve censure, the fault is not inherent in the art. It shows, too, that already they deserve commendation as well as blame; that the language is admirably suited to produce work of a still higher order; and that the poet's art is therefore as susceptible of cultivation in England, as it is worthy. The facts about contemporary literature thus confirm the general principles that have already been laid down. Sidney's digression not

1. *Institutes*, VI. i. 8 (I, 409).
2. *Works*, III, 35.   3. *De Oratore*, II. 19 (p. 104).

only is authorized by ancient usage, but it fits most neatly
into the artistic structure of the whole. Organic unity
could hardly be more complete than it is in the *Defence*.

   The peroratio is another illustration of how deftly Sidney
turned the classical oration to the purposes of a literary
essay. The ancients distinguished two species of conclusion: the "summing-up of heads" and the appeal to the
judge's feelings.[1] Accordingly, in the *Defence* there is first
a recapitulation, which runs "as briefly as possible" "over
only the principal heads"[2] of the preceding argument.
Then comes the appeal to the feelings, a passage notable
for its mock-heroic tone. "In this part of a speech,"
Quintilian could have told Sidney, ". . . allusions may be
made to *the public good*, to *the honour of the judges*, to
precedent, to *regard for posterity*. But that which produces
the most powerful impression is pity."[3] The occasion of
Sidney's *Defence* makes a serious appeal to the public
interest or to the judge's pity entirely ineffective. For if
poetry has been held in contempt, such heroics can excite
only ridicule, and it is Sidney's task to turn the laughter
against his opponents. He therefore does not venture an
allusion to the public interest, and he alludes to pity only
in such a phrase as "I conjure you all." This he robs of
all bombast by adding "that have had the evill luck to
read this inck-wasting toy of mine."[4] It is not the appeal
to pity, but allusions to "the honour of the judges," to
"precedent," to "regard for posterity," which Sidney can
use appropriately in his peroratio. By anticlimax and
other devices he gives a light touch to the whole. The
citation of such august "precedents" as Aristotle, Bem-
bus, Scaliger, and Clauserus is followed by the request
"to beleeve with me" something else; and "to beleeve
with *Landin* . . . that whatsoever [the poets] write, pro-

---

1. Cf. Quintilian, VI. i. 1 (I, 407); and Cicero, *De Oratore*, II. 81 (p. 180).
2. Quintilian, VI. i. 2 (I, 408).
3. VI. i. 22–23 (I, 413).   4. *Works*, III, 45.

ceeds of a divine furie." This last is unmistakably a
humorous exaggeration, inasmuch as Sidney elsewhere has
declared that Plato, in his doctrine of divine fury, "attrib-
uteth unto *Poesie*, more then my selfe do." [1] Through
this anticlimax, the citation of authorities (some of them
really impressive) leads to the light reference to the fame
with which the poets can reward their patrons, a reference
which ostensibly is an appeal to "the honour of the
judges" and their "regard for posterity." If you are a
friend to poets, "your name shall florish in the Printers
shops. . . . You shal be most faire, most rich, most wise,
most all." [2] But if you are their enemy, this shall be your
curse: "That while you live, you live in love, and never
get favour, for lacking skill of a Sonet, and when you die,
your memory die from the earth for want of an Epitaphe." [3]
The lofty peroration described by Quintilian has been
touched with irony.

Serious matter for thought is here in abundance. Some
of the authorities cited are names to conjure with, and the
ideas referred to are worth thinking over. But there is no
strain, no overemphasis which the comic spirit can turn to
ridicule. On the contrary Sidney, gay and urbane, can
mock his adversaries out of court. Yet he leaves no rancor: it is more than chivalrous humor, it is *sprezzatura*.

This quality of urbanity we have found throughout the
Defence — in the mock-heroic tone of the exordium and
the peroratio, in the gleams of irony which light up scattered passages and impart an air of easy confidence to the
refutation. Perhaps we can catch a glimpse of the same
quality in the underlying conception of the whole — the
use of the solemn defensive oration of the ancient law-
court for the purpose of "a pittifull defence of poore
Poetrie." In the *Arcadia* we should not be surprised to
find occasional passages of elaborate irony, or even of

1. Page 34.
2. Page 45.   3. Page 46.

parody and burlesque. In the *Defence*, however closely
Sidney has followed the rules, the humor and the lightness
of touch are more pervasive. The art is mature—perfectly
deliberate, yet so fully mastered as to give the illusion of
unstudied effort. Sidney obeys the rhetorical precepts as
a gentleman will obey the code of etiquette. His naturalness is not that of a child, but of a master of technique.

*Exordium, narratio, partitio, propositio, confirmatio,
reprehensio, digressio, peroratio* — they are all here, all the
parts of a carefully elaborated classical oration. In the
fidelity to ancient precedent, often meticulously exact, in
the fitness of style to substance, in the dovetailing of parts,
in the skilful emphasis upon such unifying ideas as the
moving power of imagination or the relation of precept to
example, and perhaps chiefly in the light touches of ironic
humor, — what do we find in all this but an art so per-
fected as to seem no art at all?

The reason is no less clear than the fact. It is partly
that Sidney has genius, partly that he has an intimate
acquaintance with the best traditions of oratory, but partly
also that these traditions offered him a sure guide. Cicero
gave a model, Cicero and Quintilian a statement of rhetorical theory; for the Renaissance model and theory alike
were universally valid. The maturity of Sidney's own workmanship is paralleled by the maturity of the general art of
rhetoric in his day. The *Defence of Poesie* has organic unity
largely because the "artificial rules" and "imitative patterns" were perfectly clear, and came to Sidney with the
stamp of ancient authority.

In *Astrophel and Stella* the author of the *Defence*, working in another clear tradition, has produced a masterpiece
of English lyric poetry. In the *Arcadia*, working in a
tradition that, as we shall see, was as yet unsettled, he has
produced a work which to the modern reader seems a
failure, though it gave delight to nearly a century of
earlier readers. Even if our own judgment of Sidney's

three works be final, can we say that the creator of two masterpieces is in the *Arcadia* a mere amateur playing at literature? Or shall we rather say that here also he is a gifted poet and conscious artist, experimenting in an art that his age was groping to reach, working in the mood of those two Renaissance types, the deliberate craftsman and the explorer of a new world?

CHAPTER III

Sidney's Classical Background

WHEN they concern themselves with criticism, nearly all, Shakespeare, Sidney, and their contemporaries, are to be admired for their moderation, wisdom, and good sense; but as soon as they take up the pen to write their imaginative works, intoxication overcomes their brain." [1] Thus does Jusserand state the common antithesis between Sidney's critical judgment and his romantic imagination. Such a contrast is familiar enough among English poets, — as in Byron, when he championed the school of Pope. Many writers neglect to follow their own principles. But an author who in one work shows a consummate mastery of form does not, in a second work, normally show a complete indifference to artistic law. To suppose, therefore, that when the author of the *Defence of Poesie* wrote — or rewrote — the *Arcadia*, "intoxication overcame his brain", is to suppose more than that he neglected his literary theories. It is to assume that in him the creative impulse itself worked in ways diametrically opposite. The common view of Sidney leaves him an enigma.

If he conceived the *Defence of Poesie* as a classical oration, may he not have looked upon the *Arcadia* as an heroic poem? And must not we expect to find again a "self-conscious art, guided by the rules of criticism"? [2]

1. J. J. Jusserand, *The English Novel in the Time of Shakespeare*, trans. Lee, 1903, p. 260.

2. J. E. Spingarn, *A History of Literary Criticism in the Renaissance*, Columbia University Studies in Comparative Literature, 5th ed., 1925, p. 258.

In the past generation, two efforts have been made to bring the *Arcadia* into harmony with Sidney's critical principles. The earlier is in Edwin Greenlaw's article, "Sidney's *Arcadia* as an Example of Elizabethan Allegory." [1] It was followed by Herr Friedrich Brie's more ambitious effort, *Sidneys Arcadia, Eine Studie zur Englischen Renaissance.*[2] The conclusions of these scholars are so frequently at variance that it would be unfair to confuse their points of view. Yet they agree in regarding the *Arcadia* as an heroic poem, and in attributing to it an allegorical significance. These views have not met with universal acceptance, and they have been sharply challenged by Mr. R. W. Zandvoort,[3] among others. He, however, bases his judgment on a comparison between the two versions of the *Arcadia*, and has not considered, except incidentally, either the theories of the *Defence* or their relation to the romance. There is clearly room for a fresh study of the problem.

In later chapters I shall show that in form the *Arcadia* is an heroic poem and shall then study the question of its allegorical content. In the present chapter I shall consider certain aspects of Sidney's classical culture without which we cannot understand his critical principles.

His idea of an heroic poem, in particular, is not easy to find. He left no complete *Ars Poetica*, and in the *Defence* he frequently is not very definite. As regards the purpose of poetry, indeed (and therefore of heroic poetry), his statements are pretty clear. But on the subject matter of the heroic poem he touches only incidentally. Of allegory he says very little. Even the didactic purpose of literature he may perhaps treat in the spirit of an advocate defending a cause, rather than of the writer discussing the principles which guide his own work. The statements of the

1. *Kittredge Anniversary Papers*, 1913, pp. 327-337.
2. *Quellen und Forschungen*, CXXIV (1918).
3. *Sidney's Arcadia, A Comparison between the Two Versions*, 1929, pp. 123 ff.

Defence must therefore be used with caution, even when they appear to be categorical. And they are not at all explicit about the technique of the epic — its language, its structure, its characters.

These are the very matters in which the modern reader finds the *Arcadia* most perplexing. The ornate and mannered phrasing and the bewildering maze of characters and incidents find no parallel in either the modern novel or the ancient epic. The elaborate design of the revised *Arcadia* is like nothing in the romances of chivalry, while the enormous bulk and the tangle of episodes can owe little to the Greek romances. If the careful design and mannered style were inspired by Heliodorus' *Æthiopian History*, and the bulk by the medieval romances, the question will still be asked whether the result is not a hodgepodge of conflicting elements, strangely at variance with the principles of good taste and classic unity which the author emphasizes in his critical essay.

Perhaps the question can be answered by asking another: Was Sidney, even in theory, a genuine classicist?

At least as regards his ideal of epic form, the testimony of the *Defence* is inconclusive, and must be supplemented with other evidence. First, there are the works of Italian criticism which lie behind the *Defence of Poesie*. Second, there is the creative literature that Sidney knew — significant for our purposes because everybody interprets critical theories in the light of his own reading. In these two sources we may hope to discover just how truly classical was his ideal of epic form. As for the first, the Italians were themselves so sharply divided about the relative merits of Ariosto and Homer that we must learn what critics Sidney trusted most fully. As to the second, the essential question is how much Greek he knew. Was he so intimate with Homer and Sophocles that he could divine better than Minturno — or as well — the theories of art laid down by Aristotle, and achieve a taste more nearly Greek than could Tasso? Or does he, like even the most classical of the Italians, belong to his own century?

From the Italians, as Mr. Spingarn has shown, Sidney learned most of his critical principles. But his problem was less simple than it appears to us, with our knowledge of the neo-classical conventions into which the Renaissance ideas were eventually to harden. For these conventions were in Sidney's time still plastic in the heat of controversy. In the 1550's there was eager debate whether romances like Ariosto's should be condemned because they lacked the organic structure proper to the ancient epic. In the 1580's, though the critics were now agreed that unity was necessary in all heroic poetry, the controversy over the *Gerusalemme Liberata* showed them to be by no means agreed on the meaning of unity.[1] A young Englishman sojourning in Padua in 1574 would have found old controversies revived and the literary world enlivened by the most recent and the most revolutionary of Italian critics — Castelvetro. In such a formative period there was no rigid canon of poetic dogma, but "a current of ideas in the highest degree animating and nourishing to the creative power"[2] and challenging to the critical faculty. For epic poetry there was not yet any tradition of criticism so authoritative as the Petrarchan for the sonnet or the classical for oratory. Sidney could not do better than select the best guides and correct them by each other.

What ones did he choose?

Mr. Spingarn has shown conclusively that Sidney knew Scaliger, Minturno, and Castelvetro. His further suggestion that he may have known Daniello, Varchi, and Trissino is less tenable.

In Trissino Mr. Spingarn finds a parallel to the passage

1. For the controversies over epic and romance, see Spingarn, *Literary Criticism in the Renaissance*, pp. 112–124. Both here and throughout my discussion of Italian criticism, my indebtedness to Mr. Spingarn is very great.

2. Matthew Arnold, "The Function of Criticism at the Present Time," *Essays in Criticism*, First Series, 1896, p. 8.

where Sidney distinguishes laughter from delight.[1] The similarities, I believe, are owing to a common original, and are less important than the differences.[2] But whether or not Sidney knew Trissino's work and was indebted to him for his theory of comedy, there is no reason to think he turned to him for his theory of epic poetry.

From Daniello Mr. Spingarn cites a parallel to Sidney's argument that philosophy, presenting but "the bare rule," is the inferior of poetry in moving power; and a second parallel to Sidney's observation that Plato, the most poetical of philosophers, was guilty of ingratitude in banishing poets from his Commonwealth.[3] But the remark about Plato might have suggested itself independently to any number of readers, and the argument that poetry surpasses philosophy in moving power may be found also in Minturno, whom Sidney certainly knew, and who was a far more important critic than Daniello. Two other specific passages in Daniello are cited by G. Gregory Smith as possible parallels to a passage in Sidney's *Defence*.[4] But the language is not identical, and the ideas, where they are similar, are common in Renaissance thought. Indeed, neither Smith nor Mr. Spingarn asserts that the parallels between the *Defence* and the *Poetica* indicate actual borrowing by Sidney. The general resemblances between the two works may be explained readily enough, since both defend poetry against her opponents and both belong to the Renaissance.

Much the same may be said of Varchi's *Lezzioni*. The

1. Spingarn, p. 288. Cf. Sidney, *Complete Works*, ed. Feuillerat, Cambridge English Classics, 1912–1926, III, 40, and Trissino, *Opere*, 1729, II, 127 ff.

2. Cf. Aristotle, *Poetics*, v. 1, trans. Butcher, in *Aristotle's Theory of Poetry and Fine Art*, 4th ed., 1923 (p. 21); Castiglione, *The Courtier*, trans. Hoby, Tudor Translations, 1900, pp. 157–158; and Cicero, *De Oratore*, trans. Watson, 1860, II, 59 (p. 151).

3. Pages 271, 274. Cf. Sidney, *Works*, III, 13 ff., 5, 33, and Daniello, *La Poetica*, 1536, pp. 19, 22–23.

4. *Elizabethan Critical Essays*, ed. G. Gregory Smith, 1904, I, 383. Cf. Daniello, pp. 12, 21, and Sidney, III, 4.

parallels to the *Defence* have been found in only a single passage, where Varchi, to establish the preeminence of poetry, compares it with some of the same subjects as does Sidney.[1] But Varchi's list includes oratory, omitted by Sidney, and does not include history, to which several very important pages are devoted in the *Defence*.[2] The two are by no means in agreement, moreover, about the function of law.[3] In this particular, closer parallels to Sidney's thought are offered in Geoffrey Fenton,[4] in Jacques Amyot,[5] and in Horace (whose very phrases are quoted in the *Defence*). In the whole discussion, moreover, a far closer parallel may be found in Amyot's preface to his translation of Plutarch's *Lives*, of which Sidney's knowledge is generally admitted.[6] His argument in defense of poetry reads for several pages like an answer to Amyot's argument for history. As the English writer compares poetry with philosophy and history, alluding briefly to law and divinity,[7] so the French writer compares history with philosophy, and alludes briefly to law and poetry. The lists are precisely the same except that Sidney, surveying all the sciences whose end is "well doing, and not . . . well knowing onely," [8] and mindful of the Puritan opposition to poetry, has added divinity to the subjects mentioned by Amyot. Again, Varchi omits history entirely. It is the special theme of the translator of Plutarch, in whose view its only rival is philosophy. Sidney, too, brings it in with philosophy as one of the two studies which can be said to compare in dignity with poetry.

1. See Benedetto Varchi, *Lezzioni*, 1590, p. 576, and Sidney, III, 12 ff. Cf. Spingarn, pp. 50–51, 272; and *Elizabethan Critical Essays*, I, 389.

2. *Works*, III, 12, 16–18.

3. Cf. Varchi, p. 576, and Sidney, III, 13.

4. "The Epistle Dedicatory," *Certain Tragical Discourses of Bandello*, The Tudor Translations,1898, I, 7. Fenton dedicated his book to Sidney's mother.

5. "Aux Lecteurs," *Les Vies des Hommes Illustres de Plutarque*, 1783, I, xxii.

6. Cf. Sidney, III, 81, 83; and *Correspondence of Sidney and Languet*, ed. and trans. Pears, 1845, pp. 9, 20, 24.

7. Sidney, *Works*, III, 13.   8. Page 11.

Finally, the arguments in favor of history, which Sidney confutes, are nearly all to be found in Amyot's preface.[1]

To discuss in further detail Sidney's interesting answer to Amyot would lead us no nearer to his theory of the heroic poem. Clearly, this is to be sought no more in Varchi than in Daniello or Trissino. We must turn instead to Aristotle and the three Italian commentators to whom Sidney was beyond all doubt indebted — Scaliger, Minturno, and Castelvetro.

Scaliger gives but little more than a page to the technique of the epic.[2] Castelvetro goes into greater detail. But Sidney, though he drew from that radical thinker the idea of the unity of place in drama, appears to have followed him with great caution. Castelvetro condemns the mingling of prose and verse in the manner of Sannazaro and Boethius, — a manner that Sidney adopted in his *Arcadia*.[3] And Castelvetro holds that the aim of poetry is to "delight and recreate the minds of the raw multitude," [4] a view utterly at variance with Sidney's aristocratic instincts and with his whole argument that poetry can teach and move to lofty virtue. As for the rule of the unity of place, which Sidney and many later critics took from the erratic and brilliant Italian, this is a natural extension of the unity of time. Thus wherever Castelvetro developed the Renaissance tradition, Sidney appears to have found him suggestive. Where he broke from the tradition, it is unlikely that Sidney would have chosen to follow him.

It is from Minturno, then, rather than from Castelvetro or Scaliger, that Sidney is most likely to have learned the theory of the epic. From that critic he took the idea of the moving power of poetry, an idea which, unlike the doctrine of the unities, is fundamental to his whole argu-

1. See especially *Les Vies*, I, xx–xxv, xxxi–xxxii; and cf. Sidney, III, 16–18.
2. *Poetices*, 1617, III. xcv (pp. 331–332).
3. See Castelvetro, *Poetica d'Aristotele*, 1576, pp. 21–22.
4. Page 29.

ment.[1] To epic poetry Minturno devotes nearly the whole of one book in both his Latin treatise and his Italian. Unlike Castelvetro, he is in the main line of the Renaissance tradition. His theories helped to shape the epics of Tasso in Italy and Ronsard in France. It would be surprising if they had no influence on the *Arcadia*. We cannot suppose Sidney to have followed Minturno at every point. That he made use, in the *Defence*, of the three most important Italian critics, and, as we shall see, goes beyond them all in insisting that an heroic poem may be written in prose, suggests that he worked in a spirit at once eclectic and critical. Seldom does he rely on one authority to the exclusion of all others. In fact, his *Defence* appears to Mr. Spingarn "a veritable epitome of the literary criticism of the Italian Renaissance." [2] But though Sidney would not lose sight of Scaliger or Castelvetro, it is fair to suppose that if in writing the *Arcadia* he was guided by definite theories, they may be found for the most part either in the *Defence of Poesie* or in the works of Minturno.

Two treatises, a Latin [3] and an Italian,[4] set forth Minturno's theory of the epic. That Sidney knew the Latin *De Poeta* has been shown by Mr. Spingarn and G. Gregory Smith, who have pointed out passages in that work which in both phrasing and idea parallel certain passages in the *Defence of Poesie*. Between the *Defence* and the Italian *Arte Poetica*, however, no specific parallels have been discovered. On *a priori* grounds, of course, it is credible enough that Sidney knew the *Arte Poetica*. Its criticism of the romances, and especially of Ariosto's

---

1. Cf. Antonio Minturno, *De Poeta*, 1559, pp. 38–39, 106; *Elizabethan Critical Essays*, I, lxxxiv, 389, 390; and Spingarn, pp. 268 ff.

2. *Literary Criticism in the Renaissance*, p. 268.

3. *De Poeta*, 1559.

4. Antonio Minturno, *L'Arte Poetica*, 1563. The title at the beginning of each book, and at the top of the verso of each leaf, is *Della Poetica Thoscana*. Mr. Spingarn, in his first edition, refers to the work as *Della Poetica*. In later editions he calls it *L'Arte Poetica*.

masterpiece, was a most important episode in a famous controversy; of that controversy a visitor to Italy, if he had any interest in literature, could hardly have escaped knowing something; and Sidney, with his eager curiosity, his instinct to go to the sources,[1] and his interest in the romances of chivalry, would have looked up (we must believe) a treatise so important as the *Arte Poetica*. It is certain that he knew the *De Poeta*. It is altogether probable that he knew also the famous *Arte Poetica* by the same author.

Whether he knew it or not is in the main unimportant. The Italian treatise is largely a translation of the Latin, differing somewhat in arrangement and illustrative material but setting forth the same theory of the epic. The important new material is the criticism of the romances of chivalry. Praise of their subject matter,[2] apparent approval of their great length,[3] strong disapproval of their want of unity and proportion[4] and of the breaking of their critical scenes in the middle[5] are all points of significance for a study of the *Arcadia*, if we could not merely believe, but know, that Sidney was familiar with this criticism. In any case, however, he could have learned the same general lesson from the *De Poeta* as from the *Arte Poetica*, and he was capable of making the application himself.

Obviously, if we would know whether Sidney wrote the *Arcadia* as an heroic poem, we must compare it with Minturno's theory of the epic, studying this theory chiefly in the *De Poeta*, and using the *Arte Poetica* only with caution.

For an understanding of the structure in the *Arcadia* these works are particularly valuable, inasmuch as Minturno, while attaching great importance to organic form, gives the idea an interpretation somewhat foreign alike to

---

1. Cf. *Works*, III, 84, quoted below (in translation), p. 96.
2. *L'Arte Poetica*, pp. 27–28, 31.
3. Page 32.   4. Pages 32–33.   5. Page 35.

ancient and to modern taste. For a charitable understanding of the mannerisms in the Arcadian style, we need to learn whether Sidney's acquaintance with the Greek and Latin classics was sufficient to set him free from vices of Renaissance rhetoric. The same inquiry should throw further light on the structure of Sidney's romance, for to appreciate his ideal of organic form, we must ask how well he knew Homer and the masters of Greek tragedy, the writers to whom we go today, as did Aristotle, for the most perfect illustrations of the principle. For comprehending Sidney's ideal of literary style our inquiry is still more significant. Classic structure he could find in the *Æneid*. But a style both simple and noble, a speech subtly adapted to every artistic purpose, he would scarcely find outside the literature of Greece.

Did Sidney read Greek?

On this point scholars are not agreed. A. S. Cook, writing in 1890, mentions Sidney's wish, during his youthful visit to Italy, to obtain Plutarch's *Lives* in the French translation; but he goes on, nevertheless, to assert, "North's version was issued in 1579, but long before this time Sidney was no doubt able to read Greek with much greater ease, and in any case must have familiarized himself with the matter of Plutarch." [1] That Sidney knew Plutarch well cannot be denied, but that he read him or the Greek poets in the original is open to question. Cook, apparently assuming a knowledge of the language, attributes to him a wide acquaintance with Greek literature.

With the two chief epic poets of antiquity, Homer and Virgil, Sidney had a familiar acquaintance. Virgil occupies the first place in his affections, but he is by no means insensible to the superior loftiness and naturalness of Homer. . . . More remarkable [than his wide knowledge of Latin writers], because less usual at that day, was his knowledge of the Greeks. Besides

1. *The Defense of Poesy*, ed. Cook, 1890, p. xv.

Plutarch and Homer, who have already been mentioned, he admires and repeatedly mentions the *Cyropædia* of Xenophon. Of the three tragedians, he was apparently best acquainted with Euripides, though typical plays of both Sophocles and Aeschylus had been included in his reading. Of Plato and Aristotle I speak under another head. . . . Here it is sufficient to say that the dialogues of Plato which he had apparently studied with most care are the *Ion, Symposium, Phædrus, Sophist, Phædo,* and *Republic*, and that he was conversant with at least the *Poetics* and *Ethics* of Aristotle, and perhaps with the *Rhetoric*.[1]

Herr Brie, though believing with Cook that Sidney was deeply influenced by Greek literature, thinks he had no great knowledge of the language. As evidence he cites the correspondence with Languet, in which Sidney, in 1574, speaks of knowing but little Greek, refers almost entirely to Latin writers as objects of study, and expresses a desire to obtain Plutarch in the French translation. Herr Brie notes further that in 1580, in quoting the *Odyssey* to his brother Robert, Sidney uses the Latin translation.[2] But Herr Brie bases his argument chiefly on the fact that even in the *Arcadia*, where the scene is Greece and the persons Greeks, Sidney gives the Greek proper names in their Latin form.[3] He concludes, therefore: "Therefore I am inclined on the whole to believe that Sidney limited himself to Latin models, and in some instances most likely to French and English translations, even though he undoubtedly had acquired enough Greek to be able easily to read an author like Homer in the original and to make use of this Malcolm W. Wallace, who on the evidence of the correspondence with Languet, concludes, "It would seem clear that neither at Shrewsbury nor Oxford had he given much attention to Greek. . . . It remains substantially true . . .

1. Pages xviii f.
2. See Correspondence, *Works*, III, 126.
3. *Sidneys Arcadia, Eine Studie zur Englischen Renaissance*, pp. 185–187.
4. Page 187.

that the education of a Shrewsbury boy was almost entirely confined to Latin." [1]

Mr. Wallace, Herr Brie, and A. S. Cook agree that in 1574 Sidney's knowledge of Greek was scanty. On this point the direct evidence of his letters to Languet is decisive. The question in doubt is whether, as Cook thinks, he was ever "able to read Greek with much greater ease." Here our direct evidence fails. Yet the reasoning of Herr Brie goes far to discredit the assertion of Cook, who has not considered that nearly all the Greek literature with which Sidney shows acquaintance was available in Latin translations.

A new study of the evidence will show Herr Brie, I think, to be nearer the truth than Cook. It is plain that Sidney had studied some Greek. In 1574 he wrote to Languet, "I should greatly like to learn some things in Greek, which for a long time I have only sipped." [2] Clearly he had studied the language a little, either in school or in university, but had let his knowledge grow rusty. One work in particular that he seems to have read in the original is Xenophon's *Cyropædia*, to which he refers very often in the *Defence*, and which was one of the texts at Shrewsbury School. [3] Sidney's eagerness to renew and extend his knowledge of Greek was not encouraged by Languet, who wrote:

About the Greek language I cannot advise you. It is a beautiful study, but I fear you will have no time to carry it through, and all the time you give to it will be lost to your Latin,

---

1. *Life of Sir Philip Sidney*, 1915, p. 44.

2. "*De Græcis vero aliqua discam quæ jamdiu supremis tantum labris attigi*" (*Works*, III, 83.) I give my own translation, because that of Pears, which I usually follow, seems inexact. Cf. *Correspondence of Sidney and Languet*, ed. and trans. Pears, pp. 23–24, "There are some things also which I wish to learn of the Greeks, which hitherto I have but skimmed on the surface." "Hitherto" for "jamdiu" seems wrong, and "skimmed on the surface" obscures the metaphor in the Latin.

3. Cf. Wallace, p. 42.

which though it is considered a less interesting language than the Greek, is yet much more important for you to know. . . . I only recommend you to learn first what is most necessary and most suitable to your condition. You are now acquainted with four languages. If in your hours of amusement you can learn enough German to understand it anyhow, I think you will be employing yourself well.[1]

Sidney's reply explains more fully his desire:

Of Greek literature I wish to drink such a draught as shall suffice for understanding Aristotle well. For though translations are made almost daily, still I suspect they do not declare the meaning of the author plainly or aptly enough; and besides, I am utterly ashamed to be following the stream, as Cicero says, and not go to the fountain head. Of the works of Aristotle, I consider the politics to be the most worth reading; and I mention this in reference to your advice that I should apply myself to moral philosophy. Of the German language, my dear Hubert, I absolutely despair.[2]

Sidney apparently agrees with Languet that he cannot hope to master all the best in Greek literature, but he desires "greatly to learn some things." These things turn out to be the works of Aristotle, and especially the *Politics*. But he might be satisfied with knowing only enough of the language to correct the translations by turning to the original. He does not mention a rapid reading knowledge as his goal. Moreover, the fact that he is still perfecting his knowledge of Latin, French, and Italian by translating and retranslating the letters of Cicero[3] argues that he had little leisure in 1574 for Greek. The indications are that he studied it, as Languet urges him to study German, in his hours of amusement. That he continued the effort through the spring of 1574 is suggested by his quoting

1. Pears, p. 26.
2. Pages 28–29. I have modified the translation of the first sentence. Cf. *Works*, III, 84.
3. Cf. *Works*, III, 83.

three Greek phrases in writing to Languet on February 26 and May 28.[1] But that even in his ardent youth he seriously hoped to gain the knowledge with which Cook credits him, there is no evidence in the correspondence with Languet.

In the *Defence of Poesie* a sprinkling of Greek terms seems to show that Sidney did not again let his knowledge of Greek grow very rusty. But these are strikingly few in comparison with the quotations from Latin, or with the Greek quotations of a real scholar like Ascham. And except for the word μισομουσοι [*sic*],[2] which Sidney appears to have coined, nearly all the phrases seem to be taken from the *Ethics* or *Poetics* of Aristotle,[3] if not from a secondary source in an Italian critic. Since his motive in studying Greek was to read Aristotle, and since according to tradition he translated two books of the *Rhetoric*, we may suspect the works of the Stagirite to have comprised the greater part of his mature studies in the Greek language.

In school or at the university he doubtless read some works by other authors. But these seem to have been few. Though he is thoroughly familiar with Plato, with Plutarch, and to a less degree with the other Greek historians,[4] he may have read them only in Latin or French translations, which were available for them all. He mentions in the *Defence* a large number of Greek authors, but his lists are taken almost wholly from Scaliger or Minturno.[5] Though he discusses comedy and refers several times to Plautus and Terence, he does not mention Aristophanes or his Greek successors. To Pindar he alludes briefly, observing that he "many times praiseth highly Victories of small moment," and ascribing to him a "gorgious eloquence";[6] but if these allusions suggest some

1. Cf. pp. 87, 94.   2. Page 26.
3. Cf. pp. 7, 9, 11, 16, 19.   4. Cf. pp. 5, 17, 130.
5. Cf. *Works*, III, 4–5, 9; Scaliger, *Poetices*, I. ii (pp. 10 ff.); Minturno, *De Poeta*, pp. 14–15; and Spingarn, pp. 268, 270, notes.
6. *Works*, III, 24.

knowledge, they do not prove that the knowledge was gained at first hand. Of the Attic orators possibly he knew Demosthenes, for he writes, "How well store of *Similiter Cadenses*, doth sound with the gravitie of the Pulpit, I woulde but invoke *Demosthenes* soule to tell: who with a rare daintinesse useth them."[1] Evidence so slight as this brief reference can prove little. But the discrimination with which Sidney speaks of Demosthenes' style seems to imply some knowledge of the Greek text, a knowledge perhaps gained by reading one or two orations at Shrewsbury or at Oxford. With Greek literature as a whole he seems to have had no very wide acquaintance, except in translations.

In particular, his acquaintance with Homer and the tragic poets appears to have been limited. To Homer as an individual he has a few scattered references in the *Defence*, which cannot show knowledge of his works. To the *Iliad* and the *Odyssey* he refers in seven passages,[2] mentioning Diomedes once, and Achilles and Ulysses each four times. But only twice [3] is his language so definite as to imply a first-hand knowledge. In both passages the references are to the *Odyssey*. To the *Cyropædia* he has eight references,[4] as many as to the *Odyssey* and the *Iliad* together, and four [5] of these are of the detailed kind that shows easy familiarity. The *Æneid* he quotes,[6] and he refers to it at least ten other times,[7] often in the language of enthusiastic admiration.[8] The contrast with the allusions to the *Iliad* and the *Odyssey* hardly indicates that Sidney was "by no means insensible to the superior loftiness and naturalness of Homer." [9] Indeed, from the *De-*

---

1. Page 42.
2. Pages 14, 15, 16, 18, 20, 25, 32.   3. Pages 14, 18.
4. Pages 8, 10, 15, 16, 17, 25, 30.   5. Pages, 8, 10, 15, 17.
6. Pages 20, 35.
7. Pages 6, 8, 14, 15, 16, 20, 25, 28, 30, 45.
8. See especially pp. 14, 20, 25.
9. *The Defense of Poesy*, ed. Cook, p. xviii.

fence of Poesie alone we might suppose that he had never made a careful study of the *Odyssey*, and that he had not read the *Iliad* at all. The *Arcadia*, to be sure, since it contains, especially in the battle scenes, a number of possible echoes of the *Iliad* besides an unmistakable reference to the *Odyssey*, shows, if we may believe Herr Brie, the direct influence of Homer.[1] But many of Herr Brie's parallels are dubious. Thus he finds "the influence of Homer's description of the aged Nestor" in the mere fact that the aged Kalander talks "of the good old times and the companions of his youth," [2] and a parallel to the siege of Troy in the siege of Cecropia's castle.[3] But even if we could accept all the supposed resemblances which the German scholar has collected, we should have no proof that Sidney had read Homer in anything but Valla's translation. The evidence of the *Defence of Poesie*, therefore, seems conclusive, that at least he had not assimilated the *Iliad* and the *Odyssey* as he had assimilated the *Cyropædia* and the *Æneid*. Clearly he was not so familiar with Homer as to learn from him the secret of organic form or the power of a style at once noble and simple.

Evidence that he knew the Greek tragedians consists in two passages, one dealing chiefly with Sophocles' *Ajax*, the other with Euripides' *Hecuba*. The first is as follows:

Anger the Stoikes said, was a short madnesse: let but *Sophocles* bring you *Ajax* on a stage, killing and whipping sheepe and oxen, thinking them the Army of Greekes, with their Chieftaines *Agamemnon*, and *Menelaus*: and tell me if you have not a more familiar insight into Anger, then finding in the schoolemen his *Genus* and *Difference*. See whether wisdom and temperance in *Ulisses* and *Diomedes*, valure in *Achilles*, friendship in *Nisus* and *Eurialus*, even to an ignorant man carry not an apparant shining: and contrarily, the remorse of conscience in *Oedipus*; the soone repenting pride in *Agamemnon*; the selfe devouring

---

1. Cf. Brie, pp. 192–197.   2. Cf. Brie, p. 197.
3. Page 194.

crueltie in his father *Atreus*; the violence of ambition in the two *Theban* brothers; the sower sweetnesse of revenge in *Medea*.[1]

This passage offers the only proof of Cook's assertion that "typical plays of both Sophocles and Aeschylus had been included in [Sidney's] reading." [2] It therefore deserves careful analysis. The references to Ulysses, Diomedes, and Achilles are to Homer; the reference to Nisus and Eurialus is to Virgil. For the moment these do not concern us. The rest of the passage falls into two parts, the first dealing with the *Ajax* of Sophocles, the second with certain characters in other ancient tragedies.

The allusions in the second part Cook explains thus: Œdipus refers to Sophocles' *Œdipus Tyrannos*, Agamemnon and Atreus to Æschylus' *Agamemnon*, "the two Theban brothers" to Æschylus' *Seven against Thebes*, and Medea to Euripides' play of that name.[3] The five allusions, according to this view, refer to four plays by three separate Greek poets. A more natural hypothesis is that the five allusions refer to five plays by the single Latin writer Seneca. These are his *Œdipus, Agamemnon, Thyestes, Phœnissæ*, and *Medea*. Sidney's knowledge of Seneca could be assumed, even if his explicit references did not make the fact obvious.[4] For his knowledge of Sophocles' *Œdipus Tyrannos*, Euripides' *Medea*, or any play by Æschylus, we have no evidence, either in the passage before us or elsewhere.

As for the reference to Sophocles' *Ajax*, it appears, indeed, to indicate first-hand knowledge. Yet it contains a curious slip. As Mr. Collins points out, "Sophocles does not 'bring Ajax on a stage, killing and whipping Sheepe and Oxen.'" [5]   G. Gregory Smith exonerates Sidney of error by assuming that he "refers to the dramatic situation

1. *Works*, III, 14–15.
2. *The Defense of Poesy*, p. xix.
3. Page 84.   4. See *Works*, III, 23, 38.
5. *Apologie for Poetrie*, ed. J. Churton Collins, 1907, p. 76.

generally."[1] If so, his language is clumsy and inaccurate, for had he known how out of keeping with Greek practice and with the dignity of Sophocles' play, would be the representation on the tragic stage of a scene so violent and so capable of degenerating into farce as the slaughter of sheep and oxen by a madman, he could hardly have used language so ambiguous. The passage does not suggest much knowledge of Sophocles' *Ajax* or of Greek tragedy in general. It suggests rather that Sidney confused Attic with Elizabethan stage practice, and that he knew the *Ajax* only at second hand.

His mistake becomes intelligible when we find in Minturno's *De Poeta* a parallel passage, in which the question of staging the episode is left ambiguous.

Atque inde pauca quædam uertamus, nónne uerisimile[2] erat, animi ægritudine Aiacem ita insanire, ut pecudes quasi Græcos sibi infensos inimicosque occideret? Atque arietem, quem Vlyssem putabat, uinctum flagello cœderet. Cùm autem resipisceret, quia pudebat, gemeret, in aliquem Deorum insaniae culpam conferret. Denique præ nimio dolore sibi mortem consciret? consolantur illum Salaminij, consolatur Tecmessa concubina, non tanquàm aliquis ex philosophorum numero, uerùm ut personæ ratio postulabat. Videtis hic morem furentis, quemadmodum actio ferebat, ita descriptum, ut ne Philosophus quidem uerius definire potuisset. At in Agamemnone, & Menelao, quos nusquàm uti sapientissimos iustissimosque leges inductos, Poeta ille quàm luculenter improbos regum mores expressit? qui ne sepultura quidem afficiendum esse Aiacem uolebant iam tunc inimicum, Sed quem bello Troiano præclarè, ac fortiter multa gessisse, & cùm de tota Græcia, tum de se benemeritum norant. Contrà, in Vlysse, quem nunquàm nõ prudẽtissimum, ac moderatissimum reperies, nónne prudẽtiæ moderationisque exempla probè admodum effinxit?[3]

Minturno goes on to quote the noble speech by which

1. *Elizabethan Critical Essays*, I, 390.
2. My emendation of the *nerisimile* in the original — an obvious misprint.
3. Page 41.

Ulysses induced Agamemnon finally to yield burial to Ajax. The passage is too long to give entire, but I have quoted enough to show numerous parallels to the passage in the *Defence*. To make these clear I will place Sidney's passage beside certain parts of Minturno's, marking with italics and letters the points of identity.

Let but Sophocles bring you Ajax on a stage, *killing*[a] and *whipping*[b] *sheepe*[c] and *oxen*,[d] *thinking*[e] them the Army of *Greekes*,[f] with their Chieftaines *Agamemnon*,[g] and *Menelaus*:[h] and tell me if you have not a more familiar *insight*[i] into *Anger*,[j] then finding in the *schoolemen*[k] his *Genus and Difference*.[l] See whether *wisdom*[m] and *temperance*[n] in *Ulisses*[o] and Diomedes . . .

ut pecudes[d] quasi *Græcos*[f] sibi infensos inimicosque *occideret*.[a] Atque *arietem*,[c] quem Ulyssem *putabat*,[e] uinctum *flagello*[b] coederet. *Videtis*[i] hic morem *furentis*,[j] quemadmodum actio ferebat, ita descriptum, ut ne *Philosophus*[k] quidem verius *definire*[l] potuisset. At in *Agamemnone*[g] & *Menelao*,[h] . . . Contra, in *Vlysse*,[o] . . . *nônne prudētiæ*[m] *moderationisque*[n] exempla. . . .

Except in the first clause, there is hardly an idea in Sidney's six lines that does not occur in Minturno. It cannot be accidental that there should be fifteen points of agreement in so short a passage, or that the characters of Ajax and Ulysses should be used to illustrate the same truth; namely, that the poet by his examples can teach the nature of anger, wisdom, or temperance more impressively and truly than the philosopher with his abstract principles. Moreover, the parallels in the passages themselves are supported by the contexts. Sidney is arguing that, unlike the poet, "the *Philosopher* setting downe with thornie arguments, the bare rule, is . . . hard of utterance, and . . . mistie to be conceived." [1] This idea, as Mr. Spingarn [2] has shown, he owes to Minturno, who introduces it within two pages of the passage about Ajax, and in almost the same phrasing. Philosophers, he says, would excite

1. *Works*, III, 13.
2. *Literary Criticism in the Renaissance*, p. 271.

popular ridicule if they discussed precepts "quæ seuerius asperiusque, quàm opus sit."[1] Again, the precepts which Minturno mentions are paradoxes of the Stoics, and Sidney observes that "Anger the *Stoikes* said, was a short madnesse."[2] Still further, "the soone repenting pride in *Agamemnon*,"[3] which Sidney mentions, is vividly illustrated in the scene described by Minturno in which Ulysses persuades the king to reverse his order and allow Ajax to be properly buried. Sidney's phrase may even echo Minturno's "regiam superbiam, regiamque . . . stultitiam."[4] And finally, the extended passage in which the Italian critic praises Homer's characterization of Achilles and other heroes, and Virgil's portrayal of Æneas, Turnus, and Latinus, may have suggested Sidney's allusion to "valure in *Achilles*, friendship in *Nisus* and *Eurialus*."[5] The leading idea, that poetry teaches better by example than philosophy by "the bare rule," the allusion to the Stoical doctrine, several incidental references, and in short the whole context of Sidney's passage confirm the evidence of similar phrasing and thought in the passage itself. There is no room for doubt that Sidney based his discussion of the *Ajax* on Minturno's.

How he used his source may be illustrated in the references to Achilles and to Nisus and Eurialus. "Valor in Achilles" is a condensation of more than half a page in Minturno. "Friendship in Nisus and Eurialus" appears to be Sidney's substitute for the Italian critic's allusions to Æneas, Turnus, and Latinus. In other words, though he often sticks close to his source, he sometimes alters it freely when he has independent knowledge. A characteristic change is from the general to the specific, or from the abstract to the concrete. Minturno's "Græcos" becomes

1. Minturno, *De Poeta*, p. 39.
2. *Works*, III, 14.
3. Page 15.
4. *De Poeta*, p. 40.
5. *Works*, III, 15. Cf. *De Poeta*, pp. 39-40.

"the army of the Greeks." "Ut ne Philosophus quidem uerius definire potuisset" is transformed into the specific and more vigorous "finding in the schoolmen his genus and difference." The substitution, though it must have been conscious, appears also to have been instinctive. Sidney visualizes what he reads. The parable of the prodigal son sets his mind in a glow. "Truly," he confesses, "for my selfe (mee seemes) I see before mine eyes, the lost childs disdainful prodigalitie, turned to envy a Swines dinner." [1]

In view, then, of Sidney's habit of thinking in images, it is easy to understand how he could write, "Let but Sophocles bring you Ajax on a stage, killing and whipping sheep and oxen." For Minturno has spoken not of seeing the play produced, but of reading it. "Inde pauca quædam vertamnus" are his words. Quite naturally, therefore, he has neglected to say that the killing and whipping is reported, and not represented. He has described the scene, however, in two vivid sentences, and Sidney's imagination takes fire as he reads. He seems to be watching the play take place on a stage before his eyes, and of course to see this striking incident among the rest. Had he read the play himself, he could hardly have failed to observe that the killing and whipping is not represented, for he elsewhere advises English dramatists to remember "the difference betwixt reporting and representing," and "the manner the Auncients tooke, by some *Nuntius*, to recount things done in former time or other place." [2] Sidney's mistake is unintelligible if we assume that he had read the *Ajax*, but becomes natural, and indeed inevitable, if we note his dependence on Minturno.

His dependence is proved, as we have seen, by similarities in thought and in context, and by numerous parallels even in the phrasing. Sidney has derived his knowledge

1. *Works*, III, 15.
2. Page 39.

of the *Ajax* from Minturno, and has not himself read Sophocles' play.

The use of a secondary source in this passage is most significant. First, it lends further support to the conclusion we have already reached, that the other five allusions point not to the Greek tragedians, as Cook supposes, but to Seneca; for if the longer and more detailed reference to the *Ajax* shows ignorance of Sophocles' play, we can hardly suppose that the shorter references show knowledge of three Greek poets instead of one Latin poet, especially since that one was familiar to all educated Elizabethans. Secondly, the passage indicates that Sidney was ignorant not only of the *Ajax* and four other specific Greek tragedies, but of nearly all others; for why should he mention only the works of Seneca and one Greek tragedy discussed by Minturno, if there were other Attic plays of which he had first-hand knowledge? At least, we must believe that he had read nothing of Sophocles or Æschylus.

The best evidence that he knew Euripides is his summary of a part of the plot of the *Hecuba*, the

storie of yoong *Polidorus*, delivered for safeties sake with great riches, by his Father *Priamus*, to *Polminester*, King of *Thrace*, in the *Troyan* warre time. He after some yeares, hearing the overthrowe of *Priamus*, for to make the treasure his owne, murthereth the Childe, the bodie of the Childe is taken up, *Hecuba*, shee the same day, findeth a sleight to bee revenged moste cruelly of the Tyrant. Where nowe would one of our Tragedie writers begin, but with the deliverie of the Childe? Then should hee saile over into *Thrace*, and so spende I know not howe many yeares, and travaile numbers of places. But where dooth *Euripides*? even with the finding of the bodie, the rest leaving to be told by the spirite of *Polidorus*.[1]

This passage, unlike the one about the *Ajax*, contains no suspicious misstatements. Cook, indeed, remarks that "notwithstanding Sidney's praise, the unities are some-

1. Page 39.

what violated in it";[1] and as authority he quotes J. P. Mahaffy's *History of Greek Literature*:

> It is to be noted that the scene being laid in Thrace, and the tomb of Achilles being in the Troad, the so-called unity of place is here violated, as often elsewhere in Greek tragedy. . . . The narrative of her (Polyxena's) death . . . forms a beautiful conclusion to the former half of the play, which is divided, like many of Euripides', between two interests more or less loosely connected.[2]

Be this as it may, an intelligent reader could have a good knowledge of the *Hecuba* without ever noting any violation of the unity of place. On the contrary, since the incidents at the tomb of Achilles and the discovery of Polydorus' body at the seashore are reported, and since Hecuba sends messengers to the shore to fetch water and to bring Polymestor to her, Sidney would naturally suppose unity of place to be preserved. Again, if the modern scholar is right in thinking unity of action to be violated, yet a man of the Renaissance could have cited Minturno's authority for the contrary view.[3] In Sidney's discussion there is a hint that his idea of a unified plot may have differed from ours, but there is no suspicious discrepancy.

Indeed, the precision of his summary of Polydorus' story may be illustrated by a comparison with Minturno's summary of the whole play.[4] The Italian, who is explaining how the plot may be divided into five acts, tells less than Sidney about the events before the drama opens. He does not, like Sidney, describe Polydorus as young, or say that "for safety's sake" he was delivered by Priam to Polymestor. He tells us that Polymestor killed the prince "per hauer l'oro del figlio";[5] Sidney tells us also that the riches were "great." Sidney calls the murderer a tyrant.

1. *The Defense of Poesy*, p. 121.
2. I, 344; quoted by Cook, p. 121.
3. See *L'Arte Poetica*, pp. 87-88.
4. Cf. pp. 105-106.   5. Page 106.

The epithet occurs in Minturno, but in another passage. [1]
These minute differences show the accuracy of Sidney's
account, and they lead me to think he had probably read
Euripides' play. His acquaintance with Minturno's
Italian treatise, moreover, in which the summary of the
Hecuba occurs, is not quite certain, though he knew and
used the Latin treatise. Possibly he was using some other
secondary source. If so, I have not found it in Scaliger or
Castelvetro. If we may judge from the evidence before us,
Sidney was drawing from his own knowledge of the play.

But whether he read it in Greek or in Latin is open to
doubt. In favor of the first possibility is the fact that he
had studied a little Greek in school or the university, and
that, as Cook points out (quoting Mahaffy), "The *Hecuba*
has always been a favorite play, and has not only been
frequently imitated, but edited ever since Erasmus' time
for school use." [2] If Sidney had read any Greek tragedy,
therefore, it is likely to have been the *Hecuba*. On the
other hand, the works of Euripides were available in a
Latin translation,[3] issued at Basle as early as 1562, which
he could easily have picked up during his wide travels on
the Continent. This book, with its parallel columns of
Latin and Greek, was well suited to Sidney if his knowledge
of Greek was never great; for his craving to "go to the
fountain head," which he expresses in the letter to Languet, could be satisfied by an occasional glance from the
translation to the original. It is not certain, therefore,
that he read the *Hecuba* in Greek, though it seems clear
that he had read it in some form.

If he had read anything else by Euripides or his great
predecessors, we have no evidence of the fact. Surely an

1. Page 101.
2. *The Defense of Poesy*, pp. 120–121.
3. *Euripides Poeta Tragicorū princeps, in Latinum sermonem conuersus,
adiecto eregionè textu Græco: cum Annotationes et Præfationibus in omnes eius
Tragœdias: autore* Gasparo Stiblino. . . . Basileæ, per Ioannem Oporinum.
[1562.]

allusion to Pylades as a constant friend is no proof of his
having read Euripides' *Iphigenia among the Tauri*, or
Sophocles' *Electra*.[1]

It seems necessary, therefore, to modify Cook's statement that "of the three tragedians, he was apparently
best acquainted with Euripides, though typical plays of
both Sophocles and Æschylus had been included in his
reading."[2] Quite possibly he had read but one play of
Euripides; almost certainly he had read nothing of Sophocles or Æschylus. We know only that he was familiar
with the *Hecuba*, and perhaps merely with the Latin
translation. Not the Greek, but, as Mr. Spingarn observes, "the Senecan drama and the Aristotelian precepts
were the sources of Sidney's theory of tragedy."[3] He
illustrated Aristotle's principles by a literature that
Aristotle did not know.

Indeed, Sidney's first-hand knowledge not only of Greek
drama, but of Greek literature in general, was very
limited.

To be specific, he seems to have read in the original not
much more than the *Cyropædia* of Xenophon, the *Hecuba*
of Euripides, perhaps the *Odyssey* in whole or in part, and
one or two orations by Demosthenes, besides at least some
parts of the *Ethics, Politics, Rhetoric*, and *Poetics* of Aristotle. His intimate knowledge of Plato would lead us to
suspect that he had read in the original some of the
dialogues of that most poetical philosopher. In translation, at least, he knew the *Odyssey* and probably the *Iliad*.
He seems to have known, no doubt in the Latin form, the
histories of Xenophon, Thucydides, and Herodotus, and
some of Plutarch's philosophical works. In French he
knew Plutarch's *Lives* and some of the Greek romances,
especially the *Æthiopian History* of Heliodorus.

1. *Works*, III, 8. Cf. *The Defense of Poesy*, ed. Cook, p. 72.
2. Pages xviii–xix.
3. *Literary Criticism in the Renaissance*, p. 284.

From such sources as these, Sidney could learn a great deal of Greek history and philosophy, but not of poetry. Studies so limited as his were, in the original language, could not easily teach Attic simplicity of style and perfection of form. From the Greeks, then, he could learn little to offset the love of ornateness, which was general even in the decadent stage of Greek literature, which was all but universal in the Renaissance, and which was authorized by so illustrious a model as Cicero, with whom Sidney was thoroughly familiar. Into classic structure he could get a better insight from Virgil, from Heliodorus, from Euripides, and even from Homer. Yet the causal connection of events, producing a sense of inevitability, had begun to weaken in Euripides, and had largely disappeared in Heliodorus and still more in the other writers of Greek romance. And even in Homer and Virgil, may not a Christian of the English Renaissance have overlooked the causal function of the portents, oracles, gods, and goddesses of the pagan religions, and have regarded them rather with wonder than with a full sense of their part in the working of inevitable law? However this may be, Sidney could hardly have seen farther into the nature of heroic poetry than the critics whom he took for his guides. Where they were not definite, we may expect the *Arcadia* to differ widely from our notion of an epic, especially in features for which there was precedent in the romances of chivalry which Sidney knew.

Sidney's classicism, in short, belonged not to the age of Boileau or Aristotle, but to the age of Minturno. If in writing the *Arcadia* he was governed by clear theories, we must expect his work to show the structure of an heroic poem as understood by Minturno, and the ornate literary style encouraged by the traditions of Renaissance rhetoric.

CHAPTER IV

The *Arcadia* as an Heroic Poem

ARTIFICIAL rules," "imitative patterns," and "exercise," not "as having known," but in order to learn, are, as we have seen, the three essentials for mastering an art, in the view both of Sidney and of the Renaissance thinkers generally.[1] The work which furnished the pattern for the revised *Arcadia*, as has been shown by William Vaughn Moody,[2] Dr. S. L. Wolff,[3] and Mr. R. W. Zandvoort,[4] was probably the *Æthiopian History* of Heliodorus. But we have yet to learn whether Sidney's work is the tentative experiment of a writer learning his craft, and whether it conforms to rules of poetry laid down by authorities.

The purpose of the present and the following chapter is to show that in subject and structure the *New Arcadia* follows Minturno's rules for the heroic poem.

In establishing this thesis I have no wish to overemphasize the importance that Sidney attached to mere rules. By his own theory, we know, craftsmanship is secondary to imagination. "A *Poet* no industrie can make, if his owne *Genius* be not carried unto it." [5] If, then, we should find

1. See *Complete Works*, ed. Feuillerat, Cambridge English Classics, 1912–1926, III, 37.

2. *An Inquiry into the Sources of Sir Philip Sidney's "Arcadia,"* 1894, pp. 49–51.

3. *The Greek Romances in Elizabethan Prose Fiction*, Columbia University Studies in Comparative Literature, 1912, pp. 351–353.

4. *Sidney's Arcadia, A Comparison between the Two Versions*, 1929, pp. 195 ff.

5. *Works*, III, 37; corrected from variant readings, III, 384.

in the *Arcadia* a close adherence to Minturno's rules, we
need not suppose that the author took as his point of
departure a set of abstract formulas. We must suppose
rather that having, as he tells us, "many many fancies
begotten" [1] in his head, he selected from those fancies
the materials, and arranged them into the form, that —
in agreement with the best opinion of his day — he recognized as most appropriate to the heroic poem. We are
considering not whether his art was mechanical, but
whether it was critical and intelligent.

Our problem is doubly complex. For the *Arcadia* exists
in two radically different versions, the second unfinished;
and Minturno's theory of the epic, as formulated in either
his Latin or his Italian treatise, is in certain obvious ways
at variance with the practice of Sidney in the *Arcadia*.

The latter problem is comparatively simple, for where
Sidney departs from the authority of Minturno we may
find in the *Defence*, as it happens, a clear indication of
his guiding principles. In discussing the theories which
guided Sidney, therefore, I shall rely primarily upon the
Defence and Minturno's *De Poeta*, supplementing the latter
work by the *Arte Poetica*.

The two *Arcadias* offer greater difficulties. The earlier,
complete version, first called to the attention of scholars
by Bertram Dobell in 1909, exists in six manuscripts, from
one of which, the Clifford Manuscript, it was published
under the editorship of M. Feuillerat in 1926.[2] Not having
access to the manuscripts, I have depended upon this
edition and upon Mr. Zandvoort's careful discussion of the
manuscripts for my knowledge of the original version of
Sidney's romance. The revised version, which breaks off
in the third book, was first printed by Ponsonby in 1590.
It makes up Volume I of M. Feuillerat's edition of Sidney.

---

1. *Works*, I, 3.
2. In the *Complete Works of Sir Philip Sidney*, Cambridge English Classics,
Volume IV.

A third form of the *Arcadia*, which appeared in 1593 under the editorship of the Countess of Pembroke, comprised Sidney's uncompleted revision together with the third, fourth, and fifth books, somewhat adapted, from the original version. In this form the work has nearly always been published since 1593.

Following Dr. Wolff and Mr. Zandvoort, I refer to the original version as the *Old Arcadia*, to the incomplete revision as the *New Arcadia*, and to the composite version published by Sidney's sister as the *Arcadia*.

The relations between the *Old Arcadia* and the *New* have been described well from different points of view by Dr. Wolff and Mr. Zandvoort.[1] But neither of these scholars has shown which version is nearer the Renaissance ideal of the epic, nor has the problem been discussed by other students of Sidney. By inference, indeed, we may draw a cautious conclusion. According to Dr. Wolff, Sidney has rewoven his story "upon the loom of Heliodorus." According to Mr. T. P. Harrison, Jr.,[2] many of his changes in the second version point equally to the influence of Montemayor. By either view, the *New Arcadia* is nearer than the original to the Renaissance ideal of an epic poem. For the romance of Heliodorus is cited by Scaliger as a model of epic structure.[3] Both that work, moreover, and the *Diana* are cited by Vauquelin de la Fresnaye as examples of poetry written in prose,[4] and he could hardly

1. On only one question I am disposed to take issue with these scholars: namely, how far the *Arcadia* as edited by the Countess of Pembroke represents Sidney's own plan. See Chapter VII.

2. "A Source of Sidney's *Arcadia*," University of Texas *Studies in English*, December 22, 1926, pp. 53–71.

3. *Poetices*, III. xcv (p. 332).

4. *L'Art Poetique*, ed. Pellisier, 1885, ii, 263–266, p. 79. Vauquelin's work, though begun in 1574, was still incomplete in 1590 and was not published till 1605. (See Spingarn, *A History of Literary Criticism in the Renaissance*, 5th ed., Columbia University Studies in Comparative Literature, 1925, p. 186.) Since Sidney died in 1586, and since he drew independently upon Minturno, he can hardly have owed anything to Vauquelin's work.

have fitted them into any class of poetry except the heroic.
This French writer, indeed, resembles Sidney not only in
his high regard for Montemayor and Heliodorus, but also
in his indebtedness to Minturno. Not improbably, therefore, Minturno also would have regarded both romances
as epic at least in structure. Whether the *New Arcadia*,
then, was modeled upon the *Æthiopian History* or upon
the *Diana*, it must in any case be nearer than the first version to an heroic poem as understood by Scaliger, Vauquelin, and Minturno. But such an inference is at best only a
plausible hypothesis. And only by inferences can I find,
in any of the existing studies of the *Arcadia*, evidence that
Sidney was guided in his creative work by the Italian
critics whose ideas he summarized in the *Defence of Poesie*.

In general, the scholars who, like Mr. Praz and Mr.
Zandvoort, have compared the two versions of the *Arcadia*, have judged them by modern standards of style or
plot or characterization. Greenlaw and Herr Brie, to be
sure, in supporting their view that Sidney regarded the
Arcadia as an heroic poem, have cited the opinions of
Sidney's English contemporaries and the theories he sets
forth in the *Defence of Poesie*. This scanty evidence Mr.
Zandvoort, however, has rejected as inconclusive. Meanwhile, no other scholar has carried the historical method
to its logical conclusion and sought to explain the *Arcadia*
by the Renaissance theory of the epic as set forth by such a
representative critic as Minturno.

This neglect is hardly surprising. For though Mr. Spingarn has shown how greatly Sidney was indebted for his
critical theories to Minturno and the other Italians, yet
even Mr. Spingarn, as we have seen, has not given up the
orthodox view that Sidney the writer contradicts Sidney
the critic. Moreover, Minturno's ideal of the epic is super-
ficially in glaring contrast with such a work as the *Arcadia*.

In neither version, of course, is that work an epic in the
full sense in which Minturno applies the term to the

Æneid and the *Iliad*. For example, Homer and Virgil begin with an invocation to the Muse, in which they lay down the main themes of their poems;[1] they write in heroic verse;[2] and they have an elaborate machinery of supernatural characters.[3] Sidney has no invocation in the ordinary sense; he writes not in heroic numbers, but in prose, interspersed with songs and eclogues in verse; and above all he has discarded the supernatural machinery almost entirely. It would be absurd to imagine that Sidney was trying to write a great epic.

And yet he may still have thought of the *Arcadia* as a more modest sort of heroic poem, differing from the epic in certain obvious ways, but resembling it in structure and in fundamental purpose.

Before considering the all-important question of structure, we may observe that in the points in which Sidney appears to disregard Minturno's theories he shows an entire consistency. Indeed, both verse and invocation, though appropriate enough to a poem which, like *Paradise Lost*, embraces within its universal sweep the supernatural no less than the natural world, would of course be fantastically out of place in a story like the *Arcadia*, which, however remote from actuality, deals yet with the purely human and natural. For a work of this kind Sidney could use neither heroic verse nor a formal invocation. He needed rather some appropriate substitute.

The flexible applications of rules is sometimes, indeed, encouraged by Minturno himself, who has some of the tact and good sense of his master, Quintilian. To regard the end, not to follow a mechanical rule, is for any classicist the first law of art.

The invocation, therefore, is described by Minturno as a means to an end. The opening, as distinguished from the

1. Cf. Antonio Minturno, *De Poeta*, 1559, pp. 111–113.
2. Cf. Minturno, *L'Arte Poetica*, 1563, p. 4.
3. Cf. p. 31.

narrative of an heroic poem, has the same function as the exordium of an oration: to make the readers "*beneuoli, dociles, attenti.*" [1] The readers will be *dociles* "if the subjects to be treated are set forth briefly and clearly." [1] They will be *attenti* when the subjects announced appear "great, new, or capable of raising wonder and awe (*admirabilia*)," as "when they concern all mankind, or numbers of them, or illustrious men, or the immortal Gods, or some city, race, or nation." [1] The readers will be *beneuoli* when they are treated with tact. Now these three aims of the opening passage may all be attained by the invocation, although the special reason for calling on the gods seems to be to render them *beneuoli*, like the human audience, and to win their aid. [2] Homer, accordingly, "was so observant of brevity that he invokes the Muse and sets forth his subject at the same time," and Virgil follows a similar course in the *Æneid* and the *Georgics*. [3] Thus for Minturno the invocation is not a mechanical requirement, but a means of making the opening effective.

Now in the *Old Arcadia* Sidney has given us nothing equivalent to the epic invocation. He begins not with setting forth the main subject, but with an exposition of the state of affairs in Arcadia — an account of the province, its people, its Duke Basilius and his family, his journey to Delphos, and his retirement from public affairs in order to avoid the misfortunes threatened by the oracle. The account reads like the narratio of the ancient oration, a "*brief, clear, plausible*" statement of the circumstances. It is not remotely like the heroic poet's address to the Muse.

In the *New Arcadia*, however, there is an episode which, whatever the author's intent, reminds us of an epic invocation. This is the conversation between the shepherds Strephon and Claius, with which the *New Arcadia* begins.

1. *De Poeta*, p. 111.   2. Page 112.
3. Page 113.

Not merely do the speeches suggest the pastoral setting of the story, and introduce the leading themes of love and friendship, which are to occasion as many heroic actions as the wrath of Achilles. The praise which the two friends lavish upon the divine Urania does more than announce the subject of the poem, for the praise is couched in just the mood of reverent adoration appropriate to the poet's prayer to his Muse. It is not unlikely, therefore, that Sidney consciously intended the passage to have the content and emotional tone of the epic invocation, and that while he abandoned the invocation, as a formal part of his poem, he achieved its purpose and general effect by a means more suited to his work. But whether or not he was thinking of Homer or Virgil or Minturno, he has at least given us an introductory sketch which fits admirably into the design of the whole narrative. Like a dumb show in an Elizabethan play, the episode in which Strephon and Claius lament their hopeless passion is set apart from the main action, while yet symbolizing what that action is to be. Thus the passage reveals the conscious artistry with which Sidney worked, and perhaps may even show him adapting the epic model to his own purposes.

These opening pages of the *New Arcadia* are nearer than those of the earlier version not only to the epic model, but also to Sidney's own theories as set forth in the *Defence*, especially in the contrast of poetry with philosophy and with history. Poetry, Sidney argues, is a better teacher than philosophy because a "speaking picture" is as clear to the mind as a dry rule, and acts far more powerfully upon the feelings and will. It is a better teacher than history because fictitious examples are more universal than the actual incidents of history. The unique thing in poetry is the speaking picture, the example which is representative of the universal. Such a speaking picture is the episode of Claius and Strephon in the *New Arcadia*. Here, in a specific dramatic situation, is the concreteness which, according to Sidney, distinguishes poetry from philosophy. We learn what two shepherds did and said and felt on a particular occasion. In the *Old Arcadia*, on the other hand, no dramatic situation is pictured until Basilius discloses to Philanax his plan to go into retirement.[1] The account of Arcadia and its duke is exposition; it makes the general statement significant, not the luminous detail; and it is, therefore, by Sidney's theory, more appropriate to philosophy than to poetry. And from another point of view it is more appropriate to history. For the facts set forth in the first two pages, though necessary to an understanding of the plot, do not introduce the large themes with which the story is to deal. The facts are but facts, like those of history. Now in the *New Arcadia*, though the episode of Strephon and Claius is highly concrete, yet it is, as we have seen, also symbolic of what is to follow. In the very first sentence, therefore, we find in the *New Arcadia* what was lacking in the opening pages of the original version, namely, a specific "example," a particular action made representative of something larger. At the outset, therefore, the *New Arcadia* shows a greater agreement than does the *Old* with the theories of the *Defence of Poesie*.

Thus in three ways the opening passage of the *New Arcadia* reveals a maturing of Sidney's art: in the possibly conscious adaptation of the epic invocation, in the appropriateness of the episode to the design of the whole, and in the agreement with Sidney's own theories of poetry.

This last is particularly significant. For where Sidney, in his mature work, departs from the epic formula of Minturno, he seems guided not only by the requirements of his immediate work, but also by his own theories. As to the invocation he has no occasion to speak in the *Defence*, but he shows clearly his attitude toward the supernatural and toward prose as a medium of poetic expression.

1. *Works*, **IV**, 3.

"It is not ryming and versing that maketh a Poet,"
writes Sidney, ". . . but it is that faining notable images of
vertues, vices, or what els, with that delightfull teaching,
which must be the right describing note to know a Poet
by." [1] In this famous statement Sidney is at one with
Minturno and Castelvetro. But he goes beyond them and
beyond the body of Italian critics, in declaring categori-
cally that "one may be a *Poet* without versing." [2] Witness
Xenophon in his *Cyropædia* and Heliodorus in his *Æthiopian History* — both "absolute heroicall Poemes." [3] The
logic of Sidney's position appears unanswerable. For if
the essence of poetry is, as Minturno says, imitation, or
fiction, rather than verse, how can he classify such fictitious works as those of Heliodorus and Xenophon, except as poetry? These works, then, show that poetry of a
high order can be written in prose. But not necessarily of
the highest order. Indeed, Sidney everywhere speaks of
verse with respect. "The Senate of Poets," he admits,
"hath chosen verse as their fittest raiment: meaning as
in matter, they passed all in all, so in maner, to go beyond them." [4] "But yet presuppose it were inseperable,
as indeed it seemeth *Scalliger* judgeth, truely it were an
inseperable commendation." [5] Apparently Sidney would
agree that the greatest epics must be written in verse,
even while he insists that "absolute heroical poems" may
be written in prose. According to Sidney's own theory,
then, the absence of meter may well remove the *Arcadia*
from the highest order of poetry, but not from all orders of
genuine poetry.

The problem of his artistic medium is further complicated by the pastoral scenes and pastoral eclogues of the
Arcadia, for the one seems inconsistent in subject, the

---

1. III, 10–11.   2. Page 27.
3. Page 10.   4. Page 11.
5. Page 27. I place a comma after *judgeth* and delete the comma after
truely. Cf. variant readings, III, 382.

other in form, with the requirements of heroic poetry. Now Sidney himself has pointed out "that some *Poesies* have coupled togither two or three kindes, as the *Tragicall* and *Comicall*, whereupon is risen the *Tragicomicall*, some in the maner have mingled prose and verse, as *Sanazara* and *Boetius*; some have mingled matters *Heroicall* and *Pastorall*." [1] Since the *Arcadia* mingles prose and verse, and matters heroical and pastoral, apparently Sidney would classify it not as purely heroic poetry, but as poetry of a mixed character. That such a mingling of the *genres* is opposed to the classic spirit is obvious enough. That it is at variance with Renaissance interpretations of the classic spirit is not so clear. At least, critical opinion in Italy was too divided to afford Sidney an authoritative guide. Now as to Sidney's own theories, though he condemns the mingling of *genres* in the "mongrel tragicomedy," yet he seems to approve in narrative what he condemns in dramatic poetry. "I know," he says, "*Apuleius* did somewhat so, but that is a thing recounted with space of time, not represented in one moment." [2] In theory, therefore, Sidney seems to approve the unclassical mingling of *genres* which is so conspicuous a feature of the *Arcadia*. The pastoral elements of that work may even be classified technically as a part of the epic fable generally recognized by Renaissance critics; for since they could be lifted out of the story without impairing its integrity, and yet are loosely connected with it, they may be described as episodes. If they are recognized parts of the narrative, they cannot destroy the epic structure of the *Arcadia*.

It is clear, therefore, that in mingling pastoral and heroical matters, in using prose as his chief medium, and in introducing eclogues in verse, Sidney is doing violence to no critical dogmas which he accepted in theory.

His abandonment of supernatural machinery is perhaps

1. Page 22.   2. Pages 39–40.

the most striking point in which Sidney seems to have ignored Minturno. For this element bulks large in both the
medieval romances and the ancient epics, though not in
the Greek romances. Moreover, Minturno, in his Italian
treatise, expressly approved "the angels, saints in heaven,
and single God," "the monks and hermits," "the sorcerers
and witches," "the fairies," "angels sent as messengers by
God," [1] and in short, the whole supernatural machinery
which the Christian religion offered in place of that in the
ancient pagan epic. Indeed, just such a Christian machinery was being employed by Sidney's friend Spenser,
and by Tasso, and with certain omissions was later to lend
grandeur to Milton's universal epic. Sidney, however,
failed to take advantage of the opportunity that other
poets seized on with eagerness. A bit of the pagan machinery, indeed, appears in the oracles of the *Arcadia*, but
these are treated consistently as vain superstitions. And
a trace of the romantic marvels appears in the *Old Arcadia*
in a dragon which serves "a man of monstruous bignes
and force and therefore comonly called a *Gyant*." [2] Even
this unimportant dragon disappears in the *New Arcadia*,
where he and his monstrous keeper are replaced by "two
brothers of huge both greatnesse & force, therefore commonly called giants." [3] Except for a passing allusion to the
"cruell monsters, & monstrous men" [3] encountered by
Pyrocles and Musidorus in Asia, the dragons and fabulous
beasts so familiar in the medieval romances have been discarded with the gods and goddesses of the pagan epic, and
the giants have dwindled into merely big men.

Now, though in its want of supernatural machinery the
Arcadia is far enough from Minturno's conception of the
epic, it is very close to the *Defence of Poesie*. In that work
Sidney shows his indifference to the supernatural, in a
passage that gains emphasis when compared with the

1. *L'Arte Poetica*, p. 31.
2. *Works*, IV, 145.   3. I, 204.

passage in Scaliger's *Poetices* on which it is based. Scaliger
had written:

Sola poesis hæc omnia complexa est, tanto quam artes illæ
excellentius, quod cæteræ (vt dicebamus) res ipsas, vti sunt,
repræsentant, veluti aurium pictura quadam. at *poeta & na-*
turam alteram, & fortunas plures etiam ac demũ sese isthoc ipso
perinde *ac Deum alterum efficit*. Nam quæ omnium opifex
condidit, eorum *reliquæ scientiæ tanquam actores sunt*. Poetica
vero, *quum & speciosius quæ sunt, & quæ non sunt, eorum speciem*
ponit: videtur sane res ipsas, non vt aliæ, quasi Hist[o]rio,
narrare, *sed velut alter deus condere*: vnde cum eo commune nomen ipsi non à consensu hominum, sed à naturæ prouidentia
inditum videatur. Quod nomen Græci sapientes vbi commo-
dissime παρὰ τὸ ποιεῖν effinxissent: miror maiores nostros sibi
tam iniquos fuisse: vt Factoris vocem, quæ illam exprimeret,
maluerint oleariorum cancellis circumscribere. eum enim solum
qui oleum facit, quum pro consuetudine caste, tum pro signifi-
catione stulte appellare licet.[1]

Sidney's passage is as follows:

Onely the Poet disdeining to be tied to any such subjectiõ,
lifted up with the vigor of his own invention, doth grow in
effect into an other nature: in making things either better then
nature bringeth foorth, or quite a new, formes such as never
were in nature: as the *Heroes, Demigods, Cyclops, Chymeras,*
Furies, and such like; so as he goeth hand in hand with nature,
not enclosed within the narrow warrant of her gifts, but freely
raunging within the Zodiack of his owne wit. Nature never set
foorth the earth in so rich Tapistry as diverse Poets have done,
neither with so pleasaunt rivers, fruitfull trees, sweete smelling
flowers, nor whatsoever els may make the too much loved earth
more lovely: her world is brasen, the Poets only deliver a golden.
But let those things alone and goe to man, for whom as the other
things are, so it seemeth in him her uttermost cunning[2] is
imploied: & know whether she have brought foorth so true a

---

1. *Poetices*, I. i (p. 6). The italics are mine.
2. I emend *comming* to *cunning*, as authorized by common sense and the
variant readings, III, 379.

lover as *Theagenes*, so constant a friend as *Pylades*, so valiant a man as *Orlando*, so right a Prince as *Xenophons Cyrus*, so excellent a man every way as *Virgils Æneas*.[1]

That in this passage Sidney made use of what I have quoted from Scaliger has already been pointed out by Mr. J. E. Spingarn[2] and by G. Gregory Smith.[3] Their view is supported even by the context of Sidney's passage. The observation by Scaliger that "the other sciences are *actores* of that which the creator of all framed" reappears in the statement of the *Defence* that the other arts "so depend" on the works of nature "as they become Actors & Plaiers, as it were of what nature will have set forth."[4] Sidney keeps the very word *actores*, but with a poet's instinct he develops the metaphor, not necessarily implied in the Latin. Again, Scaliger's regret that the Romans did not use the term *factor* for the Greek word *poet* seems to have suggested Sidney's allusion to the native English term: "I know not whether by luck or wisedome, we Englishmen have met with the Greekes in calling him a Maker."[4] And finally, the passage itself, no less than the context, shows Sidney's indebtedness to Scaliger both for phrases and for fundamental ideas. Indeed, the words "making things either better than nature bringeth forth, or quite anew, forms such as never were in nature," are a very close paraphrase of the Latin "*et speciosius quæ sunt, et quæ non sunt, eorum speciem ponit.*"

Now Sidney has done much more than clothe Scaliger's bare abstractions in poetic imagery. He develops the idea that there are two types of fiction, the one idealizing what occurs in nature in an imperfect state, the other presenting "forms such as never were in nature." Scaliger expresses the idea abstractly in a single line. Sidney elabo-

---

1. III, 8.
2. *A History of Literary Criticism in the Renaissance*, Columbia University Studies in Comparative Literature, 1925, p. 273.
3. *Elizabethan Critical Essays*, I, 385–386.   4. *Works*, III, 7.

rates it through a glowing passage which occupies thirteen lines. Of these, he gives but one to "forms such as never were in nature," merely illustrating them with a few concrete examples. But he lavishes all his eloquence on the poetry which shows the earth and man "better than nature bringeth forth." The ideas are Scaliger's. The illustrations and the emphasis are wholly Sidney's.

From the *Defence of Poesie*, therefore, we may learn that the chimeras, enchanters, monsters, and magic of the ancient epics or the medieval romances held for Sidney little interest. Exactly the same attitude appears in the *Arcadia*. In discarding the supernatural machinery which appealed to Minturno, to Tasso, and to Spenser, Sidney seems to have acted out of well-defined convictions. The rationalism of the Renaissance had not left him untouched.

Neither had the religious sense which the Reformation had quickened in England.* Scaliger claims for the poet that he "creates another nature and many fortunes, and even makes himself, as it were, another *god*." Sidney says that he "doth grow in effect into another *nature*." The alteration may spring from that dislike of extravagance which is revealed in his indifference to monsters, but it points more clearly to a sensitive reverence for religious truth. This quality is shown still more clearly when, a little below the passage I have been discussing, he goes on to develop the idea that the poet is a creator. It is not with God's creative power, but "with the efficacie of nature" that he asks leave "to ballaunce the highest point of mans wit"; [1] and he would "give right honor to the heavenly maker of that maker, who having made man to his owne likenes, set him beyond and over all the workes of that second nature, which in nothing he sheweth so much as in Poetry." [1] Sidney's phraseology is colored with Christian teaching. Scaliger's suggests rather the revival of paganism in Renaissance Italy.

[1]. Page 8.

Two reasons, then, may be found for Sidney's rejection of the supernatural machinery recommended by Minturno. His rational temper made the "forms such as never were in nature" seem absurd. His religious reverence forbade his depicting priests, hermits, angels, or the true God in any poetry short of the most sublime, or possibly even there. It is not the *vates*, or poet-seer, whose case he pleads in the *Defence*, but the poet who is a creative artist, a "maker." And in the *Arcadia* he appears as himself a creative artist of the kind he has defended.

Not only do we find in both works the same distinctive conception of a poem written in prose, and the same indifference to the supernatural machinery of epic or romance. We see also an enthusiasm for the same subjects. The very phrases which Sidney, giving his own emphasis to Scaliger's dry formulas, lavishes upon the art of divers poets, may be applied with special fitness to his own *Arcadia*. What other poets have "set forth the earth in so rich tapestry" as Sidney himself has done, "with so pleasant rivers, fruitful trees, sweet smelling flowers, [or] whatsoever else may make the too much loved earth more lovely"; as when he describes the princesses bathing in the river Ladon, or the "shepherd boy piping as though he should never be old"? When has nature "brought forth so true a lover" as Pyrocles or Musidorus and their ladies, "so constant a friend," "so valiant a man" as the same heroes, "so right a prince," "so excellent a man every way" as Sidney's Euarchus? The subject of the *Arcadia* is the pastoral world, but more especially man, not in the imperfect form attained by nature, but in the ideal form toward which nature strives, things which the poet makes "better than nature bringeth forth."

Such a work is not the universal epic of the sort that Minturno describes, yet it is built, as we can learn from the *Defence*, upon principles as definite as Minturno's. In both the *Defence* and the *Arcadia* we find the same enthusiasm for beauty of landscape and for heroic character, the same indifference to the supernatural, perhaps the same religious earnestness. The *Arcadia* is a mixed composition of a sort described in the *Defence*, written largely in prose, in accordance with Sidney's theory. With good reason does Sidney abandon heroic verse along with the supernatural machinery and the invocation of the ancient epic, for the changes are all appropriate to the work he has in hand, and are quite in accord with his own theories. Where Sidney disregards Minturno he shows the consistency of the deliberate artist, conscious alike of his principles and of his present purpose. If in certain obvious ways he has seemed to ignore the critic, yet he has only thought out his problem the more carefully, and has seen that not all the rules of the epic apply to every variety of heroic poem.

The only question, then, is whether he has seen that some rules of the epic, and these the most fundamental, do apply to all heroic poetry, and whether he has conformed to these rules in either version of the *Arcadia*.

As to which version is more nearly an heroic poem we have thus far found a few vague hints. In the use of prose as its chief medium, in introducing considerable bodies of verse, in mingling matters heroical with matters pastoral, the two versions offer no contrast. In the avoidance of the supernatural, however, the *Old Arcadia* is somewhat less consistent than the *New*, and yet is not measurably nearer to Minturno's requirements for the epic. Again, the *Old Arcadia* has nothing that suggests the classic invocation. Finally, the expository paragraphs with which it opens do not, like the opening passage of the *New Arcadia*, suggest a poetic example of the kind Sidney discusses in the *Defence*. In general, therefore, the art of the original version seems less consistent with itself and with the author's theories than does that of the *New Arcadia*, without showing a greater conformity to Minturno's rules for the epic. The art of the *Old Arcadia* is therefore comparatively immature. If either version conforms to fundamental principles of heroic poetry, it is likely to be the later and more mature work.

What, then, is the fundamental part of Minturno's theory?

He defines the epic as

the imitation of actions grave and illustrious (*chiari*), of which the perfect and complete interweaving is of an appropriate magnitude, with embellished diction, without music or dancing, now simply narrating, now introducing others in action and in speech; in order that through pity and fear of the things imitated and described, the soul may be purged of such emotions with a mingling of pleasure and wondering awe (*mirabil piacere*), and with profit.[1]

This definition (an adaptation of Aristotle's definition of tragedy) may possibly have been unknown to Sidney, for it occurs only in the *Arte Poetica*, which we cannot be quite certain that Sidney knew. It sums up conveniently, however, the theory that Minturno sets forth also in his *De Poeta*, with which Sidney unquestionably was familiar.

With many parts of that theory we have no present concern. The purgative or ennobling power of the epic does not bear directly on the problem of organic form which we are now considering. Of the four elements of epic poetry — action, character, *sententiæ*, and diction — distinguished by Minturno, as by Aristotle, only action is of first importance to our problem. The analysis of the action is the most distinctive part of Minturno's discussion of heroic poetry, and the plot of the *Arcadia* is what for a modern reader seems to violate Sidney's supposedly classical theories. If the story in either version of the *Arcadia*, therefore, can be shown really to conform to Minturno's requirements for the heroic poem, we can hardly escape the conviction that Sidney deliberately cast his work into this poetic form.

1. *L'Arte Poetica*, p. 9.

Minturno's requirements for epic action concern either the kind of incidents or their arrangement into a plot — either the subject matter, that is, or the structure.

In regard to subject matter his requirements are vague. Although in his Latin treatise he declares heroic poetry to be essentially the imitation of an action,[1] and implies that the action should be "grave and illustrious" (as he states definitely in the *Arte Poetica*), yet he is nowhere very explicit as to what subjects meet this description. The material of the *New Arcadia*, however, if not of the *Old*, he could hardly fail to approve. In his Italian treatise, indeed, his general endorsement of the chivalric themes of the romances [2] shows that among the subjects peculiarly suited to heroic poetry he would include not only war and adventure, but love. Similarly, his citing the *Trionfi* [3] of Petrarch as a model for the epic seems to emphasize the view that love is a theme as heroic as war. Even war, apparently, is not indispensable, for Minturno cites the *Divine Comedy* [4] as a model epic, though it does not treat of fighting. On the other hand, he refers to Homer as the chief of epic poets, Homer, who treats war, not love, as the great activity of men. In short, this Renaissance critic seems little interested in explaining what actions are "grave and illustrious." The vagueness of his discussion leaves the poet a wide freedom. Minturno might endorse the themes of either version of the *Arcadia*.

Yet if the term "heroic" is interpreted strictly, it can be applied with greater truth to the subjects of the *New Arcadia* than to those of the *Old*.

Here Sidney's own statements in the *Defence* correct the vagueness of Minturno's statements. We have Sidney's bantering allusion to love — "that even to the *Heroical*, *Cupid* hath ambitiously climed" [5] — and his reference to

1. *De Poeta*, p. 109.   2. *L'Arte Poetica*, pp. 27–28, 31.
3. Pages 36–37.   4. Page 38.
5. *Works*, III, 30.

the "sugred invention of that picture of love in *Theagenes
& Chariclea*," to show he thought "an absolute heroicall
Poeme" [1] might deal largely with love. And from the
other subjects treated in the romance of Heliodorus, in
Xenophon's *Cyropædia*, and in Virgil's *Æneid* — all works
which are praised enthusiastically in the *Defence* — we
may infer that adventure, politics, warfare, and great
national events all come within the province of the heroic
poem.

Adventure, politics, and love are conspicuous themes of
the *Old Arcadia*. Fighting, in that version, however, is
limited to the combats of the two heroes with the lion and
the bear, to the defense against the mob that assailed the
duke's lodge, to the brief struggle of Musidorus against
the rascals who captured him and Pamela on their flight
from Arcadia, to the skirmish in which Philanax's soldiers
cut these same rascals to pieces, and to a few incidents,
briefly narrated, in the careers of the princes before their
arrival in Arcadia. Now in the revised version the fighting
includes all the foregoing combats, and many new ones in
addition. Argalus slays Demagoras, Amphialus kills his
friend Philoxenes, Phalantus jousts against all who deny
Artesia's preeminence in beauty, Zelmane wounds Amphialus in the very midst of an idyllic bathing scene, and the
two heroes perform many new exploits in Asia Minor.
Nor is the fighting confined to personal combats. Laconia
is plunged into civil war by the insurrection of the Helots,
and Arcadia by the great rebellion of Amphialus, the latter
involving, in addition to many duels, several skirmishes
and a pitched battle. War, traditionally the special
province of the heroic poem, plays in the *New Arcadia* an
enormously larger part than in the *Old*.

The earlier version, indeed, is largely a story of love
and lovers' devices, thrown against a background of
politics in a Greek province. Politics are introduced

1. Page 10.

chiefly by way of debates — a discussion between Basilius and the faithful Philanax about the wisdom of Basilius' retirement, or the lengthy arguments during the trials of Gynecia and the two princes. In the *New Arcadia* politics appear not only in debate but also in action — in the prudent government of King Euarchus, in the various follies of Asiatic monarchs, in the shrewd conduct of Amphialus when he stirs up a civil war. We now see the love stories against a background of war and great political events involving, not only Arcadia, but also all Greece and Asia Minor. The events of the *Old Arcadia* concern one province. Those of the *New Arcadia* concern a kingdom and two continents.

Love, adventure, politics, heroic warfare, and great national and even international events,— the subjects in which Sidney shows an interest in his *Defence of Poesie*,— all appear in the *New Arcadia*. Warfare and great events are absent from the *Old Arcadia*. And these are the very subjects which add dignity to the story. The action of the *New Arcadia* can be described truly as "grave and illustrious." To the events of the *Old Arcadia* the terms are far less appropriate. In subject matter, at least, the revised version is much nearer than its predecessor both to Minturno's and to Sidney's conception of what an heroic poem should be.

Not in the themes of the story, however, but in the organic form, do the two *Arcadias* offer the most striking contrast. "In the first 'Arcadia'," according to Bertram Dobell, "we have the unity of effect of a Greek temple; in its second form we have a rococo erection, fine in some of its parts, but formless and grotesque as a whole."[1] This impression will be shared by almost any modern reader on first examining the revised version. And it is in the apparently loose and rambling structure

1. "New Light upon Sir Philip Sidney's 'Arcadia'," *The Quarterly Review*, CCXI (July, 1909), 90.

that Sidney's romance appears most at variance with the theories of the *Defence*. In introducing into England the unities of time and place, Sidney is the advocate of neo-classicism. In writing a formless novel is he not betraying his underlying romanticism? Perhaps. But if so, why has he given a rigid structure to the earlier, unrevised version of his work, which might be expected to reveal his natural imaginative processes, unchecked by critical judgment?

As a matter of fact, the later version is not without form. Dr. Wolff has made plain the "almost incredible skill" with which Sidney has rewoven "the Old Arcadia upon the loom of Heliodorus." [1] A design which is not readily apparent is remote enough from the noble simplicity of the ancients. But was Sidney, or was Minturno, even in theory, a genuine classicist? Precisely how far is the Italian critic's ideal of epic structure truly Aristotelian? In what respects is it now the common property of all students of literature, and in what does it belong distinctly to the sixteenth century? These are questions which we must answer if we are to understand the complex design of the *New Arcadia*.

The emphasis which Minturno places on the epic fable is clear from a glance at either the *De Poeta* or the *Arte Poetica*, and suggests the care with which he had thought out his theory. It is important to keep the whole theory in mind. The epic fable, we learn, is what distinguishes heroic poetry from history. The historian tells what has happened, the poet what ought to happen. [2] The poet, perhaps beginning with an historical subject, is free to omit some incidents and to invent others. The historian, describing what has actually happened, must often show many unrelated actions of divers men in many times and places. Here is the opportunity of the poet, for being free to omit or to invent incidents, he does not tell all the

1. *The Greek Romances in Elizabethan Prose Fiction*, pp. 352–353.
2. *De Poeta*, p. 123.

events of an historical period, or the whole life of his hero. Unlike the historian, he presents only a single great action. Homer is to be praised because he does not write a complete biography of Achilles [1] or a history of the Trojan War,[2] but begins the *Iliad* in the ninth year of the war, and confines himself to the wrath of Achilles and the events to which it led, introducing earlier and later incidents as episodes. In the close-knit, unified action of the epic, events follow one another as cause and effect. Not so with history, for in actual life the causal connection of events cannot always be observed. The historian, therefore, often recording the inexplicable, shows a less general aspect of truth than the poet. As Sidney states this familiar doctrine of Aristotle, "the *Poet* doth so farre exceed him, as hee is to frame his example to that which is most reasonable, be it in warlike, politike, or private matters, where the *Historian*, in his bare, was, hath many times that which we call fortune, to overrule the best wisedome. Manie times he must tell events, whereof he can yeeld no cause, and if he do, it must be poetically." [3]

From the distinction between history and heroic poetry it follows that Minturno has no use for the theory, advocated first by Giraldi Cinthio and later by Castelvetro, that the laws of heroic poetry outlined by Aristotle apply only to the ancient epic, and that the romance and the biographical poem are equally legitimate species of poetry, with very different laws of their own. Epic structure is fundamental in every heroic poem. It is always necessary that the fable "be the imitation of a single action, which is entire and complete, and that its parts cling together in so close a union that nothing can be altered or omitted without the whole being changed and disturbed." [4]

Such a fable may be either complex or simple, according as it has or has not a "change of fortune" or "recogni-

1. Page 123.   2. Page 131.
3. *Works*, III, 17.   4. *De Poeta*, p. 123.

tion" or both. It is the complex type that chiefly interests
Minturno. He analyzes recognition scenes into several
kinds, after the manner of Aristotle, and has a careful discussion of change of fortune, or *peripeteia*. This is an event
which turns the fortunes of the central characters suddenly
from good to bad, or from bad to good, falling quite contrary to our expectations, and yet according to what we
recognize as probable or necessary.[1] The *peripeteia* divides
the fable into two parts — the knitting together of incidents (*colligatio*) and the unraveling, or solution (*solutio*).[2]
It is essential to have the solution arise from the necessities
of the story, not, as in the *Medea* of Euripides, from an
agency external to the main action.[2] Not only the change
of fortune, but all the events should fall "unexpectedly,"
yet according to an inner connection, and not by chance,
for such events produce an impression of wonder, admiration, and awe (*admiratio*) — the impression of sublimity
which only the greatest art can give.[3]

Thus far Minturno's conception of plot offers nothing
novel. Except for the place given to recognition scenes, it
is perfectly familiar to every modern student of literature.
Based directly upon Aristotle, using even his very phrases,
it is truly — almost slavishly — classical.

If Minturno had stopped here, then Sidney's original
Arcadia would have conformed more closely to his requirements than the revised version. Everything in the
Old Arcadia fits together exactly. "Nothing can be altered
or omitted without the whole being changed and disturbed." Pyrocles' sight of Philoclea's picture causes him
to love her and to disguise himself as an Amazon in order
to gain admittance to her father's household. Musidorus'
friendship for Pyrocles causes him first to protest against
his action, then to lend him assistance, then, being near the
duke's lodges, to see Pamela, to love her, to disguise him-

1. Page 126.   2. Page 133.
3. Page 124.

self as a shepherd, and to apprentice himself to the clown Dametas, who is her guardian. The appearance of the lion and the bear is accidental, but the courage of the princes springs from their love. Once they are in favor, their disguises become the chief obstacles to their love, and once they have won their ladies, the strange retirement of Basilius, and his and his wife's infatuation for Pyrocles, become further obstacles. The devices by which the princes overcome these difficulties lead to still greater distress, but also to the final happy ending. For the device by which Pyrocles brought Gynecia and Basilius together in the cave leads to Basilius' confusion, to the love potion's being administered him, to his apparent death, and to his awakening just in time to save the prisoners from execution. Even in very small points the story is admirably coherent. The rascals who recaptured Pamela and Musidorus are a remnant of the mob which had already attacked the lodges, and their later action was dictated both by their remembrance of Musidorus' earlier injuries to them, and by their wish to regain the duke's favor by bringing back his daughter. Again, in the trial scene, the recognition between Euarchus and his son and nephew whom he had just condemned to death, is brought about naturally through Musidorus' old servant, whose sudden arrival was prepared for in an earlier incident.

The events fall unexpectedly enough, "yet according to an inner necessity, and not by chance." There is an abrupt *peripeteia* when Basilius wakes from his apparent death. There is a long rising action, during which the threads of the plot are knitted together. There is a swift unraveling once Basilius awakens, recognizes the dangerous folly of his past behavior, exonerates his wife, and gives his consent to the marriage of his daughters. And this solution springs not from an agency external to the main action, but from the necessities of the story itself.

In the *Old Arcadia*, therefore, the plot conforms in

nearly every particular to Minturno's requirements as I
have so far described them — requirements made not
only by the more classical critics of the Renaissance, but
by the ancients, by the neo-classicists of the seventeenth
and eighteenth centuries, and by most critics of today. To
understand the plot of the *New Arcadia*, however, we
must look especially at those parts of Minturno's theory
which offer a contrast to our own ideas.

Like Scaliger and Horace, Minturno insists that the epic
poet should not begin *ab ovo*, but plunge *in medias res* at
the point where his single main action begins.[1] Events
before the time of the main action should be narrated as
episodes, especially through the words of the *dramatis
personæ*. In two places he discusses the distinction between direct and indirect narration. In one he explains
that the direct method is the relation of incidents in the
poet's own words, and that the indirect is the relation
through the speech of his characters. The dramatist, he
continues, can use only the indirect method, while the
epic poet uses both.[2] In the second passage Minturno tells
us that only by narrating through his characters can the
writer prove himself truly an imitator, and that therefore
the epic poet will speak little in his own person, much in
the persons of others.[3]

In his famous attack upon the *Orlando Furioso* and other
romances, Minturno objects specifically to the habit of
breaking off a narrative in the midst of an exciting scene,
such as a battle or a storm, in order to take up another
thread of the story. "Variety in the events narrated," he
admits, is naturally agreeable;[4] but the method of the
romances causes confusion.

The illuminating discussion of episodes, and the vague
remarks about the length of an epic, do not concern us for
the moment. Suffice it to say that Minturno's theory is all

1. *De Poeta*, p. 131.   2. Page 114.
3. Page 154.   4. *L'Arte Poetica*, p. 35.

of a piece. The poet who uses the dramatic method to relate "things done in former time or other place" will be able to plunge at once into his main action, to preserve the continuity of his narrative, and to introduce a large variety of episodes without breaking his single action into several independent stories.

"Things done in former time or other place" is a phrase of Sidney's, in a passage of the *Defence of Poesie* where he discusses the structure of tragedy in terms that recall Minturno's discussion of the epic.

> But they will say, how then shall we set foorth a storie, which contains both many places, and many times? And do they not know that a Tragidie is tied to the lawes of *Poesie* and not of Historie. . . . Againe many things may be told which cannot be shewed: if they know the difference betwixt reporting and representing. As for example, I may speake though I am here, of *Peru*, and in speech digresse from that, to the description of *Calecut*: But in action, I cannot represent it without *Pacolets* Horse. And so was the manner the Auncients tooke, by some *Nuntius*, to recount things done in former time or other place. Lastly, if they will represent an Historie, they must not (as *Horace* saith) beginne *ab ovo*, but they must come to the princi-pall poynte of that one action which they will represent.[1]

In this passage Sidney recommends for tragedy two of the rules which Minturno recommends for the epic, namely, plunging *in medias res*, and reporting through the characters "things done in former time or other place." The third rule, not to break off the narrative in the middle of an important scene, he does not discuss; and since Minturno has enunciated it only in his Italian trea-tise it is just possible that Sidney had not run across this rule in his study of Italian criticism. In any case, however, in revising the *Arcadia* he has adhered to the third rule along with the first two, though in the original version he has disregarded all three.

1. *Works*, III, 39.

In the *Old Arcadia*, as we have seen, Sidney begins with exposition, sketching first the circumstances which led to Basilius' retirement, and then the events which brought the two princes into Arcadia. In the revised version he plunges at once into the story, with the scene between Strephon and Claius, or, if we regard that scene as a kind of prologue, he begins with the arrival of Musidorus' half-drowned body on the shore near where the shepherds are standing. Whichever view we take of the scene between Strephon and Claius, the *New Arcadia* plunges *in medias res*. The *Old Arcadia* begins *ab ovo*.[1]

Again, since he has begun the *New Arcadia* with the main action, Sidney has necessarily used the dramatic method of narration to describe "things done in former time." To Kalander he has given the account of Arcadia and of Basilius' retirement, excepting only the words of the oracle, which Kalander could not know,[2] and which he reports to us by Basilius himself in a conversation with Philanax at the end of Book II.[3] These changes to a dramatic narration are typical of the new technique which Sidney has developed. He drops the numerous references to "fair ladies" in his audience (which nearly every writer upon the *Arcadia* has observed in the original version) and he uses the pronoun *I* much more sparingly than in that more immature work. He now follows Minturno's rule to narrate little in his own person, much through the reports of his character. Moreover, in adhering to this rule he has also adhered to the third — not to break off an important scene in the middle. Indeed, in each book of the

1. That in plunging *in medias res* and in "having 'the story of one's life' narrated by a personage in the course of the current story," Sidney is following epic convention, has been pointed out by Dr. Wolff (*The Greek Romances in Elizabethan Prose Fiction*, pp. 351 ff.) and by other scholars. (Cf. Moody, *An Inquiry into the Sources of Sidney's "Arcadia,"* pp. 49-51.) I would emphasize the fact not as a discovery, but as evidence that Sidney was trying to write an heroic poem.

2. *Works*, I, 19 ff.   3. Page 327.

New Arcadia he keeps his narrative continuous from beginning to end.

How scrupulously Sidney now obeys these two rules
may be seen from a glance at the events of Book I. It is as
though he were taking the reader forward on a journey, in
the guidance now of one set of characters, now of another,
never leaving the first set till he is already in the company
of the second, and pausing only to hear a story occasionally
from the lips of one new acquaintance or another. This
will be clear from a brief summary.

With Strephon and Claius we see the body of Musidorus
cast on the shore of Laconia, run to.his assistance, accompany him in his effort to rescue Pyrocles from a wreck at
sea, and return when the oarsmen take fright at some approaching pirates. With the two shepherds as guides we
now travel with Musidorus to seek assistance from Kalander, in Arcadia. Arrived at that gentleman's house,
the shepherds leave us, and we remain with the young
prince during his long illness. From Kalander we learn
the state of affairs in Arcadia, and from his steward we
hear the story of Argalus and Parthenia, and learn of the
rebellion of Helots in Laconia, and of their having captured Argalus and Kalander's son Clitophon. With Musidorus we join the rescue party, find Pyrocles the leader
of the Helots, and now remain with that prince while his
friend returns to Arcadia. We return with Pyrocles to
Kalander's house, learn from Parthenia how her beauty
was restored, witness her reunion and later her marriage
with Argalus, hear Pyrocles tell Musidorus of his adventures since being captured by pirates, observe his interest
in the picture of Philoclea and her parents, note the change
in his behavior, hear his friend's over-wise remonstrances
broken off by Kalander, accompany the princes on Kalander's hunting party, and remain with Musidorus while
Pyrocles disappears. With Musidorus we travel for two
months in search of his cousin, meet Queen Helen of Cor-

inth, and hear from her the tragic story of how her love for Amphialus, though unrequited, had caused him to slay his friend Philoxenus. At last we find Pyrocles, disguised as an Amazon lady and calling himself Zelmane, witness the quarrel between the friends and then their reconciliation, and hear from Pyrocles the full account of how he fell in love, gained admittance to the royal household, and found his suit to Philoclea hindered by the king's loving him as an Amazon woman and the queen's loving him as the man she guesses him to be. Leaving Musidorus, we return to the lodge with Pyrocles, hear from Basilius an account of Phalantus and Artesia, and with the general company witness Phalantus' prowess in the jousts. We remain with the general company while Pyrocles disappears on the second day of the jousts, see him reappear in plain armor and overthrow Phalantus, and hear how he had obtained horse and armor. Remaining now with Pyrocles, we witness his reunion with Musidorus, hear from that prince how he had seen Pamela, had loved her, had obtained shepherd's clothes from Menalcas (whom he had sent off to Thessalia lest he betray him), and now, as the shepherd Dorus, was seeking to join Basilius' pastoral sports. We see him apprentice himself to Dametas, the clown who is guardian to the Princess Pamela; we return to the lodge, leave Basilius to wait for the shepherds, go with the princes and the ladies to the place appointed for the pastoral games, and, when the lion and bear appear, hurry after Pyrocles and Philoclea to the spot where Basilius is still standing. There we are joined first by Gynecia, then by the rest of the company, hear from Pamela how Dorus has slain the bear and what cowardice Dametas has shown, learn from a messenger that the beasts had belonged to Cecropia, whom Gynecia mistrusts, and turn finally to the pastimes of the shepherds, with which the first book ends.

"Things done in former time or other place," it will

readily be seen, are consistently reported by the characters in the story, not represented by the author. Kalander's account of Basilius' retirement, his steward's account of Argalus and Parthenia and the revolt in Lacedæmon, and Queen Helen's account of Amphialus, all deal with "things done in former time." Pyrocles' summary of his adventures up to the time that his friend found him the leader of the Helots, Parthenia's report of how her beauty was restored by Queen Helen's physician, Pyrocles' detailed story of his progress in love, Basilius' account of Phalantus and Artesia, Musidorus' account of how he fell in love and obtained a disguise, and Pamela's description of how the young shepherd had slain the bear,— all deal with events simultaneous with the action which the reader has been following, but events which happen "in other place." It is by this use of the dramatic method of narration that Sidney is able to keep the unbroken forward movement of his story. For the different reports which we hear are themselves incidents in the action which we are following.

Some of these episodes belong only to the revised version, but those which are common to both versions are, in the *Old Arcadia*, regularly narrated by the author himself — with the exception of a few brief passages, such as the single sentence in which Pyrocles tells how he fell in love with Philoclea from her picture.[1] Some of the episodes, because of the simpler plot in the original version, belong there to the main story, and so do not interrupt the continuity. Others, such as the account of how Musidorus fell in love with Pamela,[2] do interrupt the forward movement of the narrative, because the author stops to explain what has been happening "in other place."

The contrast in narrative technique is especially clear in the accounts of how Pyrocles slew the lion and Musidorus the bear. In the *Old Arcadia* Basilius' love meditations

---

1. *Works*, IV, 14-15.   2. Pages 36 ff.

are interrupted "by the hasty and fearefull ronning unto him, of moste parte of the Shepeardes, who came flying from the pastorall sportes." [1] The shepherds report what has happened, says the author, "but after suche a broken maner, that I thinke yt not best, to truble yo^w, fayre Ladyes, with theyre panting speeches, but, to make a full Declaracõn of yt my self." [1] Sidney then leaves the bewildered duke and goes back to tell what has been happening to the ladies and the two princes. First he describes how Pyrocles has saved Philoclea from the lion. Then, breaking off again, he goes back to explain at length that Gynecia, observing Pyrocles' manner of fighting, has been confirmed in her earlier suspicion that the supposed Amazon was really a man. [2] Sidney then returns to Philoclea and Pyrocles, and describes the dressing of Pyrocles' wound. Next, when the company, their sudden anxiety set at rest, "all see *Pamela* coming betwixt *Dametas* & *Dorus*," [3] the author once more breaks off his account of what is now happening, to tell in his own words what has just been happening to Pamela, Musidorus, and the bear. [4] Four times in this one episode, therefore, Sidney breaks his narrative.

In the revised version, as we have seen, he describes the episode without any interruption. He leaves Basilius without mentioning his meditations, and accompanies the princes and the ladies to "the faire field, appointed for the shepherdish pastimes." [5] He greatly condenses the passage about Gynecia and the description of how Pyrocles' wound was dressed. And he tells the exploit of Musidorus in the words of Pamela. Except for an incidental reference to Gynecia, which occupies but two sentences, [6] he is enabled by these changes to make his action constantly progressive. In the *Old Arcadia*, on the contrary,

---

1. Page 41.   2. Page 44.
3. Page 46.   4. Page 47.
5. I, 118.   6. Page 120.

his narrative moves forward with Basilius, then back to the entrance of the wild animals and forward to Pyrocles' rescue of Philoclea, then back to Gynecia and again forward to the dressing of Pyrocles' wound, then back a fourth time to Pamela and the bear, and so forward once more. The narrative method in the original version is precisely that against which Minturno inveighs in the *Arte Poetica*. The method in the revised version would meet with his hearty approval.

The two versions of Book II offer a yet plainer contrast. In the *Old Arcadia* the narrative is interrupted twice in a most exciting scene. When Pyrocles and Basilius are fighting a band of dangerous rioters and suddenly receive a timely aid from shepherds led by Musidorus and Philisides, the story breaks off and leaves the battle raging while we are told what Musidorus has been doing, and how Pamela has found safety in a cave.[1] Then as soon as the ducal party have entered the lodge, and while the mob are preparing to burn it, the author intrudes himself into the narrative in order to explain the origin of the riot.[2] In the *New Arcadia*, on the other hand, the beginning of the riot is described by Clinias to Basilius,[3] after everything is over; and the account of what Musidorus has been doing is condensed from two pages to two sentences.[4]

Again, in the original version of Book II there are, all told, seven breaks in the story[5] — two on a single page.[6] None occurs in the second version, unless we except one passage of half a page in which Sidney explains the character of Clinias, and his relation with Cecropia.[7] This passage, since it occurs after the mob have begun to cheer for Basilius, does not violate Minturno's requirement, for

1. IV, 118 ff.   2. Pages 120 ff.
3. I, 321 ff.
4. Page 311.
5. See IV, 92, 93, 103, 112, 116, 118, 120.
6. Page 93.   7. I, 319.

it does not interrupt the scene at a time of excitement, and indeed serves to emphasize the fact that the danger is past. In the *Old Arcadia*, on the contrary, the story of the riot is broken twice by long passages and at critical moments.

To obtain the greater continuity of the *New Arcadia*, Sidney has employed various devices. He often condenses the original material or changes its order. He sometimes invents a connecting incident — such as Philoclea's evening walk to her sister's lodge [1] — which enables the reader to go from one place to another in the company of one of the characters. But most commonly he uses dramatic narration. "Things done in other place," but simultaneous with the main action, he narrates through a reporter — as when Musidorus tells Pyrocles how he wooed Pamela,[2] and when Pamela reveals to her sister the love she will not yet confess to her princely shepherd.[3]

Still more conspicuous is the reporting of "things done in former time." Except for Basilius' account of the oracle which caused him to go into retirement,[4] these events fall into two apparently independent stories, dealing respectively with the birth, education, and famous adventures of the two heroes, and with the love of Plangus and Erona. The one is related by Musidorus and Pyrocles to their ladies.[5] The other is divided among three narrators — Philoclea, Pamela, and Basilius.[6] These stories constitute a special problem. Occupying more than half the prose portions of Book II, they distract the reader's attention from the main action. Not only unity, but continuity, is wanting, for the account is broken into five parts. To any modern reader or to a true classicist the episodes are a glaring defect in the artistic structure of the *New Arcadia*.

1. Pages 168 ff. Cf. also p. 308.   2. Pages 153–166.
3. Pages 177–182.   4. Pages 326–327.
5. Pages 184–214, 262–307.
6. Pages 232–236, 242–250, 329–338.

Whether they are equally faulty from the point of view of Minturno I shall discuss in the next chapter. Here we need only note that they are related by the *dramatis personæ*, and therefore technically do not break the forward movement of the narrative. Two of Minturno's rules for the epic which Sidney disregarded in Book II of the *Old Arcadia* he follows consistently in the revised version; and one of those rules he has himself laid down for tragedy.

In Book III the earlier and the later forms cannot be easily compared, for the stories overlap at no point. Yet the differences in technique, though not thrown into high relief by identity of material, are nevertheless plainly discoverable.

Nowhere, indeed, is there a more startling example of what Minturno condemned than in Books III and IV of the *Old Arcadia*. In Book III Musidorus and Pamela, during their attempted flight from Arcadia, are attacked by "a Doszen Clownish villeynes" at the moment when Musidorus, overcome by the charms of the sleeping Pamela, is about to break his oath and violate her chastity. Here the narrative comes to an abrupt stop.[1] The reader's attention is forced away to the story of Pyrocles. Ninety-five pages intervene before the reader learns, in Book IV, that Pamela's chastity was preserved, and that the "clownish villains" brought the prince and princess back to Arcadia.[2] Had Sidney lived to rewrite the episode, it is scarcely possible that he would have left in his narrative so startling an interruption. Indeed, the confinement of the two princes in the same tent,[3] and of the two heroines in the same lodge,[4] gave him an opportunity to tell the whole episode by dramatic narration, in the words either of Pamela or of Musidorus — a change quite in keeping with the new technique of the revised version.

This new technique is apparent in the unfinished Book

1. IV, 190.   2. Pages 285 ff.
3. Page 298.   4. Page 299.

III of the *New Arcadia*. Though Sidney has employed dramatic narration less than in the earlier books, where he had to relate events anterior to the main action, yet he has used the device whenever it was appropriate. When Cecropia carries off the two princesses and the disguised Pyrocles, it is from her talk with her son that we learn her motives; and when Pyrocles has apparently seen both Philoclea and her sister executed, it is from Philoclea's words to her agonized lover that we discover the truth. At the point where the *New Arcadia* ends, the author has left untold the story of Musidorus during his absences from the scene of battle, a story which he must have planned to tell through Musidorus or his companions. Sidney has learned to speak little in his own person, much in the persons of others.[1]

Quite as certainly, he has learned to keep his story unbroken in exciting scenes. In the third book, as in the first two, he betters Minturno's instruction, for he carries the reader forward with only the most trifling interruptions of the journey. But his technique is a little less rigid than heretofore.

Occasionally, for example, he allows us to pass from one scene to another without the guidance of some person in the story. We do not follow a character, but merely turn to the subject uppermost in our minds when we pass from Cecropia's arguments with Pamela to the state of the siege, or from Amphialus' victories over his challengers to the grief of Basilius.[2] In such instances, be it noted, our journey continues, for the temporal sequence of events is preserved. In other instances we pass to events simultaneous with those we have just witnessed; as when we turn from the grief in Basilius' camp for the death of Parthenia to the remorse of Amphialus for his deed.[3] Yet

1. Cf. *De Poeta*, p. 154.
2. See *Works*, I, 384, 419. Cf. also pp. 401, 428.
3. Page 450. Cf. also p. 464.

here, too, we are not carried backward in time, and in a moment we resume our progress, without doubling and redoubling back upon our tracks as in the *Old Arcadia*. Moreover, the occasions when Sidney has interrupted the journey with even the most trivial break are far outnumbered by those, too numerous to mention, when he takes pains to have us follow a character from one scene to the next.[1] Especially noteworthy are the nameless messengers with whom we often travel, and whose prominence is hard to understand except as a device for connecting two incidents.[2]

Only one transition in Book III can be said in any real sense to break the narrative. This occurs when, after hearing the punishment of Clinias and Artesia for their conspiracy against Amphialus, we go back to learn the cause of a tumult in the camp of Basilius, which has occurred earlier and has been mentioned half a page back.[3] Not only do we pass to this tumult without a guide (though we have seen it from Pamela's window) but we pause now to learn from the author himself the character of Anaxius, his acquaintance with Amphialus, and his history since parting with Pyrocles, before we learn of his success in breaking through Basilius' lines and joining forces with Amphialus.[4] Even this marked, though momentary, interruption of the forward movement of the plot may be considered appropriate; for it emphasizes the fact that Anaxius, in pushing through Basilius' lines, has thrust himself also into the main story. To break the narrative here is far more effective than to continue it without interruption.

Thus in relaxing somewhat in Book III the rigid methods of the earlier books, Sidney shows at times a surer

---

1. Cf., for example, pp. 357, 362, 376, 394, 402, 411, 413, 415, 418, 423, 434, 445, 466, 476, 482, 492, 495, 496, 512.

2. Cf. pp. 420, 469, 478–479, 503, 509–511.

3. Pages 438–439.   4. Pages 439–440.

mastery of his art. Nowhere does he abandon his own
principle. Still less does he offend against Minturno's, for
he never interrupts a critical scene in the middle. In the
combats between Amphialus and his challengers [1] or the
scenes in which Cecropia tyrannizes over her nieces,[2] there
is nothing like Sidney's abandonment of Pamela and Musidorus in the *Old Arcadia* at a time when the princess is in a
double danger.

In the *New Arcadia*, therefore, Sidney has followed certain laws of form as unmistakably as in the *Defence of
Poesie*. He has begun *in mediis rebus*. He has used dramatic narration. He has avoided interruptions in important
scenes. He has adhered also to the similar rules for tragedy
which he himself has laid down in the *Defence*. And finally,
he has made his practice consistent with itself. By the
use not only of dramatic narration, but of connecting incidents, he has maintained a continuity of narrative which
even Minturno does not require. Thus in the *New Arcadia*
Sidney reveals a more conscious artistry than in the *Old*,
and in at least three important particulars he has attained
what he did not there approach — an epic technique.

What he has not attained is the rounded symmetry
which marks the *Defence of Poesie*. So plain to modern
readers is his failure that Dobell thinks Sidney should have
left the *Arcadia* "in its original state, since in that form it
is much better as a work of art. . . . Even had the author
lived to complete his work in its second form, it could
never have been made anything more than a series of
stories, all of them, it is true, interesting in themselves, but
so unskilfully pieced together that it is hard for the reader
to understand exactly where he is." [3] To be sure, Dobell
has overlooked the technical skill in plotting, which Dr.
Wolff was the first modern scholar to reveal in the *New*

1. Cf. pp. 412 ff., 422 ff., 445 ff., 453 ff.
2. Cf. pp. 376 ff., 402 ff., 469 ff.
3. "New Light upon Sir Philip Sidney's 'Arcadia'," p. 82.

Arcadia. But "such marvellous involution and complexity," Dr. Wolff hastens to add, "defeat their own artistic ends. One who reads for pleasure simply cannot understand the 'Arcadia'." [1] Has not Sidney neglected Minturno's fundamental requirement — a single great action bound together by causal connection?

Now the chief difficulty which Dobell and Dr. Wolff encounter in following Sidney's story is the episodes of Book II — the long narratives of the princes' former exploits in Asia and of Plangus' love for Erona. These, as has been remarked, constitute a special problem which will be considered in the next chapter. By setting them aside for the moment, we can gain a better perspective on the plan as a whole.

In view of Dr. Wolff's elaborate analysis of the plot, we need do little more here than enforce his conclusions with a few illustrations. Sidney, in "re-weaving the Old Arcadia upon the loom of Heliodorus"— and of Minturno — "has not dropped a single thread in the whole enormous design. As far as he recast it, the grandiose pattern is perfect." [2] Of the new incidents almost none could "be altered or omitted without the whole being changed and disturbed." [3] In Book I nearly every event is occasioned by two incidents — the separation of the heroes in the sea fight, and Pyrocles' falling in love with Philoclea, on seeing her picture in Kalander's summer house. Some episodes seem, on a first reading of the *Arcadia*, quite unnecessary to the central love story. Examples are the marriage of Argalus and Parthenia, the tragic love of Queen Helen for Amphialus, and the jousts in which Phalantus celebrates the beauty of Artesia. But in the third book all of these people have important rôles to play. How carefully these minor actions are woven into the rest of the story may be seen from two details. The ladies whose pictures are borne

1. *The Greek Romances in Elizabethan Prose Fiction*, p. 352.
2. Pages 352–353.   3. Cf. *De Poeta*, p. 123.

in triumph before Phalantus and his mistress nearly all appear in person in the adventures of Musidorus and Pyrocles in Asia; [1] and Queen Helen's marvelous physician, who in Book I restores Parthenia's beauty, is apparently the same to whom in Book III the queen takes Amphialus to be cured of his desperate wounds. [2]

In Book II, where the episodic material becomes so unwieldy, the main narrative is still as closely knit as Minturno could wish. The love stories are told from the point of view first of the heroes, then of the heroines. Gynecia and Basilius provide necessary obstacles. And the appearance of Amphialus is a preparation for Book III. Even the episodic material comes in naturally, for Pamela and Philoclea wish to hear the exploits of their lovers, and Pyrocles is eager to know the fate of Queen Erona, to whom he once gave assistance.

In Book III the unified design is still clearer. The sufferings which the lovers now encounter all spring immediately from Cecropia's ambition for her son, his passion for Philoclea, or Anaxius' pride; and ultimately from Basilius' neglect of his kingly duties. Each event, moreover, arises from the preceding action. From Phalantus' combat with Amphialus there results a long series of conflicts, and finally the defeat of Amphialus at the hands of Musidorus. His desperate condition then allows his mother to govern in his stead, and so leads to her new cruelties, and thence to his discovery of them, her death, his attempted suicide, his being carried by Queen Helen to her physician, and Anaxius' new tyrannies during his absence.

Certain incidents could perhaps be omitted. The combats between Dametas and Clinias and between Amphialus and the Knight of the Tombs, who turns out to be Parthenia, have no bearing on Musidorus' victory over Amphialus and little upon the later course of the action. They exist largely for themselves, the one as a comic, the

1. *Works*, I, 101–104.   2. Pages 50, 496–497.

other as a pathetic, interlude. And yet they bear some relation to the main story. Amphialus' victory over Argalus gives the occasion for them both. Then, as the story proceeds, Clinias' defeat leads to his abortive conspiracy, to the execution of his accomplice Artesia, and to the cruelest of all the tortures inflicted upon Philoclea.[1] The death of Parthenia, moreover, intensifies Amphialus' gloom, and so becomes a contributing cause for his attempted suicide,[2] and for the deliverance of the heroines and Pyrocles from captivity. Even if some episodes in Book III could be altered or condensed, perhaps none could be omitted without lessening the impression we receive of a mysterious providence governing the fortunes of men. Such amplifications of the main plot received, as we shall see in the next chapter, the full sanction of Minturno.

In only one way can Book III be said to violate epic unity: Amphialus, with Cecropia and Anaxius, occupies the center of the stage, and we seldom see the heroes. Perhaps if Sidney had finished the *New Arcadia*, this violation of unity would trouble us no more than Hamlet's absence from the stage in the fourth act. In any case, everything in Book III bears ultimately upon the central love stories. There is one great action, governed by cause and effect. Sidney has fairly earned Dr. Wolff's praise of his technical skill. "As far as he recast it, the grandiose pattern is perfect."

Is not its very magnitude, however, too great for the mind to grasp as a whole?

This and other questions must be answered before we can describe Sidney's work as an heroic poem, but it is time to bring together the evidence thus far considered. The *New Arcadia* is not an epic; for it has no formal invocation, it is written in prose, it introduces pastoral elements, it lacks a supernatural machinery. In all these points, however, it has the consistency of conscious art,

1. Pages 475 ff., 488.   2. See p. 493.

and is in perfect harmony with the author's critical theories
as described in the *Defence of Poesie*. Again, in its enormous complexity the *New Arcadia* is remote from the
simple and noble outlines of the Homeric epic. Its subject
matter, however, is heroic; for from the Renaissance point
of view love is a theme appropriate to epic no less than to
romance, and in the *New Arcadia* there are also the other
stock themes of heroic poetry — adventure, war, and great
national and even international events. Again, the narrative technique — the beginning *in mediis rebus*, the reporting by dramatic narration "things done in former time or
other place," the scrupulous avoiding of unnecessary
breaks, particularly in critical scenes — is precisely that
which Minturno demands in the epic and is perfectly
consistent with what Sidney requires in tragedy. Finally,
in its structure it has in general the single great action and
the causal connection of events on which Minturno puts
his greatest emphasis. The art of the *New Arcadia* is more
conscious than that of the *Old*, and more consistent
with the author's theories. Its structure is no less appropriate to the epic, its subject and above all its narrative
method are conspicuously more appropriate, than those of
the original version. That Sidney regarded the *Old Arcadia* as an heroic poem there is little or no evidence. There is
strong reason for believing he so regarded the *New Arcadia*.

Certain features of the revised version remain to be
discussed. Two which have already been mentioned are
its great length and the mass of episodic material in Book
II; another is the ornateness of the prose style. These
features, though uncongenial enough to the classical epic,
lend support to the view that in organic form the *New
Arcadia* is a sixteenth-century heroic poem. Elaborate
style, varied episode, and large design all reflect the love of
magnificence which distinguishes the art of the Renaissance from that of the ancients. And both Sidney and
Minturno shared the tastes of their age.

CHAPTER V

Ornament in the *New Arcadia*

BEAUTY, to a true classicist, resides in form. To the men of the Renaissance it often lies in ornamental detail. In the characteristic architecture of the period, in the splendid garments of courtiers, in the tournament or the royal progress, in all the varied pageantry of life, the sixteenth century shows a love of spectacle, a delight in profusion and richness of detail, which, though altogether foreign to the Greek ideal, touched even the men most deeply imbued with the classic spirit. The poets gloried in ornamentation, and the humanists raised no clear note of protest. It was a student of the New Learning who wrote the great narrative poem of Elizabeth's reign, a work notable for richness of imagery, harmony of line and stanza, stateliness of pageantry, variety of incident, and elevation of mood, but wanting in classic design. Another university graduate gave us in *Tamburlaine* unforgettable bursts of poetry, and all the "pomp and circumstance of glorious war"; but Marlowe's plot is episodic, the sort that Aristotle stigmatized as the very worst. Spenser and, in his early work, Marlowe, show a similar weakness in structure, and a similar power in line and episode. Thus the Renaissance love of ornament appears in poetry in sumptuous phrase or splendid incident, the very elements which in the *New Arcadia* have obscured for modern readers the design of the whole.

The sixteenth century, in taste as in all else, was a time of quick growth. In its early and middle decades the humanists, in their enthusiasm for choice language, too often conceived style as an end in itself, the ornament, not the inevitable expression, of thought — a tendency against which Bacon was to raise so powerful a voice.[1] But among English writers Bacon is only one of those who, toward the end of the sixteenth century, were beginning to grasp more clearly than the Ciceronians the meaning of artistic form. Shakespeare felt his way from chronicle history to tragedy. Daniel and Jonson showed that poetry may be simple. "Eloquence and gay wordes," said Daniel, "are not of the substance of wit."[2] Within three years after Sidney's death, the author of the *Arte of English Poesie* was calling "the phantasticall part of man (if it be not disordered) a representer of the best, most comely, and bewtifull images or apparances of thinges to the soule and according to their very truth."[3] Oddly enough, Spenser, in spite of his own practice, gave perfect expression to the Greek view of art:

> That Beautie is not, as fond men misdeeme,
> An outward shew of things that onely seeme;[4]

> For soule is forme, and doth the bodie make.[5]

In this maturing of English taste, Sir Philip Sidney, had he lived, would doubtless have had an important part; but dying in his thirty-second year, while he was still learning the poetic art, he stands as a transitional figure. While Sidney was a boy at Shrewsbury School, Roger Ascham was writing, from the point of view of the Ciceronians, "Euen as a faire stone requireth to be sette in the finest gold, with the best workmanshyp, or else it leseth moch of the Grace and price, euen so, excellencye in learning, and namely Diuinitie, ioyned with a cumlie personage, is a

---

1. *Advancement of Learning*, ed. Wright, 1880, I. iv. 2, pp. 28–30.
2. *Defence of Rhyme, Elizabethan Critical Essays*, ed. G. Gregory Smith, 1904, II, 372.
3. *Elizabethan Critical Essays*, II, 20.
4. "An Hymne in Honour of Beautie," ll. 90–91, *Complete Poetical Works*, Cambridge edition, 1908, p. 747.
5. L. 133, p. 748.

meruelous Iewell in the world." [1] Had Sidney lived to the
age of sixty, he could have read in Bacon's essays: "Vertue
is like a Rich Stone, best plaine set: And surely, Vertue is
best in a Body, that is comely, though not of Delicate Features: And that hath rather Dignity of Presence, then
Beauty of Aspect." [2] Bacon's words show a significant
change in the idea of "comeliness," or artistic fitness. "A
fair stone" should indeed "be set in the finest gold, with
the best workmanship" — but it is "best plain set." Ornament may be excessive.

Now when Bacon published his essay on beauty, Sidney
had been for nearly thirty years in his grave. If he groped
for the classic idea

> That soul is form, and doth the body make,

he was not destined to reach it. The Ciceronians have left
their mark on the theories of the *Defence of Poesie* and on
the style of the *Arcadia*, while the luxuriance of episode in
that *magnum opus* was encouraged by the very critic who
had argued the cause of classic art against the romances.
In his conception of poetic ornament Sidney stands mid-
way between Ascham and Bacon, in one of the formative
moments of English literature.

It was perhaps the only time in history when such a book
as the *Arcadia* could be written under the influence of a
great interpreter of Aristotle. In its elaborate style, its
length, and its wealth of episode, it disregards the principles laid down by the Greek thinker; and yet it does no violence to the rules announced by his Renaissance disciple.
"Epic poetry," writes Minturno, "grows in magnitude by
a magnificent and sumptuous pomp of incidents and language." [3] If in this generalization one can find the Aristote-

---

1. *The Scholemaster, English Works*, ed. Wright, Cambridge English Classics, 1904, p. 194.
2. "On Beauty," *Bacon's Essays*, ed. Wright, 1887, p. 176.
3. *De Poeta*, 1559, p. 152.

lian doctrine of magnificence, a man of Sidney's time could
find in it the authority for a literary art quite as ornate as
that of the *Arcadia*. Sidney's style, it will be seen, appears
to have been fairly well fixed before he made a careful study
of the *De Poeta*. But the length and baffling complexity of
his plot seem due at least in part to the direct influence of
Minturno, and in any case are in harmony with that critic's
conception of an heroic poem.

No part of Minturno's theory is more distinctive than
that which deals with episodes. These bear the same relation to the fable as the digressions in an oration to the main
argument. They "are introduced either for the sake of enlarging or adorning the poem, or because they must not be
omitted." [1] In the fable itself, as we have seen, the "parts
must cohere in so close a union that nothing can be altered
or omitted without the whole being changed and disturbed." [2] Not so with the episodes. Some, indeed, like the
arrival of Æneas at Carthage, the love and death of Dido,
or the descent into Hell, are closely "attached" to the main
action. Others, however, like the account of the fall of
Troy and the wanderings of Æneas, or the story of affairs
among the Latins, lie "outside" the fable. [3] Minturno adds,
somewhat inconsistently, that "whatever is not in the
fable may be said to be attached to it, as, for example, the
arrival at Carthage, the descent into Hell, the games at the
obsequies of Anchises." [1] Apparently Minturno has used
the word "attached" (*afficta, affinguntur*) [4] with different
meanings. All episodes, in one sense, are "attached" to the
fable, since they bear some relation to it. In a stricter
sense, however, episodes are attached to the main action
only if they are simultaneous with it. They are "outside"
it if they comprise events which occur before it begins or
after it ends. [5]

1. *De Poeta*, p. 132. 2. Page 123.
3. Page 130. 4. Cf. pp. 132, 130.
5. Cf. p. 132.

Now in the *Arcadia*, as in any other story which has a central action, the events must necessarily belong either to the fable or to the episodes. Sidney's fable, we have seen, is "single," "entire, and complete," and therefore meets every requirement of Minturno unless it is too long. The episodes present the chief difficulty. To a true classicist, those which are "attached" to the main action, as, for example, the joust held by Phalantus, the "combat of cowards," or the death of Parthenia, may make the whole work too long and too varied; while those which lie "outside" the fable, particularly the events in Asia Minor related in Book II, will certainly appear to encumber the story with unnecessary material.

But Minturno, especially in his discussion of episodes, is not purely a classicist. To describe the fable as a complete and perfect whole, and then to say that the episodes are additions to what is already complete, is to say that the episodes are no organic part of the poem. Even though Minturno would have them "attached" to the fable, and says they sometimes "cannot be omitted," yet he leaves the poet free to introduce them merely "for the sake of enlarging or adorning the poem"; to make them, in other words, a comparatively superficial ornament. On the one hand, there must be a unified design. On the other, there may be decorative episode. Between the epic as Aristotle understood it and as Minturno conceived it there is a difference like that between a Greek temple and a church of Renaissance Italy. What judgment the author of the *De Poeta* might have passed on the *Arcadia* it is not easy to guess. But his statement of theory gave Sidney every reason for calling it an heroic poem.

Certainly the episodes of Books I and III are as closely connected with the main story as Minturno could ask. Nor can it be argued that from the sixteenth-century point of view the episodes in Book II are logically unrelated to the fable. The real questions are whether these episodes bulk so large, and whether the *New Arcadia*, if it had been finished, would have been so inordinately long, as to destroy the unity of the plot.

On these questions, however, Minturno could give a poet no definite guidance. There is, of course, some limit to what may be included within a single work of art. Thus Homer and Virgil could not have related every incident in the wars at Troy or in Latium,

> even if either war had been so clearly a whole as to be treated without obscurity; since those writers had seen plainly that if so many great events had been described, the poem would have turned out to be almost endless, and hard to understand, or if it had not grown longer than was fitting, it would at least have been overloaded with too much variety. For if they had set forth briefly in historical manner what occurred, and had adorned the work with no episodes, they would have deprived the poetry of its beauty. But those incidents which seemed more notable and more worthy of being commemorated and especially whatever was included within an entire and single action — these things they undertook to relate. Then they introduced many varied matters to enrich the work.[1]

For most readers of the twentieth century, such expressions as "almost endless, and hard to understand," or "at least overloaded with too much variety" are only too applicable to the revised *Arcadia*. And yet if we look closely, we find Sidney doing just what Minturno supposes Homer and Virgil to have done. He chooses not to tell everything that occurred during Musidorus' two months' search for Pyrocles, or during the rebellion of Amphialus. He tells rather the "more notable" incidents — such as Musidorus' meeting with Queen Helen — and especially whatever concerns the love stories of the two heroes. Then, besides the things which bear directly on that central action, he introduces "many varied matters to enrich the work." Thus

---

1. Page 148.

Sidney could reasonably have thought he was adhering faithfully to Minturno's principles.

Indeed, a grandiose plan like that of the *New Arcadia* can be justified by several passages in the *De Poeta*. Witness what is said of the appropriate length for the fable (which it will be remembered does not include the episodes):

But indeed how great this action is to be, and how long, you will not easily define. It is agreed by common consent that it ought not to be too large for us to see the whole at one time, and keep in the memory what we have seen, and that it should not be carried further than where there is a change of fortune. On the latter subject, indeed, we have made many observations in the appropriate place. But this requirement will be met if the complications shall be fewer than the ancients formerly made, but shall be extended until several tragedies suited to one sitting have been completed. Nor should they include so many tragic fables as are contained in either the *Cypria* or the *Little Iliad*. For from those which the *Little Iliad* includes, the following tragedies are made: *The Judgment of Arms*, the *Philoctetes*, the *Neoptolemus*, the *Euryphilus*, the *Mendicant Ulysses*, the *Laconian Women*, *The Fall of Ilium*, *The Return of the Greeks*, the *Sinon*, *The Trojan Women*. But yet both from the *Iliad* of Homer and from the *Odyssey* you will produce one, or at most two tragedies, and from the *Æneid* a like number, unless you will add the fall of Troy, the fortunes of Priam, the ruin of Laocoön, the dismemberment of Polydorus, and how Dido and Amata committed suicide, and whatever else is introduced aside from the fable. For the heroic poem by its very nature has taken to itself these additions (a matter in which no other kind of poetry can rival it), in order to increase in magnitude, as is the genius of narrative. Indeed, since narrative can include not a few things which occur simultaneously, it invents many things which happen together, by which the mass of the work is enlarged, and, if one may use the expression, the womb swells. . . .

This prerogative secures great magnificence, and continually relieves the hearer. For various dissimilar incidents and characters which are outside the fable are added to assure the richer

abundance of both. . . . For nothing has more power to relieve
the audience than variety in the things related. But in order
that now at last we may prescribe in some degree what bulk
this kind of poetry should have, if you will examine the poems
of Homer and Virgil, you will find that the action each under-
takes to relate comprises events which occur within a year.[1]

The foregoing passage contains Minturno's most definite statements about how long the epic fable should be.
As to the episodes, a discussion of why they are placed outside the fable gives some hints of their right number and
length:

Although the heroic fable has been said to include a great deal
of material, one is not to understand it is so complicated as to
seem overloaded, or so long that all parts cannot be seen alike,
and easily be brought within the scope of the understanding.
For its end, middle, and even beginning ought to be in plain sight
at the same time. Nevertheless, since epic poetry increases in
grandeur by a magnificent and sumptuous pomp of incidents and
language, and even by a kind of majesty; and especially because
there must be variety to give delight, certainly many events
ought to be added, and unless they are placed outside the proposed action, neither the nature of the fable nor the heroic
genus of writing will be preserved. For if the fable were busied
with all these things, which, though brought in from outside,
could seemingly be connected with it, then either it would not be
unified, or it would be so complicated and so long that in exceed-
ing the limits of magnitude it would produce *ennui*, and could
scarcely if at all be untangled, and indeed would be considered
as written in the historical rather than the poetic manner. For
the historian begins far back, and carries his narrative down to
a later time, in whatever sequence and order the events are
naturally connected, and sticks together many and diverse elements, even if he do it fitly and suitably. Hence the poet
omits many things which so cohere with the fable as to appear
to be in it, but which nevertheless ought to be placed outside of
it; and neither narrates them himself, nor introduces others to

1. Pages 148–149.

describe them as having performed them. For Homer and Virgil made Ulysses and Æneas relate what had happened to themselves. This they did, so that they would not crowd the narrative with these matters, in case they touched them but lightly, though related to matters in the main action; or again, in case they handled them more fully (as they would have done if they had introduced them just as part of the action), so that they would not prolong the poem beyond the limits of a just magnitude.[1]

Imagine an ambitious young poet studying these broad generalizations of the *De Poeta* in the effort to find a practical guide for his own literary work. The heroic poem, he would find, must have design, magnitude, and variety. To maintain a fit balance of these qualities, he must reject the totally unrelated materials which an historian would have to treat; and of what he retains he will arrange part into a close-knit fable, the rest into episodes less intimately connected with the central action. The fable will provide his poem with the necessary design, and to a degree with magnitude and variety. The special function of the episodes is to give still further magnitude and variety, and thus to clothe the heroic poem in a suitable magnificence.

All this is clear. Moreover, as was shown in the preceding chapter, the ways of giving design through the fable are equally unmistakable. But just how is variety to be obtained, and what are the proper limits to magnitude?

The length of the fable is to be governed by four elastic principles:

(1) It should allow but one reversal of fortune.

(2) It should contain the materials of only one or two tragedies.

(3) The events should fall within one year.

(4) The reader should be able to see the central action as a whole, and retain it in the memory.

As to the episodes, the requirements are less clear. They

1. Page 152.

should be numerous and varied, and should contain the materials of many tragedies. Though often outside the fable, they will be related to it. How far, if at all, they are to be limited in bulk by the rules for the fable is an obscure point which will be discussed later.

Vague, indeed, is most of what Minturno says of epic magnitude. Even the rules for the fable seem to apply equally well to a short-story like the *Masque of the Red Death*, an epic like *Paradise Lost*, or (except in not containing the elements of tragedy) a novel so long as *Tom Jones*. And none are violated in the *Arcadia*, for all its vast bulk. Test the work by each rule, and what do we find?

(1) What look like reversals of fortune occur several times in the stories of Argalus and of Amphialus, but only if one considers the action from the point of view of those characters. In the lives of Argalus and Parthenia a long series of disasters is ended by their reunion and marriage; then their happiness is ruined by the king's call to arms. Amphialus loses his battle with Musidorus after a long period of uninterrupted success, and again, just as he begins to recover his health, he suffers the shock of learning how Cecropia has treated Pamela and Philoclea. In a larger sense, however, the fortunes of Amphialus never change, from the time that he slays his foster brother until he causes his mother's death. Even his victory over Argalus gives him little cause to rejoice, since Philoclea is still inflexible. He is always a tragic figure, doomed to win by wrecking his peace of mind. Toward him fortune shows herself ironical, but only too constant. Toward Argalus she is more fickle. But his story must be called an episode, however closely bound up with the main plot. Thus so far as the central action is concerned there is no reversal until the very end. Pyrocles and Musidorus, like Amphialus, perform their exploits only to find themselves in greater difficulties than before. Their much-desired reunion leads to Pyrocles' falling in love. To win their ladies soon proves

easier than to wed them, and meanwhile captivity intervenes. Unless the unwritten parts of the *New Arcadia* were
to disregard the original plan — an hypothesis not to be
reconciled with the version authorized by the Countess of
Pembroke — fortune was not to turn her wheel until Basilius awoke from his supposed death, established the innocence of the heroes, and approved their marriages to his
daughters. In the fable of the *Arcadia* there is but one *peripeteia*.

(2) Nor are there the materials of more than one or two
tragedies. Consider again the story of Amphialus. It is
admirably suited to a tragedy on the Greek model. The
play might begin with the captives talking about the con-
valescence of Amphialus and the cruelties inflicted on them
by his mother. After this preparation, the hero would
enter. Gradually, in a "scene of recognition," he would
observe the cold demeanor of his cousins, and at last would
learn the truth in one horrible moment. Then, after he had
rushed out, there would come a report of how his mother,
terrified at his look, had fallen from the roof and been
killed, and how he had attempted to end his own sufferings
by death. Finally there could be a "scene of suffering"
when the wounded hero was carried in, writhing in pain
and tormented with remorse. Here, as Aristotle would
have said, is the downfall of a great though not eminently
just man, not through "vice or depravity," but by human
"errors and frailties." So dramatic is the material, that
the poet could preserve the unities of time and place and
have the horrible events occur off stage, as in the Greek
drama.

Besides the tragedy of Amphialus, can any other be
found in the main action of the *Arcadia*? The story of Argalus and Parthenia, as has been shown, hardly lies within
the fable, since it could be omitted without affecting the
outcome. Is there any other? Obviously the downfall of
Anaxius and his brothers does not constitute a tragedy, for

it stirs neither pity nor terror. To be sure, Sidney's formula for tragedy, as we shall see in discussing the episodes, is not purely Aristotelian. The phrase in the *Defence of Poesie* is not "pity and terror," but "*Admiration* and *Comiseration*."[1] The fall of Anaxius may indeed stir admiration in the Elizabethan sense of the word, but cannot be said to move "commiseration." In this respect the overthrow of the savage blusterer offers a powerful contrast to the moving close of Amphialus' story. If neither Anaxius nor Argalus can be said to add to the number of tragedies within the main action, still less can any other character. Sufferings crowd upon Queen Gynecia, Philoclea, Pamela, and the two princely heroes, but everything turns out happily in the end. So far as the incomplete state of the book allows us to form an opinion, Sidney intended that the story of Amphialus should constitute the only tragedy in the fable of the *New Arcadia*.

(3) Do the events fall within a single year? Here again we can only show what the author probably intended. More than once he indicates only vaguely the time that elapses between important events. We cannot say just how long it took to end the war begun by Amphialus and continued by Anaxius. Often we can be more definite. Musidorus' illness in Kalander's house lasted six weeks,[2] and his search for Pyrocles after his friend's second disappearance occupied two months.[3] The last two books in the original version concern the events of only a very few days. Thus, even if the first three books were to occupy ten or eleven months, Sidney could still have kept the action within the time set by Minturno.

Only one fact seems to point to a different hypothesis: in revising the *Old Arcadia* Sidney omitted from the

1. Sidney, *Complete Works*, ed. Feuillerat, Cambridge English Classics, 1912–1926, III, 23.
2. I, 16.
3. Page 74.

oracle's prophecy the statement that all the events shall fall within "this fatall yeare." [1]

Yet he made another change which seems to limit the action of the revised version, like that in the original, to the single year required by Minturno. Queen Artaxia, when she imprisoned Erona, announced that she would have her executed if Pyrocles and Musidorus, within two years from the date when they slew Artaxia's brother Tiridates, did not come to the rescue.[2] Since the death of Tiridates occurred some months before the events with which the *New Arcadia* begins, and since in Book V Erona is still alive, the action must fall within considerably less than two years.

But the time is still further limited. Shortly after Pyrocles and Musidorus had sailed for Greece, Artaxia, hearing reports of their death, besieged "the Nobleman who had *Erona* in ward, . . . demaunding present delivery of her, whom yet for his faith given, he would not, before the day appointed, if possibly he could resist, which he foresaw, lŏg he should not do for want of victuall." [3] In this crisis, while everything cried for haste, Plangus came into Greece to seek aid of Euarchus, some time before Pyrocles went in disguise to the lodge where Philoclea was living,[4] and therefore within eight or nine weeks from the opening of the action.[5] Now Plangus did not find Euarchus until a few days before the events of the last book, unless we are to reject from Book V a passage first published by the Countess of Pembroke, but doubtless written or at least sketched by Sidney himself.[6] During Musidorus' two months' search for Pyrocles, therefore, and through all the time occupied by the events of Books II and III, including Amphialus' rebellion, Plangus was seeking Euarchus, pursuing him

1. I, 327; IV, 2.   2. I, 336.
3. Page 337.   4. Page 226.
5. The illness of Musidorus occupied six weeks (cf. p. 16).
6. II, 149 ff.

from one place to another. He "made all possible speede,"[1] attaining his purpose at last "extremely wearied with his long journey (desire of succouring *Erona* no more relieving, then feare of not succouring her in time aggravating his travaile)."[2] "Soone after" Plangus' hurried departure in Euarchus' ship, that king, "with so great a fleete as haste would suffer him to assemble, forthwith imbarqued for *Byzantium*,"[3] but "in short time" was carried out of his course and, arriving in Arcadia, was called to preside at the trial with which the epic fable comes to an end.

In view of the critical state of Erona's affairs, and the haste shown by both Plangus and Euarchus, these events, though they include a long journey, could hardly have occupied nearly so much as a year's time. The simultaneous action of the main story must therefore also fall within the same period, unless we are to imagine Sidney to have been guilty of what for him would be a rare inconsistency. In any case, he could not have exceeded by more than a very few months the maximum time set by Minturno, and there is every reason to think he kept well within it.

Thus so far as we can judge, in the *New Arcadia* Sidney has observed at least three of the elastic rules by which the Italian critic sought to limit the magnitude of an heroic fable.

(4) What of the last rule? Can the action of the *New Arcadia* be grasped as a whole and retained in memory?

To try to answer this question is to show the rule to be very flexible. How long a plot can be kept in mind will depend a great deal on the reader. In the twentieth century, few persons, on first encountering the *Arcadia*, can grasp it as a whole. With our habit of reading short-stories; with our want of leisure and the multiplicity of our tasks or pleasures; with our custom of reading hastily in scattered moments, alone instead of in company; with

---

1. II, 149.   2. Page 150.   3. Page 151.

our memories comparatively untrained in modern schools; we find ourselves irritated and baffled by so complex a work as the *Arcadia*. But consider the audience of Sidney's day — the ladies, courtiers, and literary men who gathered round the Countess of Pembroke and reproduced in some degree the conditions at the court of Urbino. With minds alive with the spirit of discovery, but with their freedom for adventure hampered by the queen's will, they had at once the restless energy of modern times and a forced leisure which is outside our experience. They read not singly, but in companies, where in the occasional pauses they could compete with one another in recalling the complex details of the story. And some of them, including the author of the *Arcadia*, had had their memories disciplined in the schools of the Renaissance. Must we not believe that when the reading of the book was at last finished, most of the auditors could grasp the fable, at least, as a unit, and remember its beginning, middle, and end? From the lovers of Poe the notion will provoke a smile. Yet even under modern conditions one need but run through the *Arcadia* a second time to see the unity of design.

From the point of view of the sixteenth century, it cannot be argued that Sidney has violated any of the rules which govern the length of the heroic fable.

But the episodes are what most try our patience today. Because of them Bertram Dobell found the second version of the *Arcadia* "a rococo erection, fine in some of its parts, but formless and grotesque as a whole," [1] and regretted "that Sir Philip did not leave his work in its original state." [2] And because of the episodes Dr. Wolff can declare, and most of us must agree out of our own experience, "One who reads for pleasure simply cannot understand the 'Arcadia'." [3]

1. "New Light upon Sir Philip Sidney's 'Arcadia'," *The Quarterly Review*, CCXI (July, 1909), 90.   2. Page 82.

3. *The Greek Romances in Elizabethan Prose Fiction*, Columbia University Studies in Comparative Literature, 1912, p. 352.

In attempting to explain the labyrinth of episodes which distinguishes the *New Arcadia* from the *Old*, Dobell saw in the revised work a return "to the older form of chivalric fiction."[1] Mr. Mario Praz sees rather "the Spanish fashion of dovetailing many side-stories into the main plot."[2] Dr. S. L. Wolff showed the influence of epic technique in the *Æthiopian History*. In all of these suggestions there is probably some truth, yet even taken together they are incomplete. Why should the student of Minturno, after first writing a straightforward, unified story, return to the narrative method of the writers whom Minturno especially attacks? Why should he include so many more episodes than are to be found in the romance of Heliodorus? What peculiar authoritativeness should the example of Montemayor and other Spaniards possess over a young English poet? By what principle, if any, did Sidney select his literary models?

To all these questions the answer is to be found in the theories of Minturno. His most emphatic statements urge the virtue of magnificence: "The heroic poem by its very nature takes on these additions in order to increase in magnitude, as is the genius of narrative. In this matter no other kind of poetry can rival it." Besides the straightforward and unified plot, Homer and Virgil "introduced many varied matters to enrich the work. . . . Epic poetry increases in grandeur by a magnificent and sumptuous pomp of incidents and language." "Nothing has more power to relieve the audience than variety in the things related."[3] Beside these strong, clear words, Minturno's warnings against overdoing a good thing are vague and feeble.

Do any of the rules for limiting the fable apply also to the episodes? Certainly not the laws that there be but one reversal of fortune and that there be the materials of but

1. Page 89.
2. "Sidney's Original *Arcadia*," *The London Mercury*, XV (March, 1927), 509.   3. *De Poeta*, pp. 148-149. See pages 156-158 above.

one tragedy; for the episodes are to contain the elements of many tragedies, and therefore are to have many reversals. Certainly no time limit can be deduced from the example of Homer or Virgil, for the wanderings of Æneas occupy seven years, those of Ulysses ten, and the Trojan War ten. There remains the elastic fourth requirement. Did Minturno expect the reader to grasp in a single view not only the fable, but the episodes, and keep them all in mind? On this crucial point he is obscure.

Only in this doubtful matter, then, could the Renaissance critic take exception to the episodes in the *Arcadia*. They contain, as we shall see, the materials of many tragedies. Unlike the romances of chivalry, they do not extend over several generations, but except for the brief account of the parentage and early life of the heroes, fall within a year or two, a much shorter period than that occupied by parallel incidents in the classical epics. But do the episodes bulk too large?

If Minturno expected them to be included within a single view, we may doubt whether even the Countess of Pembroke and her friends could have performed the feat except on a second reading. Yet we can only surmise what they would have done, and what Minturno would have expected. By itself each episode is easy enough to grasp on a first reading. The difficulties are not due to their number or length, but to a further cause. The number of characters and places is so great that when, after an interval, they reappear in the story, they are hard to identify. The obscurity is due to the very effort to weave all the episodes into a single design.

Thus when Plexirtus has descended suddenly upon Pyrocles, Musidorus, and their new friend Leonatus, and when the king of Pontus appears most opportunely, the difficulty is to remember who in the world he is, and to distinguish him from the new king of Phrygia. Again, a particularly obscure passage occurs in the latter part of

Pyrocles' narration, where on one page we find references to "Otaves (brother to *Barzanes* slaine by *Musidorus* in the battaile of the six Princes)," to the new king of Pontus, to "two mighty *Giants*, sonnes to a couple whom we slue in the same realme," to Plexirtus, and to Tydeus and Telenor,[1] not to mention Zelmane, disguised as the page Daiphantus, who is the center of interest for the moment. A few pages later we find a great gathering of princes, "as, the Kings of *Phrygia*, *Bythinia*, with those two hurte, of *Pontus* and *Galatia*, and *Otaves* the prisoner, by *Musidorus* set free; and thither came *Plexirtus* of *Trebisonde*, and *Antiphilus*, then King of *Lycia*; with as many mo great Princes." [2] These lists of characters, by parading the chief actors in the adventures of the heroes, serve the obvious purpose of bringing together all the threads of the story, like the summaries which tie up the argument in various parts of the *Defence of Poesie*. There is obscurity, not so much because the incidents, as because the characters and places, are hard to keep clear in the mind. For the Elizabethans, of course, with their custom of reading in companies, the difficulty was much less serious than for us.*

Again, obscurity is produced by having the story of Plangus and Erona related to Pyrocles by three different speakers who are separated at wide intervals. This queer technique produces suspense, of course, as Dr. Wolff has pointed out; [3] but it does more. It sets the story of Plangus and Erona apart from the occurrences related by Musidorus and Pyrocles. It thus emphasizes certain events which are central in the story of those two heroes. When, in defending Erona, Pyrocles kills Euardes, and he and Musidorus surprise and kill Tiridates, they gain the inveterate hatred of Euardes' nephew Anaxius, and of Tiridates' sister Artaxia. The enmity of these revengeful spirits is to hang over their destinies like the wrath of Juno over the fortunes

---

1. *Works*, I, 296.   2. Page 301.
3. *The Greek Romances in Elizabethan Prose Fiction*, pp. 350–351.

of Æneas. It leads to Pyrocles' first combat with Anaxius, and so to his rescue of Dido, to his betrayal by her father for the sake of reward from Artaxia, and to his rescue by Musidorus and by Plangus' father. Thence it leads to the imprisonment of the heroes by Plangus' stepmother, Queen Andromana, to their escape, to the pathetic love of Zelmane for Pyrocles, and, in short, to the whole train of incidents up to the time when the heroes arrive in Greece. Even there they are still entangled in the same web of circumstance. Anaxius prolongs the war begun by Amphialus, and Artaxia, through her treatment of Erona, is the occasion of Plangus' long journey, and so of Euarchus' coming into Arcadia just in time to preside at the trial of his nephew and his son. Besides Artaxia and Anaxius, only one other villain is the occasion of so many events. This is Plexirtus, and he is half-brother to Plangus' stepmother, father to Zelmane, and later the husband of Artaxia. Thus the story of Plangus and Erona is central in the episodes. Not merely for suspense, therefore, but for emphasis and structural design does Sidney relate it in so odd and striking a way.

If he had left all his episodes independent, they would be easy enough to follow. They could be read once and forgotten, without greatly confusing the unity of the fable. They are obscure not, as Dobell supposes, because the author was returning to the loose structure of the medieval romances, but just because he was dissatisfied with that kind of art, and was trying to weave every episode into the central pattern. Of course, Sidney could have carried the process further, by dropping out the episodes of Pontus and Phrygia, reducing the number of characters, and centering attention wholly upon Plangus and Erona and their oppressors. But had he made the unification so complete, he would have had not the decorative episodes prescribed by Minturno, but a second fable, like the story of Roger in *Orlando Furioso*, to which exception is taken in the *Arte*

Poetica.[1] To reduce the number of episodes, moreover, would have been to limit very greatly the number of tragedies. What Sidney has done is to introduce an abundance of episodic material, but to weave it into a pattern without creating a second fable. Faithful to the teachings of Minturno, he introduces many minor stories by way of ornament to the central action, setting them outside it, but connecting them with it and with one another.

By the standards of true art, the result was a failure. But the mere effort is significant; first, because it is directed toward design and not chaos, and second, because it emphasizes the experimental temper in which Sidney wrote, — not "as having knowne," but in order "to know."[2]

Was his material too unwieldy for a single heroic poem? In the *De Poeta* no clear answer can be found. In the *Arte Poetica*, however, one passage would encourage just such an experiment as Sidney undertook. Discussing romances even vaster than the *Arcadia*, Minturno objects chiefly to their want of unity. For this fundamental quality no other excellence can be a substitute. Now the great size of the romances had been advanced as a point in their favor. Minturno's reply is significant:

> Even if the giant is more beautiful than the pigmy, and if it is better that one sin in magnitude than in little stature, yet the animal does not look at all beautiful who is large beyond measure, and in whose members we find no proportion.[3]

Magnitude without design produces not a comely giant, but a hideous monster. Yet suppose design be imposed upon the amorphous materials of the romances; may not their colossal size then become magnificence? Minturno gives no real answer. Did he fear to injure his case by arguing against the less important prejudices of his audience? Or did he share their tastes? Whatever his reason, he

1. Page 28.   2. *Works*, III, 37.
3. *L'Arte Poetica*, p. 32.

tacitly allows the poet to make his work as long as the medieval romances, provided only he keeps unity of design.

Thus, just as Tasso sought to mould the romantic material into truly epic form, so Sidney, using the liberty that
Minturno gave him, tried to unite the magnitude of the
romances with the harmonious proportions of classic art.
The conception may be bad, although for the age it was an
intelligent experiment. But however faulty, the *Arcadia* is
not a return to a medieval narrative art, in defiance of the
author's classical principles. Nor is it the result merely of
imitating Heliodorus or Montemayor. In its profusion of
ornamental detail, just as clearly as in the singleness of its
action, the work is perfectly consistent with the theory of
epic structure held by the most classical of Italian critics.*

Not alone by its design and by its colossal bulk does the
Arcadia illustrate the Renaissance idea of magnificence.
No less does it do so by its inexhaustible variety. In character, in subject matter, and in style, it shows a diversity
which Minturno expressly recommends for the epic, and
particularly for the "mixed" type. The critic distinguishes this type of fable from the simple, or single, kind.

Of a single kind are those in which no variety of characters is
introduced, and no dissimilar fortunes ensue. . . . But the mixed
sort are those in which unlike characters are depicted, as for
example the *Odyssey*, in which Homer makes not only good and
bad men take part, but also princes and shepherds, like the
Amphitrio of Plautus, which he called a tragi-comedy, as if it
were of two orders of poetry.[1]

This mingling of the *genres*, which is encouraged by
diversity of characters, is for the Renaissance critic absurd
in a play, but in the epic is justified by a precedent no less
august than Homer. Accordingly, Sidney, in the *Defence
of Poesie*, draws a distinction between "a thing recounted
with space of time" and what is "represented in one mo-

1. *De Poeta*, p. 125.

ment"; and though his attack on the "mongrell Tragi-comedie" of the English stage is one of the most famous in our critical literature, yet he can speak without disapproval of Apuleius for "somewhat" mingling comic with serious matters in a narrative.[1]

Minturno attributes to Homer a blending of even more diverse elements.

This heroic genus is that in which we give the preference to Homer and Virgil as by all means the first. For from that fount every variety of poem has flowed. It is apparent in the case of Tragedy, which has adopted the epic dignity. But Comedy too not only has imitated the *Odyssey* (in which they will have it that what is called comic is expressed), but also has sought an example in several places of the *Iliad*, as, for instance, when Homer brings in Vulcan, who limping round as he passed the drinking cup to the Gods, excited laughter; so that really I am inclined to think that it was not quite truly said that Menander wished to be unlike Homer at all times. In this point, certainly, he must have chosen to be very near him, since the same Homeric Vulcan could stir one to laughter in the theater of Athens as well as when he is in divine company. Again, the same Homer shows how to sing the praises of gods and men, as when he has Phemius or Demodocus sing. In the variety of song, moreover, there is so great a power that other orders of poet may be seen to treat the very same themes in a different manner. Love is treated more intemperately by the elegiac poets, and more jocosely by the comic. Pitiful events are set forth with less moderation by the tragedians, and praises with more agreeable flattery by the lyric poets, than by the heroic, who notwithstanding present all these matters with greater decorum and with much greater ornamentation.[2]

"Any Epic poem," Aristotle had remarked, "will furnish subjects for several tragedies." [3] Minturno, going further

1. *Works*, III, 39–40.
2. *De Poeta*, pp. 105–106.
3. *Poetics*, XXVI. 6, trans. Butcher, in *Aristotle's Theory of Poetry and Fine Art*, 4th ed., 1923 (p. 111).

than his master, calls it the source of every other variety of poem, and mentions specifically comedy, lyric, and elegy. Why not, therefore, mingle pastoral eclogues in an heroic poem? Traditionally the bucolic poem was written in an epic measure. Moreover, Minturno himself observes in the *Arte Poetica*, "You will find poetry mingling both epic manners, that is, prose and verse, as in the *Arcadia* of our countryman Sannazaro, and the *Ameto* of Boccaccio, and my own *Amore Innamorato*." [1] Yet Sidney need not have read the Italian treatise to justify the mingling of prose and verse, and "matters *Heroicall* and *Pastorall*." [2] For if the epic is the source of every variety of poem, and if in the *Odyssey* Homer introduced shepherds along with men of princely rank, what more natural than to let some of the shepherds enrich the heroic poem with their eclogues?

Thus critical principles and ancient authority, no less than the example of Montemayor, justified Sidney in ornamenting his work with profuse variety. Making his fable of the mixed sort, like that of the *Odyssey*, he introduced characters of every rank and every degree of vice and virtue. With the thoughtful laughter of comedy or the varied passions of the lyric or the artful simplicity of the pastoral, he interwove the pathos and awe of tragedy. And he used a style as flexible as it was elevated and ornate, suiting it to the constant changes of mood and theme.

The multitude of characters in the *Arcadia* has often been noticed. Their variety is equally striking. Even in the original version there are princes and kings, dukes, duchesses, shepherds, artisans, and farmers; there are the stern and noble Philanax, the absurd though rather engaging Basilius, and his passionate wife and flawless daughters, not to extend the list further. In the *New Arcadia* the range of character has grown with the number. Of royal rank there are women so ambitious, yet so different, as

1. *L'Arte Poetica*, p. 4.
2. *Works*, III, 22.

Cecropia and Andromana; so passionate as Gynecia, Helen, and Erona; so unrelenting as Artaxia; so "matchless every way" as the gentle Philoclea and her more austere sister. Of lower rank are the devoted Parthenia, and the yet more unfortunate Zelmane; such types of unchastity as Dido and Baccha; not to mention the peasant Miso and her equally agreeable daughter. Among the men there is perhaps even greater diversity — usurpers like the subtle bastard Plexirtus or the lowborn coward Antiphilus; knights as different as Argalus and Anaxius; the unfortunate lovers Plangus, Palladius, and Amphialus; trusting characters like Tydeus, Telenor, and the noble Leonatus; and more complete heroic types like Euarchus and his son and nephew. In lower rank there are the clown Dametas, the shifty coward Clinias, and also the courteous shepherds Claius and Strephon. Here are parents, both wise and foolish, with children loyal, careless, or treacherous; tyrants and true monarchs; clowns, parasites, and upstarts, or shepherds made by education the fit companions of a prince; lovers and knights, the false and the true; women of every type or rank — high and low, chaste and loose, bold and gentle. In the *Old Arcadia* there is no parallel to this stately and crowded pageant, embracing the whole range of human life.

No less striking is the variety of poetic material. Of the pastoral and the love lyric, and their diversity in form and in mood, there is little occasion to speak. No reader can miss them, and they have been discussed in detail by numerous students of Sidney. What scholars have not pointed out is the obvious relation of these elements to the plan of an heroic poem, in the Renaissance meaning of the term. A glance at Minturno's treatises reveals how naturally they fit into the whole grandiose scheme. So, too, do certain passages of strong feeling which are written in prose — the lament of Leucippe for her lover's infidelity,[1]

1. I, 289.

Queen Helen's praise of Amphialus,[1] and complaint of his and fortune's cruelty, or Pamela's beautiful prayer to the "eternal Life of all things." [2] Are not these the materials for the elegy, for the song in praise of a hero, and for a hymn to the divine powers?

Conspicuous among the varied elements is comedy. The fight between the cowards Clinias and Dametas illustrates the less refined aspect of Sidney's humor. So does the skirmish between the rabble and the defenders of the lodges, when one fellow, whose nose had been chopped off, bent down "to bring his nose to his head," and "*Zelmane* with a blow, sent his head to his nose" [3] — to the indignation of Mr. Praz.[4] Better comedy appears in the scene between Pyrocles and his cousin where the now lovesick and repentant Musidorus is reminded of his former heresies against Cupid — a scene which Dr. Wolff calls "the high-water mark of Sidney's humor." [5]

The best comedy of the *Arcadia* provokes a smile rather than laughter. Witness Kalander's mocking himself for keeping his guest from supper with his "idle discourses," [6] or his amusement that Strephon and Claius should impute to love the superiority they owe to learning.[7] Of similar quality is the humorous treatment of Basilius, not so much in the situation — an old king falling in love with a young man whom he takes for a girl — as in the airs which he sometimes puts on to impress his mistress.[8] Again, in the account of Phalantus' tournament, "there is," as Mr. Zandvoort points out, "an unmistakable undertone of irony running through these chapters, which is foreign to the *Amadis*. . . . It is all no more than an elegant pastime, and

---

1. Pages 67 ff. See especially pp. 67, 69.
2. Pages 382–383.
3. Page 312.
4. "Sidney's Original *Arcadia*," p. 513.
5. *The Greek Romances in Elizabethan Prose Fiction*, p. 331.
6. *Works*, I, 29.
7. Page 27.   8. See p. 100.

when it is over, the lady is conducted back to her seat, as after a dance." [1]

In these passages of quiet humor — a phrase here and there, or sometimes a scene — one finds the urbane author of the *Defence of Poesie*.

A more detailed discussion of Sidney's comic art must be reserved for a later chapter. Here it is sufficient to have pointed out its presence in the *Arcadia*. In accordance with the precepts of Minturno and the supposed example of Homer, Sidney has used comic relief to lend variety to his heroic poem. Particularly to be noted is its presence in two episodes, the combat between Dametas and Clinias, and the tournament held by Phalantus.

But of all the diverse poetic materials which adorn the *New Arcadia*, by far the most conspicuous is tragedy. Consider in particular the events described by dramatic narration — the steward's account of Argalus and Parthenia; Queen Helen's story of how Amphialus scorned her love, slew his foster brother, and caused his foster father to die of grief; and the narrative of occurrences in Asia Minor with which Pyrocles and Musidorus were concerned directly or indirectly — the overthrow of the tyrants of Phrygia and Pontus; the misfortunes of the blind king of Paphlagonia; the fall of Tiridates; the exile of Plangus; the deaths of Dido and her miserly father; the suicide of Andromana after she causes the death of her son Palladius; the fatal combat between the brothers Tydeus and Telenor; Zelmane's death of a broken heart; the cruel sufferings of Erona; and the capture and execution of Antiphilus. To these events related by a character in the story, we must add the deaths of Argalus and Parthenia at the hands of Amphialus. In all this mass of episodes what is there but tragedy?

Not every one, of course, meets the ideal requirements of Aristotle as well as does the downfall of Amphialus in

1. *Sidney's Arcadia, A Comparison between the Two Versions*, 1929, p. 107.

the main fable. In the deaths of Antiphilus, Andromana, Tiridates, and the unnamed kings of Phrygia and Pontus, we have the overthrow of vicious tyrants, not of great though humanly frail heroes. In Zelmane, Argalus, and Parthenia, we have sufferings that are wholly undeserved. Dido and her father, not to mention the wretched Pamphilus, are not elevated in either character or rank. Amphialus, to be sure, is a tragic hero of the Aristotelian stamp, in the episodes no less than in the main story. So, too, are Plangus, the king of Paphlagonia, and the brothers Tydeus and Telenor, all of whom are great in rank or nature and suffer through their own mistakes. But such tragedies as theirs are but one of the many kinds furnished by the episodes of the *Arcadia*.

In all this material so somber in general character, there is very wide diversity. Sidney's tyrants are not at all like one another. Zelmane and Parthenia, too, though both suffer innocently, are different enough in all other circumstances of their fates. Zelmane's love was not reciprocated, as was that of Parthenia for Argalus.

> She never told her love,
> But let concealment, like a worm i' the bud,
> Feed on her damask cheek: she pined in thought,
> And with a green and yellow melancholy
> She sat like Patience on a monument,
> Smiling at grief.

Zelmane has nothing of Parthenia's wild desperation. She could never have disguised herself as a knight, have challenged the man who has slain her husband, have rushed upon her own death, and so have won an ironical revenge. Parthenia, with her energy of character, is the more truly tragic figure.

The two heroines are typical of Sidney's art. He sometimes puts several characters into nearly identical situations, or endows them with certain traits in common, but always with a difference. Parallels and contrasts, there-

fore, are conspicuous in his *Arcadia*, but not mere same-
ness. Especially varied are his episodes. In the sufferings
of innocent ladies, in the fall of tyrants or of great but
faulty heroes, in comic passages of boisterous fun or urbane
irony, in elegiac lament, in pastoral eclogue, in love lyric,
and in prayer, the episodic materials in the *New Arcadia*
provide the universal range of poetic mood which, in the
view of the Renaissance critics, lends to the greatest of
poetic forms the quality of magnificence.

For a work of so grandiose a plan, the fit accompaniment
is a style both varied and sumptuous. In classic manner
the heroic poets will "suit the action to the word, the word
to the action," "and even if in many places and most often
they are full, vehement, and copious, yet sometimes they
cultivate directness and simplicity, and in a few places do
not hesitate to employ a due temperance or sweetness." [1]
But with all the appropriate variety of their style, they will
habitually employ a "magnificent and sumptuous pomp of
incidents and language." [2]

Fully to treat the complex Arcadian rhetoric would take
us far beyond the limits of the present study. The influence of Cicero and (as Dr. Wolff shows) of the Greek romances, the possible parallels in contemporary Italian or
Spanish literature, the analysis of poetic figures by Scaliger
might all prove but parts of a still wider investigation. So
large is the subject that I should not approach it at all,
were not the style of the *Arcadia* so striking a feature of
Sidney's literary art, and did it not seem to many readers
at variance with the principles of good taste set forth in the
Defence of Poesie.

Thus Mr. Mario Praz, for example, cannot see "why the
man who wrote *The Defence of Poesie* should have thought
his trifling pastoral" worth recasting into the form of the
New Arcadia, especially in "*la razon de la sinrazon* style." [3]

1. *De Poeta*, p. 105.   2. Page 152.
3. "Sidney's Original *Arcadia*," p. 509.

Jusserand, too, is puzzled, and offers an explanation of the supposed contradiction:

> Sidney who in his 'Apologie' had laughed at these extravagances in the poets and dramatists, could not himself avoid them when he wrote his romance. When they concern themselves with criticism, nearly all, Shakespeare, Sidney, and their contemporaries, are to be admired for their moderation, wisdom, and good sense; but as soon as they take up the pen to write their imaginative works, intoxication overcomes their brain, a divine intoxication that sometimes transports them to heaven, an earthly intoxication that sometimes leads them into bogs and gutters.[1]

Elsewhere Jusserand explains the Arcadian *préciosité* as due to feminine influence.

> [Sidney's] aim was to amuse a clever and elegant lady, and the ladies of his time were fond of immense frills, double and treble rows of lace, gold-enamelled jewels, studded with precious stones. He therefore attired his phrases in elaborate style, he frilled his sentences, and marshalled forth his periods as for a court pageant.[2]

No doubt the Elizabethan ladies encouraged Sidney in the paradoxes, jingles, personifications, and other figures which mar his English. But we need not assume that either feminine tastes or some half-divine poetic frenzy could have led him to disregard well-thought-out principles of art.

Indeed, the most casual observation will suggest points of obvious contact between the language of the romance and the theorizing of the essay. Any reader may find in the *Arcadia*, as also in *Astrophel and Stella*, "compositions of two or three wordes togither," in which Sidney declares English is "neare the Greeke, farre beyond the Latine,"

---

1. *The English Novel in the Time of Shakespeare*, trans. Lee, 1903, pp. 259–260.

2. *A Literary History of the English People*, 2nd ed., II (1926), 534–535.

and which, he adds, "is one of the greatest bewties can be in a language."[1] Again, the discussion of rime and classical measures in the *Defence*, and the opinion there expressed that "truly the English, before any Vulgare language, I know is fit for both sorts," [1] must gain point when one considers the sonnets, songs, and eclogues which crowd the pages of the *Arcadia* with all manner of verse, both ancient and modern. Examples such as these raise the question whether the critic who writes the *Defence* is not the craftsman of the *Arcadia*, deliberately studying his materials in the endeavor to see what effects he can produce.

As a matter of fact, the supposed contradiction disappears when one really understands Sidney's theories. Jusserand himself, apparently not realizing the full implications of his words, has said with admirable precision, "Sidney hated euphuism, but loved ornament."[2] In the *Defence of Poesie* the classic principle of fitness leads the author to despise affectation, but the Renaissance delight in ornament leads him to set a high value upon gorgeous phraseology. Greek taste and sixteenth-century profusion are no better reconciled in the critical work than in the romance, and Sidney himself seems to have been not quite satisfied with the result.

In the name of common sense and good taste he attacks "a Courtisanlike painted affectation," "farre fet words," "coursing of a letter," and the injudicious use of "figures and flowers, extreemlie winter-starved." [3] He laughs at the "diligent Imitators of *Tully* & *Demosthenes*" who "keepe *Nizolian* paper bookes of their figures and phrases," [3] without learning the fine art of using them with discrimination. For euphuism, with its "stories of beasts, foules, and fishes . . . rifled up, that they may come in multitudes to waite upon any of our conceits," he has only scorn. In place of all such "moste tedious pratling" he advocates "a plaine

1. *Works*, III, 44.   2. *A Literary History*, II, 534.
3. *Works*, III, 42.

sensiblenesse" like that cultivated by Antonius, Crassus, Demosthenes, and Cicero, and the observance of what is "fittest to nature." [1]

All well enough for a general discussion, but precisely what use of "figures and phrases" will be appropriate in an heroic poem? The models that Sidney mentions are those of orators, not of narrative writers. Teachers of rhetoric like Quintilian wrote for men who would be public speakers. Where could one find either a clear critical guide or a suitable model for a narrative prose fiction of an ambitious order? Malory, perhaps, and the Italian followers of Boccaccio might show a style both plain and refined. But were they writing heroic poems? "To haue the stile decent & comely," writes the courtly author of the *Arte of English Poesie*, "it behooueth the maker or Poet to follow the nature of his subiect, that is if his matter be high and loftie that the stile be so to, if meane, the stile also to be meane, if base, the stile humble and base accordingly: and they that do otherwise vse it, applying to meane matter hie and loftie stile, and to hie matters stile eyther meane or base, . . . do vtterly disgrace their poesie and shew themselues nothing skilfull in their arte." [2] Here is the classic view of fitness. Now can such words as "high" and "lofty," be said to describe the style or themes of Italian prose tales? And even granting that some may be of a high order, have they the authority of such a writer as Heliodorus, who was one of the ancients, and supposedly a Christian bishop as well?

If there were few right models for an heroic poem in prose, critical guides were inevitably still more rare. Ancient rhetoric, as I have remarked, dealt with oratory, not prose fiction, and the English humanists show the same preoccupation. From their generalizations a writer could get little more than vague hints as to the appropriate kind

1. Pages 42–43.
2. *Elizabethan Critical Essays*, II, 155.

of style in another literary form. Indeed, in all matters of taste the English humanists leave the final decision to the writer's own good sense. "A right wise man vnlearned," writes Thomas Wilson, "shall doe more good by his Naturall witte, then twentie of these common wittes that want Nature to helpe Arte."[1] And Sidney, too, has "found in divers smal learned Courtiers, a more sound stile, then in some professors of learning."[2] To be sure, native good sense can most safely be trusted in persons of education. "The highest flying wit," in Sidney's view, must "have a *Dedalus* to guide him."[3] And Wilson writes in the same spirit, "There is none so wise but counsaill may doe him good. Yea, he shall doe much better that knoweth what arte other men haue vsed, what inuention they haue followed, what order they haue kept, and how they haue beste doen in euery parte. If he like not theirs, he may vse his owne."[4] Not rules, not models, but intuitive good taste is the final criterion. Though Sidney's poet may have a "Dedalus to guide him," yet he soars "onely reined with learned discretion,"[5] "freely raunging within the Zodiack of his owne wit."[6] By Sidney and his contemporaries the classic principle of fitness is stated without the pedantry of neo-classic rules, and without the definiteness. Rightly to apply it in narrative fiction was not easy.

The practical difficulties in letting "your discretion be your tutor" are greatly increased by the Renaissance doctrine of "exornation." This doctrine Sidney, like Minturno, explicitly accepts. He describes verse as "but an ornament and no cause to Poetrie,"[7] though its "fittest raiment."[8] The simple directness of an English ballad is not the highest form of art. If "the old Song of *Percy* and *Duglas*" move his heart "more then . . . a Trumpet,"

1. *Arte of Rhetorique*, ed. Mair, 1909, p. 159.
2. *Works*, III, 43.   3. Page 37.
4. Page 160.   5. *Works*, III, 10.
6. Page 8.   7. Page 10.
8. Page 11.

though "so evill apparelled in the dust and Cobwebbes of that uncivill age, what would it worke, trimmed in the gorgious eloquence of *Pindare*?"[1] The heroic poet, accordingly, is to deck out virtue "to make her more lovely in her holliday apparrell."[2]

Sidney had not learned that "virtue is like a rich stone, best plain set." With Ascham, the classical scholar, he would have delighted to have "a fair stone . . . set in the finest gold, with the best workmanship." Few men, indeed, in his generation or earlier could grasp the intimate relation between form and substance. Sidney's theory of style, therefore, is not that

> Soul is form and doth the body make,

but that, as Pope was to say,

> Expression is the dress of thought, and still
> Appears more decent, as more suitable.[3]

Spenser, in a classic mood, would have style to be something inevitable, as inseparable from meaning as body from life. Sidney thinks of it as a garment that may be changed at will, and though decent and suitable, yet gorgeous. He agrees in part with Castelvetro:

Although verse and prose are not the essential difference between poetry and history, nevertheless verse accompanies and adorns poetry, and prose history, as their appropriate raiment and habits. History should not or cannot put on verse without blame, nor poetry put on prose, just as ladies should not or cannot use the habits of men, or men the habits of ladies.[4]

Sidney, rejecting the notion that a poet should write in verse,[*] keeps the essential idea that "expression is the dress

1. Page 24.
2. Page 25.
3. "Essay on Criticism," ll. 318-319.
4. Castelvetro, *Poetica d'Aristotele*, 1576, p. 190.

of thought." Both Xenophon in his *Cyropædia*, he says, and Heliodorus in his *Theagenes and Chariclea*, gave examples of "an absolute heroicall Poeme."

And yet both these wrote in prose, which I speake to shew, that it is not ryming and versing that maketh a Poet, (no more then a long gown maketh an Advocate, who though he pleaded in Armour, should be an Advocat and no souldier) but it is that faining notable images of vertues, vices, or what els, with that delightfull teaching, which must be the right describing note to know a Poet by. Although indeed the Senate of Poets hath chosen verse as their fittest raiment: meaning as in matter, they passed all in all, so in maner, to go beyond them: not speaking table talke fashion, or like men in a dreame, words as they chanceably fall from the mouth, but peasing each sillable of eache word by just proportion, according to the dignitie of the subject.[1]

Here Sidney appears to be meditating the problem of a truly literary prose, not necessarily, as has often been said, a "prose-poetry" of the sort produced by De Quincey or Ruskin, but a refined speech that may be a suitable medium for artistic expression. He is farsighted enough to see that great narrative fiction need not be written in verse. On the other hand, "words as they chanceably fall from the mouth" are quite unfit for any order of poetry, certainly not for the loftiest of them all. The true epic, of course, will choose verse as its "fittest raiment." But just below that supreme literary form is another, the heroic poem in prose, for which a suitably gorgeous "holiday apparel" must be found. Here is an opportunity for fruitful experiment. "Artificial rules" for such a narrative style are hard to find, and "imitative patterns," except perhaps for Heliodorus or Xenophon, are rare and lack authority. The writer must therefore rely on his own practice, not "as having known," but in order "to know."[2]

1. *Works*, III, 10–11.   2. See p. 37.

And as he experiments, he will take as his guides the two fundamental principles of fitness and ornamentation.

These principles, according to Greek and to modern taste, cannot be reconciled, until the conception of style as "the dress of thought" is given up. In Sidney's theory, therefore, there is a basic contradiction. But there is none between theory and practice. The elaborate intricacies of the Arcadian manner are but examples of what Sidney calls "gorgeous eloquence." The conflict does not lie between the style of the romance and the principles of taste set forth in the *Defence*. The principles themselves are in opposition.

The Arcadian style, therefore, is not to be ascribed chiefly to the influence of the Countess of Pembroke and her friends. Their love for "immense frills, double and treble rows of lace, gold-enamelled jewels, studded with precious stones," was but one phase of the Renaissance love for lavish ornamentation. And in this taste the literary critics and the humanists shared. Still less can we ascribe Sidney's *préciosité* to a kind of poetic frenzy, for his art is nothing if not self-conscious.

Consider, for example, the following passage, over which Jusserand makes merry, and in which he thinks it "difficult to recognize the author of the 'Apologie'": [1]

But when they came so neere as their eies were ful masters of the object, they saw a sight full of piteous strangenes: a ship, or rather the carkas of the shippe, or rather some few bones of the carkas, hulling there, part broken, part burned, part drowned: death having used more then one dart to that destruction. About it floted great store of very rich thinges, and many chestes which might promise no lesse. And amidst the precious things were a number of dead bodies, which likewise did not onely testifie both elemēts violence, but that the chiefe violence was growen of humane inhumanitie: for their bodies were ful of grisly wounds, & their bloud had (as it were) filled the wrinckles of the

---

1. *The English Novel*, p. 259.

seas visage: which it seemed the sea woulde not wash away, that it might witnes it is not alwaies his fault, when we condemne his crueltie.[1]

"At the thought of this sea that will not wash itself" Jusserand finds it "impossible to keep serious."[2] One would not lose the jest. To use Sidney's own language, he has "cast Suger and spice uppon everie dish," if we may trust our modern taste, "like those *Indians*, not content to weare eare-rings at the fit and naturall place of the eares, but they will thrust Jewels through their nose and lippes, because they will be sure to be fine." [3]

Yet is it so "difficult to recognize" here "the author of the 'Apologie'"? Pass over as insoluble the question whether "to wear ear-rings" at all be "fit and natural"; grant that excess marks this passage; yet does not also the most careful craftsmanship? Take even so stilted a phrase as "a ship, or rather the carcass of the ship, or rather some few bones of the carcass"; even here one suspects something more than mere "cadenced repetition." Throughout the passage the images appear in the same order as they did to Musidorus and his companions while they were approaching the wreck. First they got a general impression of "piteous strangeness." Then they centered their attention on the most conspicuous object, the ship. A second glance showed it was but the carcass. As they drew nearer, they found it "rather some few bones of the carcass," and observed it in greater detail. Part was "broken, part burned, part drowned." Hence the spectators realized that death had "used more than one dart to that destruction." Turning from the central object, they noticed in the water "rich things and many chests." Again they inferred that in the chests there must be other rich things. Finally, what absorbed all their attention was the dead bodies in the water. On a close view they found the cause of the

1. *Works*, I, 9–10.
2. *The English Novel*, p. 259.   3. *Works*, III, 42.

whole strange spectacle. It was neither fire nor the treachery of the sea, but a battle, as evidenced by the "grisly
wounds" in the dead bodies. For a moment the prince and
his companions gazed at the blood filling the troughs between the waves, and reflected that many an unexplained
tragedy at sea may be due to man's inhumanity, and not
to the cruelty of the elements against which we so often
cry out.

Thus, precisely as in his narrative technique Sidney
keeps the reader constantly moving forward in the company of some one of the *dramatis personæ*, so here also he
has him assume the point of view of the men moving
rapidly toward the scene. The images are of the things
they saw. The reflections are what the sights would easily
suggest to an active mind. Bad taste there may be in this
conscious word painting, but hardly an imagination run
beyond the artist's control.

The intellectual quality of the art, indeed, is noteworthy. It appears, for example, in the generalness of the
description. The thoughts suggested by the sight of the
wreck are not those of Strephon or Claius in particular.
The pun on "the bones of the carcass" is not the remark
of some witty Greek sailor. The things the men saw do not
appear in realistic detail. To give, like Defoe, the illusion
of actuality was no part of Sidney's plan. Accordingly,
when he describes the objects in the water, he mentions
only the classes to which they belong — "rich things,"
"chests," "dead bodies." Without attributing to his art
the "grandeur of generality" in the full sense of the term,
we can find here a broad treatment, at once suitable to the
large scope of the story, and natural in a person trained to
think in logical categories.

The same temper appears in the elaborate antitheses
which disturb a modern reader. Even a jingling paradox
like "human inhumanity" carries a real idea. Though unpleasant, the phrase has meaning enough, like debaters'

jargon. Again, the "cadenced repetition of the same words" is not, as Jusserand charges, "written merely for effect." [1] As we have seen, the repetition of "ship" and "carcass" conveys a distinctly new image. Tricks like these, one suspects, may be due to the author's long discipline in logic and rhetoric. Whatever their source, Sidney, alike in these verbal quips, in the generalness of his description, and in his carefully maintained point of view, shows in his art a conspicuous intellectual quality.

Can one say, then, with Jusserand, "Intoxication overcomes [his] brain"? Is not his mind only too alert? The tendency to dazzle the reader with dexterity cannot easily be explained as arising from a naïve indifference to artistic law. But is it not a natural product of self-conscious art? The same mind which could follow critical principles with fidelity could take delight in every kind of ingenious turn of speech.

Another sort of ornamental phraseology is personification. Frigid and far-fetched at times, it still reveals, in the description of the wreck, a poet's imagination at work. "The bones of the ship's carcass" is a graphic metaphor. Even a roundabout expression like "their eyes were full masters of the object" is something more than fine writing, suggesting, as it does, the sense of achievement with which one finally gets a clear view of something in the distance, after straining hard to make it out. Again, "the wrinkles of the sea's visage," though we laugh at their being filled with blood which the sea leaves in proof of its innocence, are, if taken alone, no bad description of a calm sea lightly roughened with little waves. What offends us is the development of the metaphor into an intricate conceit. Not the figurative language alone reminds us that Sidney conceived the *Arcadia* as an heroic poem. For the courtiers and ladies who first heard it read aloud, the cadence of the periods, and perhaps the very artificiality of the style,

1. *The English Novel*, p. 255.

must have had an effect analogous to that of meter, in creating the illusion of a world other than the actual. In prose we moderns expect reality. But Sidney had not yet learned what can be done in prose, and what can be done well only in verse.

He could not learn the lesson except by experiments like the *Arcadia*. The bad tendencies of the first version, to be sure, he did not correct in the revision. Mr. Mario Praz can even argue plausibly, if not so as quite to carry conviction, that "almost each sentence of the first draft has been subjected to a process of stucco decoration." [1] Yet however firmly the mannerisms may have been fixed in Sidney's style, the path toward improvement could be found only by experience. Meanwhile, the habit of regulating creative work by critical rules will encourage an ingenuity which, even if not further stimulated by bad models like the Greek romances, may easily run beyond all bounds; especially when the limits which mark prose from poetry are not well understood, and gorgeous phraseology is conceived as admirable.

With entire consistency, therefore, the man who laughed at euphuism could argue that his own jingles, paradoxes, repetitions, personifications, and other elaborate mannerisms are no mere "tedious pratling, rather overswaying the memorie . . . then anie whit enforming the judgement." [2] Too ingenious or too poetical though they are when judged by any true standards of taste, they are for the sixteenth century only a gorgeous "holiday apparel," investing a real idea in language of suitable magnificence. The faults are inherent in self-conscious art of an experimental character.

The poetic sincerity of *Astrophel and Stella*, and Sidney's dying wish to have the *Arcadia* burned afford a hint that he thought he had by no means "achieved perfection." [3]

---

1. "Sidney's Original *Arcadia*," p. 511.
2. *Works*, III, 43. 3. Cf. Praz, p. 509.

The same impression is suggested by a passage in the *Defence of Poesie*:

> I think this digression will make my meaning receive the fuller understanding: which is not to take upon me to teach *Poets* how they should do, but only finding my selfe sicke among the rest, to shew some one or two spots of the common infection growne among the most part of writers; that acknowledging our selves somewhat awry, wee may bende to the right use both of matter and manner.[1]

Finding himself "sick among the rest," Sidney revises his original *Arcadia* in the light of critical principles. The result is an exaggeration of the conceits, and a vast increase in the complexity of the plot — faults that the best thought of his age either overlooked or encouraged. The result is also a far more impressive work, and certain passages of unforgettable beauty, — those most quoted pages which have no parallel in the *Old Arcadia*. For his own times the "Sidneian showers of sweet discourse" came as a revelation of what beauty there might be in English prose. And if we today see more clearly the evils of *préciosité* and the limits of prose and verse, yet we can see also the debt of English literature to just such experiments as Sidney's.

We may think of him as an Elizabethan voyager, not a mere vagabond or adventurer but a scientific explorer seeking with compass and map a northwest passage to the golden land; failing like many an explorer, yet also succeeding. The barriers between prose and poetry have thus far defied the efforts of English writers to find a passage through them. But by other paths, men like Bacon, Taylor, Fielding, and Thackeray, have reached the goal that Sidney was seeking — a prose both free from affectation and capable of noble artistic effects. In the effort to relate fiction of high quality in some medium other than

1. *Works*, III, 43.

verse, as in the similar experiment in writing English poetry in classical measures, the style of the *Arcadia* is an intelligent, if too ambitious, experiment, inspired by the conflicting ideals of good taste and ornateness to be found alike in the works of Renaissance critics, the traditions of English humanism, and the *Defence of Poesie.*

How constantly the author changes his manner, as he describes now "a shepherd's boy piping as though he should never be old," now the princess Philoclea bathing in a river or coming in prison to speak with her lover, now her sister Pamela in prayer, and now Musidorus engaged in mortal combat with Amphialus, or the peasant Miso interrupting a tragic narrative with her old wives' tale — all this endless diversity requires no analysis. Suffice it to show that in its variety, as in its "gorgeous eloquence," the style of the *Arcadia* meets the requirements laid down by Minturno for an heroic poem.

In all that relates to form, therefore, Sidney's work is in harmony with Renaissance critical principles as they are set forth in the *Defence of Poesie* or the *De Poeta.* The ornate style, ever changing with the theme; the songs and eclogues, the prose passages of elegiac or religious mood, the scattered bits of irony, the comic scenes, the tragic episodes each so different from the rest; the characters, representing every rank in society, and every degree of virtue or vice — all contribute to the endless variety which for Minturno, partly because of the supposed example of the *Odyssey,* was essential to epic magnificence, especially in a poem of "mixed" type. The size of the work, though out of all proportion to ancient models, does not exceed that of the longer medieval romances, tacitly conceded by the classical theorist to be a point in their favor; while the fable, so far as can be judged from its imperfect state, keeps within all the limits prescribed for an appropriate magnitude. Yet though the material is immense and varied, every detail fits into a plan. The episodes, related to the main plot, though lying outside it, are but the ornamental additions authorized in the *De Poeta*. The narrative technique is epic, as was shown in the last chapter; for the work begins *in mediis rebus*, "things done in former time or other place" are reported by dramatic narration, and all unnecessary breaks, particularly in critical scenes, are consistently avoided. The fable has unity and gives the poem the necessary design. The themes it treats — love, war, and great national and international events — are from the sixteenth-century point of view lofty and serious. Written in prose, without formal invocation or supernatural machinery, the *New Arcadia* is not an epic; but in these very particulars it shows consistent art, and conforms to the author's well-known theories. Theme, fable, episodes, central design, profuse and varied ornament, sumptuous style, changing with the subject — here are all the elements of an heroic poem as the form was understood by Minturno.

The *Old Arcadia*, on the other hand, by its more trivial subject, simpler technique, shorter action, narrower range of characters, and comparative want of episodes, possesses the epic magnificence to a very small degree, or not at all.

What conclusions may we draw?

(1) The *Old Arcadia*, which shows little or no influence of Minturno or of other critics, could hardly have been conceived as an heroic poem. Yet in its admirably clear outlines it reveals in the author a deep-seated instinct for form — an instinct which led him in a few years to make a careful study of critical theory.

(2) The *New Arcadia* was written under the direct influence of Minturno's theory of the epic, as shown particularly in its quality of magnificence; and therefore "by Sidney" no less than by "his contemporaries," it indubitably "was regarded as an heroic poem." [1] But though it is

---

1. Greenlaw, "Sidney's *Arcadia* as an Example of Elizabethan Allegory," *Kittredge Anniversary Papers*, 1913, p. 327. His opinion is attacked by Zandvoort, *Sidney's Arcadia, A Comparison between the Two Versions*, p. 123.

a far more serious and ambitious work than the original version, it must be judged as an experiment.

(3) Sidney, rather than Ben Jonson, was the Englishman with whom first "the study of the art of poetry became an inseparable guide to creation; and it is this element of self-conscious art, guided by the rules of criticism, which distinguishes him from his predecessors." [1]

(4) The supposed antithesis between Sidney's classical theories and romantic imagination must be discarded or wholly revised, since both versions of his *Arcadia* show a strong instinct for form, and the second a remarkable fidelity to critical law.

In poetic content, therefore, as well as in form, may we not expect his work to show a consistent art?

1. Spingarn applies the words to Jonson alone. See *A History of Literary Criticism in the Renaissance*, 5th ed., Columbia University Studies in Comparative Literature, 1925, p. 258.

CHAPTER VI

Sidney's Theory of Poetic Truth

WHEN Sidney changed his pastoral romance "into a complicated heroic 'poem',"[1] revealing in every part the most studied craftsmanship, what purpose did he have in view? Surely we may wonder if it could have been only "to amuse a clever and elegant lady."[2] The pains he took with his work ought to have produced something more than a summer's light reading for his sister, however devoted to her he may have been. The simplest hypothesis is that he tried to make the *Arcadia* an heroic poem in its purpose, no less than in its form.

To find his idea of the function of poetry, we need not go to Minturno. Sidney's own statements in the *Defence* are definite. And yet they have led scholars to widely different interpretations. Herr Brie and Greenlaw find a belief in allegory and the didactic purpose of poetry. Miss Phoebe Sheavyn thinks that in emphasizing "the positive ethical value of poetry," Sidney was "laying aside for a time his conviction of the value of imaginative art simply for its pleasure-giving power,"[3] in "the endeavour to meet the moralists upon their own ground."[4] Mr. J. E. Spingarn sees the *Defence of Poesie* as "a veritable epitome of the

1. Edwin Greenlaw, "Sidney's *Arcadia* as an Example of Elizabethan Allegory," *Kittredge Anniversary Papers*, 1913, p. 330.
2. J. J. Jusserand, *A Literary History of the English People*, 2nd ed., II (1926), 535.
3. *The Literary Profession in the Elizabethan Age*, University of Manchester Publications, No. XLIX, 1909, p. 179.
4. Page 178.

literary criticism of the Italian Renaissance." [1] Mr. R. W. Zandvoort agrees with a student of Mr. Spingarn's, Mr. D. L. Clark, in the view "that while the ideas on allegory of such men as Lodge and Harington were still largely mediaeval, Sidney rather stood for the classical view of rhetoric as applied to poetry by the critics of the Italian renaissance. According to Sidney, the purpose of poetry is to win men to virtue by pleasant instruction; it accomplishes this end primarily by *examples*." [2]

Thus from the *Defence of Poesie* conflicting views of the function of poetry have been derived: that it is to give pleasure alone, to teach by allegory, or to teach by "examples."

The confusion is due in part to the failure to distinguish between telling arguments and real convictions. Even Mr. Spingarn treats like a scientific statement the remark that poetry "is more Philosophicall and more studiously serious then History." [3] "Sidney, in the assertion of this principle," according to Mr. Spingarn, "follows Minturno and Scaliger, and goes farther than Aristotle would probably have gone." [4] Has exaggeration, one wonders, never been employed as a debater's device? In an argument, of course, Sidney can maintain that poetry "in the most excellent worke, is the most excellent workeman," [5] surpassing not only history, but also philosophy. Yet in his correspondence we find him giving to these two studies, and to rhetoric, an almost exclusive attention, both when he seeks advice from Languet,[6] and when a few years later he assumes the rôle of adviser to his brother Robert.[7] Even in

1. *A History of Literary Criticism in the Renaissance*, Columbia University Studies in Comparative Literature, 1925, p. 268.

2. *Sidney's Arcadia, A Comparison between the Two Versions*, 1929, p. 123, n. 1. Cf. D. L. Clark, *Rhetoric and Poetry in the Renaissance*, 1922, pp. 145 ff.

3. Sidney, *Complete Works*, ed. Feuillerat, Cambridge English Classics, 1912–1926, III, 16, corrected from variant readings, p. 380.

4. Page 273.

5. *Works*, III, 22.

6. Pages 81, 83, 84.   7. Pages 124 ff., 130 ff.

the *Defence of Poesie*, does he not deprecate "civill warre among the Muses"? [1] To be sure, he tells us the lofty titles conferred in ancient days upon the poet, but he continues, with great persuasiveness, "I hope though we get not so unmatched a praise as the *Etimologie* of his names will graunt, yet his verie description which no man will denie, shall not justly be barred from a principall commendation." [2] When Sidney writes as a cultivated gentleman of catholic tastes rather than as an advocate, he does not claim for poetry a more "unmatched praise" than does Aristotle.

Generally in the *Defence of Poesie*, however, he speaks as an advocate in behalf of a client. The work, as we have seen, is a classical oration. According to the established view the purpose of this literary form is to teach, to delight, and to persuade.[3] Teaching is important. Cicero would even have the orator master philosophy and from that source draw many large principles to illumine his discussion and raise it above the petty contentions of the moment.[4] Yet teaching, as also delight, is but a secondary aim, for a lawyer must win his case. His chief task is persuasion, or as Quintilian insists, persuasion to good ends.[5] He must therefore often state his general truths as a skilful debater rather than as a philosopher, and must omit many ideas which have no bearing upon the point at issue.

Hence when Sidney cites the broad principle that poetry "is more philosophical and more studiously serious than history," he states it not with the scientific detachment of an Aristotle, but with the skilful emphasis of a Cicero. Hence, too, he cannot find room in the *Defence* for all his ideas about poetry, expressly waiving the question

1. Page 4.
2. Page 9.
3. Cf. Thomas Wilson, *Arte of Rhetorique*, ed. Mair, 1909, p. 2, and Cicero, *De Oratore*, trans. Watson, 1860, II. 28 (p. 116).
4. *De Oratore*, III. 14 ff. (pp. 206 ff.).
5. *Institutes*, trans. Watson, 1856, II. xv. 1 ff. (I, 139 ff.).

whether verse can make a poem without the element of fiction,[1] and not even mentioning the structure of an heroic poem; though as we have seen, his views upon the latter subject were perfectly definite. In short, the principles which he makes prominent are not always intrinsically the most important, but the most essential for his argument. Of course, since only a sophist will deliberately employ false reasoning, we must ordinarily take Sidney's statements at their face value. But since any man, to prove one thing true, may honestly stress some of his beliefs to the exclusion of others, we must ask whether his emphasis would have been the same had he not been defending a cause.

Keeping this question in mind, we may now try to decide between the conflicting interpretations of the *Defence of Poesie*.

In the opinion of Greenlaw, Sidney shared "the view, inherited by the Renaissance from the mediæval period, that the great epics should be regarded as allegories." [2] Hence a "concrete application of the theories of the province of poetry laid down in his *Defense*" will produce "an 'historicall fiction,' a prose counterpart of the *Faerie Queene*, having for its object 'to fashion a gentleman or noble person in vertuous and gentle discipline,' and to portray 'a good governour and a vertuous man.'" [3] With Greenlaw's view Herr Brie is in substantial agreement.[4] On the other hand, Mr. Spingarn thinks the element of allegory "is minimized in the *Defence of Poesy*," [5] and is replaced by the Aristotelian idea of imitation.

Did Sidney conceive poetry as ideal imitation, or as allegory?

1. Cf. *Works*, III, 9.
2. "Sidney's *Arcadia* as Elizabethan Allegory," p. 327.
3. Page 337.
4. *Sidneys Arcadia, Eine Studie zur Englischen Renaissance, Quellen und Forschungen*, CXXIV (1918), 32 ff.
5. *Literary Criticism in the Renaissance*, p. 276.

These conceptions are alike, at least for the Renaissance, in emphasizing the teaching function of poetry. Their difference may be shown conveniently by the treatment of similar themes in the *Faerie Queene* and *Paradise Lost*; as, for example, repentance in the Red Cross Knight (Book I, Cantos X and XI) and in Adam and Eve (Books X to XII). The Red Cross Knight, sojourning in the House of Holiness, has his diseases cured by the instructions of Dame Cœlia's daughters, Fidelia and Speranza; by the ministrations of the leech Patience and his servants Penaunce, Remorse, and Repentaunce; and then by the further teachings of Dame Cœlia's third daughter, Charissa, and of those whom she appoints to show him a vision of Paradise and tell him the secret of his birth. Restored to health, he fights a dragon, at the end of each day falling exhausted into life-giving waters, rising next morning stronger than ever, and on the third day winning a glorious victory. The lesson which Spenser teaches by allegory Milton conveys by example. Adam and Eve, after their fall, spend the first fruitless hours "in mutual accusations," "but neither self-condemning." Then each is overwhelmed with a sense of his own guilt, suffers an agony of remorse, forgives his partner in sin, and humbly takes the blame all on himself. God, accepting their repentance, imposes on them the penance of leaving Paradise, but in a vision of the future comforts them with the promise of the Messiah, who will cure the evil they wrought. Milton and Spenser both teach that self-blame, humility, and penance, associated with hope, faith, and love, lead to renewed strength; and that then God's free grace intervenes beyond our hopes or deserts to enable us to achieve the final victory over sin. Imitation and allegory both teach, but by different methods.

The unlikeness lies in the significance of the literal story. No warrior, tired out by labor and wounds, would rise stronger than ever because he had spent the night in a pool of water. But Adam and Eve, when each first blames the other and then forgives the other and humbles himself, show how they might have acted, and how offending husbands and wives do act every day — or ought to. Both accounts are fiction. But one, taken literally, is absurd; the other is representative of life. Spenser's allegory, to be sure, is not very successful. Bunyan and Dante are never absurd. But always in allegory the literal story is the husk or veil, hiding a moral lesson which is to be discovered by the eager watchfulness of the mind, if not by deliberate analysis. In ideal imitation, on the other hand, the literal story, showing things as they ought to be, moves the reader with desire to follow that high example, made beautiful by the poet's art. The ethical effect comes not from hidden meanings detected by a watchful mind, but by an instantaneous effect upon feeling and imagination. In allegory the fiction is so distinct from the lesson that the story may even be indecent — as with Ovid — or preposterous — as with Ariosto. In fact, it was the absurdity or the evil of certain episodes in Homer that first inspired the ancients to seek a hidden lesson behind the literal meaning. With representative or imitative art, on the other hand, there is no meaning but the literal, and the lesson cannot be separated from the imaginative effect of the fiction.

In specific cases, of course, the line between the two kinds of poetic teaching is difficult to draw. The parable of the sower is clearly allegory. Is the story of the good Samaritan an allegory, or an idealized example of neighborly kindness? The parable of the prodigal son is an allegory of heavenly love, yet it is at the same time a moving human story. Great allegory may be the loftiest poetry, and imitative art may thrust upon the mind a commonplace lesson. The same man may appreciate both types of literature, may indeed write both, and may, like Dante, even unite them into one great architectonic whole.

It is no wonder, then, that critics have disagreed as to

whether Sidney conceived poetry as allegory or as imitation. The most significant evidence, of course, is the direct
testimony of the *Defence of Poesie*. But contemporary
writings furnish collateral evidence which may affect the
interpretation of Sidney's own statements.

On this collateral evidence Greenlaw and, more especially, Herr Brie, lay great weight. In favor of allegory
Greenlaw cites Webbe, and gives particular attention to
Nash, Harington, and Spenser. As for Spenser, whether
Sidney's relations with him were intimate or casual is a subject so complex, and at the present time so highly controversial, that I shall not enter upon it here; only observing
that the man who could befriend both Campion, the Catholic martyr, and Bruno, the martyr of free thought, and
who could yet remain himself an earnest Protestant, might
have been much drawn to Spenser without sharing all his
opinions about poetry. As for Nash and Harington, it is
unexpected to find so careful a scholar as Greenlaw treating
their views as serious evidence. Both men were essentially
humorists and satirists, who, with a genuine enthusiasm
for poetry, felt called upon to defend it with the best reasons they could muster. The argument from allegory is a
plausible defense against Puritan opposition. Is it anything more serious for these mad wags? In the opinion of
Mr. B. M. Hollowell, a recent student of Elizabethan
criticism (whose researches were not available to Greenlaw
or Herr Brie) Nash "does not care greatly even if the accusations of immorality are true, but answers for the sake of
showing that he has an answer."[1] And of Harington this
same scholar says, "One is never sure just when he is serious
and when he is talking with his tongue in his cheek."[1]
How significant are such witnesses? These as well as the
other writers mentioned by Greenlaw are cited also by
Herr Brie. And with exhaustive thoroughness the German
traces the idea of allegory from its ancient beginnings in the

1. *The Beginnings of English Criticism*, 1922, p. 128.

study of Homer, down through Strabo, Servius, Donatus, Petrarch, Boccaccio, and the Renaissance humanists, to Wilson, Lodge, Puttenham, and others of Sidney's contemporaries. He takes pains to show that Sidney had read Strabo and probably Donatus, that he was personally acquainted with Wilson, and that Wilson's *Rhetoric* and *Logic* are described by Harvey as "the dailie bread of our common pleaders, & discoursers."[1] "At length, the long line of [his] disputation makes a point in this":[2] that allegorizing lingered long in Renaissance England — which nobody denies.

Neither Greenlaw nor the learned Herr Brie considers whether there was not already developing a different interpretation of poetry. Mr. Hollowell, who has studied afresh the whole problem of allegory in Elizabethan critical theory, concludes that the "contradictions of the theory of allegorization will serve to show that the age was not accepting the principle without question, although they do not equal by a good deal the number of expressions on the affirmative side."[3] His conclusion is confirmed by Mr. D. L. Clark, who, writing in the same year, has independently shown "the displacement of allegory by example" in the theories of English criticism, a change in which Sidney stands out with Jonson as a pioneer.[4] Both Mr. Clark and Mr. Hollowell distinguish Sidney sharply from his contemporaries.[5] And in so doing, they follow Mr. Spingarn, whose authoritative work is ignored by Greenlaw and Herr Brie. According to Mr. Spingarn, Harington "differs from Sidney . . . in laying particular stress on the allegorical interpretation of imaginative literature. This element is minimized in the *Defence of Poesy*; but Harington accepts,

1. Brie, pp. 33–45; see especially p. 41.
2. Cf. Sidney, *Works*, III, 13.
3. Page 478.
4. *Rhetoric and Poetry in the Renaissance*, pp. 154–161.
5. Cf. Clark, p. 148, and Zandvoort, p. 123; cf. also Hollowell, pp. 124, 131.

and discusses in detail, the mediæval conception of the three meanings of poetry, the literal, the moral, and the allegorical." [1] If Mr. Spingarn, Mr. Hollowell, and Mr. Clark are right in thinking that Sidney minimized allegory, the fact is very significant. For Sidney must have been perfectly well aware that his contemporaries were stressing this argument in order to answer the Puritan attack. "The frequency with which the idea was used in and about the eighties," according to Mr. Hollowell, "was due to its association with the defence of poetry which was going on at just that time." [2] Greenlaw expresses the same view.[3] If, therefore, Sidney neglects an argument generally considered plausible, he neglects it in order to stress the newer idea of imitation which he found in the Italian disciples of Aristotle. Thus all Herr Brie's imposing evidence from collateral sources may only bring into clearer relief the truth of Mr. Spingarn's view: "The introduction of Aristotelianism into England was the direct result of the influence of the Italian critics; and the agent in bringing this new influence into English letters was Sir Philip Sidney." [4]

What is the direct evidence of the *Defence of Poesie*?

According to Greenlaw, "Sidney sees in Æneas the portrait of the 'excellent man'; 'a virtuous man in all fortunes'; 'no philosophers precepts can sooner make you an honest man than the reading of Virgil . . . there are many mysteries contained in poetry which were of purpose written darkly'." [5] "Finally," continues Greenlaw, "we have, in a single sentence in the *Defense*, evidence of Sidney's acceptance of the view that an heroic poem may be written in prose, and that it should have allegorical significance: 'For Xenophon, who did imitate so excellently as to give us

---

1. *Literary Criticism in the Renaissance*, p. 276. Cf. *Elizabethan Critical Essays*, ed. G. Gregory Smith, 1904, II, 201–202.
2. Pages 479–480.
3. "Sidney's *Arcadia* as Elizabethan Allegory," p. 327.
4. Spingarn, p. 268.   5. *Op. cit.*, p. 328.

effigiem justi imperii . . . under the name of Cyrus, . . . made therein an absolute heroical poem'." [1] These sentences appear to indicate that Greenlaw has not distinguished sharply between allegory and ideal imitation. A "portraiture of a just empire" need not be allegory. In the relations of Adam and Eve Milton gives us "the portraiture of a just" family government, and in the rule of the Omnipotent, "the portraiture of a just empire," at least as he conceived them. Adam, before the Fall, is an image "of the 'excellent man'," and the angel Abdiel behaves like "a virtuous man in all fortunes." An admirer of *Paradise Lost* could assert with some plausibility that "no philosophers precepts can sooner make you an honest man than the reading of" Milton. Yet Milton's heroic poem is not allegory. It does not contain "many mysteries . . . which were of purpose written darkly." Only this one phrase quoted by Greenlaw can be said to describe allegory and not ideal imitation.

The distinction, though of first importance for an understanding of Sidney's artistic methods, is perhaps less necessary for a discussion of his ideas, such as Greenlaw gives in so suggestive a form. And it is only fair to say that he does attempt to distinguish Renaissance allegory from the medieval type. The sixteenth-century variety, as he describes it, shows many of the features of imitation, and an example of such a hybrid art may be found in the *Faerie Queene*. But before assuming Sidney's *Arcadia* to be a work of this sort, we must see whether he differentiated between allegory and representative fiction. If he did, we can justly ask the modern critic to make the same distinction.*

Herr Brie, like Greenlaw, treats the distinction as of no importance. In support of his interpretation he cites numerous statements in the *Defence*; [2] as that poetry aims

1. Pages 328–329.
2. *Sidneys Arcadia, Eine Studie zur Englischen Renaissance*, pp. 29–32.

to teach and delight, and is a better teacher than philosophy or history; or "that it is not ryming and versing
that maketh a Poet, . . . but it is that faining notable
images of vertues, vices, or what els, with that delightfull
teaching." [1] Yet all this and much more of the same sort
can be applied to a work like *Paradise Lost*, and therefore
does not show Sidney accepting the theory of allegory.
The only new evidence relative to this question which
Herr Brie produces is a passage in the peroration, where
Sidney conjures his readers "to beleeve with *Clauserus*, the
Translator of *Cornutus*, that it pleased the heavenly deitie
by *Hesiod* and *Homer*, under the vaile of Fables to give us
all knowledge, *Logicke*, *Rhetoricke*, *Philosophie*, naturall
and morall, and *Quid non*?" [2] The climax of the erudite
German's argument is Sidney's further conjuration, already quoted by Greenlaw, "to beleeve with me, that there
are many misteries contained in *Poetrie*, which of purpose
were written darkly, least by prophane wits it should be
abused." [2] Thus the entire body of the evidence mustered
by both Herr Brie and Greenlaw to prove Sidney's acceptance of the allegorical theory of poetry amounts to just
two sentences in the peroration.

Neither of these scholars considers the context of the
passages. In the chapter on the *Defence* as a work of art I
have already remarked upon the tone of ironical exaggeration in the peroration.[3] The very next sentence after those
quoted by Herr Brie prays us to believe that poets "are so
beloved of the Gods, that whatsoever they write, proceeds
of a divine furie"; [2] a prayer obviously not meant too
solemnly, inasmuch as in an earlier passage Sidney has
disavowed this Platonic doctrine.[4] Is there no hyperbole
when Sidney speaks of the pretentious claim that in Hesiod
and Homer "all knowledge" is contained "under the veil

1. Sidney, III, 10–11.
2. Page 45. Cf. Brie, pp. 31–32.
3. See above, pp. 80–81.   4. Page 34.

of fables"? And when he describes poetry as too mysterious for profane wits to understand, are we quite sure it is
without a little polite mockery of his opponents? Partial
truths, no doubt, we may look for here. But to pick out
two observations in a passage not more than half serious,
and on them to rear an elaborate superstructure of argument, hardly reveals in the critic the urbane good sense of
his author.

Herr Brie might have cited also the allusions to the
parables of the prodigal son and of Dives and Lazarus; [1] to
the "prettie Allegories" [2] in Æsop's tales; to the story of
the conspiracy of the parts of the body against the belly, by
which Menenius Agrippa was said to have quieted a
Roman mob; [3] to the parable that Nathan told David, "of
a man whose beloved lambe was ungratefully taken from
his bosome"; [3] to the rationalization of the legends that
"*Amphion*, was said to moove stones with his Poetry, to
build *Thebes*, and *Orpheus* to be listned to by beasts, indeed stonie and beastly people"; [4] and especially to the
statements that pastoral poetry "can shewe the miserie of
people, under hard Lords, and ravening souldiers," and
"sometimes under the prettie tales of Woolves and sheepe,
can enclude the whole considerations of wrong doing and
patience." [5] If all this evidence, added to Greenlaw's and
Herr Brie's, is not imposing, neither is it quite negligible.

Just how much is it worth?

Doubtless the statement that many mysteries have been
written darkly in poetry — a statement confirmed by Sidney's rationalizing of the legends of Orpheus and Amphion
— proves that Sidney interpreted allegorically some ancient authors whom we interpret literally — perhaps Ovid,
for example. From his discussion of the pastoral it would
be surprising if his own efforts in that form contained no
veiled references to contemporary politics, as does Mil-

1. Sidney, III, 15.   2. Page 16.   3. Page 21.
4. Page 4.   5. Page 22.

ton's *Lycidas*, or to his personal friends, as does Sannazaro's *Arcadia*; for he praises the *Shepheardes Calender*,
which has examples of both; and the *Eglogues* of Barnabe
Googe show that Spenser's pastoral does not stand alone
in its time. On the other hand, none of the evidence points
to a strong interest in allegory. With few exceptions, all
the passages cited could be omitted without impairing the
integrity of the argument. The inclusion of several would
be urged merely by good strategy. A debater's examples
ought to be familiar and ought to command respect. Now
nothing could be more familiar than Æsop's fables or the
"notorious" tale of the belly and the rebellious members.
And what authority could be more august than Nathan the
prophet, David, and Jesus himself? To describe as
"pretty" the fables of Æsop or the pastoral "tales of
wolves and sheep" hardly suggests enthusiasm. Unmistakable fervor appears in the reference to "the divine
narration of *Dives* and *Lazarus*," and to "that heavenly
discourse of the lost childe and the gracious Father." [1]
Yet the first is not an allegory at all, but an example illustrating the relations of rich and poor in this world and the
next. Even the parable of the prodigal son seems to appeal
to Sidney's imagination directly, like the inspiring actions
in imitative poetry: "Truly," he says, "for my selfe (mee
seemes) I see before mine eyes, the lost childs disdainful
prodigalitie, turned to envy a Swines dinner." [1]

Why does he place so little emphasis on allegory?

Does he, like some of his modern critics, merely lump it
together with representative fiction? Unquestionably he
does not call attention to the distinction. He cites parables
and fables to show how clearly poetry can teach and how
powerfully it can move. Yet what is pertinent to the debate is not the difference between the two kinds of poetry,
but the similarity. Both use fiction to teach and to move.
Since allegory is one form of the art which Sidney is de-

1. Page 15.

fending, he would need to include it, yet he would unneces-
sarily complicate his argument by first distinguishing it
from imitation, and then defending both. Moreover, as a
shrewd advocate he would not wholly ignore the familiar
arguments that his audience considered effective. Rather
he would glance at them, but rest his case on others more
unusual and more powerful. In other words, whether he
distinguished between the two conceptions of poetry or
not, the requirements of debate would make his procedure
much the same.

Since his contemporaries, however, were emphasizing
allegory at just the time when he was emphasizing the
Aristotelian ideas, we must suppose him to have seen a distinction, and to have made a deliberate choice.

Would he have shown more interest in allegory had he
not been writing an argument? Apparently not. Indeed,
one may question whether all his courtly readers could follow his novel reasoning. Sir John Harington, though in his
own *Apology* he takes over many ideas from Sidney, has
comparatively little to say of imitation, and reverts to the
more familiar argument of allegory. Sidney's emphasis on
the Aristotelian doctrines, therefore, reveals not only the
debater, but the eager humanist, bringing to his half-
civilized countrymen the best new ideas.* There is no hint
that he cared more for allegory than the brief allusions in
the *Defence* would indicate.

Indeed, what won his enthusiasm, it appears, was the
direct impression of poetry upon the imagination. He himself confesses, "I never heard the old Song of *Percy* and
Duglas, that I founde not my heart mooved more then with
a Trumpet." [1] This flash of quick ardor hardly suits the
mood of the allegorist, picking useful doctrine out of
"pretty tales of wolves and sheep." It is equally foreign
to the dilettante. But it fits precisely the temper of the
soldier and poet — the Sidney who yearned to fling him-

1. Page 24.

self into noble action, and who turned some of his eager energies to the creation of literature.

Quite possibly such a man would throw into a fictitious narrative veiled allusions to his contemporaries and friends, and to events which stirred him deeply. But that he would care to make a studied allegory of political and moral philosophy, such as Herr Brie conceives the *Arcadia* to be, there is in the *Defence of Poesie* no substantial proof.

On the contrary, the basis of Sidney's theory of poetry is the Aristotelian idea of representative fiction, or imitation. The evidence given by Mr. Spingarn is so accessible and so complete that there is no need here for more than a summary. The doctrine of imitation underlies the allusion to Plato's fictitious dialogues between "many honest Burgesses of *Athens*"; [1] the statement that the essence of poetry is not verse, but "that faining notable images of vertues, vices, or what els, with that delightfull teaching"; [2] the contrast between historic facts and poetic inventions; [3] and the skilful reply to the charge that poetry is an art of lies. [4] The idea is made especially prominent in Sidney's very definition of poetry: "an Art of *Imitation* — for so *Aristotle* termeth it in the word μίμησις, that is to say, a representing, counterfeiting, or figuring forth; to speake Metaphorically, a speaking *Picture* — with this end, to teach and delight." [5]

The poet, of course, is not merely to copy life. In the literary criticism of the Renaissance, as Mr. Spingarn reminds us, "there are scarcely any traces of realism, in anything like its modern sense." [6] The artist imitates not what is, but "what may be and should be." [7] The actual "world is brasen, the Poets only deliver a golden." [8]

1. Page 5.   2. Page 11.
3. Pages 16 ff.   4. Pages 28 ff.
5. Page 9. The punctuation is mine.
6. *Literary Criticism in the Renaissance*, p. 37.
7. Sidney, III, 10.
8. Page 8.

The "maker" will teach and delight through an idealized fiction.

Which function is for Sidney more fundamental?

Greenlaw and Herr Brie think it is instruction. Miss Sheavyn boldly says it is pleasure. Sidney's emphasis on the teaching function of poetry, she asserts, is merely the best way of meeting the Puritan attack. "The trend of his treatment implies the belief, — however imperfectly formulated even in the writer's own mind, — that to arouse pure emotion by artistic means is a legitimate end in itself." [1] What critical doctrine, then, really lies behind the advocate's pleading?

Even in answering the Puritans, Sidney never forgets, as does Herr Brie, that poetry gives delight, though it also can impart wisdom. The "maker's" "effects be so good as to teach goodnes, and delight the learners of it." [2] The right kind of English comedy would afford "delightfull laughter, and teaching delightfulnesse." [3] "The *Philosophers* as they think scorne to delight, so must they be content little to moove." [4] In the words of Mr. Spingarn, the aim of poetry is "not instruction alone, or delight alone, as Horace had said, but instruction made delightful; and it is this dual function which serves not only as the end but as the very test of poetry." [5]

Mr. Spingarn has emphasized what has often been overlooked: that however much in his argument Sidney may stress the teaching function of poetry, in theory he stresses it hardly more than delight. Yet Sidney himself appears to go farther than even Mr. Spingarn has observed. In his general definition, where he describes the end of poetry as equally to teach and delight, he has included the didactic works of the religious and the philosophical poets, who

1. Sheavyn, *The Literary Profession in the Elizabethan Age*, p. 184.
2. *Works*, III, 26.
3. Page 41.   4. Page 20.
5. Pages 270–271.

manifestly are not chiefly entertainers. But in the restatement of his definition, where he is concerned only with what we should call the creative artists, he seems to give to delight a higher importance than to at least one kind of teaching.

These third be they which most properly do imitate to teach & delight: and to imitate, borrow nothing of what is, hath bin, or shall be, but range onely reined with learned discretion, into the divine consideration of what may be and should be. These be they that as the first and most noble sort, may justly be termed *Vates*: so these are waited on in the excellentest languages and best understãdings, with the fore described name of Poets. For these indeed do meerly make to imitate, and imitate both to delight & teach, and delight to move men to take that goodnesse in hand, which without delight they would flie as from a stranger; and teach to make them know that goodnesse wherunto they are moved; which being the noblest scope to which ever any learning was directed, yet want there not idle tongues to barke at them.[1]

Delight is indispensable, though not as an end in itself. For Miss Sheavyn to ascribe to Sidney the "conviction of the value of imaginative art simply for its pleasure-giving power"[2] is to brush aside the plainest sort of evidence. The idea had been set forth by some of the Italian critics, as Mr. Spingarn has shown,[3] and it was taken up by the French writer Amyot, in the preface to his translation of Heliodorus.[4] But Sidney, whom Greville, though he "knew him from a child, . . . never knew . . . other than a man,"[5] says nothing whatever of poetry merely as an agreeable experience. Delight is indispensable in art because it alone can "move men to take . . . goodness in hand." Explicit instruction, on the other hand, can only "make them know

1. *Works*, III, 10.   2. Page 179.
3. Page 55.
4. Heliodorus, *Histoire Æthiopique*, trans. Amyot, Paris, 1585, fols. 3 ff.
5. *Life of Sir Philip Sidney*, ed. Nowell Smith, 1907, p. 6.

that goodness whereunto they are moved." The value of teaching is to make clear to the mind the impressions that the moving power of fiction has already made on feeling and will, and the first purpose of the feigned example is not to tell what goodness is, but to move men to "take it in hand." Moving is more fundamental than either delight or instruction.

Yet of course to convey clear ideas of excellence was for Sidney a far more important end of poetry than it seems to us. Like philosophy and history, it may teach the most valuable kind of learning, "which stands . . . in the knowledge of a mans selfe, in the Ethike and Politique consideration." [1] Hence "all vertues, vices, and passions," [2] all "warlike, politike, or private matters" [3] come within the poet's range. He can teach the nature of patriotism, anger, wisdom, temperance, valor, friendship, remorse of conscience, pride, cruelty, ambition, and revenge.[4] He can direct princes and give the order of a whole commonwealth — witness Xenophon's Cyrus and More's *Utopia*.[2] With his "speaking picture" he can teach these lessons more simply and clearly than the philosopher, with his "bare rule." He can even give practical instruction in politics and war, for "whatsoever counsaile, pollicie, or warre [5] stratageme, the *Historian* is bounde to recite, that may the *Poet* if hee list with his imitation make his owne." [6] He excels the historian, moreover, because he can make his examples more philosophical, and therefore more clearly illustrative of general truth; he can show more truly the causes of events, and above all he can show that providence ultimately overrules fortune to reward virtue and to punish vice.[7]

Each form of poetry has its appropriate lesson. Comedy

---

1. *Works*, III, 11.   2. Page 15.
3. Page 17.   4. Cf. pp. 14–15.
5. I delete the comma after *warre*. Cf. the variant readings, p. 381.
6. Page 17.   7. Pages 16–18.

of the right character represents "the cõmon errors of our life, . . . in the most ridiculous & scornfull sort that may be: so as it is impossible that any beholder can be content to be such a one." [1] Tragedy "maketh Kings feare to be Tyrants, and Tyrants manifest their tyrannicall humours, . . . teacheth the uncertaintie of this world, and . . . maketh us know, *Qui scæptra sævus duro imperio regit, Timet timentes, metus in authorem redit.* But how much it can move, *Plutarch* yeeldeth a notable testimonie of the abhominable Tyrant *Alexander Pheræus.*" [2] Above all, in heroic poetry, "as the Image of each Action stirreth and instructeth the minde, so the loftie Image of such woorthies, moste enflameth the minde with desire to bee woorthie: and enformes with counsaile how to bee woorthie." [3]

Sidney never forgets the lessons of poetry, but neither does he forget that each form of the art can move no less than instruct. Indeed, though "in furnishing the minde with knowledge" [4] the poet excels the historian and often equals the philosopher, yet it is in stirring men to action that he stands without a rival. "And that mooving is of a higher degree then teaching, it may by this appeare, that it is well nigh both the cause and effect of teaching." [5] Of all human learning, Sidney says, poetry is "the most familiar to teach [goodness], and most Princely to move towards it." [6] Moving, then, is *par excellence* the function of poetry.

This fact becomes clearer when we consider the nature of the poet's lessons. They are important not because we do not know them, but because we do not act upon our knowledge. The "errors of our life" which comedy represents are all "common." The lesson of tragedy — "the uncertainty of this world" — is not unfamiliar. That tyrants "fear those who fear them, and the dread returns

---

1. Page 23.
3. Page 25.
5. Page 19.
6. Pages 21–22.

2. Pages 23–24.
4. Page 18.

upon its author," is indeed a useful warning to princes who are tempted to abuse their power, but have they never heard it except from Seneca? If few men understand what temperance and wisdom are, do they not know pretty well the nature of anger, valor, friendship, remorse of conscience, pride, cruelty, ambition, or revenge?

Certainly even our Saviour Christ could as well have given the morall common places of uncharitablenesse and humblenesse, as the divine narration of *Dives* and *Lazarus*, or of disobedience and mercy, as that heavenly discourse of the lost childe and the gracious Father.[1] . . . Nay truly learned men have learnedly thought, that where once . . . the minde hath a free desire to doo well, the inward light each minde hath in it selfe, is as good as a *Philosophers* booke, . . . but to be moved to doo that which wee know, or to be mooved with desire to know, *Hoc opus, hic labor est*.[2]

The poet's lessons are great commonplaces. Only his power to move is unique.

Hence there is in poetry a special opportunity and a special danger. "By the reason of his sweete charming force, it can do more hurt then anie other armie of words."[3] Yet one can truly say, not "that *Poetrie* abuseth mans wit, but that mans wit abuseth *Poetrie*."[3] Sidney, unlike Ascham and the elder English humanists, does not distrust the imagination. For lacking it, he censures many English love lyrics, "so coldly they applie firie speeches."[4] By "that same forciblenesse or *Energia*,"[4] he finds his "heart mooved more then with a Trumpet" when he hears "the old Song of *Percy* and *Duglas*."[5] The essential thing is "the right use of the materiall point of *Poesie*."[6] In its moving power, therefore, lies the poet's unique opportunity. He can bring home to us great truths that we have

1. Page 15.
2. Page 19. I substitute a comma for Ponsonby's period before *Hoc*.
3. Page 30.   4. Page 41.
5. Page 24.   6. Page 42.

heard and have disregarded all our lives, since, as Sidney reminds us in a different context, "our erected wit maketh us know what perfectiõ is, and yet our infected wil keepeth us frõ reaching unto it." [1]

The subjects he will illustrate will be "warlike, politike, or private matters"; [2] perhaps especially "vertues, vices, and passions." [3] As to how full and systematic the treatment will be, Sidney leaves the individual poet a wide latitude. Apparently he would wish at least as much instruction as may be found in a poem like *Amadis of Gaul*, to which he refers with mingled praise and condescension. In that poem there are lessons chiefly in courtesy, liberality, and courage.[4] In others the instruction rivals what philosophy can give. "Even in the most excellent determination of goodnesse, what *Philosophers* counsaile can so readily direct a Prince, as the feined *Cirus* in *Xenophon*, or a vertuous man in all fortunes: as *Aeneas* in *Virgill*, or a whole Common-wealth, as the Way of Sir Thomas Moores *Eutopia*." [3] Between *Amadis of Gaul* and the *Utopia*, the heroic poet has great freedom of choice. Perhaps the only requirement is that in general effect his work should be ennobling.

As to what Sidney himself would choose to do, we may draw a cautious inference from one passing remark: "For suppose it be granted, that which I suppose with great reason may be denied, that the *Philosopher* in respect of his methodical proceeding, teach more perfectly then the *Poet*, yet do I thinke, that no man is so much φιλοφιλοσοφος, as to compare the *Philosopher* in mooving with the *Poet*." [5] Apparently an ordinary poet will not attempt the comprehensiveness and explicitness that belong to the philosopher "in respect of his methodical proceeding." Yet we may fairly suppose that Sidney, at least, will attempt far more deliberate teaching than his critics before Greenlaw were

1. Page 9.   2. Page 17.   3. Page 15.
4. Page 20.   5. Page 19.

disposed to believe. His method in the *Defence* affords us
a hint of what he might do in the *Arcadia*. Of the eight
ways which Wilson distinguishes for examining a subject
logically, Sidney, as we have seen in an earlier chapter,
uses five in his confirmatio. Of the four kinds of argument
which Wilson describes, Sidney uses two. He never fails
to consider the rules of logic and of rhetoric; they guide
him at every moment, but they do not fetter him. He is
controlled only by his central purpose. Now in the *Arcadia* we should expect his central purpose would be to
"move men to take . . . goodness in hand." In the accepted treatises on ethics and politics, then, we may guess
that he will find an indispensable guide, as he found a guide
in the handbooks of rhetoric and logic. But in the *Defence
of Poesie* we can find no ground for thinking that he would
attempt to cover all the eleven virtues described by Aristotle, or perhaps even all those in which he shows an interest in the *Defence*. He will presumably select what suits
his purpose.

We may therefore infer that to read Sidney as primarily
a thinker is to misunderstand him. The lessons that he
ascribes to poets are simply the common property of his
age, like the principles of rhetoric. They are not the
writer's original studies in moral and political science.
Moreover, Sidney's own creative genius does not seem to
have lain in philosophic thought. To be sure, his keen interest in ideas is clear from both the *Defence of Poesie* and
from his translation of Du Plessis Mornay's *Vérité de la
Religion Chrestienne*. But though in the *Defence* he gives
his own emphasis to the critical theories, he derives them
from Plato, Aristotle, Horace, the tradition of rhetoric,
and the Italian critics. The unique feature is the skill with
which he selects and harmonizes the most representative
ideas of the best thinkers, and with a view to the purposes
of debate moulds them into the form of the classical oration. The originality is artistic, not philosophical. Again,

when Sidney really wishes to discuss ethics and religion, he does not make a treatise of his own. He translates the work of Du Plessis. He is not so much a thinker as a persuasive advocate of other men's thought. His political writings, it is significant to note, are all *defenses*. The *Discourse on Irish Affairs* is a defense of his father's administration. The letter to Queen Elizabeth on her proposed marriage to D'Alençon is a defense of the views of Walsingham and Leicester. His only other political treatise is a defense of his uncle against a scurrilous pamphlet. Sidney is a peerless debater, a poet, a man of action, but unless the *Arcadia* contradicts all that we know of him from other sources, he is not an original thinker.* "Well doing" interests him more than "well knowing," [1] as moving seems to him more important than teaching. A procedure so philosophical as Herr Brie ascribes to Sidney in the *Arcadia* is out of harmony with what we know of his mind and temper, and it is not required by the theories that he sets forth in his *Defence*.

Moreover, it is entirely hostile to "that high flying libertie of conceit propper to the Poet," [2] in which Sidney rejoices no less than in the ideal world of art. The poet "ranges onely reined with learned discretion, into the divine consideration of what may be and should be"; [3] the historian is "bound to tell things as things were." [4] Yet "whatsoever action or faction, whatsoever counsaile, pollicie, or warre stratageme, the *Historian* is bounde to recite, that may the *Poet* if hee list with his imitation make his owne; bewtifying it both for further teaching, and more delighting as it please him: having all frõ *Dante* his hevẽ to his hell, under the authority of his pen." [5] In all other arts man is compelled to follow nature.

Onely the Poet disdeining to be tied to any such subjectiõ, lifted up with the vigor of his own invention, doth grow in effect

1. Cf. p. 11.   2. Page 6.   3. Page 10.
4. Page 16.   5. Pages 17-18.

into an other nature: in making things either better then nature bringeth foorth, or quite a new, formes such as never were in nature: . . . so as he goeth hand in hand with nature, not enclosed within the narrow warrant of her gifts, but freely raunging within the Zodiack of his owne wit.[1]

For the courtier fettered by poverty and empty duties there must have been an irresistible appeal in the poet's glorious exercise of free power. In spite of all his moral earnestness, all his debater's emphasis upon moral teaching, it is difficult to conceive the author of the *Defence of Poesie* tying down his inventive genius in order to give his readers a complete body of political and ethical doctrine.

On the other hand, it is quite impossible to think of him as merely playing with literature. Even if one disregards the unanimous testimony of contemporaries that he was grave beyond his years, one cannot by any ingenuity explain away the sustained and powerful reasoning of the *Defence* as a mere *tour de force*. In both this work and the *Arcadia*, moreover, Sidney guides his "high flying wit" by the laws of form. Clarity of conception and deliberateness of method mark his work to a notable degree. Thus although the creative impulse is with him most fundamental, he may certainly control it so as to illustrate a multitude of philosophical truths. Sidney conceived the poet as more a teacher than a dilettante, though still more as a serious artist with a sense of ethical values.

The moving power of poetry comes from the "speaking picture," but Sidney implies that the poet has also other means of making clear his lesson. He praises *Gorboduc* because "it is full of stately speeches, and wel sounding phrases, clyming to the height of *Seneca* his style, and as full of notable morallitie, which it dooth most delightfully teach, and so obtaine the very ende of *Poesie*." [2] In discussing tragedy, as we have seen, Sidney quotes with ap-

1. Page 8.
2. Page 38.

proval a precept of Seneca's.[1] The indications are that he regards with favor the judicious use of "moral sentences" when the author speaks in his own person, and of more extended discussion when a fictitious character is allowed to make "stately speeches." Of course Sidney is speaking here of tragedies, not epics, but in an age that delighted in apothegms and proverbs and in every variety of rhetorical exercise, both speeches and sententious observations would be natural in any form of literature. They would be quite sufficient to make the readers "know that goodness where-unto they are moved."

But they would not always be necessary. The poet's special medium is the feigned example; the adage and the discussion belong rather to the philosopher. Though at times the poet may use them to call attention to the idea implicit in the fiction, much as an editor might add a marginal comment, yet at other times the idea will be clear from the example alone without a gloss. "See whether wisdom and temperance in *Ulisses* and *Diomedes*, valure in *Achilles*, friendship in *Nisus* and *Eurialus*, even to an ignorant man carry not an apparant shining." [2] The heroic poet in particular is one "who maketh magnanimitie and justice shine through all mistie fearfulnesse and foggie desires; who if the saying of *Plato* and *Tully* bee true, — that who could see vertue, woulde bee woonderfullie ravished with the love of her bewtie, — this man setteth her out to make her more lovely in her holliday apparrell, to the eye of anie that will daine not to disdaine untill they understand." [3] Here is no reference to explicit moralizing. The idea shines through the fiction, without the aid of a commentary.

To see why the "application," as Sidney calls it, can be so clear, we need only turn to the chapter on example in

1. Cf. above, p. 212, and *Works*, III, 23.
2. Page 15.
3. Page 25. The punctuation is mine.

Quintilian's *Institutes*. As we saw in considering the artistic method of the *Defence*, Sidney's familiarity with this work is next to certain. There may be some significance in his employing, to illustrate the moving force of poetry, two of the examples used by Quintilian — Æsop's fables, and Menenius Agrippa's story about the belly and the mutinous members — though of course these were common property. In any case, Quintilian is representative of a whole tradition, in which Sidney was steeped; and, as Mr. D. L. Clark has shown, Sidney's theory of example is ultimately derived in large measure from the rhetoricians' discussion of its power in argument.

Now "example . . . partakes of comparison," [1] writes Quintilian. It may be "similar, or dissimilar, or contrary." [2] Between the feigned images of poetry, therefore, and the situations of real life, the reader sees certain striking resemblances or contrasts. Thus the rage, remorse, and penitence of Adam and Eve after the Fall suggest to an orthodox Christian the common experience of sin, and the one way of escape. The comparison, it is to be observed, is made not only with situations in real life, but with the teachings of philosophy or religion. Again, the parallel may be found within the fiction itself; as in *Paradise Lost*, where Satan's refusal to humble himself before the Almighty stands in marked contrast to the repentance of Adam and Eve. By comparison, more often unconscious and instantaneous than deliberate, the behavior of fictitious characters becomes a model of what to avoid or shun.

Most effective in exhortation, according to Quintilian, are "unequal comparisons."

Courage is more deserving of admiration in a woman than in a man; and, therefore, if a person is to be excited to a deed of valour, the examples of Horatius and Torquatus will not have so much influence over him as that of the woman by whose

1. *Institutes*, trans. Watson, 1856, v. xi. 1 (I, 362).
2. v. xi. 5 (I, 363).

hand Pyrrhus was killed; and, to nerve a man to die, the deaths of Cato and Scipio will not be so efficient as that of Lucretia; though these are arguments from the greater to the less.[1]

In the same way, the captivity episodes in the *Arcadia* show the heroines enduring torture,[2] and the heroes preserving their chastity in the face of strong temptation.[3]

Thus whether or not the poet brings in wise "sentences" and "stately speeches" "full of notable morality," his lesson, by the very nature of example, will be as clear to the discerning reader as it is simple and familiar. But he will not make it too conspicuous.

Hee beginneth not with obscure definitions, which must blurre the margent with interpretations, and loade the memorie with doubtfulnesse: but hee commeth to you with words set in delightfull proportion, either accompanied with, or prepared for the well enchanting skill of *Musicke*, and with a tale forsooth he commeth unto you, with a tale, which holdeth children from play, and olde men from the Chimney corner; and pretending no more, doth intend the winning of the minde from wickednes to vertue; even as the child is often brought to take most wholesome things by hiding them in such other as have a pleasaunt taste: which if one should begin to tell them the nature of the *Alloes* or *Rh[u]barbarum* they should receive, wold sooner take their phisick at their eares then at their mouth, so is it in men (most of which, are childish in the best things, til they be cradled in their graves) glad they will be to heare the tales of *Hercules*, *Achilles*, *Cyrus*, *Aeneas*, and hearing them, must needes heare the right description of wisdom, valu[r]e, and justice; which if they had bene barely (that is to say Philosophically) set out, they would sweare they be brought to schoole againe.[4]

Have we not here the means of reconciling the divergent views of the *Arcadia*? Most readers feel that its only end was recreation. Greenlaw, Herr Brie, and Miss Lois

---

1. v. xi. 10 (I, 364).   2. Sidney, I, 471 ff.   3. Pages 278 ff.
4. III, 19–20, corrected from variant readings, p. 381.

Whitney [1] think that it aims to present the author's ripest thinking. Are not both impressions precisely what Sidney's theory would lead us to expect in his romance? The poet will really win men to virtue, but he will conceal his purpose in an illusion of pure entertainment, just as the courtier will hide his serious interest in an air of nonchalance. He will not preach wisdom, valor, and justice, but will show the inspiring examples of Cyrus, Æneas, Pyrocles, Musidorus, and the good king Euarchus, which "even to an ignorant man" will "carry an apparant shining." For the majority who will not read "with attentive studious painfulnesse," [2] the ethical effect will be delightful and almost unconscious; it will be not so much a moral lesson as an instantaneous lifting of imagination. The more studious reader will be conscious of what is happening to him. He will find in the poem much thought, if not a complete body of doctrine. He will find familiar truths of which he needs often to be reminded, here made irresistibly appealing by the power of fiction to inflame the mind.

The most significant thing, then, is not that Sidney stresses the teaching function of poetry, or even that he lays greater emphasis on its imaginative appeal, but that he insists they should not be separated. He does not, as Miss Sheavyn supposes, imply "the belief . . . that to arouse pure emotion by artistic means is a legitimate end in itself." [3] Nor is it accurate to say, with Miss Mona Wilson, "In Sidney's hands, as in Shelley's, and in Blake's, the defence of poetry becomes a defence of the imaginative life." [4] Doubtless his ideal poem will give only delight in scattered passages, and in others will merely teach useful lessons. But essentially it will be an inseparable fusion of

1. "Concerning Nature in 'The Countesse of Pembrokes Arcadia'," *Studies in Philology*, XXIV (1927), 207–222.
2. Page 19.
3. *The Literary Profession in the Elizabethan Age*, p. 184. Cf. above, p. 209.
4. *Sir Philip Sidney*, 1931, p. 161.

both elements into an image of luminous beauty, which will fill men with the love of excellence.

For Sidney, therefore, the stuff of poetry is not merely imagination, but what the late Professor Babbitt called imagination of an ethical quality. He is approaching the view of Aristotle that poetry is "an imitation of men in action," and (to use Goethe's phrase) gives the "illusion of a higher reality." Yet Sidney's idea of the world revealed by art differs from Aristotle's in the importance he assigns to character as compared with action, and to the possible as compared with the probable.

The views of Aristotle are set forth especially in his discussion of tragedy, but as he observes, "whoever . . . knows what is good or bad Tragedy, knows also about Epic poetry." [1] Either poetic form, therefore, may be said to be "an imitation, not of men, but of an action and of life, and life consists in action, and its end is a mode of action, not a quality. Now character determines men's qualities, but it is by their actions that they are happy or the reverse. Dramatic action, therefore, is not with a view to the representation of character: character comes in as subsidiary to the actions. Hence the incidents and the plot are the end of a tragedy [or an epic]; and the end is the chief thing of all." [2] Imitating an action, poetry must relate not "what has happened, but what may happen,—what is possible according to the law of probability or necessity." [3] "Accordingly, the poet should prefer probable impossibilities to improbable possibilities." [4] The events should "follow as cause and effect." [5] The poet, therefore, shows a great action governed by universal law.

Thus only does he produce an ethical impression, although, strangely enough to our modern notions, universal

---

1. *Poetics*, v. 5, trans. Butcher, in *Aristotle's Theory of Poetry and Fine Art*, 4th ed., 1923 (p. 23).

2. vi. 9–10 (p. 27).   3. ix. 1 (p. 35).
4. xxiv. 10 (p. 95).   5. ix. 11 (p. 39).

law may appear to flout our ideals of justice. Indeed, apparent injustice is the theme of tragedy. For tragedy arouses pity and fear, and "pity is aroused by unmerited misfortune, fear by the misfortune of a man like ourselves." [1] The ideal tragic hero, therefore, is neither entirely virtuous nor entirely wicked, but is "a man who is not eminently good and just, yet whose misfortune is brought about not by vice or depravity, but by some error or frailty." [2] Whether the epic hero may be more nearly perfect, Aristotle does not say; but he certainly thinks he need not be flawless. Painters, he says, "while reproducing the distinctive form of the original, make a likeness which is true to life and yet more beautiful. So too the poet, in representing men who are irascible or indolent, or have other defects of character, should preserve the type and yet ennoble it. In this way Achilles is portrayed by Agathon and Homer." [3]

The world of poetry, therefore, is not, according to Aristotle's view, a "land of heart's desire." Though it is more nearly perfect than what we find in life, it is still a place where "men like ourselves," though greater, can suffer "unmerited misfortune" because they have been caught in a chain of events, events governed not by human notions of justice, but by "the law of probability or necessity." Such a view as Aristotle's is perhaps possible only for minds of a scientific temper like his own, which observe both in nature and in man's life the workings of universal law.

It is not the view of Sir Philip Sidney. He, to be sure, can draw on the Greek thinker for the argument that poetry "is more Philosophicall and more studiously serious then History," [4] since "poetry tends to express the universal, history the particular." [5] But whereas Aristotle

1. XIII. 2 (p. 45).   2. XIII. 3 (p. 45).   3. XV. 8 (p. 57).
4. *Works*, III, 16, corrected from variant readings, p. 380.
5. *Poetics*, IX. 3 (p. 35).

means by the universal "how a person of a certain type will on occasion speak or act, according to the law of probability or necessity," [1] Sidney gives to the idea a very different turn. "If the *Poet* do his part aright, he wil shew you in *Tantalus*[,] *Atreus*, and such like, nothing that is not to be shunned; in *Cyrus*, *Aeneas*, *Ulisses*, each thing to be followed: where the *Historian* bound to tell things as things were, cannot be liberall, without hee will be Poeticall of a perfect patterne." [2] Aristotle says nothing of characters who are "perfect patterns" of what is "to be shunned" or "to be followed." Moreover, Sidney's illustrations imply a distinction between the heroes of tragedy and of epic poetry which the Greek thinker does not make. "Cyrus, Æneas, Ulysses," whose examples are to be followed, are the heroes of three epics. "Tantalus and Atreus," who are held up as warnings, are characters in one of Seneca's most horrible tragedies. Apparently Sidney conceived the hero of a tragedy as often a villain, but, like Tasso,[3] thought the hero of an epic should be a man "eminently good and just."

Nor is he nearer to Aristotle in what he says of poetic action. Here again he states the general principle in language that Aristotle would have approved.

The *Poet* doth so farre exceed [the historian], as hee is to frame his example to that which is most reasonable, be it in warlike, politike, or private matters, where the *Historian* in his bare, was, hath many times that which we call fortune, to overrule the best wisedome. Manie times he must tell events, whereof he can yeeld no cause, and if he do, it must be poetically.[4]

Here Sidney commits himself to Aristotle's "law of probability or necessity." Yet a moment later he subscribes to

1. IX. 4 (p. 35).
2. *Works*, III, 16.
3. Cf. Spingarn, *Literary Criticism in the Renaissance*, p. 122.
4. *Works*, III, 17.

a doctrine which is the very negation of that law. He declares that to show "vertue exalted, & vice punished" is a

commendation . . . peculier to Poetrie, and farre off from Historie; for indeed Poetrie ever sets vertue so out in her best cullours, making fortune her well-wayting handmayd, that one must needs be enamoured of her. Well may you see *Ulisses* in a storme and in other hard plights, but they are but exercises of patience & magnanimitie, to make thē shine the more in the neare following prosperitie. And of the contrary part, if evill men come to the stage, they ever goe out (as the Tragedie writer answered to one that misliked the shew of such persons) so manicled as they litle animate folkes to follow them. But the Historie beeing captived to the trueth of a foolish world, is many times a terror from well-dooing, and an encouragement to unbrideled wickednes.[1]

Just as the "perfect patterns" of virtuous or wicked characters will move men to admire the one and loathe the other, so the different fates which poetry gives them will move men with the hope of reward and the fear of punishment, though not necessarily in this "foolish world." Not by showing the eternal laws of causation at work in human life will Sidney's poet produce an ethical impression, but by feigning idealized pictures of good and evil persons, and by creating another world in which poetic justice reigns.*

Yet this view does not imply a total disregard of the law of probability which Sidney has himself stated. The purely irrational, at least, holds no meaning for him. It is "absurd," like the plays which take you over the whole world and through the events of a lifetime, all in two hours.[2] As I pointed out in Chapter IV, neither Sidney's *Defence of Poesie* nor the *Arcadia* reveals any interest in "Heroes, Demigods, Cyclops, Chymeras, Furies," and other "forms such as never were in nature" — the stock-in-trade of ancient legend or medieval superstition. The absurd, the

1. Page 18.
2. Cf. p. 38.

monstrous, the irrational either disgusted Sidney or amused him. Only what is possible is in his judgment a fit subject for art.

From a Greek or a modern point of view he preferred the possible to the probable. Yet Sidney's theory may rather imply a different conception of probability from that which prevails in an age when men see in both nature and human affairs the rule of law. It is near the view of Boethius, that fortune, however capricious she may appear, is really the agent of an all-wise providence. The view was a natural one for the men of the Renaissance. Though they awoke to the value of the actual world and to the presence in it of law, they had not shaken off the medieval conception that in comparison with the eternal life, the things of here and now are transitory, insignificant, and often irrational. "Love my Memory, cherish my Friends," said Sidney, recognizing the claims of this world even as on his death-bed he took leave of his brother Robert; "their Faith to me may assure you they are honest. But above all, govern your Will, and Affections, by the Will and Word of your Creator; in me, beholding the end of this World, with all her Vanities." [1] In Sidney's death an Elizabethan chronicler beheld "a notable lesson to our good (though in this example we be taught to our griefe) [of] the variablenesse of fickle fortune, and the small securitie in all humane and worldlie things whatsoeuer." [2] Feeling the uncertainty of life, and in some moods its vanity, the Elizabethans must have conceived as probable, things that to a pagan* of the fourth century B.C. or to a man of our own age might seem highly improbable. For the contemporaries of Sidney it was normal to find many events whereof they could "yield no cause," which appeared to be the work of "that which we call fortune," but which in reality were the work of a

---

1. Greville, *Life of Sidney*, ed. Nowell Smith, pp. 139–140.
2. Edmund Molyneux, in Stow's continuation of Holinshed's *Chronicles*. See Holinshed, 1808, IV, 881–882.

providence that made fortune the "well-waiting hand-maid" of virtue.

The poet, therefore, who wished to create the "illusion of a higher reality" would need to include within his view what Aristotle did not have to consider — the reward of the just and the punishment of the unjust, not in this world, but in the next. The imaginative insight of the Greek showed him changeless laws governing human life. The poet described by Sidney, if he belong to the lofty order of inspired seers, will celebrate the divine truths of Christianity. The humbler "maker" will feign a golden world, different alike from earth and from heaven, for it will be at once a picture of the capricious events of this world, and of the overruling providence which in actual life we can perceive only vaguely, and must accept on faith. Disregarding what is merely impossible, the artist will reveal the perfect forms which nature strives unavailingly to reach.

Nature never set foorth the earth in so rich Tapistry as diverse Poets have done, neither with so pleasaunt rivers, fruitfull trees, sweete smelling flowers, nor whatsoever els may make the too much loved earth more lovely: her world is brasen, the poets only deliver a golden. But let those things alone and goe to man, . . . & know whether she have brought foorth so true a lover as *Theagenes*, so constant a friend as *Pylades*, so valiant a man as *Orlando*, so right a Prince as *Xenophons Cyrus*, so excellent a man every way as *Virgils Aeneas*.[1]

Thus poetic truth is for Sidney neither the realism of modern fiction, nor the classic imitation of men in action, according to the law of probability. Nor is it an arid moral lesson. None the less, poetry is a serious effort to interpret life. It is no mere escape in holiday mood into a land of heart's desire; for delightful as the golden world may be, its function is to move men to love ideal goodness and to hate evil. In the perfect poem there is room for scattered

1. *Works*, III, 8.

bits of moral allegory, or veiled allusions to persons and events that touched the author in his life. There will be much reflection upon ethics, politics, and religion, expressed sometimes in memorable "sentences" or "stately speeches," but more often in the fiction itself, in idealized portraits of what is good and bad in human nature, and in a story that shows in all the vagaries of fortune the rule of providence. But though there are to be lessons, they will be familiar to most educated readers, they will perhaps not be too systematic or complete, and they will be subordinate to imaginative appeal. An exultant energy will create scenes of great beauty and of stirring action, which will appear to exist for themselves, and will veil, if not supersede, the philosophic purpose. The art will seem no art.

In short, if Sidney tried to achieve his poetic ideal, he would write like neither a dilettante nor a moral reformer, but like a born poet, a conscious workman, and an urbane man of action who coveted earnestly the best things.

CHAPTER VII

Poetic Truth in the *New Arcadia*

TO WRITE on the imaginative quality of a work of fiction is to invite controversy. Yet although I cannot hope to make a definitive critical study of Sidney's *Arcadia*, the present conflict of opinion in regard to the work makes necessary some attempt at clarification. The romance has most often been described as an amateurish effort without artistic sincerity. Greenlaw and Miss Whitney [1] show that it contains much serious thought. But in the opinion of the reviewer in *The Year's Work in English Studies*, "This only proves that Elizabethan ladies liked their romances thick and slab, not that Sidney was unlikely to compose an idle tale to beguile a summer's holiday." [2] Herr Brie, on the contrary, believes the *Arcadia*, even in its first version, to be a solemn political allegory.[3] This view is commonly said to have the support of Fulke Greville, but most scholars are ready to set aside his apparently first-hand testimony. Miss Wilson thinks "Sidney may be credited with intentions less portentous and rather more artistic," [4] and Mr. Zandvoort takes vigorous exception to the whole allegorical theory, whether expounded by Greville, by Herr Brie, or by Greenlaw. To call instruction "Sidney's prime motive in writing

1. Lois Whitney, "Concerning Nature in 'The Countesse of Pembrokes Arcadia'," *Studies in Philology*, XXIV (1927), 207 ff.
2. H. J. C. Grierson and A. Melville Clark, in *The Year's Work in English Studies*, VIII (1927), 187.
3. *Sidneys Arcadia, Eine Studie zur Englischen Renaissance, Quellen und Forschungen*, CXXIV (1918), 53.
4. Mona Wilson, *Sir Philip Sidney*, 1931, p. 143.

the *Arcadia*," declares this scholar, is to disregard "the composite texture of the romance, which is by no means woven of one single thread, and it is, moreover, in flat contradiction to Sidney's dedicatory letter to his sister. . . . In it, Sidney refers to his book as 'this idle worke of mine'; and the conclusion of the letter is emphatic in urging Mary to look 'for no better stuffe, then, as in an Haberdashers shoppe, glasses, or feathers'." [1]

In this chaos of critical opinion, three general views may be distinguished: (1) the *Arcadia* is merely the pastime of a summer's holiday; (2) it is a political and moral allegory or treatise; (3) it is primarily a work of literary art.

To the first of these interpretations I have replied in Chapters I to V of the present study. The letter to the Countess of Pembroke, of which scholars have made so much, refers almost certainly to the first youthful version of the *Arcadia*, which in comparison with the elaborate revised work is "but a trifle, and that triflingly handled." Even so, the words are an example of *sprezzatura*, the courtly nonchalance which conceals a profound enthusiasm. Sidney's mastery of form, moreover, and his fidelity to critical law, not only in the *Defence of Poesie*, but also in the *New Arcadia*, make simply untenable the view that the revised work, at least, can be an idle tale, composed "to beguile a summer's holiday."

But even though Sidney regarded it as serious art, he may not necessarily have tried to give it philosophic depth and range. What, then, of the second and third interpretations? Is the *Arcadia* an allegory or treatise? Is it purely a work of literature, inspired by a poet's love for beauty?

The simplest answer is that of Mr. Zandvoort: "The *Arcadia* is at once a romance and a treatise." [2] It contains a great deal more thought than was suspected by the

---

1. R. W. Zandvoort, *Sidney's Arcadia, A Comparison between the Two Versions*, 1929, p. 121.   2. Page 120.

scholars who wrote before Greenlaw, but its end is not chiefly to teach.

> Neither the original *Arcadia*, nor the revised version, in themselves lend sufficient support to the theory that Sidney wrote the romance primarily as a political allegory. But a comparison of the two texts shows that, as time went on, his mind was increasingly occupied with questions of government and warfare.[1]

In other words, according to the view of Mr. Zandvoort, Sidney's book contains much thought, but largely because it mirrors whatever happened to be uppermost in his mind when he wrote. It is hardly an organic whole, but a work of "composite texture," "at once a romance and a treatise," not to be taken too seriously. Sidney did not consciously set out to illustrate the truths of philosophy.

This conception of the *Arcadia*, though it explains the differences between the two versions — the subject which Mr. Zandvoort has made his special study — does not relate Sidney's literary art to the ideas which guided its creation. In form the *New Arcadia* is an heroic poem, conceived and executed in accordance with well-defined laws.

In fundamental purpose also we must expect it to reveal a fidelity to critical principles.

What those principles were, I tried to show in the foregoing chapter. The *Defence of Poesie* says nothing about idle tales which give only delight. It emphasizes instruction, but still more the power of poetry to move, not chiefly by allegory, but by illustrative examples, in which the ethical impression cannot be divorced from the imaginative. An heroic poem, of course, contains varied elements; on this point the Renaissance critics are agreed. But its effect need not be merely miscellaneous. Delight, instruction, and "sweet charming force" may all blend in a single swift impression on the imagination. If the *Arcadia* is an

1. Page 158.

heroic poem of this kind, it may well have both philosophic content and romantic adventure, but it cannot be a
hodgepodge of contradictory elements. It must be essentially a work of literary art, though art of a very special
kind. Characters and action will constitute a series of
"examples," illustrating a number of philosophic truths.
The teaching will be part of the fundamental plan; and
yet, though conscious and deliberate, will not make the
work either an allegory or a treatise.

Fully to discuss Sidney's ideas on politics and ethics is
quite beyond the scope of the present chapter. For since
the example, as we have seen in the last chapter, is a kind
of comparison, to find all the author's ideas we must be
able to show the parallels he intended not only between
the examples within the fiction itself, but also between
these and the concrete problems of his day. For such a
study of Sidney as a thinker, we should have to "be familiar with the course of his life," as Mr. Zandvoort observes, "with his letters and other writings, and with the
history of Europe in the latter half of the sixteenth century." [1] Nor could we stop here. We should need to make
a special study of the ways of life in Sidney's own social
group. And we could not get far without knowing well the
great ideals which came to Sidney with the authority of
long tradition — from the codes of chivalry; from the
classical philosophies, as set forth especially by Plato,
Aristotle, Seneca, Plutarch, and Cicero, and by their
Renaissance commentators; from the Italian courtesy
books; and from Protestant Christianity as it was taking
shape in the still formative period when the *Arcadia* was
written — not to mention the unorthodox views of Lucretius and Machiavelli, which Sidney viewed with distrust. It is a large field.

Obviously, I must limit sharply the present study. My
chief endeavor, therefore, will be to show how the *Arcadia*

1. Page 164.

conforms to Sidney's theory of example. After first showing that it is not primarily an allegory, I shall consider the
much larger question, whether it is a philosophic treatise.
I shall examine the methods used by Sidney to convey his
ideas, and some of his specific lessons in warfare, politics,
and ethics. My endeavor will be not to exhaust the subject, but to show in general the range of problems treated
by Sidney, the deliberateness of his teaching, and the relative importance he attaches to the lessons and the imaginative appeal of his work.

First, as to allegory. Does the *Arcadia* contain either of
the kinds of allegory so familiar to us in the *Faerie Queene*,
namely, covert allusions to persons and events of contemporary history, and symbolic representations of abstract ideas?

Sidney's fictitious characters have often been thought to
stand for persons with whom he came into contact in real
life. In support of this view Herr Brie has collected considerable evidence from among Sidney's early readers.[1]
He cites the anonymous author of the *Arte of English
Poesie*, Sir Thomas Wilson, and Sir William Alexander, besides Aubrey, who, a hundred years after Sidney's death,
obtained from one Tyndale, who claimed to be "conversant amongst his relations," a "key" to the *Arcadia*.[2] Of
these witnesses, Wilson merely links Sidney's book with
the *Diana* of Montemayor, "wherein under the names and
vai es [*sic*] of Sheppards and theire Lovers are covertly dis-
coursed maine [*sic*] noble actions & affections of the Spanish nation." [3] The statement is comprehensive, but hardly
specific. The author of the *Arte of English Poesie* lends
support to the traditional view that Philoclea is to be

1. *Sidneys Arcadia, Eine Studie zur Englischen Renaissance*, pp. 264–266,
273.
2. Aubrey, '*Brief Lives*,' ed. A. Clark, 1898, II, 250–251.
3. MS. Additional 18,638, quoted by Brie, p. 265.

identified with Lady Rich: "Sir *Philip Sidney*," he writes, "in the description of his mistresse excellently well handled this figure of resemblaunce by imagerie, as ye may see in his booke of *Archadia*." [1] More definite evidence is offered by Sir William Alexander, who, in the passage he wrote to fill the gap between the *New Arcadia* and the last books of the *Old*, ascribes to Philisides an unrequited love for Philoclea. Since the name Philisides, like Astrophel, is of course an anagram on the name of Philip Sidney, and since the account of the mournful shepherd's death is obviously colored with memories of Zutphen, it is clear that Alexander has in some sense identified Philisides with his creator, and Philoclea, the object of his hopeless passion, with the Stella of the sonnets. Tyndale not only equates Philoclea with Lady Rich and Philisides with Sidney, but Amphialus also with Sidney, Queen Helen with Frances Walsingham, Sidney's wife, and Pamela with Lady Rich's sister. The suggestions are interesting, but are rendered dubious by the lateness of the period when Tyndale wrote, and by certain obvious errors in his account. Of Sidney's relations with Stella's husband he writes: "Lord Ri[ch] being then his friend, he perswaded her [Penelope's] mother to the match, though he repented afterwards: she then very young and secretly in love with him but he no consern for her." [2] Beside the fierce indictment of Lord Rich in the sonnets the statement looks a bit absurd. Tyndale himself describes his key as "not worth anything," and "all a guesse," and he seems to have been about right.

The evidence collected by Herr Brie cannot be entirely dismissed. The first readers of the *Arcadia*, even when so close to the Sidney circle as Alexander, seem to have found living prototypes for some of the characters in the ro-

1. *The Arte of English Poesie*, ed. Arber, 1869, pp. 250–251. The passage is omitted by G. Gregory Smith in his *Elizabethan Critical Essays*, 1904. Cf. Brie, pp. 264–265, n. 2.

2. Aubrey, II, 251.

mance, in particular for Philoclea and Philisides. The view is made credible enough by the example of Montemayor's *Diana*, and it has been accepted in a general way by Sidney's modern biographers. How far the characters in the fiction are accurate portraits from life is a very different question, nor is it easy at this date to find a key worth more than the guesses recorded by Tyndale.

Herr Brie, with his usual confidence, identifies Philoclea and Mira with Penelope Devereux; Pyrocles, Amphialus, and Philisides with Sidney; Queen Helen and Basilius with Queen Elizabeth; Urania with the Countess of Pembroke; and Corydon with Dyer. The last two characters figure so little in the *Arcadia* that we may disregard them. What must we think of the other suggestions?

To equate two fictitious characters with one real person is on the face of it somewhat puzzling. Things equal to the same thing are equal to each other, but Philoclea is not like the shadowy Mira; Pyrocles, Amphialus, and Philisides are as different as could well be imagined; and Queen Helen bears little resemblance to Basilius either as a ruler or as a human being. Clearly, not all of these characters can be wholly identified with their alleged prototypes.

At the same time Sidney, like any other artist, must have drawn on his own first-hand knowledge of men and women. Here and there we can recognize an unmistakable personal allusion. For example, the meeting between Argalus and Parthenia, after Demagoras had destroyed her beauty with poison, must owe some of its strong feeling to a meeting between Sidney's father and mother when Philip was in his ninth year. "I left her a full fair lady, in my eyes at least the fairest," wrote Sir Henry twenty years later, "and when I returned I found her as foul a lady as the small-pox could make her, which she did take by continued attendance of her Majesty's most precious person, sick of the same disease; the scars of which, to her resolute discomfort ever since, remain in her face, so as she liketh solitariness." [1] This "mischance of sicknesse" [2] is one of the few circumstances in Lady Sidney's life which Fulke Greville thought worth recording. In the beauty of their married life, moreover, Parthenia and Argalus bear some relation to Sidney's parents. Sir Henry often had to sacrifice domestic happiness to public duty, as did Argalus when he answered Basilius' call to arms; and we may fancy that Elizabeth's summons may once have broken in upon a scene like that where the king's messenger found Argalus "sitting in a parler with the faire *Parthenia*, he reading in a booke the stories of *Hercules*, she by him, as to heare him reade." [3] Yet surely we cannot in any complete sense identify Argalus with Sidney's father, who may also have furnished hints for the character of Euarchus; nor need we try to find in the life of Sidney's mother a parallel to Parthenia's seeking to join her husband in his death, especially when there is a known literary source in the suicide of Panthea in the *Cyropædia*. A few scattered allusions do not identify the characters of fiction with persons in real life.

Turning now to Herr Brie's key to the *Arcadia*, we must admit that in Philisides and Mira, Sidney intends some sort of reference to himself and Penelope Devereux. Philisides' autobiography in the *Old Arcadia* [4] corresponds in a general way to what we know of Sidney's life (though there is also a source in Sannazaro). In the *New Arcadia*, one passage, sharply emphasized by the words of Pyrocles, "Thus I have digrest," contains a reference to the "*Star*, wherby his course was only directed." [5] Obviously, this is

---

1. Quoted by H. R. Fox Bourne, *Sir Philip Sidney*, 1891, p. 23, from Sir Henry Sidney's letter to Walsingham, March 1, 1582/3. The passage, except for one phrase quoted in a note, is omitted from the extracts in the *Carew Manuscripts*, ed. Brewer and Bullen, II (1868), 359.

2. Greville, *Life of Sir Philip Sidney*, ed. Nowell Smith, 1907, p. 5.

3. Sidney, *Complete Works*, ed. A. Feuillerat, Cambridge English Classics, 1912–1926, I, 420.   4. IV, 312 ff. Cf. Brie, pp. 272 ff.

5. I, 285. Cf. Brie, p. 267.

an allusion to Stella. In both versions of the *Arcadia* the passages about Philisides and Mira are consistent with the tone of *Astrophel*, and must be intended as compliments to Penelope Devereux. That they are anything more serious there is no tangible evidence. Certainly they afford us little help in estimating the biographical and fictitious elements in the sonnets.

Much the same may be said of Philoclea. When the author, departing from his almost invariable custom in the *New Arcadia*, suddenly addresses her in his own words, "And alas (sweete *Philoclea*) how hath my penne till now forgot thy passions, since to thy memorie principally all this long matter is intended?" [1] we may suspect a compliment to some lady of Sidney's acquaintance. And we may guess at her identity when we remember that her eyes, like Stella's, were of the unfashionable color of black; "blacke indeed, whether nature so made them, that we might be the more able to behold & bear their wõderfull shining, or that she, (goddesse like) would work this miracle in her selfe, in giving blacknes the price above all beauty." [2] The very same conceits are further elaborated in the seventh sonnet of *Astrophel and Stella*.[3] Even without the tradition recorded by Sir William Alexander and by Tyndale, we could reasonably infer that in Philoclea Sidney was giving at least a partial and idealized portrait of Penelope Devereux. But, as with the more shadowy figures of Philisides and Mira, it seems a hopeless task to discover the elements of fact which enter into the fiction.

Again, Amphialus undoubtedly bears in some particulars a striking resemblance to Sidney himself. They are alike in courtesy, in energetic leadership, in courage and skill in the tourney, perhaps in melancholy. Each, until he reached manhood, was heir to his uncle, Basilius and Leicester respectively; and each had his hopes of inheritance cut off by

1. I, 168–169. Cf. Brie, p. 279.
2. Page 90. Cf. Brie, p. 279.   3. II, 245.

his uncle's marriage, though Leicester's son, unlike the princesses of Arcadia, died in infancy. Amphialus was disappointed in his love for Philoclea as Sir Philip may have been in his love for her living prototype. Moreover, since Penelope Devereux was stepdaughter to the Earl of Leicester, she stood to Sidney in the relation of cousin, just as did Basilius' daughter to Amphialus. Certainly the parallels are numerous and striking, but so are the differences — Cecropia's Machiavellian influence over her son, his leading an insurrection, the taint of egoism which poisons his whole life. Perhaps a Freudian critic could argue that Amphialus represents the author as he might have been, had he not suppressed one side of his nature. Only by thus letting our imaginations run wild can we really identify Sidney with the noble but sinister figure of Cecropia's son, although the resemblances seem to show at least some degree of self-portraiture.

So, too, with the other characters. Queen Helen suggests Queen Elizabeth only in her beauty and her ability "to governe a people, in nature mutinously prowde, and alwaies before . . . used to hard governours; . . . & which was notable, even in the time that many countries were full of wars." [1] In the rest of her conduct she resembles nobody that we know anything about. Basilius, too, may suggest Elizabeth in his unwillingness to let his daughters marry (paralleled by the queen's reluctance to approve the marriage of her courtiers); and by his retirement from kingly duties, which, as Greenlaw points out, bears some likeness to the queen's slowness to defy Spain. But an equally good parallel may be found in the lassitude of the German princes. Moreover, to find "in the frequently ludicrous, sometimes contemptible figure of Basilius" [2] a portrait of Sidney's sovereign, is the merest nonsense. "Basileus [*sic*], of course, is not Elizabeth," writes Greenlaw, "but the Prince, the type of a prince misguided by

1. I, 283.   2. Zandvoort, p. 126.

want of perception of his duties, set over against Evarchus, type of princely wisdom." [1]

Personal allusions may be found here and there in the *Arcadia*, perhaps most strikingly in the characters of Amphialus and Philoclea; but they cannot easily be recognized, and no evidence justifies us in describing anyone in the story as merely a portrait from life.

To do so would be to disregard a fundamental principle in Sidney's theory of art. Not the actual world, but forms "better then nature bringeth foorth," [2] stir his enthusiasm. In this view he is in agreement not simply with his age, but with a long tradition. Patient Griselde and the saintly Custance (in Chaucer's *Tale of the Man of Law*) do not strike one as drawn from life. Castiglione's courtier is more perfect than the servant of any living prince, just as Cicero's orator furnishes the ideal pattern which men may approach, but never quite reach. In a different field, Plato's *Republic* furnishes the same sort of flawless model. The point of view is all but universal in the sixteenth century, and meets us in the most unexpected places. Ascham, for example, in his treatise on archery, advises a man to

folowe in learnynge to shoote faire, the noble paynter Zeuxes in payntyng Helena, whyche to make his Image bewtifull dyd chose out .V. of the fayrest maydes in al the countrie aboute, and in beholdynge them conceyued & drewe out suche an Image that it far exceded al other, bycause the comelinesse of them al was broughte into one moost perfyte comelinesse. [3]

In similar fashion, the conception of Euarchus may owe something to Sir Henry Sidney, Languet, and William the Silent, yet he is to be identified with no one of them. When has nature "brought foorth so true a lover as" Pyrocles and Musidorus, "so constant a friend" and "so valiant a

1. "The Captivity Episode in Sidney's *Arcadia*," *Manly Anniversary Studies*, 1923, p. 57.   2. *Works*, III, 8.

3. *Toxophilus, English Works*, ed. Wright, Cambridge English Classics, 1904, p. 100.

man" as either youthful hero, "so right a Prince, . . . so excellent a man every way" [1] as Euarchus? No doubt these idealized figures were partly suggested by real persons. The book could not have been written without reference to experience any more than could Castiglione's *Courtier* or Cicero's treatise *On Oratory*. Further allusions to contemporary events and to real persons may be discovered in the *Arcadia* from time to time. But the parallels must be far more numerous and striking than those now established before we can safely identify Philoclea with Lady Rich, Pyrocles and Amphialus with Sidney, or Basilius and Queen Helen with Elizabeth. In painting forms "better than nature bringeth forth" Sidney probably followed the example of Zeuxis, chose several of the noblest characters he had known or had read about, and "in beholding them conceived and drew out such an image that it far exceeded all other." He may well have followed a similar method in creating evil types such as Plexirtus, Andromana, Clinias, and Cecropia, who, we may hope, are worse "than nature bringeth forth." Sometimes a fictitious character may be drawn largely from one particular living model. Perhaps Cecropia, as Greenlaw believes, "is the Queen Mother of France." [2] But in the main, so far as can be learned now from the allusions which have been traced and from the ideal quality of the art, a fictitious character probably includes traits from several real persons, and the same living man or woman often afforded hints for more than one character in the story.

We do not know. And from the intangible nature of the evidence we cannot know, unless research should give us many new facts. At present, therefore, we can arrive at no more intelligent opinion than Greenlaw's:

I do not believe that Sidney wrote with propagandist design. . . . His knowledge of life, his acquaintance with the great actors

1. Cf. *Works*, III, 8.
2. "The Captivity Episode," p. 57.

on the stage of Europe, and his ideal of what a prose poem should be, all combined to color his narrative. That Cecropia equals Catherine, therefore, indicates not so much formal allegorical intent as the sort of influence that we find in the writings of many other novelists.[1]

If the characters and events of the *Arcadia* are not to be regarded chiefly as copies from reality, are they, on the other hand, symbolic representations of abstract ideas? In the view of Greenlaw, "Anaxius represents Pride,"[2] and the two giants (who rebelled against the tyrant of Pontus) "a mistreated populace, useful to a wise prince, but a source of danger made greater through their ignorance."[3]

In one sense, undoubtedly, Anaxius represents pride; but is he therefore an allegorical abstraction? Is he not rather an "example" of a proud man, brave and skilful, but boastful, discourteous, fundamentally barbaric in contrast with the civilized gentleman, Amphialus; in short, a type character, simpler than real persons often are, and yet a man and no mere personification? As for the giants, if they "represent a mistreated populace," why do they wreak their fury on the populace? Rather are they types of strong but ignorant men, who, rightly used, are valuable servants, but when mistreated turn outlaws, and take vengeance on the innocent. When Sidney shows a populace driven to desperation by bad government, he does not give us allegorical abstractions, but the examples of Helots or of Arcadian commoners rising against their masters.

Symbolism may be intended, I have sometimes thought, in the figures of Strephon and Claius, who remain warm friends though they both love the divine Urania. The very name of the lady suggests the heavenly study of ideal

1. Page 58, note.
2. "Sidney's *Arcadia* as an Example of Elizabethan Allegory," *Kittredge Anniversary Papers*, 1913, p. 333.
3. Page 335, n. 2.

beauty, goodness, and truth. "Hath in any, but in her, love-fellowship maintained friendship betweene rivals?"[1] As was observed in Chapter IV, the scene in which the two shepherds appear resembles in some ways the dumb show in Elizabethan plays, which, of course, was often allegorical. Moreover, a symbolical representation of the love of heavenly beauty, goodness, and truth would be an appropriate opening for a story of love, heroic virtue, and political activities. And yet we must be on our guard. The traveling companions of Musidorus are real persons with a fine sense of tact. The wise Kalander tells us that Strephon and Claius "are beyond the rest by so much, as learning commonlie doth adde to nature. . . . Which all notwithstanding, it is a sporte to heare howe they impute to love, whiche hath indewed their thoughts (saie they) with suche a strength."[2] In giving to Urania the praise that belongs to divine philosophy, the two shepherds, therefore, merely speak in their characters of eloquent lovers. Even here what looks like allegory turns out to be "an imitation of men in action."*

Allegorical personification may here and there be woven into the varied pattern of the *Arcadia*. But none whatever has been proved, and for all practical purposes it may safely be ignored. Of allegory in the sense of allusion to real persons and to political events, there is much more. The parallels, however, cannot easily be recognized, they are seldom complete, and they may mean only that Sidney, like any other poet, drew on his knowledge and experience in creating his "feigned images"; though in accordance with the prevailing fashion he used his idealized fictions to convey compliments to his sovereign and his personal friends. The significant thing in the *Arcadia*, as in all imitative poetry, is the literal story. In the strict sense of the term, allegory of any sort is of comparatively little im-

1. *Works*, I, 8.
2. Page 27.

portance. At least in its artistic method, Sidney's work is not what Greenlaw calls it, "a prose counterpart of the *Faerie Queene*." [1]

For once, Herr Brie comes nearer to the truth.

From the aesthetic point of view the significant thing about this is that here we are not considering an allegorical romance in the medieval sense, as for example Stephen Hawes' *Pastime of Pleasure*, nor yet an allegorical Renaissance epic like the *Faery Queene*, where the characters are still readily felt in medieval fashion as allegories, and where everything still centers on the warfare between the virtues and the vices, but rather we are dealing with a purely narrative work of art with conflicts of a political and genuinely human character which is intended to meet the difficult requirement of presenting at one and the same time a concrete and a symbolic action.

Herr Brie has stated the case with great precision, except for his last clause, where he returns to his thesis that the real purpose of the *Arcadia* is philosophic.

Is the work, then, essentially either a treatise, or even, as Mr. Zandvoort calls it "at once a romance and a treatise"? [3] I believe neither view to be accurate. Both are at variance with Sidney's critical principles, according to which a poem will be more truly a work of the imagination than Herr Brie supposes, and yet will contain more conscious teaching than Mr. Zandvoort can find in the *Arcadia*. The lessons, it is to be remembered, will be contained chiefly in the "example."

The *New Arcadia* meets these requirements far better than the *Old*. In the original version, where Sidney so often disregards the principles of the *Defence*, he frequently drops his rôle of "maker" and comments upon the story. Thus, after describing how Basilius came to favor Dametas

---

1. "Sidney's *Arcadia* as Elizabethan Allegory," p. 337.
2. '*Sidneys Arcadia, Eine Studie zur Englischen Renaissance*,' p. 112.
3. *Sidney's Arcadia, A Comparison between the Two Versions*, p. 120.

and even to "putt his lyfe into his handes," the author observes, "Hee grounded uppon a greate errur: For his quality was not to make men, but to use men according as men
were, no more then an Asse woulde bee taughte to man-
neage[,] a horse to hunt, or a hounde to beare a saddle,
but, eche to bee used acording to ye force of his owne
nature." [1]   This comment, much condensed, is in the *New
Arcadia* given to Kalander, who there describes the political situation in Basilius' kingdom.   Moreover, the
thought is expressed less bluntly by the experienced
Kalander than by the youthful author of the first *Arcadia*.
"I doubt me (I feare mee in deede)" [2] are the words with
which the old knight prefaces his wise remark, and so conceals from the unwary reader the fact that he has been
given a lesson in political philosophy.   Again, in the original version, when Pyrocles, in subduing the riot before the
lodges, invites the loyal Arcadians to "turne theyre backes
to the gate, with theyre weapons bent ageanst suche as
woulde hurt the sacred person of the *Duke*," the author
comments in his own person:

O weyke trust of the many headed multitude, whome inconstancy onely dothe guyde at any tyme, to well dooyng.   Let no
man lay confidence there where Company taketh away shame,
and eche may lay, the faulte in his fellowe. . . . And in deede no
yll way yt ys in suche mutinyes to give them some occasyon of
suche service as they may thincke in theyre owne judgmentes
may Counterveyle theyre trespas.[3]

In the *New Arcadia* the first two sentences are uttered by
"a craftie felow among them, named *Clinias*, to himselfe."[4]
The last is given as the unspoken thought of Pyrocles.[5]
Any number of other instances might be cited to show how
the dramatic method of narration has taken from the *New
Arcadia* the appearance of deliberate instruction.

1. *Works*, IV, 28.   2. I, 22.
3. IV, 125.   4. I, 319.
5. Page 318.

In this fact lies the explanation of a divergence of views between Herr Brie and Greenlaw, which Mr. Zandvoort has thought worth emphasizing. Brie believes that in the original version "the intentions as sketched by Greville are much more obvious."[1] Greenlaw, on the other hand, describes the *Old Arcadia* as merely "a pastoral romance,"[2] and looks for philosophic seriousness in the revised version. This apparent division in the ranks of his opponents is made the most of by Mr. Zandvoort.[3] Yet if one remembers the more dramatic narrative method of the second version, one sees both Greenlaw and Herr Brie to be right. The thought lies in plainer view in the *Old Arcadia*, but there is more of it in the *New*.

It appears not only in wise "sentences," but also in discussions. In the original story, Philanax makes a formal address to Basilius about the duke's proposed retirement;[4] Musidorus and Pyrocles debate about leisure and honorable action, virtue and love;[5] Pyrocles harangues the Arcadian mob;[6] and in the last two books half-a-dozen characters join in a tremendous finale of speech-making. In the *New Arcadia*, these rhetorical passages, so far as they lie within the story covered by the uncompleted revision, are all retained. In addition we have Pyrocles' oration to the Helots,[7] Pamela's reply to her aunt's atheism,[8] Clinias' skilful account of how the Arcadian riot began,[9] and the debate between Kalander and Philanax whether Basilius should raise the siege of Cecropia's fortress.[10] Yet the great mass of the new material is concerned not with men in counsel, but with men in action. Witness the adventures of the two heroes in Asia Minor, and the multifarious activities of Amphialus. The "distinctly rhetorical

---

1. Page 53.
2. "Sidney's *Arcadia* as Elizabethan Allegory," p. 330.
3. Page 128.   4. *Works*, IV, 3 ff.
5. Pages 10 ff.   6. Pages 123 ff.
7. I, 46–47.   8. Pages 403 ff.
9. Pages 321 ff.   10. Pages 466 ff.

cast that is characteristic of Greek Romance," [1] Dr. S. L. Wolff has shown, is "more prominent in the Old Arcadia than in the New." [2] The second version, therefore, is proportionately nearer to Sidney's ideal of imitative poetry. In it we are to look for his thought not in wise discussions or moral "sentences," but chiefly in "examples."

Of course an exhaustive study of Sidney's philosophy would take full account of his passages of moralizing. The point of departure would be his own words in the first version, which would frequently show a character in the *New Arcadia* to be his mouthpiece. The rôle seems to be filled even by a clever rogue like Clinias, when he has no motive to deceive, as well as by virtuous and wise persons like Pyrocles, Kalander, and Philanax. But to think of any character as always the author's mouthpiece would be misleading. The noble Philanax and the humane Kalander take opposite sides on two occasions. [3] Pyrocles' falling in love is represented as natural and right, but when he argues in favor of a life of leisure we may, with Mr. Zandvoort, suppose Musidorus to have the better of the dispute. [4] Yet there is another possibility, which Mr. Zandvoort has overlooked. Pyrocles and Musidorus may both express views that in the author's mind have real force. Though Sidney sought to make his own life one of honorable action, as Musidorus recommends, yet if we may trust a letter of Languet's he sometimes felt powerfully the attraction of a life passed among "friends in dignified ease," and devoted, perhaps, to intellectual pursuits. [5] In the debate between the cousins, therefore, though he gives the decision to Musidorus, he may recognize much truth in what Pyrocles says. To some extent he may be only posing a question. Again, in the trial scene, Euarchus' carefully weighed de-

1. *The Greek Romances in Elizabethan Prose Fiction*, Columbia University Studies in Comparative Literature, 1912, p. 355.
2. Page 354. 　　　　　3. Cf. *Works*, I, 466 ff., and II, 136–137.
4. I, 56–59. Cf. Zandvoort, p. 150.
5. *Correspondence of Sidney and Languet*, ed. and trans. Pears, 1845, p. 184.

cision is right, I believe, according to the evidence before him and the laws of Arcadia. But we know the evidence to be incomplete and misleading, and the laws to be unduly severe. Human justice, then, even when administered impartially, is not infallible. Now the king's verdict is set aside only by what seems a divine intervention — the awakening of Basilius at just the right moment. From the best human justice the only appeal is to the divine. There is truth in both sides of the argument, though more on one side than on the other.

To get the author's meaning, then, we cannot look upon any single speaker as his mouthpiece, though Herr Brie and Mr. Zandvoort so regard Euarchus [1] and Musidorus [2] respectively, on different occasions. When the classical Milton allows Satan to utter a glorious tribute to Hellenic culture, are we to suppose he feels no force in even the Devil's arguments? In the whole tradition of the literary debate the opposition is frequently not between bad and good, but between good and better; and sometimes it is resolved entirely in a larger truth.

These considerations must not be overlooked by the scholar who would make a definitive study of Sidney as a thinker, but for the relation between his literary work and his critical theories they are less important. For our present purposes the facts are simple and clear. In both versions of the *Arcadia*, as is to be expected from the *Defence of Poesie*, there are "stately speeches" and brief "sentences" "full of notable morallitie." [3] But in the *New Arcadia* the debates have been subordinated to the action, and the aphorisms have been half concealed in dramatic narration. A learned reader may find in Pamela's energetic answer to her aunt, Sidney's own reply to the philosophy of Lucretius. [4] But those who would not "be

---

1. Brie, pp. 147–148.   2. Zandvoort, pp. 149–150.
3. Cf. *Works*, III, 38.
4. I, 407 ff. Cf. Greenlaw, "The Captivity Episode," pp. 59 ff.

brought to schoole againe," [1] and who find little meaning in the rational language of argument, will see the same contrast between religion and foul impiety in Pamela's prayer and the fiendish cruelties with which Cecropia flouts the laws of heaven. For the great majority of readers, the discussion will merely "teach to make them know that goodnesse wherunto they are moved." [2] The ideas are implicit in the story itself. The *Arcadia* is not a miscellany of romance and philosophy, therefore, as Mr. Zandvoort seems to believe, but a work of art in which the scattered passages of moralizing serve to emphasize the underlying thought. Chiefly in the "notable images of vertues, vices, or what els" [3] the ideas are set forth. They are to be sought in the examples — in the plot, that is, and the characters, of the fiction itself.

The plot of the *Arcadia* is of just the sort we should expect from the *Defence of Poesie*. Nothing is quite impossible, but there are plenty of surprises. The events therefore illustrate not the Aristotelian law of probability, but the Christian doctrine of a providence which overrules "that which we call fortune." [4]

Consider some of the surprises in the plot. The captain of the Helots knocks off Musidorus' helmet, then kneels to his foe, and turns out to be Pyrocles. Parthenia, after her beauty has been ruined by poison, suddenly comes on the scene quite as lovely as ever. In Phrygia, when Musidorus and Pyrocles were fighting against fearful odds, there arose a mutiny which ended in Musidorus' being chosen king. More than once during their adventures, help arrived thus just in the nick of time. Equally surprising are the sham executions of Pamela and Philoclea, and the manner of Cecropia's death. And in the last books, the apparent death of Basilius, the unexpected arrival of Euarchus, the appearance of Musidorus' servant from Thessaly, and

1. III, 20.   2. Page 10.
3. Page 11.   4. Page 17.

Basilius' coming to life again, all are sufficiently startling. Certainly they do not conform to Aristotle's law of probability.

Yet these wonderful events all result from natural causes. Pyrocles' being captain of the Helots is due to a chain of events which is fully explained.[1] Parthenia recovers her beauty through Queen Helen's physician, "the most excellent man in the worlde."[2] The sudden mutiny in Phrygia is carefully accounted for,[3] as are also the arrival of help in the heroes' other hairbreadth escapes,[4] the sham executions of Pamela and Philoclea,[5] the manner of Cecropia's death,[6] and the surprises which crowd upon us in the last two books.

This union of the strange and the logically possible may have seemed less improbable to Sidney, as I have remarked in the foregoing chapter, than to persons who see in life the rule of law rather than of providence. In any case, it is what we are to expect from the *Defence of Poesie*, and it is recommended by Minturno:

We feel admiration at things which occur contrary to expectation, particularly when they are interrelated. For things of that kind move more admiration than what happens by accident or fortune. For among fortuitous events those are seen most strongly to inspire admiration which are believed to happen either by divine intervention or of their own free power, as when the statue of Mitys at Argis collapsed and killed the spectator, by whom Mitys had himself been slain; or when at Rome C. Cæsar fell pierced with wounds at the base of Pompey's statue. These things, even if perhaps they occurred by fortune, seem nevertheless to arise not by haphazard, but by divine plan, or with the express purpose that one should take vengeance on his enemy.[7]

This passage, though largely a translation from Aris-

1. I, 52–53.   2. Page 50.
3. Page 200.   4. Cf. pp. 211, 276–277.
5. Page 488.   6. Page 492.
7. Antonio Minturno, *De Poeta*, 1559, pp. 124–125.

totle,[1] is capable of an interpretation quite foreign to the Stagirite's way of thinking, namely, that wonders are admissible if they are accounted for logically and if they seem a part of poetic justice. Now "the providential plot" of the *Arcadia* has been studied in detail by Dr. Wolff,[2] and is clear to any careful reader. Musidorus, unselfishly trying to rescue the son of his host, finds the friend whom he had wished to seek. The tyrant of Phrygia, when he is about to commit his worst atrocity, is overthrown by the malcontents his bad government has fostered. Cecropia's death is caused by the son for whom she has practiced her villainies. Euarchus, seeking a just revenge for the murder of his son and nephew, is carried out of his course by a storm to the place where they are, judges them to death, and receives his reward when by a miracle they are proved innocent. These wonders arise not from fortune, but from a chain of events which are part of a divine plan.* They do not belong to the actual world. Do we not see there "the just *Phocion* and the accomplished *Socrates*, put to death like Traytors?"[3] They belong to the more intelligible world of poetry where we view the facts of this life with reference to the ideal distribution of rewards and punishments which is to be actually attained only before a divine tribunal.

The plot of the *Arcadia* conforms to poetic justice not only in the contrasting fates of the very good and the wicked. The foolish, like Basilius, suffer for their folly. Heretics against love, such as Musidorus and Erona, are forced to acknowledge their errors. The faulty but high-minded Amphialus escapes the ignominious death of his wicked mother, and after many agonies is spared to marry Queen Helen. If Zelmane, Argalus, and Parthenia suffer

1. *Poetics*, ix. 11–12, trans. Butcher, in *Aristotle's Theory of Poetry and Fine Art*, 4th ed., 1923 (p. 39).
2. *The Greek Romances in Elizabethan Prose Fiction*, pp. 320 ff.
3. *Works*, III, 18.

without desert, they at least do not occupy the center of attention. "Well may you see" Pyrocles and Musidorus "in a storme and in other hard plights, but they are but exercises of patience & magnanimitie, to make thẽ shine the more in the neare following prosperitie." In the total picture, fortune is the "well-wayting handmayd" [1] of virtue.

The plot of the *Arcadia*, then, is an example of human action, not "of what is, hath bin, or shall be," but "of what may be and should be." [2] Like the rhetorical example, it partakes of comparison. We perceive the working of providential law by comparing almost unconsciously the deed with the reward, and the fate of the wise and good with that of the foolish or wicked. By still less consciously comparing the feigned example with the ideal, or with what we ourselves ordinarily achieve, we even contemplate virtue in its native beauty and vice in its ugliness, without reference merely to rewards and punishments. "Who readeth *Aeneas* carrying old *Anchises* on his backe, that wisheth not it were his fortune to performe so excellent an Act?" [3] And who (if, like the Elizabethans, he can read the *Arcadia* without fatigue) can avoid sympathizing with every brave and disinterested act, and scorning any which are foolish or vicious?

In the characters, even more than in the "providential plot," the ethical quality of the art is clear. Types of perfect heroism, like Argalus, Euarchus, and the two princes, or of pure villainy, like Plexirtus, Andromana, Clinias, and Cecropia, "carry an apparant shining." [4] Even the more complex characters, compounded of good and ill, produce on our feelings an impression hardly less swift, and show perhaps still more plainly the element of comparison which belongs to the rhetorical example.

In Amphialus, for instance, do we not admire courage, courtesy, skill, high-mindedness, humanity toward his

1. III, 18.   2. Page 10.
3. Page 20.   4. Page 15.

followers, and yet at the same time deplore his rebellion and injustice? We never view him without judging him by ideal patterns, of which we are reminded by Philanax, Anaxius, and Argalus, who serve as foils to him. When, against all show of justice, Amphialus is about to execute the just and loyal Philanax, and then, in response to a message from Philoclea, releases his prisoner with a courteous speech, is not his indifference to justice made clearer by his foe's disinterested loyalty, and even by his own graceful action?[1] On the other hand, when Amphialus entertains Anaxius as a guest, are not his hospitality, his modest bearing, his chivalry, his good taste in music, all contrasted favorably with the coarse pride and barbaric violence of the other knight?[2] Yet while we admire the gentleman we cannot approve the rebel who has come to associate with one so shallow and cruel as Anaxius. A still more striking contrast is offered by Argalus because he has so many of Amphialus' high virtues. The one seeks unavailingly to win Philoclea by constraint; the other has won Parthenia of her own free will, when her mother has tried to force another match. Amphialus, rebelling against his uncle and native prince, "justifieth the unjustice"[3] by his hopeless passion for Philoclea. Argalus sacrifices a happy love to die for his king, though not born his subject. In both love and war the disinterested conduct of the one knight throws into sharp relief his rival's breach of loyalty and justice, and his underlying egoism. The contrasts of character in the *Arcadia* perhaps explain in part the antithetical style.

Egoism is revealed in Amphialus from the time when we first hear of his having slain his foster brother Philoxenus. One may be forgiven for defending himself against a desperate man. But when one's life-long friend hurls such epithets as "traitor and coward," and offers blows, one

1. I, 399-400.   2. Pages 440 ff.
3. Page 422.

who is not thinking too much of one's self will suspect that there is some misapprehension. He does not answer in Amphialus' words, "Thus much villany am I content to put up, not any longer for thy sake (whom I have no cause to love, since thou dost injure me, and wilt not tell me the cause) but for thy vertuous fathers sake, to whom I am so much bound." [1] If even his friendship is not quite disinterested, Amphialus' love of honor is still more clearly tainted with egoism. He jousts with a long succession of knights in single combat, "though against publike respect, & importunity of dissuaders," [2] merely in order to impress Philoclea. Musidorus, on the other hand, fights him without even telling his name,[3] in selfless devotion to the lady who has rejected him. Cecropia's Machiavellian nature has left its mark upon her son.

Thus by comparison and contrast the flaws and the high merits in Amphialus are made distinct and vivid for the reader. Explicit teaching may be found here and there, as in Argalus' wish that his rival's honor might "flie up to the heavē, being caried up by both the wings of valure & justice; whereof now it wants the latter." [4] But these words are only a comment on the lesson which is implicit in the character. The career of Amphialus, a totally new part of the revised *Arcadia*, shows how far Sidney has discarded moralizing for illuminating examples. He fixes our attention on what the characters do, but stirs our sympathies only by what our judgments can approve.

In this sense, of course, the art of Shakespeare has ethical content, but few readers will find in it the deliberate teaching which Sidney conceives as one function, though a secondary one, of the poet. Milton achieves better than Shakespeare the ideal set forth in the *Defence*. In *Paradise Lost* imaginative appeal is fundamental, but the characters and incidents are made to illustrate great truths —

1. Pages 70–71.   2. Page 419.
3. Page 453 ff.   4. Page 422.

the justice of God, and the right conduct for men. In like manner Sidney's heroic poem shows the hand of providence, and various kinds of right and wrong behavior.

Herein lies the explanation of one defect which all modern critics observe in the *Arcadia* — the simplicity of the characterization. An exception is perhaps Gynecia, with whom, according to Jusserand, "for the first time, the dramatic power of English genius leaves the stage and comes to light in the novel." [1] Mr. Zandvoort applies the remark to Erona, and has words of praise for Cecropia and her son. "Yet somehow," he adds, "Amphialus just fails of being a truly tragic character." [2] Of course he does. For Sidney, in harmony with his poetic creed, is not creating personalities like Hamlet or Cleopatra, but is "faining notable images of vertues, vices, or what els." [3]

By characters which invite comparison with one another, and by a plot which in the midst of the apparent vagaries of fortune shows the working of providential law, far more than by "stately speeches" and wise maxims, Sidney has given to his heroic poem its power of "delightful teaching." His general method, therefore, is quite in accord with his theory in the *Defence*. But does he keep consistently before him the teaching function of poetry? Does he often forget all about it, as Mr. Zandvoort seems to hold, or does he subordinate all else in the *Arcadia* to it, as Herr Brie maintains? How systematic is his instruction? how important a part of his work? and just what does he teach?

In general he deals with the subjects which in the *Defence* he describes as suited to heroic poetry — "warlike, politike, or private matters." [4] Particularly does he mention in his critical work stratagems of war,[4] the difference

---

1. *The English Novel in the Time of Shakespeare*, trans. Lee, 1903, p. 247.
2. *Sidney's Arcadia, A Comparison between the Two Versions*, p. 117.
3. Works, III, 11.
4. Page 17.

between kings and tyrants,[1] and the relations of aristo-crats and commoners to the body politic.[2] Among virtues he refers several times to friendship[3] and the relation of father and son.[4] "Patience & magnanimitie," he says, are illustrated in Ulysses;[5] "wisdom, valu[r]e, and jus-tice" in *"Hercules, Achilles, Cyrus, Aeneas"*;[6] "courtesie, liberalitie, and especially courage" even in *Amadis de gaule*;[6] "magnanimitie and justice" in heroic poetry gen-erally.[7] Among vices, he mentions pride and cruelty;[8] and among passions, anger, ambition, revenge, and re-morse of conscience.[8] To love he gives an important place. The ideal lover, Theagenes, is worthy to stand with Pylades, Orlando, Cyrus, and Æneas.[9] Heliodorus' "sugred invention of that picture of love in *Theagenes & Chariclea*" is "an absolute heroicall Poeme."[10] In short, "even to the *Heroical, Cupid* hath ambitiously climed."[11] These subjects — love, remorse, anger, revenge, ambition, cruelty, pride, justice, magnanimity, courage, liberality, courtesy, wisdom, patience, filial piety, friendship, anar-chy, tyranny, stratagems of war — are illustrated in the *Arcadia*, not once, but many times.

Friendship, valor, and love are leading themes. A strata-gem of war, which is recounted in detail, is the means by which Musidorus and Kalander's other friends are able to get into the city of the Helots;[12] others, mentioned but not described, are employed by Musidorus and Pyrocles against Tiridates,[13] and by Plangus against Artaxia.[14] Tyr-anny of various sorts is illustrated in the kings of Phrygia and Pontus, in Plexirtus, Tiridates, Antiphilus, Andro-mana, and Cecropia. Anarchy is only too apparent in

1. Page 23.
2. Page 21.
3. Pages 8, 15, 21.
4. Pages 15, 20.
5. Page 18.
6. Page 20.
7. Page 25.
8. Page 15.
9. Page 8.
10. Page 10.
11. Page 30.
12. I, 40.
13. Page 236.
14. Page 334.

Arcadia, not to mention Laconia and Asia Minor. Filial piety is the theme of one of the most famous episodes in the *Arcadia*, which found its way into *King Lear*. Courtesy is exemplified in Amphialus and in nearly all the better characters. Liberality may be learned from the evil example of the miser Chremes, who, for gold that he could not use, was ready to betray a guest who had saved his daughter's life.[1] Magnanimity and justice "shine" in Euarchus, condemning his own son to death, though suffering a father's feelings. Basilius and Amphialus, in their different ways, illustrate the disregard of justice. The love of it inspires many of the exploits which Musidorus and Pyrocles perform in Asia Minor. Magnanimity appears in the younger hero when, in obedience to his promise to Zelmane, he risks his life for Plexirtus, whom he knew to be a scoundrel, even though he had to leave his friend at a critical time.[2] It appears also in Musidorus, who, while his cousin was saving Plexirtus, conquered, set free, and made a friend of Otaves.[3] To extend the list would be tedious. Plainly, the topics illustrated in the *Arcadia* include those described in the *Defence* as suited to the highest form of poetry.

The thoroughness with which the subjects are handled varies widely.

Least informing are the "warlike matters." A skilful stratagem, a pitched battle, a siege, a successful effort to carry reinforcements to the defenders, almost exhaust the list of military activities which are related in detail. A conspicuous exception is the single combats which Sidney delighted to describe. "He that would skilfully and brauely manage his weapon with a cunning Fury," wrote Gabriel Harvey with enthusiasm, "may finde liuely Precepts in the gallant Examples of his valiantest Duel-

1. Pages 274–275.   2. Pages 299 ff.
3. Page 301.

lists."[1] No doubt these "Heroicall Monomachies" reflect the Elizabethan interest in dueling as Harvey suggests, and derive in large part from the romances of chivalry. Yet they are not handled as in the older fiction. Amphialus' skill and courage are admirable enough, but his policy of challenging all comers is represented as dangerous to his cause. When he insists on fighting Phalantus, "his olde governour with perswasions mingled with reprehensions, (that he would rather affect the glorie of a private fighter, then of a wise Generall) . . . sought . . . to dissuade him."[2] One thinks of Languet's earnest admonitions to the same effect.[3] His protégé, who as military governor of Flushing was to show discretion and skill, no less than heroism, must have felt the combat of champions to be an anachronism in warfare. There is always the danger of bad faith: witness Tiridates[4] and the brothers of Anaxius.[5] A victory is indecisive, as was Musidorus' victory over Amphialus, and therefore the public benefit is slight. Yet the cost is heavy. Basilius cannot replace Argalus. Amphialus, too, loses more than honor when he is disabled, for even though the king raises the siege, matters within the castle go from bad to worse as the leadership passes first to Cecropia and then to Anaxius. Heroism is no substitute for strategy. To be sure, the man who challenged Oxford to a duel and was ready to prove the lie upon the defamers of Leicester probably found his "heart moved more than with a trumpet" by the personal combats of chivalric days; and in the similar episodes of the *Arcadia* he teaches the reader to "manage his weapon with a cunning fury." But though he "enflameth the mind" with valor, he also "enformes with counsaile"[6] how *not* to use it.

1. *Pierce's Supererogation, Elizabethan Critical Essays,* ed. G. Gregory Smith, 1904, II, 264.
2. *Works,* I, 414.
3. Cf. Pears, *Correspondence,* p. 137.
4. *Works,* I, 234.   5. Page 462.
6. III, 25.

Even in "warlike matters" Sidney likes to dwell on the larger problems which belong hardly more to strategy than to politics. Bad government occasions the civil conflicts in Laconia and Arcadia, the wars with which he is chiefly concerned. With strictly military affairs he deals far less than with political.

By Fulke Greville [1] the "politike matters" in the *Arcadia* were emphasized to the exclusion of nearly all else, and they have been discussed by Greenlaw,[2] Herr Brie,[3] and Mr. Zandvoort.[4] Greenlaw gives special attention to Sidney's "exposition of the Machiavellian theory of statecraft," [5] and to "the contrast between Evarchus, the wise prince, and Basilius, king in name only." [6] He sees in the *Arcadia* some reference to Elizabeth's delay in "checking the increasing Spanish aggression," [7] but does "not believe that Sidney wrote with propagandist design." [8] Herr Brie also emphasizes the same crisis,[9] but he concerns himself in particular with the influence of Aristotle's *Politics* and Xenophon's *Cyropædia* upon Sidney's theories of government, as, for example, in the various kinds of tyrants illustrated in the episodes.[10] Herr Brie thinks that probably "Sidney originally intended to write a political romance and at first conceived of the love story as of only secondary importance, until the relationship gradually shifted and the love story together with the Eclogues made up the main content of the romance." [11]

1. *Life of Sir Philip Sidney*, pp. 11-15.
2. "Sidney's *Arcadia* ˙ Elizabethan Allegory," pp. 334–336.
3. *Sidneys Arcadia, Eine Studie zur Englischen Renaissance*, pp. 66–107.
4. *Sidney's Arcadia, A Comparison between the Two Versions*, pp. 149–159.
5. "Sidney's *Arcadia* as Elizabethan Allegory," p. 334.
6. Page 335.
7. "Sidney's *Arcadia* as Elizabethan Allegory," p. 336.
8. "The Captivity Episode," p. 58, n. 1.
9. *Sidneys Arcadia, Eine Studie zur Rnglischen Renaissance*, pp. 57 ff.
10. Pages 69 ff.   11. Page 87.

Mr. Zandvoort calls attention to "the account of Amphialus' preparations for war against Basilius," which involve political as well as military strategy, and suggests that "the writer of this chapter must have been an accomplished man of action himself." He sums up well the present scholarly opinion on Sidney's concept of a well-governed state.

A wise and strong monarch, who knows how to keep the great nobles in their places, and acknowledges that he with his people makes all but one politic body; lords and gentlemen admitted into counsel; the commons to abstain from prying into matters of government: such was Sidney's political creed, and considering the time in which he lived and his own station in life, it could hardly have been otherwise.[2]

In illustrating these and similar political ideas, just what sort of appeal was Sidney making to his aristocratic audience? Did he write "with propagandist aim," was he trying to teach a whole political philosophy, was he merely reflecting the prejudices of his class, or had he still another purpose? I believe he was trying to quicken in his courtly readers a sense of responsibility toward the state.

In the opinion of Mr. Zandvoort he was encouraging something very different.

But if Sidney's view of democracy need cause no surprise, the brutal tone he adopts whenever referring to the lower classes as a whole or to any single member of them is harder for a modern reader to understand. When revising the riot scene, he expressly interpolated a would-be facetious passage full of gruesome details of the massacre of the rebels. He delights in their agonies like a boy torturing a cockchafer or a frog. Every plebeian in the *Arcadia* is fair game to his love of ridicule. A man like Kalander goes out of his way to repeat some verses containing a ludicrous description of Dametas' daughter Mopsa. . . . Evidently, one could be 'the president of Noblesse and of chevalree' and hold a base-born rustic of less account than a hound or a horse.[2]

1. Page 157.   2. Page 156.

On first reading the *Arcadia*, I felt much as does Mr. Zandvoort. "A man's a man for a' that," as we democrats never forget, and we share not only the creed of Burns, but his touchy class pride. Hence it is easy for us to mistake the point of view of an Elizabethan aristocrat. In reality our first judgment may be little better than nonsense. Of democracy Sidney says very little. Of anarchy he says much more, but he does not hold the lower classes chiefly responsible.

Five times in the *Arcadia* the common people are represented as acting *en masse*: in the rebellion of the Helots, in the revolt against the tyrant of Phrygia, in the confused battle at sea just before Musidorus and Pyrocles arrive in Greece, in the riot before Basilius' lodge, and in the anarchy after his supposed death. Toward all these events the attitude of Sidney is aristocratic in the best sense.

In the *Old Arcadia* his view may be seen in the results which follow the apparent death of Basilius. The fundamental cause of the anarchy is not the commoners, but the king: "there was a notable example how great Dissipations Monarchiall governmentes are subject unto: For nowe theyre Prince and guyde had lefte them, they had not experyence to Rule, and had not whome to obay, Publique matters had ever beene privatly governed, so that they had no lyvely taste what was good for them selves, but every thing was eyther vehemently Desyrefull, or extremely terrible." [1] The responsibility for confusion, then, lies first with the king, because he made his government too personal. It lies also with the nobles. Timantus and Kerxenus, from very different motives, stir up dangerous factions.

The lower classes are at least no worse than any other.

Great Multitudes there were wch having bene acquaynted wth the Just government of *Philanax*, went to establish hym as

---

1. *Works*, IV, 299.

Livetenaunt of the State, and these were the moste populer sorte, who judged by the Comodityes they felt. But the Principall men in honor and mighte who had longe before envyed his greatenes with *Basilius*, did muche more spurne ageanst any suche preferment of hym.[1]

The commoners are no more selfish than the nobles, and have a much better appreciation of just government. To be sure, they resort to violence. The Mantineans run "to delyver the twoo Princes." But they are stirred up by Kerxenus, "a Man bothe grave in yeares & knowne honest."[2]

The "popular sort" can recognize virtuous men among their leaders, and can appreciate good government, even if they cannot foresee the wisest course of action. Though they can become a danger to the state, the chief fault lies with an irresponsible king and a factious nobility. How do these views show a brutal contempt for the lower classes?

The ideas set forth in the *Old Arcadia* remain essentially unchanged in the revised version.

Even the minor episodes enforce the same doctrine. In Phrygia the ultimate cause of the anarchy is tyranny. It breaks out when one soldier, "to pike a thanke of the King,"[3] strikes another for running away from Pyrocles and Musidorus. To maintain order, a tyrant must depend not upon disinterested patriots, but upon pick-thanks and cowards, who protect neither him nor the state. The king of Phrygia gives further occasion to anarchy by fleeing as soon as the tumult arises. The citizens, hating tyranny as the Arcadian populace love the just government of Philanax, overthrow the guard. "But some of the wisest (seeing that a popular licence is indeede the many-headed tyranny) prevailed with the rest to make *Musidorus* their chiefe."[4] The people cannot govern, but they can respond to leadership, which "some of the wisest" must provide.

1. Page 300.
2. Page 305.
3. I, 200.
4. Page 201.

Again, in the sea fight,[1] the ultimate cause of the trouble is a tyrant, Plexirtus. The immediate cause is the conflicting orders of the captain and of the counselor who sought to protect Musidorus and Pyrocles. Divided authority will produce wild confusion, for people will respond to either good or bad leadership.

A striking illustration is shown in the civil war in Laconia "betweene the gentlemen & the peasants."[2] Under Demagoras, says Kalander's steward, the Helots "have committed divers the most outragious villanies, that a base multitude (full of desperate revenge) can imagine."[3] Yet although they are "villanously cruell," Pyrocles, when he becomes their leader, "tempereth thẽ so, sometimes by folowing their humor, sometimes by striving with it,"[4] that he is able to save both Argalus and Clitophon from their rage. At first they "fought rather with beastly furie, then any souldierly discipline," but experience and skilful captains have "now made the[m] comparable to the best of the *Lacedæmonians*," so that their former masters have "sent unto them, offering peace with most reasonable and honorable conditions."[5] In the absence of Pyrocles, however, they fall unwarily into the trap laid by Musidorus, and are losing the battle when their leader returns, and at once changes their fortunes.[6]

Obedience to the right leaders is a first step toward civilized society. The next is the rule of law and the responsibilities of citizenship. The Helots, Pyrocles tells them, have won the following terms of peace:

The Townes and Fortes you presently have, are still left unto you, to be kept either with or without garrison, so as you alter not the lawes of the Countrie, and pay such dueties as the rest of the *Laconians* doo. Your selves are made by publique decree, free men, and so capable both to give and receive voice in elec-

1. Pages 304 ff.   2. Page 14.
3. Page 34.   4. Page 37.
5. Page 39.   6. Page 41.

tion of Magistrates. The distinction of names betweene *Helots* and *Lacedæmonians* to bee quite taken away, and all indifferently to enjoy both names and priviledges of *Laconians*. Your children to be brought up with theirs in *Spartane* discipline: and so you (framing your selves to be good members of that estate) to bee hereafter fellowes, and no longer servaunts.[1]

The task of governors is to insure peace, respect for law, fair taxation, personal freedom, and civilized life. Classes hitherto held in slavery are to be given citizenship, with a voice in choosing their own magistrates, and with an opportunity to give their children the best education. If this arrangement illustrates Sidney's political ideal, it is a little absurd to say he held "a base-born rustic of less account than a hound or a horse."

Yet as Mr. Zandvoort insists, "when revising the riot scene, he expressly interpolated a would-be facetious passage full of gruesome details of the massacre of the rebels." Mr. Zandvoort's distress is shared by others. "In Sidney's would-be funny accounts of the slaughter," writes Dr. Wolff, ". . . there is an ugly vein of cruelty." [2] Mr. Praz makes a more damning charge. "There is very little originality," according to his view, in what he, too, is pleased to call the "would-be funny account of the slaughter." [3]

Grant that Sidney's humor cannot satisfy the refined taste of our age, though Greenlaw [4] has thought it good. Grant that he treats the mob none too gently. Yet can he truly be said to show an "inhuman contempt for the rabble," [5] or to "delight in their agonies like a boy torturing a cockchafer or a frog"? [6]

After all, it is hard to see what mercy they deserve, ex-

1. Pages 46–47.
2. *The Greek Romances in Elizabethan Prose Fiction*, p. 331.
3. "Sidney's Original *Arcadia*," *The London Mercury*, XV (March, 1927), 512.
4. "Sidney's *Arcadia* as Elizabethan Allegory," p. 335, n. 4.
5. Wolff, p. 331.
6. Zandvoort, p. 156.

cept from the point of view of eighteenth-century senti-
mentalism. Dangerous rebels, in arms against a kindly
monarch, threatening highborn ladies with a horrible
death, the Elizabethan sees them as outlaws from decent
society. What compassion do they deserve until they lay
down their arms? Clumsy alike in their fighting and their
thinking, why should they not be laughed at? In an age
when men enjoy watching the antics of madmen, it is not
"inhuman" to feel scorn for a dangerous rabble. Not they,
indeed, but Cecropia, by her machinations, and Basilius,
by his shirking of kingly duties, are chiefly responsible for
the disorders. But Sidney is not sentimentalist enough to
regard them as free from blame because their rulers are
still more seriously at fault. Here is harsh Elizabethan
justice, no doubt, but not merely an aristocratic disdain
for the vulgar. Indeed, it is as if Sidney invited his courtly
audience to laugh at the rascals caught in their own folly,
in order to show that the serious danger to the state comes
not from them, but from their natural leaders who betray
their trust.

Thus wherever in the *Arcadia* Sidney introduces the
populace, he inculcates the same lesson. Without guidance
they are helpless. They respond quickly to wise captains
like Pyrocles, brutal outlaws like Demagoras, clever
trouble-makers like Clinias, virtuous but factious noblemen like Kalander, or just governors like Philanax. The
great need, therefore, is leadership at once wise, disinterested, and unified.

Hence the value of a good monarchy. Hence also the
duties of the privileged classes to which Sidney belonged.
His overwhelming emphasis, therefore, is not upon the
follies of the vulgar, but upon the crimes of the great. In
the long narrative of events in Asia Minor, the worst of-
fenders are monarchs — the tyrants of Phrygia and Pontus, the usurpers Plexirtus and Antiphilus, Plangus' weak
father, and his unscrupulous queen, Andromana, to whom

he passes over his authority. A factious nobility, on the other hand, was the first danger that confronted Euarchus when he ascended the throne, and is the main cause of the turmoil in Arcadia after Basilius quits his post. In the revised version of Sidney's romance, nearly one-third the space is devoted to a rebellion led by the chief nobleman of the country. If Sidney believed in a government by kings and lords, he saw their vices without illusion. Of course he was no democrat. But privilege, in his political philosophy, is another name for duty, and the great danger to the state is selfish ambition or equally selfish indifference in the upper classes.

His handling of this idea is not merely theoretical. He touches on living issues. In the age of the Tudors and Stuarts, the difference between monarchy and tyranny was a very practical question. Greenlaw has shown how the international crisis of the 1580's is reflected in the contrasting behavior of Basilius and Euarchus; how several characters in the *Arcadia* are contemporary Machiavellian types, Cecropia in particular bearing a strong resemblance to Catherine de' Medici; and how in the field of religion Pamela's reply to her aunt's atheism is Sidney's answer to the newly-revived heresies of Lucretius.

The timeliness of Sidney's discussion may be further illustrated from the Ireland of Elizabeth's reign. Without equating Euarchus with Sir Henry Sidney, we can find striking parallels in the conditions which they had to face. The Irish lords, like the Macedonian, "had brought in . . . the worst kind of *Oligarchie*. . . . For they having the power of kinges, but not the nature of kings, used the authority as men do their farms, of which they see within a yeere they shal goe out: making the Kinges sworde strike whom they hated, the Kings purse reward whom they loved: and (which is worst of all) making the Royall countenance serve to undermine the Royall soveraintie." [1] Of

1. *Works*, I, 185.

this last evil, Queen Elizabeth's favorite, the Earl of Ormonde, gave more than one example, to the great annoy-
ance of the lord deputy. Sir Henry, like Euarchus, each
time he took up the government of Ireland, "thundred a
duetie into the subjects hartes" by "some fewe (but in
deede notable) examples," [1] as when he cowed the Earl of
Desmond in 1567,[2] and some years later the Earl of Clan-
rickard.[3] The activities of the lord deputy find a parallel
not only in the government of Euarchus, but in the careers
of Pyrocles and Musidorus. The great assembly of rulers
which gathered to honor the two princes on their departure
for Greece bears a family likeness to the triumphal recep-
tions sometimes accorded Sir Henry. In one official report
he writes:

> I came to this Cittie, . . . accompanied withe the Earle of
> *Desmound*, the Bisshoppes of *Casshell* and *Corck*, my Lord of
> *Lowth*, and some others of the Nobilitie, dyvers Knights and
> principall Gentlemen of the Countrie; where I was received
> with farre greater Pompe, then either I my selfe have heretofore
> had, or sawe yeelded to any other in this Lande.[4]

To Pontus, in like fashion, there

flocked great multitudes of many great persons, and even of
Princes. . . . So as in those partes of the world, I thinke, in many
hundreds of yeares, there was not seene so royall an assemblie:
where nothing was let passe to doo us the highest honors.[5]

Some of the parallels are more general. In Asia Minor,
as in Ireland, a chief task is to establish justice through
force. Again, the need of able and honest leaders is not
emphasized more in the *Arcadia* than in the official correspondence of Sir Henry Sidney. In 1575-6 he calls for "a
discreate and active Governor, to be contynuallye resident

1. Page 186.
2. *Letters and Memorials of State*, ed. A. Collins, 1746, I, 26-27.
3. Pages 120-121.   4. Page 93.
5. *Works*, I, 301-302.

in" Munster. "The like . . . is as necessarie for *Connaught*," and there must also be "a Chauncelor, for the whole Realme." [1] The same year the lord deputy writes at length to Queen Elizabeth about the urgent need for ministers in the Irish church.[2] He asks also for three lawyers. "This is so necessarie, that, if I should write a whole Quier of Paper onelye of this Pointe, I were not able to expresse the Necessitie of it." [3]

Perhaps the most striking parallel to Irish affairs is to be found in the revolt of the Helots.

They were a kinde of people, who having been of old, freemen and possessioners, the Lacedemonians had conquered them, and layd, not onely tribute, but bondage upon them: which they had long borne; till of late the *Lacedæmonians* through greedinesse growing more heavie then they could beare, and through contempt lesse carefull how to make them beare, they had with a generall consent (rather springing by the generalnes of the cause, then of any artificiall practise) set themselves in armes, and whetting their courage with revenge, and grounding their resolutiõ upon despaire, they had proceeded with unloked-for succes.[4]

Substitute "English" for "Lacedæmonians" and we have no bad description of the Irish in Sidney's time. Was he thinking of Lord Grey's recent failure when he wrote these lines? Perhaps not exclusively, for throughout Elizabeth's reign the Irish, like the Helots under Demagoras, committed beastly atrocities under their rebel leaders; [5] but under wise and firm government, like that which Pyrocles exercised over his followers, they showed rapid and notable improvement. More than once a group of them secured terms like those which the peasants of Laconia wrested from their masters: freedom, provided they obeyed the

1. *Letters and Memorials*, I, 95.
2. Pages 112–113.   3. Pages 109–110.
4. *Works*, I, 39.
5. Cf. *Letters and Memorials*, I, 24.

laws and paid their taxes. In the county of Limerick, writes the lord deputy, they

crave, that they may have the Forces of their meane Lordes suppressed, and that they may be equallye cessed to beare an *Inglishe* Force, and to have *Englishe* Lawes planted amongest theim, and *Englishe* Sheriffs to execute those Lawes, and to surrender their Landes to her Majestie (as maney as may, and have not donne alredie).[1]

Equal distribution of burdens, for which the Helots fought, was a cardinal principle with Sir Henry. It won him the enmity of the Earl of Ormonde, and involved him in a long struggle with the gentry and nobles of the English pale. "The onelye Gawle of the Pale, for this Present," he reports near the beginning of the trouble, "is the wilfull Repininge at the Cesse, which is stirred vp, by certeine busye hedded Lawyers, and miscontented Gentlemen."[2] Two months later he writes:

In Troth the Bourden is great, as the Prices and Rates of Things are nowe. . . . But I entende to make it generallye more easye, by makinge it more indifferent. The Gentlemens Resistaunce is onelye for their owne Particuler, which nether furthereth Service, nor benifitteth the Common Wealth. The poore Fermors and Tenaunts, who beare the Bourden in deede, are verye desierous to geve fyve Marke out of a Ploughland, to be easied of the rest.[3]

On one occasion the lower gentry told the lord deputy, "What the Lords would do, they would followe; they were but Inferiors, and therefore they would do as their Betters did."[4] Of selfishness in the upper classes Sidney must have learned something from his father's experience.

How he used the materials of real life is illustrated well in the revolt of the Helots. They are like the poor farmers

1. Page 94.   2. Page 151.
3. Page 167.   4. Page 237.

and tenants of the English pale in being oppressed by the
gentlemen. They are like the Irish in their racial difference
from their masters, their natural barbarism, their response
to good leadership, and their satisfaction in being made
equal subjects before the law. Yet in one way they are
like neither the Irish natives nor the English farmers. For
whereas these were stirred up by the gentlemen or tribal
chiefs to resist the government, the Helots are revolting
against the gentlemen. Ireland saw no peasants' rebellion
in the sixteenth century, though the interests of the humbler folk were often at variance with those of their betters.
The problems of Ireland, moreover, were complex and confused, and were never really settled. The illustrative examples in the *Arcadia* are simple, clear, and capable of
final adjustment. To equate the Helots with the Irish
peasants, the Macedonian lords with the Irish chiefs, and
Pyrocles or Euarchus with Sir Henry, would be to ignore,
as I have remarked earlier in this discussion, the philosophic and ideal side of Sidney's poetic art. His picture is
faithful not to historic fact, but to general truth. Anarchy,
Machiavellian intrigue, national indifference in the midst
of great crises — these dangers were real enough in the
Ireland or the Europe of Sidney's day, yet he treats them
in the spirit not of propaganda, but of humanistic education. The *Arcadia* is not directed merely to the specific
problems of a moment. Rather does it illustrate the sort
of duties which an active Elizabethan courtier would some
time be called upon to face.

That the teaching is deliberate I think there can be no
question. No doubt Sidney did not expect a casual reader
to identify all his allusions to contemporary events, but he
aimed to make his general lessons unmistakable. Inevitably the tyrants of Asia Minor force comparison with one
another. So also do Andromana and Cecropia. Both are
artful, ambitious, unscrupulous. One imprisons the heroes
of the story, the other the heroines. Both have to do with

well-meaning but weak and credulous kings. Each has a son whom she labors to make heir to the throne, displacing the rightful claimant; each ruins her son and brings destruction on herself. Cecropia is shameless in suggesting passionate thoughts to her nieces; Andromana is unchaste. Their similarities, indeed, are enforced by contrast. Andromana, carried headlong by a mad passion, inadvertently causes the death of her son, and then kills herself. Cecropia's son, likewise overmastered with passion, accidentally causes her death, and then tries to kill himself. Parallels like these cannot be accidental; and they serve to emphasize the same lesson — the evils of Machiavellian politics — just as the various examples of tyrants present another theme in varied aspects which cannot be mistaken.

The five passages which deal with the common people acting *en masse* show an art no less deliberate. The rebellion of the Helots gives occasion for the first combats in the *Arcadia*; it first introduces Pyrocles; and it is therefore one of the most conspicuous episodes in the romance. The riot before the lodge brings one book to a close, and ushers in the great rebellion of Amphialus. The anarchy which follows the supposed death of Basilius involves the very last incidents in the story, standing, as it does, at the end of Book IV, and setting the stage for the dramatic choice of Euarchus to judge his own son and nephew. Of the events during the heroes' wanderings, the very first includes the insurrection in Phrygia, and the very last is the fight at sea between the two factions of the crew. These five passages, therefore, stand in perhaps the most conspicuous positions in the *Arcadia*, the beginning, middle, and end of the main action, and the beginning and end of the leading story related in the episodes. Sidney's readers cannot overlook the dangers of anarchy, and the responsibility of kings and nobles not to encourage it.

Not merely was Sidney's mind "increasingly occupied

with questions of government and warfare"[1] when he revised the *Arcadia*. The striking arrangement of the examples and the unmistakable parallels between them prove the political lessons to be part of the fundamental plan, inseparable from the plot and from the conception of important characters. The author consciously set out to illustrate important political truths.

How complete an art of politics Sidney included in the *Arcadia* is a question which I must leave unanswered. Clearly enough, he treats some problems quite thoroughly. Others he may not consider at all. Again, how original is his thought I am also unable to say with assurance. The evidence suggests, however, that in the *Arcadia*, as in the *Defence of Poesie*, Sidney is trying, not to give a novel or complete system of thought, but to apply to living issues large principles endorsed by the highest authorities. His ideas are widely current in the sixteenth century, and appear to be as old as Aristotle. In both his heroic poem and his critical essay he makes clear a few fundamental conceptions, like the nature of poetry or of true monarchy. Other matters, such as the structure of an epic or the question of whether able men of low birth should be admitted into the aristocracy, he barely touches on. In both works, his method appears to be to select a few great commonplaces, to set them before the reader in varied aspects, and to lend them the persuasive power of his literary art. There is no evidence, however, for the view that he looked upon the *Arcadia* as a political treatise. The instruction, though part of the fundamental plan, does not lie upon the surface, and the ordinary reader need not be conscious of how the book has helped to shape his political philosophy. The story does not exist entirely for its own sake, but the specific lessons are subordinated to the moving power of the fiction.

1. Zandvoort, p. 158.

In ethics, no less than in "warlike" and "politike matters," the *Arcadia* conforms to Sidney's theory of example. In general, as we have seen, it deals with the "private matters" which are emphasized in the *Defence of Poesie*. From the many subjects illustrated in the prose poem, I shall select for consideration only a few — friendship, revenge, forgiveness, loyalty to one's word, filial relations, and love. Though I shall try to show in a broad way Sidney's thinking upon these matters, I shall make no effort to study his philosophy exhaustively. As in discussing his political ideas, my aim is chiefly to show that his teaching is at once deliberate and unobtrusive, and is admirably suited to his courtly audience.

To begin by removing a misconception. Mr. Zandvoort, as we have seen, charges Sidney with using a "brutal tone" not only toward "the lower classes as a whole," but also toward "any single member of them." He complains especially of the ridicule heaped upon Dametas and his family. Is it true, then, that "one could be 'the president of Noblesse and of chevalree' and hold a base-born rustic of less account than a hound or a horse"? [1]

Strangely enough, Mr. Zandvoort forgets the idealized portraits of Strephon and Claius. They, like Dametas, are only shepherds. But as the wise Kalander remarks, "they are beyond the rest by so much, as learning commonlie doth adde to nature: for, having neglected their wealth in respect of their knowledge, they have not so much empayred the meaner, as they bettered the better." [2] Moreover, even the ordinary shepherds far surpass the clown Dametas. They excel in making "Songes and Dialogues in meeter"; "neither are our shepheards such, as (I heare) they be in other countries: but they are the verie owners of the sheepe." [3] Throughout his description of Arcadia, Kalander, as we have seen,[4] appears to express

1. Zandvoort, p. 156.   2. *Works*, I, 27.
3. Page 28.   4. See above, p. 244.

the views of the author. His remarks about Dametas, therefore, are particularly significant: "Neyther doo I accuse my maister for advauncing a countriman, as *Dametas* is, since God forbid, but where worthinesse is (as truely it is among divers of that fellowship) any outward lownesse should hinder the hiest raysing."[1]

The ordinary yeoman is worthy of respect. The exceptional person, like Strephon or Claius, if civilized by education, is not to be barred from as high a position as his merit deserves. But Dametas is no representative English peasant. Not his low rank or his physical ugliness, but, as Kalander says, "the basenesse of [his] minde,"[1] makes him the object of scorn. He is like his beldame Miso: "Onley one good point she hath, that she observes *decorū*, having a froward mind in a wretched body."[2]

This conception of decorum is central in Sidney's art. His heroes and heroines appropriately join high birth with rare beauty and lofty virtue. Amphialus, on the other hand, illustrates the want of decorum, for with his great personal beauty, noble rank, and princely virtues, his egoism and injustice form a shocking contrast. Basilius, too, has violated the principle of fitness, for he has left the station allotted him by fortune, has put an unworthy constraint upon his daughters, and has placed Dametas in a position to which he is not entitled by fortune, character, or education. Strephon and Claius have made themselves gentlemen. Dametus is a natural boor. He was well enough in the low station to which he was born, but when he steps beyond it he becomes fair game for comedy, like Basilius, the old man in love, the monarch who would not reign. When fitness is not observed, we may smile even at a king's folly. Why not laugh at a clown's?

The law of decorum, then, is a basic principle of Sidney's ethics. Far from making the courtier a snob, it imposes upon him the duty of self-discipline. In Sidney's scale of

1. Page 28.   2. Page 21.

values a high or low rank is but the symbol of the virtues which should accompany it. He certainly would not hold the democratic creed:

> The rank is but the guinea's stamp,
> The man's the gowd for a' that.

For Sidney a natural boor is not composed of precious metal. The aristocrat, on the other hand, if he is not to degenerate from his ancestors, must have the good breeding and the high qualities suited to his station. Born a gentleman, he must cultivate every human excellence, whether chivalric honor, Christian charity, or the classic virtue of friendship.

Turning now to Sidney's treatment of particular problems in ethics, we shall find every evidence of careful thought and systematic teaching, though concealed by the courtier's graceful art.

As for friendship, Sidney's handling of the subject has been studied so often that it need not detain us long. What concerns us is the evidence of deliberate teaching. Not merely is the theme treated in a general way wherever Musidorus and Pyrocles appear in the *Arcadia*. The very arrangement of the examples is made to enforce a lesson. The brothers Leucippus and Nelsus, servants and friends of the two heroes, leave to them the rib of the ship to which they have all been clinging, and cast themselves into the sea.[1] In the very next episode each of the princes tries to outdo the other in willingness to lay down his life for his friend. Does not Sidney invite a comparison between these successive episodes? Again, a striking parallel to the conduct of Leucippus and Nelsus is that of another pair of brothers, Tydeus and Telenor, servants and friends of the villain Plexirtus. Risking their lives for his honor, they are betrayed by the suspicious tyrant into killing one another, "leaving fewe in the world behind them, their

1. Page 194.

matches in any thing, if they had soone inough knowne the ground and limits of friendship." [1] The incident is one of the very last related by Pyrocles, as that of the first pair of brothers is one of the very first described by Musidorus. The arrangement emphasizes the parallel, and reveals the unobtrusive but conscious art with which Sidney has given his lesson: that friendship welcomes any sacrifice, but can exist only where there is virtue on both sides.

To avenge the wrong to a friend is a clear duty. Leucippus and Nelsus, who managed after all to reach Pontus, are at first favored by the tyrant there, but then are cast into prison and killed. The two princes march into the country, and have the king "slaine upon the tombe of their two true Servants." [2] Yet vengeance must not exceed justice. On the very same page where we learn the end of this adventure, we hear of another pair of brothers, "of huge both greatnesse & force, therefore commonly called giants," who "had a while served the King of *Pontus*" [2] with great fidelity. Suddenly losing the king's favor, they had not intelligence enough to see the proper limits of revenge. "Being men indeed by nature apter to the faults of rage, then of deceipt," [2] and "thinking nothing juster thē revenge, nor more noble then the effects of anger, . . . they immediately gave themselves to make all the countrie about them (subject to that king) to smart for their Lords folly: not caring how innocent they were." [3] Revenge of this kind merits the punishment inflicted upon the giants.

In the next episode we meet still another pair of brothers, the sons of the blind king of Paphlagonia. Again the theme is revenge. Leonatus forgets his father's "abhominable wrongs," [4] in order to protect him in his exile. A generous man could take no other course, for the old king has repented, and has himself been more deeply injured than his son. In contrast to this example is Leonatus' ill-

1. Page 295.
2. Page 204.
3. Page 205.
4. Page 210.

advised treatment of Plexirtus. He, too, seems entirely repentant and appears the victim of bad advisers,[1] but when pardoned by his brother he soon makes an effort to poison him; Leonatus' "goodnesse being as apt to be deceived, as the others crafte was to deceive."[2]

The episode shows Sidney's teaching at its best. Certainly he "could as well have given the morall common places"[3] of forgiveness to the repentant sinner and sternness to the unregenerate, as this most famous "example" in the *Arcadia*. Was he thinking of "that heavenly discourse of the lost childe and the gracious Father"?[3] His story is of a lost father and his gracious son, one who is ready to forgive his brother seven times, or seventy times seven. The Christian mood suggests the wisdom of seeking other sources besides Aristotle and Plato for some of Sidney's characteristic ideas.

The nobility of friendship, of just revenge, and of forgiveness, and the appropriate limits of these virtues, are set forth, as we have seen, in an unbroken narrative. One theme leads into another, and one example invites comparison with another. Throughout the story of the heroes' exploits in Asia, the same artistic method is maintained, and justifies the view of Greenlaw that here "Sidney presents the chief exposition of his 'Ethice, or vertues of a private man'."[4]

The episodes fall into two groups, according to Greenlaw, the first ending with the story of Leonatus. In the second, "unity is gained through the fact that the misfortunes which the heroes now seek to correct proceed not from tyrannical or unjust government, but from sins against love."[5] Certainly the power of love is the dominant theme not only in the episodic material, but in the main narrative at this point. Musidorus breaks off his

---

1. Page 213.   2. Page 293.   3. III, 15.
4. "Sidney's *Arcadia* as Elizabethan Allegory," p. 331.
5. Pages 332-333.

story in order to woo Pamela.[1] In the same chapter Pyrocles composes a song in honor of Philoclea, while he watches her bathing in the river, and then draws his sword on Amphialus, "madded with finding an unlooked-for Rivall."[2] In the next chapter a poetical dialogue between the middle-aged Plangus and the elderly Basilius further illustrates the power of love over men in every time of life. There follows the story of Erona, "irreligious against love,"[3] and of Plangus; which is interrupted by Miso with a poem in scorn of Cupid,[4] and then by Basilius,[5] who dotes on the disguised Pyrocles if ever any man sighed for a lady. When finally the narrative is taken up by Pyrocles, the episodes of Dido, Andromana, and Zelmane keep before us the same leading theme of the sovereignty of love.

Interwoven with it are many other ideas which are hardly less evident. Fidelity to one's word, and the natural relations between brothers or between child and parent are set forth in a great variety of illustrations.

We may begin with the first. Plexirtus' treachery does not stand alone. Tiridates[6] and Erona[7] both violate their oath, and in the next episode Plangus lies to protect Andromana.[8] In Pyrocles' narrative, Pamphilus, after betraying numerous women,[9] makes peace with Dido,[10] but immediately breaks his oath,[11] and tries to kill her in her father's sight. Chremes, in turn, attempts to betray his guest to Artaxia.[12] In the following episode the wicked arts of Andromana are contrasted with the legitimate use of a stratagem by her son Palladius,[13] in the effort to free the princes whom she has unjustly imprisoned. Next we find a new victim of Pamphilus' infidelity,[14] and then re-

---

1. *Works*, I, 215.
2. Page 223.
3. Page 232.
4. Pages 239–240.
5. Page 250.
6. Page 234.
7. Page 236.
8. Page 243.
9. Page 268.
10. Page 269.
11. Page 272.
12. Pages 275 ff.
13. Pages 282 ff.
14. Page 289.

turn to Plexirtus. In spite of Plexirtus' falsity to Leonatus [1] and to his friends Tydeus and Telenor,[2] Pyrocles
leaves his cousin at a moment of great need, "to go save
him whom for just causes," as he tells Philoclea, "I hated.
But my promise given, & given to *Zelmane*, & to *Zelmane*
dying, prevailed more with me, then my friendship to
Musidorus." [3] With Pyrocles' notable example of fidelity
we compare the conduct of the old nobleman who held
Plexirtus prisoner, but yet delivered him "(according to
faith given)," when Pyrocles fulfilled the conditions on
which the scoundrel was to be released. On the same page,
too, we learn that Otaves is now the friend of Musidorus,
"for so he gave his worde to be, and he is well knowen to
thinke him selfe greater in being subject to that, then in
the greatnes of his principalitie." [4] In return for Pyrocles'
having saved his life at extreme peril to himself, Plexirtus
now devises a plot to kill both heroes, while pretending the
warmest friendship.[5] In the final episode of Book II, the
falsity of Antiphilus [6] and Artaxia,[7] in their different ways,
is contrasted with the honorable dissimulation of Plangus
in attempting to free Antiphilus by a stratagem; [6] and with
the conduct of "the Nobleman who had *Erona* in ward,"
and who refused, "for his faith given," to surrender her
"before the day appointed." [7]

The multitude of these examples is not less striking than
their variety. Tiridates and Erona are impelled by love,
Pamphilus at first by mere whim, and later by revenge;
Chremes by avarice; Plangus by love for an unworthy
woman; Plexirtus by fear and ambition; Artaxia by her
thirst for vengeance; Antiphilus by cowardice. Lies occasioned by passion, it seems, are all hateful, though they
are least evil when caused by love. Deceit of a very differ-

1. Page 293.   2. Pages 292 ff.
3. Page 299.   4. Page 301.
5. Pages 303 ff.   6. Page 334.
7. Page 337.

ent sort appears in stratagems like those used by the two heroes to surprise Tiridates in his camp,[1] by Palladius to free his mother's prisoners, and by Plangus to deliver Antiphilus. In these cases there is no violation of a promise, the motive is honorable, and the deceit is therefore right.

Even a lie is sometimes unavoidable. Though Pyrocles, with his extraordinary fidelity to his word, stands in contrast to the utterly false Plexirtus, yet when Philoclea asks him what became of Musidorus after the fight at sea, his answer is, "Lost."

Ah my *Pyrocles*, said *Philoclea*, I am glad I have takē you. I perceive you lovers do not alwaies say truely: as though I know not your cousin *Dorus*, the sheepeheard? Life of my desires (said *Pyrocles*) what is mine, even to my soule is yours: but the secret of my friend is not mine. But if you know so much, then I may truely say, he is lost, since he is no more his owne.[2]

This incident, coming at the conclusion of Pyrocles' narrative, in which his own behavior makes so striking a contrast with that of Plexirtus, gives added emphasis to the whole discussion. A promise, — though merely implied, as when a secret has been confided by one friend to another, or though given to a mortal enemy or the meanest traitor, — must be kept at any cost, even at the cost of a verbal lie. Sometimes it is right to deceive, but never to break a pledge.

Thus in the episodic materials of Book II there are about twenty examples of true or false dealing, which not only invite comparison with one another, but also lay bare the motives which cause men to deceive, show the varying degrees of evil they involve, and reveal the author's exacting standards. The teaching is not unpleasantly obvious, but is it not deliberate and systematic?

Some of these same examples illustrate the nature of in-

1. Page 236.   2. Page 307.

gratitude. The vice is conspicuous in Plexirtus, Andromana, Chremes, and Antiphilus, the very meanest characters that the heroes meet in their wanderings. Sidney's
art is too complex to allow one person to represent only a
single quality.

These characters, with others, illustrate the relations between members of one family. Three pairs of brothers, as
we have seen, appear in the earlier group of adventures,
always acting in harmony. Even the gigantic outlaws are
faithful to one another. In contrast to such conduct, the
behavior of Plexirtus to Leonatus is all the blacker. In the
very instant when he is trying to destroy his brother and
father, Tydeus and Telenor show the mutual fidelity natural between nearest kin.[1] The monstrous behavior of
Plexirtus is further contrasted with the course pursued by
his wife Artaxia, whose one redeeming feature is loyalty to
her brother Tiridates.

Of the relations between parents and children there are
many examples. Just after Musidorus finishes the story of
the blind king of Paphlagonia, Miso breaks in upon our
attention,[2] to remind us of another king's ill-advised conduct toward his children, in giving to her the authority
over them. When the narrative of the earlier events is resumed, Philoclea tells how Erona defied her father's authority by choosing for her husband the lowborn Antiphilus. Her behavior is to be contrasted not only with the
gentle character of Philoclea herself, but with the prudent
conduct of her sister toward the shepherd Dorus, even
after she knows him to be a prince in disguise. When
Pamela takes up the story, it is to tell how Plangus' father
was led to persecute him through the influence of Andromana, after having supplanted him in her favor.
Pamela's own father is at this moment longing for a second
marriage, and her mother is seeking to supplant Philoclea
in the affections of Pyrocles. The resemblance between the

1. Page 211.   2. Page 215.

situations in the episodes and in the main story cannot be accidental.

In a more general way the churlish behavior of Chremes toward his daughter Dido, the effort of Andromana to advance her son, the grief of Zelmane for her father Plexirtus' crimes, and her continued love for him, all continue the same theme of filial relations. So, too, do events outside these episodes. In the story of Cecropia and Amphialus the relation of mother and son is constantly emphasized. Parthenia offers a striking contrast to Erona. Each comes into conflict with her only parent by falling suddenly in love with a man of her own choice. Neither can marry till after her parent's death, then finds a new obstacle in a barbarous suitor, but is able at last to achieve her desires. These resemblances only throw into stronger relief the differences. Before falling in love, Erona has set herself violently against Cupid. Parthenia shows no such morbid asceticism, but on the contrary is merely passive about love, and is ready at first to acquiesce in her mother's plans for her marriage. Equally normal is her choice of Argalus, a worthy man of her own rank. Erona's husband is as mean in character as in birth. In the one case the parental objections are as unreasonable as they are well founded in the other. Erona's passion is a kind of madness, which makes her the aggressor in the conflict with her father. Parthenia's is a beautiful and natural love, and her opposition to her mother is as modest as it is unyielding. She merely denies the parent's right to dictate the man she must marry. Erona denies her father even the right to veto her choice. In short, the one is the victim of circumstances; the other brings tragedy upon herself by her own headlong folly.

The contrast, I believe, was part of the author's plan, but proof is not easy. In the other cases we have been considering, the very arrangement of the examples in relation to one another almost forces the reader to make a comparison; but in the stories of Parthenia and Erona the author has used no such means to call attention to the parallel. That is, his art is becoming more purely an imitation of human action. We still judge the heroines by the author's standards, as we do when reading Thackeray or Shakespeare. But though the ethical quality of the art is apparent, the element of direct instruction is tending to drop out. It is most conspicuous in the episodes of Book II, which in so many other ways are at variance with modern taste.

In any case, throughout his work Sidney has made perfectly evident his views upon the reciprocal duties of parents and children. Arbitrary conduct in the elders he always represents unsympathetically. Witness Parthenia's mother, Plangus' father, and Basilius. On the other hand, to exercise authority for the child's own good, as does Erona's father, is a clear duty. Whatever the parent's derelictions, he is to be treated with reverence. Fathers may be foolish, like Philoclea's and Pamela's, unjust, like Leonatus' and like Plangus', or wicked, like Zelmane's; but obedience, gentleness, undiminished love are most becoming in the children. "They are but passions in my father, which wee must beare with reverence," [1] wrote Sidney on one occasion to his brother Robert. So important in his eyes is filial duty, that even toward Cecropia he has her son show respect, and the climax of his tragic career comes when he inadvertently causes her death.

One question which not unnaturally appears frequently in such a story as the *Arcadia*, is the proper authority for a parent to exercise in his child's love affairs. To fear or seek to prevent them, as does Basilius, is represented as absurd. To aid a child in a hopeless suit, after the manner of Cecropia, is wrong. To become his rival, like Gynecia and Plangus' father, is as unworthy as it is undignified. Obstinately to oppose his reasonable wishes, as does the

1. III, 130.

mother of Parthenia, is wilful and irresponsible. And yet it is the parent's right and duty to prevent a foolish match, although, as Erona's father discovered, it is no easy task. The child, on the other hand, should recognize the parent's position of adviser, and yield him even the right of veto; but, like Parthenia, must not consent to marry where there can be no love. In a day when forced marriages too commonly showed the abuse of parental authority, Sidney's treatment of the theme must have had lively interest.

Marriage, from his point of view, is both a personal and a social matter. For a guardian or a violent lover like Tiridates to flout the wishes of an individual is to be guilty of heartless tyranny. Yet for Erona to choose an unworthy person far below her in rank is to be guilty of injustice to the country she is to rule. Plangus' father is heavily punished for raising a commoner to be his queen. In both cases there is disparity not only in rank, but in character. The ideal marriage, then, will be one of mutual consent, between persons of similar virtue and social rank, like those between Parthenia and Argalus, Philoclea and Pyrocles, Pamela and Musidorus; or between less flawless but well-matched persons like Amphialus and Helen, or Plangus and Erona. Marriages of this sort are best initiated by the parties themselves, but quite properly by the parents, as when, in the *Old Arcadia*, Euarchus hopes "to provyde the Mariage of *Basilius* twoo Daughters, for his Sonne and Nephewe."[1] In short, the individual must have an assurance of happiness in marriage, but must recognize, especially if he is an aristocrat, the interest which his family, his social class, and his country have in his choice.

Sidney's views on marriage, filial relations, and fidelity to one's word, not to mention revenge and forgiveness, cannot easily be attributed to any single influence, whether of Greek philosophy or medieval chivalry. Rather do they

1. IV, 332-333.

seem typical of Elizabethan times, when so many currents of thought converged to enrich English life. If one may hazard a guess, they owe more to the early guidance of Sir Henry Sidney than to the philosophy of Aristotle. Yet Sir Henry was himself a product of the complex Renaissance culture; and in the ethical opinions of his son, as in the poetic art, it is hard to see anything out of harmony with the best contemporaneous theory, which was so deeply affected by Aristotle's *Ethics* and *Politics*.

Upon the particular subject of love — the leading theme, as we have seen, in Book II, where the discussion of conduct is so plain — Sidney's views appear also to spring from the social experience of his generation, but to be in harmony with tradition. A different interpretation, however, is elaborated by Herr Brie, and still another by Mr. Zandvoort. The Platonic element in Sidney's idea of love is emphasized by the one scholar, and the sensual element by the other. In both interpretations there is truth, but even when taken together there is not, I think, the whole truth.

Herr Brie's argument shows his characteristic method in both its strength and its weakness. He points out that Sidney, following Aristotle, classified love as a passion rather than as a virtue or a vice,[1] and that to justify its dignity he had recourse to Plato.[2] This much may be admitted. But when Herr Brie proceeds to argue that Sidney placed love below friendship, on the ground that a passion is inferior to a virtue,[3] one wonders what other reader ever derived such a lesson from the *Arcadia*. In handling evidence, the German scholar disregards what makes against his own case. After postulating a theoretical conflict between Sidney's ideas of love and virtue, he assumes that the problem had a deep personal meaning for him, on ac-

1. *Sidneys Arcadia, Eine Studie zur Englischen Renaissance*, pp. 146 ff.
2. Pages 149 ff.
3. Pages 146 ff.

count of his passion for Penelope Devereux,[1] just as if nobody had ever questioned the meaning of *Astrophel and Stella*. Whenever Herr Brie finds Platonic language in the sonnets or the *Arcadia*, he takes it to be of solemn philosophic import, not considering whether it may not be only a courtly way of speaking. Basing much of his argument upon a single passage — the disputation between the cousins, when Musidorus finds Pyrocles dressed as an Amazon [2] — he does not trouble to read it in the light of the later passage [3] where Musidorus recants his heresies, or to ask whether the whole debate is not somewhat of a *tour de force*. Is it not, indeed, a bit of urbane mockery, directed against folk who argue pompously about love, which, when all is said, still remains a force to be reckoned with? Humor is generally lost upon the subtle German scholar. He can even argue seriously that the character of Philoclea proves women incapable of virtue,[4] a suggestion of which Mr. Zandvoort makes the most. In short, Herr Brie has treated the evidence without tact or discrimination. Undoubtedly the Platonic doctrines colored Sidney's thinking about love, but there is no proof that the philosophic problem meant half as much to him as to his modern critic.

Mr. Zandvoort has a most welcome grasp of fact. "Sidney's lovers," he declares, "have not assimilated Platonism to the extent Brie seems to suppose. They treat love quite frankly as a passion; the claims of reason are not recognised till the day after." [5] The reference in the last sentence, of course, is to two scenes in the *Old Arcadia* which were altered by the Countess of Pembroke. In one Pyrocles and Philoclea consummate their love before the wedding ceremony; in the other Musidorus is about to

1. Pages 149 ff. 2. Pages 152 ff. Cf. *Works*, I, 77 ff.
3. *Works*, I, 113 ff.
4. Page 121. Cf. *Works*, I, 260, and Zandvoort, p. 132.
5. *Sidney's Arcadia, A Comparison between the Two Versions*, p. 145.

break his oath of continence when he is prevented by the sudden attack of certain rascals. Dobell,[1] who discusses only the second of these scenes, Mr. Praz,[2] and Mr. Zandvoort[3] suppose that in expurgating the more sensual passages the countess was acting on her own responsibility; and among scholars who have considered the question, only Miss Wilson takes a contrary view.[4] According to Mr. Zandvoort, Sidney displays "in the revised books . . . the same fondness for the sensual aspect of love that characterizes the first draft," and in one passage in particular shows an "unmistakable gusto." [5]

Without doubt, Sidney treats the physical side of love frankly, and perhaps at times with relish, in the *New Arcadia* no less than in the *Old*. But Mr. Zandvoort, in recoiling from Herr Brie's Platonic theorizing, has overstated the case. He does, indeed, recognize that even in the *Old Arcadia* Sidney represents the misfortunes of the heroes as a punishment inflicted by "the Everlasting Justice" [6] for their offense against ideal standards. But Mr. Zandvoort, like other scholars, has overlooked evidence which gives strong support to the opinion put forth by Miss Wilson: "There can be little doubt that the alteration, though made by the Countess of Pembroke, follows Sidney's general directions." [4]

Certainly he had planned some kind of alteration. The song which in the *Old Arcadia* appears in the scene in Philoclea's chamber [7] comes in an entirely different place in Sidney's revision. Again, the details of the conflict between Musidorus and the outlaws who assailed him seem to be reworked, as Mr. Praz has observed, in the revised

1. "New Light upon Sir Philip Sidney's 'Arcadia'," *The Quarterly Review*, CCXI (July, 1909), 100.
2. "Sidney's Original *Arcadia*," pp. 513–514.
3. Pages 31–32.   4. *Sir Philip Sidney*, p. 154.
5. Page 148.
6. *Works*, IV, 247, 286.
7. Cf. *Works*, IV, 223 ff., and I, 218 ff.

account of the riot before the lodges.[1] Clearly, the scenes were to be changed somewhat.

The one in which Musidorus figures was to be changed radically. For in the first place, "Pamela's character," as Mr. Zandvoort himself has remarked, "had, in her creator's mind, developed a degree of austerity and augustness to which she had by no means attained in the first draft."[2] When Musidorus merely offers to kiss her, the princess,

as if she had bin ready to drinke a wine of excellent tast & colour, which suddenly she perceived had poison in it, so did she put him away frõ her: loking first unto heaven, as amazed to find herselfe so beguiled in him; then laying the cruel punishment upon him of angry Love, . . . Away (said she) unworthy man to love, or to be loved. Assure thy selfe, I hate my selfe for being so deceived; judge then what I doo thee, for deceiving me. Let me see thee no more, the only fall of my judgement, and staine of my conscience.[3]

Musidorus does not see her again for several months, while she is imprisoned by Cecropia, and during this entire period he is stricken with melancholy and goes arrayed in black. Is it likely that he would offend a second time, and much more seriously? There is another reason for thinking the countess' expurgation represented her brother's wishes. The flight of Pamela and her lover from Arcadia is one of the "things done in other place" than the main story, which in the original version, as I showed in Chapter IV, are regularly described in the author's own words, but which in the *New Arcadia* are invariably reported by one of the characters. It is hard to see how an attempt on Pamela's honor would be related either by herself or by her lover. Beyond question, therefore, Sidney planned to strike out the incident.

As to the scene in Philoclea's chamber the evidence is

1. Cf. IV, 287–288, and I, 312–313. Cf. also Praz, p. 512.
2. Page 75.   3. *Works*, I, 355.

less certain. Yet she, too, like her sister, has developed great firmness of character in the *New Arcadia*, for all her gentleness. In her captivity she shows great power of endurance. One may question whether after the tragic sufferings in this episode (which occurs only in the revised version) the scene in Philoclea's chamber, as first written, would not be somewhat of an anticlimax. In any case, it is at variance with her new character. When she accepts Pyrocles' suit, she firmly repels his too ardent advances, which in the original account of the incident are not mentioned at all.[1] From the change in the position of Pyrocles' song, we know that Sidney planned some alterations of the scene in Philoclea's chamber; and those made by the Countess of Pembroke were quite in keeping with the character of his heroine.

According to Fulke Greville, to whom we owe the first reference to the two versions of the *Arcadia*, even the new was "to be amended by a direction set down under his own hand, how and why."[2] Among the notes he left, in the opinion of Mr. Zandvoort himself,[3] there was a sketch of the circumstances leading to Euarchus' arrival in Arcadia, an incident which is occasioned by very different circumstances in the two versions,[4] although it occurs in a book which Sidney did not rewrite as a whole. It is more than likely that among his notes there were also some hints about his intended revision of the scene in Philoclea's chamber and the account of the flight from Arcadia. Either from his papers, therefore, or from conversations with him, his sister, for whom he originally wrote the work, may well have known his plans and have made her most radical changes in accordance with his wishes. According to her editorial assistant, Henry Sandford,[5] her alterations

---

1. Cf. I, 261, 307; IV, 116.
2. Quoted by Malcolm W. Wallace, *Life of Sir Philip Sidney*, 1915, p. 232, from *State Papers — Dom. Eliz.*, Vol. CXCV.
3. *Sidney's Arcadia, A Comparison between the Two Versions*, pp. 38–39.
4. Cf. *Works*, II, 149 ff., and IV, 331 ff.   5. Cf. Wallace, p. 234.

went "no further then the Authours own writings, or knowen determinations could direct. Whereof who sees not the reason, must consider there may be reason which hee sees not." [1] There appears every ground for thinking Sidney's sister knew his intentions better than the modern scholars who have so readily accused her of prudishness and dishonesty.

Sidney's motive for the change, I believe, is supplied by Greville. He directed that the *Arcadia* be burned, says this biographer, because on his deathbed he "discovered, not onely the imperfection, but vanitie of these shadowes, how daintily soever limned: as seeing that even beauty it self, in all earthly complexions, was more apt to allure men to evill, than to fashion any goodness in them." [2] To no other part of the *Arcadia* are these remarks so applicable as to the scenes expurgated by the Countess of Pembroke. The author's intention is to represent the behavior of the princes as imprudent and faulty, though not criminal. But the examples are dangerous, in spite of the punishments bestowed by the heavenly powers. Perhaps in the solemnity of his last days Sidney thought the same of "the scene where Pyrocles watches the princesses bathing in the river Ladon," or the description of "Pyrocles' sensations on coming into close bodily contact with Philoclea, owing to the narrowness of the coach," or "the dalliance between the two lovers," [3] which Mr. Zandvoort cites to prove Sidney's "fondness for the sensual aspect of love" in the revised version as well as in the original. But if in these and similar passages beauty may be "apt to allure men to evill," the discriminating reader will not find the physical side of love described with quite so much gusto as Mr. Zandvoort imagines.

Certainly the sexual passion is represented as all but

1. The address "to the Reader" prefixed to the folios. Cf. *Works*, I, 524.
2. *Life of Sidney*, p. 16.
3. Zandvoort, p. 148. Cf. *Works*, I, 217 ff., 168, 307-308.

irresistible. Not only men and women in their youthful prime, but elderly kings, like Basilius and Plangus' father, matrons like Gynecia and Andromana, and persons as young as Palladius and Zelmane, all bow to the same sovereign authority, and all echo the prayer of Musidorus: "O thou celestial, or infernal spirit of Love, or what other heavẽly or hellish title thou list to have (for effects of both I finde in my selfe) have compassion of me."[1] Whatever love may be is largely an academic question. In any case, it responds less readily to our wills than fear, anger, joy, sorrow, and other passions, which the wise man, as Musidorus maintains so confidently before he meets Pamela, can control by reason.[2]

In its power over men's actions love bears some analogy to poetry, which "may not onely be abused, but . . . being abused by the reason of his sweete charming force, . . . can do more hurt then anie other armie of words."[3] The dangers may be illustrated by the passion of Erona for Antiphilus, of Plangus for Andromana, and of Gynecia for Pyrocles. Love tempts the virtuous Pyrocles and Musidorus into grave mistakes, causes Zelmane to die of grief, and drives Parthenia to suicide. From its power there is no escape in asceticism, for resistance only makes its expression the more destructive. Witness Erona, who is punished for having caused the naked statues and pictures of Cupid to be pulled down and defaced.[4] Witness also Basilius and Plangus' father. The one remains for many years a bachelor, the other a widower; and then each marries a woman much younger than himself. The queens are still in their prime when their husbands have reached old age. Gynecia is drawn irresistibly toward Pyrocles, Andromana toward both him and his cousin. Plangus' father allows his wife to govern his every action. Basilius' late marriage keeps the succession to the throne in doubt until

1. *Works*, I, 114.   2. Pages 77 ff.
3. III, 30.   4. I, 232.

the next heir has grown to manhood only to have his hopes dashed. If the examples of these kings mean anything, it is that sooner or later the resistance to love breaks down, and that from every point of view the surrender had better come early than late.

If asceticism is impracticable, unchastity is vicious. In women, of course, Sidney represents it as an offense of the first magnitude. Andromana and Baccha are utterly evil. Dido and the other victims of Pamphilus are to be pitied, but are not innocent. In Gynecia infidelity would have been a crime, while in her husband it is an absurd vice. In men unchastity is far less serious than in women. The noble Pamela has only loathing for Andromana, but speaks with pity of Plangus. "The errors in his nature were excused by the greenenes of his youth, which tooke all the fault upon it selfe." [1] Yet forbearance would have been better. Musidorus and Pyrocles can resist Andromana, even at the cost of imprisonment and the threat of worse, though she must have had physical charm to win both Plangus and his elderly father. Chastity is not a matter merely of prudence. Yet it brings a reward, as Pyrocles finds when he is able to tell Philoclea that he did not yield. Purity is the duty of women; for men it is the ideal.

But even for heroes the normal expression of love is physical. When, in the *New Arcadia*, Pyrocles begs his princess to "be gracious unto" him,[2] Sidney hints a disapproval only by Philoclea's resolute denial. Her modesty is admirable, but Pyrocles' ardor may be excused. The consummation of their love before marriage would be a matter not so much of right or wrong, as of better or worse. In the *Old Arcadia* it is described in language beautified with poetry and rhetorical colors. It is not wicked, but may easily appear so to other persons, as it did to Euarchus, and is, to say the least, extremely imprudent. Herr

1. Page 243.
2. Page 307.

Brie is right, I think, in saying that the lovers are portrayed as blameworthy, although he greatly exaggerates
the guilt.[1] Indeed, Philoclea's yielding to her lover, and
Pamela's flight from the kingdom are made all but inevitable by the arbitrary restrictions which their father
has placed upon them. With Basilius the chief fault lies,
as he is very ready to admit.[2] The love between his daughters and the two princes is wholly natural and fitting. If
thwarted, love will take its own course, but if allowed its
normal expression in marriage, it will be a power for good.
Where there is virtue, this dangerous passion may be
trusted.

In the last analysis, therefore, the responsibility lies
chiefly with the parents, not merely to prevent bad matches
and to encourage suitable ones, but also in a more general
way to raise their children in habits of virtue. Argalus and
Parthenia, Pyrocles and Philoclea, Musidorus and Pamela
have been thus educated. These lovers have no morbid
asceticism, but even the men have been continent until
they fall in love. Thereafter it is their ladies' task to im-
pose self-restraint upon them. To seek physical expression
of love before marriage is blameworthy, but is no great
dereliction from virtue. It is imprudent rather than
wicked, and should be viewed more charitably than by the
harsh laws of Arcadia. But though Sidney's ideal lovers
find the passion is not always to be resisted, yet in them
"that sweete and heavenly uniting of the myndes, w^{ch}
properly ys called Love, hathe no other knott but vertue."[3]

The words I have just quoted have a Platonic coloring,
as Herr Brie points out.[4] They are spoken, however, by no
mere theorist, but by Euarchus, a man of wide experience
in practical affairs, who, like Chaucer's Franklin, knows
how to reconcile idealism with common sense. Sidney's

---

1. *Sidneys Arcadia, Eine Studie zur Englischen Renaissance*, pp. 147 ff.
2. *Works*, IV, 388.   3. Page 379.
4. Page 155.

treatment of love suggests not the academic philosopher, but the gentleman, seeking to make noble and beautiful his actual conduct in the real world.

The same is true of all the teaching in the *Arcadia*. It has philosophic range and depth. Direct influence of Plato and Aristotle is often obvious to any reader of the romance who is familiar with the *Symposium*, the *Republic*, the *Ethics*, or the *Politics*. Perhaps further investigations will even justify the view of Herr Brie, that "for the first time in English literature the traditional medieval notions of 'Honor,' 'Truth,' 'Virtue,' and 'Love' are here consciously supplanted by a definite ethical system." [1] The deliberateness of Sidney's art lends support to this hypothesis. But however this may be, Sidney's emphasis is not chiefly upon philosophic theory. Love, marriage, the relations of young men and women to their parents, faithful dealing in word and act, the limits of friendship, what offenses ought to be forgotten, and what may justly be revenged — these matters, like the political problems which Sidney discusses, would be living realities to a young Elizabethan, passing from the control of tutors or parents to the opportunities and temptations of an active life at court or in the field. Sidney treats these topics with some fullness, and analyzes the appropriate virtues and the corresponding vices; but he writes less in the spirit of Plato and Aristotle than of Cicero and Castiglione, men of affairs whose minds were enriched with humanistic studies. Like them, he has little novelty of thought, but represents the best culture of his age, and is interested chiefly in the practical action befitting a gentleman.

With great justice, therefore, Greenlaw regards the *Arcadia* "as an 'historicall fiction,' a prose counterpart of the *Faerie Queene*, having for its object 'to fashion a gentleman or noble person in vertuous and gentle discipline,' and to portray 'a good governour and a vertuous man'." [2]

1. Page 120.   2. "Sidney's *Arcadia* as Elizabethan Allegory," p. 337.

Little objection can be made to this view, except that the *Arcadia*, unlike the *Faerie Queene*, is not an allegory, and that the didactic purpose is veiled in fiction.

Fulke Greville's view of the ethical and political lessons in Sidney's romance is much like Greenlaw's, but he understood better his friend's poetic art. In speaking of the *Arcadia*, he lays stress upon the value of its ideal examples as a guide of life.

In all these creatures of his making, his intent, and scope was, to turn the barren Philosophy precepts into pregnant Images of life; and in them, first on the Monarch's part, lively to represent the growth, state, and declination of Princes, change of Government, and lawes: vicissitudes of sedition, faction, succession, confederacies, plantations, with all other errors, or alterations in publique affaires. Then again in the subjects case; the state of favor, disfavor, prosperitie, adversity, emulation, quarrell, undertaking, retiring, hospitality, travail, and all other moodes of private fortunes, or misfortunes. In which traverses (I know) his purpose was to limn out such exact pictures, of every posture in the minde, that any man being forced, in the straines of this life, to pass through any straights, or latitudes of good, or ill fortune might (as in a glasse) see how to set a good countenance upon all the discountenances of adversitie, and a stay upon the exorbitant smilings of chance.[1]

This is one aspect of the truth, which deserves emphasis because it is often overlooked. On the other hand, Sidney's works

were scribled rather as pamphlets, for entertainment of time, and friends, than any accompt of himself to the world. . . . But the truth is: his end was not writing, even while he wrote; nor his knowledge moulded for tables, or schooles; but both his wit, and understanding bent upon his heart, to make himself and others, not in words or opinion, but in life, and action, good and great.[2]

1. Greville, *Life of Sidney*, pp. 15–16.
2. Pages 17–18.

In this "Architectonical art," continues Greville, Sidney "was such a master" that

> into what Action soever he came last at the first, he became first at the last: the whole managing of the business, not by usurpation, or violence, but (as it were) by right, and acknowledgment, falling into his hands, as into a naturall Center.
> By which onely commendable monopolie of alluring, and improving men, looke how the sunn drawes all windes after it in fair weather: so did the influence of this spirit draw mens affections and undertakings to depend upon him.[1]

Allowing for exaggeration in Greville's eulogy of a friend long dead, and for the grave and anxious mood of the Stuart era in which he wrote, one finds in his account as good a description as an elderly man could be expected to give of a book conceived in the ardor of youth, and in the "spacious times of great Elizabeth" when men exulted in the beauty of life. The *Arcadia*, as he says, has a serious purpose, and contains many definite lessons about public and private affairs. But the author's interest is "in life and action," rather than in "knowledge moulded for schools"; and his method of teaching men, whether in books or in personal relations, is to "allure" them with "pregnant images."

If taken alone, however, Fulke Greville's interpretation is misleading. Perhaps in reaction against a current tendency to view the work merely as a delightful tale, he has not mentioned the love story, and has omitted to say that the poet conceals his art.

The *Arcadia* is not a treatise about public and private virtue. Still less is it an idle tale, composed "to beguile a summer's holiday." Nor is it merely a composite work of varied texture, as Mr. Zandvoort suggests. It is an heroic poem which makes noble conduct beautiful. In both ver-

1. Page 18.

sions, to be sure, the lessons are numerous and quite as definite as is required by Sidney's theory. In the first draft, however, they are to be found in theoretical discussions no less than in the deeds of the characters and in their fates. Only in the revised work do the examples of men in action assume the importance that they have in the *Defence of Poesie*. The teaching is especially plain in the narrative of events prior to the main story, where time after time it is made clear by comparison or contrast. In the fable, too, the same method is often used, notably in the account of Amphialus; and at all times we judge men's behavior by the ideal standards which are so unmistakable in the episodes. In fact, just as these digressions help us to understand the course of events in the main action, so do they enable us to view the events from the author's ethical point of view. The teaching is deliberate, but even in the episodes it is unobtrusive; and to call the *Arcadia* a treatise is to overlook its pervading beauty. Not merely are there glowing passages, like the description of the princesses bathing in the river Ladon, which appear to exist for their own sake. Consider the very nature of some of the instructive examples — tact in Strephon and Claius; hospitality in Kalander; noble horsemanship in Musidorus; personal beauty not only in ladies but in men, and most notably in one of such valor as Pyrocles; courtesy in Amphialus; poetical skill in heroes and shepherds generally. To delight in those "pregnant images" one must regard life not only as a moral task, but as an art. Throughout the *Arcadia* an underlying idea is that of decorum, the fine instinct for fitness which requires action to be wise and good, of course, yet also beautiful.

The teaching, moreover, though often clear and definite, tends to be fused into the very substance of the story. To be sure, the *Arcadia* is not purely a work of fiction with ethical seriousness. The fusion of elements is not complete, for Sidney's art is of the Renaissance. The style, as we have seen in an earlier chapter, is more ornate, and the episodes are longer and more numerous, than is consistent with classical taste; but one who finds in the work only variety and rich excess has overlooked its design and its close adherence to critical law as understood in the sixteenth century. In the same way, the lessons are more explicit than Aristotle would have approved, just as the allusions to actual persons are a little more definite than in purer forms of art; but these elements could be dropped out of the *Arcadia* without altering its essential character. It would still show noble conduct as beautiful, and so would inflame "the minde with desire to bee woorthie." [1] The lessons, like the rhetorical colors, the episodes, and the personal allusions, are additions to something more fundamental. The work is tending to become, therefore, not only in form, but in ethical and imaginative quality, an heroic poem, "an imitation of men in action," giving "the illusion of a higher reality." It cannot easily be described in the language of Aristotle or of modern criticism, but with the author's own principles it is in complete harmony. Implicit in its fine, though immature, art there is a view of life both heroic and beautiful. And yet the author does not take himself too seriously.

Hee commeth to you with words set in delightfull proportion, either accompanied with, or prepared for the well enchanting skill of *Musicke*, and with a tale forsooth he commeth unto you, with a tale, which holdeth children from play, and olde men from the Chimney corner; and pretending no more, doth intend the winning of the minde from wickednes to vertue. [2]

1. *Works*, III, 25.
2. Page 20.

CHAPTER VIII

Sprezzatura

THROUGHOUT the present study I have not tried to make a complete analysis of Sidney's ideas, or to settle questions of what is intrinsically good and bad in his art. My endeavor has been to learn the spirit in which he worked. On a superficial examination, it is easy to regard *Astrophel and Stella* as the story of a headlong passion, the *Defence of Poesie* as an eager endorsement of the newest critical ideas, and the *Arcadia* as the recreation of a summer's holiday; and from the apparent differences of mood and treatment, it is easy to conclude that Sidney troubled little about consistency, and never regarded his literary work as anything "more than a pleasant pastime." [1] His habitual disparagement of his writings appears to give this interpretation the final proof. And yet the view, however plausible, cannot be reconciled with the facts.

Far from proving a lack of deep interest, Sidney's disparagement of his work is but an example of *sprezzatura*, the courtly grace which conceals a sober purpose and is, indeed, the mark of consummate artistry. The servant of a prince could not afford to be thought chiefly a poet; but in daily conduct he needed the artist's fine tact, and Sidney in particular shows an eagerness and poise which made him by nature a poet, together with an earnestness which would have made it difficult for him to regard his compositions merely as an agreeable pastime.

1. H. R. Fox Bourne, *Sir Philip Sidney*, 1891, p. 255.

Nor does the variety of his work reveal any inconsistency. The sonnets raise so many problems of their own, that they have hitherto been omitted from the present study. But the *Arcadia* and the *Defence of Poesie* reveal at every point a conscious art, and are very closely related. The one, a Ciceronian oration in form, follows with studious care the rules elaborated by ancient rhetoricians, and yet conceals its deliberate method in an air of urbane nonchalance. The other follows the principles laid down in the *Defence* and in the Italian criticism on which that work is based. In narrative technique, and in its union of central design with sumptuous adornment by episode or rhetorical figure, it conforms to Minturno's laws for an heroic poem; while in its want of epic verse and of supernatural machinery it reflects the same point of view as the *Defence*. In ethical and imaginative quality, moreover, the *Arcadia* is in entire harmony with the author's doctrine of "delightful teaching" through example. But although the work has educational value, it is to be regarded not as a solemn treatise, but as a work of art, seeking to allure men from vice to virtue by what appears to be only a tale. The *Arcadia* and the *Defence of Poesie* belong together; for the one exemplifies what the other states as theory, and both reveal the master craftsman, inspired by a serious purpose, mindful of critical law, but concealing his art.

These remarks apply, however, only to the *Arcadia* in its revised form. The earlier version frequently disregards both Minturno's rules for an heroic poem, and Sidney's theory of example. Not the *Old Arcadia*, but the *New* belongs to the same period of composition as the *Defence of Poesie*. Some time after completing his original version in 1580 or 1581, Sidney must have undertaken a more thorough study of criticism than he had hitherto attempted, a study which led him to set before his countrymen an epitome of the best contemporary thought about literature, and to recast his pastoral romance as an heroic poem.

Here is presumptive evidence that the *Defence*, written perhaps in 1583, is not essentially a reply to Gosson, whose *School of Abuse* had been published in 1579; and that it need not be supposed to represent the joint opinions of Sidney and Spenser, whose personal contact, whether intimate or not, belongs likewise to the earlier period.

More important for our purpose is the evidence of how Sidney took up his creative work. He began without a mature theory, and learned by experience. Whether the original stimulus came from his dissatisfaction over the proposed marriage of Elizabeth to a French prince, or from his delight in Montemayor's *Diana* or the *Æthiopian History*, we do not know. In any case, his imagination was on fire. "In summe, a young head, not so well stayed as I would it were, (and shall be when God will) having many many fancies begotten in it, if it had not ben in some way delivered, would have growen a monster, & more sorie might I be that they came in, then that they gat out." [1] Only after he has finished his first draft, and found himself "somewhat awry," does he "bende to the right use both of matter and manner." [2]

Fundamental in Sidney's literary work, therefore, is a restless creative energy. His thirst for action, we must believe, appears in the kaleidoscopic variety of incident in the *New Arcadia*; just as in the elaborate conceits and intricate plots there appears a delight in intellectual dexterity. His is not merely a romanticism of adventure. Well might he say,

> Peace foolish wit, with wit my wit is marde. [3]

Yet with all his spontaneity Sidney has a reverence for established form. His medium for argument and exposition is the ancient oration; for poetic feeling it is the Pe-

---

1. Sidney, *Complete Works*, ed. Feuillerat, Cambridge English Classics, 1912–1926, I, 3.
2. III, 43.   3. II, 256.

trarchan sonnet sequence — conventional forms which he
has learned to handle with such easy mastery that at times
they seem but the inevitable expression of his thought.
Even in the *Old Arcadia* he follows models like Heliodorus
and Montemayor, and his narrative is anything but formless. And for the poems in both versions of the work he has
used measures which, in spite of their extraordinary variety, are nearly all authorized by ancient or modern custom. Sidney loved novelty, but he felt no compelling urge
to give his art such individuality of form as may be found
in the work of Shelley, Browning, or Swinburne. Even the
ornate style and grandiose structure of the *Arcadia* do no
violence to the most classical opinion of his age. The
sources of his philosophy, whether they are in Plato and
Aristotle, in Cicero and Castiglione, in Protestant Christianity, or in the traditions of chivalry, lie along the beaten
highways of human culture. In thought, and in art, Sidney, eager child of the Renaissance as he was, has learned
to discipline his nature in the school of an experience far
wider than his own.

Regard for law is a quality of classic art. The passions
for adventure and for mental activity have been described
as romanticism of action and of the intellect. Is the classic
or the romantic quality deeper in Sidney's courtly temper?

We cannot answer the question without defining the
terms. Since no definition has thus far won general approval, none that I can offer is likely to meet a better fate.
All I can hope is to attach some meaning to the terms, and
to make that meaning clear.

A classicist, then, I take to be one who in life and in art
shows an instinct for what is central in human experience.
His ideas are representative of "the best that has been
thought and said." His form is authorized by tradition, or
fixes a mode of expression for men who come after. A
romanticist I take to be one who in life and in art shows an
instinct for what is highly individual, in disregard of the

conventions established by experience. His ideas and his form are likely to be peculiarly his own. To illustrate: Lamb and Addison have equally a fondness for odd characters. But Addison asks us to regard Sir Roger de Coverley from the point of view of a humane and cultivated man of the world, and to measure his behavior by that norm. Lamb asks us to consider Mrs. Battle simply as an interesting fellow-creature, and not to judge her at all. So, too, in their form — Lamb rebelled against convention, Addison fixed it.

No one need be alarmed lest Sir Philip Sidney turn out to be a Queen Anne wit. And yet the common view, that his classicism is but theoretical and is belied by his literary practice, cannot be accepted. His art is in accord with his doctrine. The one is not purely romantic, nor the other purely classic. Is it useful to describe Sidney merely as a romanticist?

In the *Arcadia* not merely are the elements which seem least Greek quite in harmony with the taste even of the best interpreters of Aristotle known to Sidney. Not merely is the work infused with humane learning. Like Addison's essays, it looks to the future. Written in a form less fully matured by long tradition than the sonnets or the *Defence of Poesie*, the *Arcadia* could not endure. And yet its popularity continued for seventy-five years. In substance it foreshadows the seventeenth-century romances, in style the school of conceits. But its chief significance lies elsewhere. Though a failure,* it shows Sidney groping toward a fiction written in a prose at once elevated and free from affectation, an ideal eventually to be made actual by Fielding and Thackeray. Again, the great experiment, conceived as an heroic poem, reaches out not only toward *Tom Jones*, but toward *Paradise Lost*. In short, the *Arcadia* does more than reflect the tastes of one generation. The age was the springtime of English literature, and the seeds not only of the romances, the school of conceits, and the grand prose-poetry of the seventeenth century, but also of classicism, of the novel, and of the greatest modern epic, all found root in Sidney's fiction, and flourished side by side. If the instinct for what is permanent is the mark of the classic temper, then Sidney's grasp of some of the enduring tendencies in English literature makes the classic elements in his art more important than has often been recognized.

Again, experience has proved the essay to be a better medium for thought than a feigned narrative can be; it has shown personalities to be more interesting than type characters, and Aristotle's idea of probability to be more satisfying in art than the conception of a golden world governed by poetic justice. Considered absolutely, therefore, the *Arcadia* is anything but a classic. Considered as indicating the currents of literature, however, it shows a pronounced tendency away from allegory in the direction not of art for art's sake, but of poetry in which the ethical impression is one with the imaginative. The book fails of being a masterpiece, not because the author did not regard it seriously, but largely because his idea of prose fiction had not been tested and clarified by a long tradition. Had Sidney written when the novel was a mature literary form, his love of action, interest in character, ready invention, conscious artistry, and ethical temper might well have made the *Arcadia* one of the supreme classics of English fiction. For of his literary genius I think there can be no doubt.

If Sidney could never have been an Augustan, he seems equally remote from some of the nineteenth-century poets who have claimed kinship with him. Somehow, one finds it hard to imagine him announcing to mankind his "passion for reforming the world." That is not the language of the courtier, nor is it the mood. The man of the world may hope to make his countrymen more civilized by introducing them to the best traditions of thought about politics, ethics, or poetry, and by helping to create a literature worthy the leisure of thoughtful men. He may even repre-

sent the final stage in such an educational movement as the
New Learning, and be a better humanist than Ascham or
Elyot. But his air of nonchalance is no mere affectation of
false modesty. It is the easy grace of one who has mastered the art of life. Fundamentally serious, loving honor
in any true form, ever mindful of the law of decorum, the
ideal courtier attaches no monstrous importance to himself or to his work. Yet his devotion is none the less real
because he keeps a sense of proportion.

This courtly temper helps us to understand the problem
with which we set out: how the same man could produce
works so different one from another as the three on which
Sidney's fame rests, and yet be the trusted friend of Walsingham and William the Silent. A key alike to his literary
work and to his personal character is to be found in the
urbane quality of *sprezzatura*. In an earlier chapter we
have recognized it in the *Defence of Poesie*. Our task will
be complete if we find it to be significant also in the *Arcadia*
and in *Astrophel and Stella*.

In the *Arcadia* the fundamental seriousness is to be seen
in the ethical tone, the heroic adventures, the tragedies
which mark the episodes and the career of Amphialus.
Yet the crowded pageantry, the lavish wealth of incident
and character, the passages of sheer beauty give it an exuberant spontaneity, a movement and color which is natural
enough to find in a knight who won fame in the Elizabethan tournament. With all this earnestness and vitality
there is a striking sophistication. Irony lurks in scattered
sentences, or comes into the open in scenes like those where
Musidorus confesses the power of love, or Phalantus holds
a tourney in behalf of Artesia.

The element of comedy in Sidney's art is worth particular emphasis.

When Dametas is betrayed into a victory over Clinias,
when the Arcadian rioters awkwardly allow themselves to
be cut to pieces, or when Miso tumbles out of a tree at a

word from her father, whom she takes for a god, "there is physical absurdity," as Dr. S. L. Wolff observes, "that almost amounts to horseplay." [1] Yet even here Sidney preserves a courtly sense of fitness. Unless we ought to pity the rascals who are slain for attacking their king and queen, has he not avoided "the great faulte . . . forbidden plainly by *Aristotle*" of stirring "laughter in sinfull things, which are rather execrable then ridiculous: or in miserable, which are rather to be pitied then scorned"? [2] "Wee laugh at deformed creatures, wherein certainly wee cannot delight." [3] Witness the marvelous ugliness of Mopsa,[4] or her father's efforts to emulate a prince's skill in horsemanship.[5] Even the coarser fun of the *Arcadia* has in it the element of incongruity which for Sidney is the occasion of laughter.

There is more refined humor in some of the comic characters. Is not Phalantus "a busie loving Courtier," Dametas "a hartlesse threatning" coward, Basilius "a selfwise seeming" old gentleman? Are not Pyrocles and Musidorus "wry transformed" [6] by love? The highborn personages in particular afford "both delight and laughter: for the representing of so straunge a power in Love, procures delight, and the scornefulnesse of the action, stirreth laughter." [7]

Whole scenes of the *Arcadia* illustrate this kind of comedy. Mention has been made of Phalantus' tournament. Two other cases in point, if I am not mistaken, are the incident of the lion and the bear, and the lovers' quarrel between Pamela and Musidorus, by which the prince is driven almost to madness. Like the tournament, of course, these are stock themes of romance; and like it, they are handled with a touch of irony.

The lion and the bear are rather more formidable in the

1. *The Greek Romances in Elizabethan Prose Fiction*, Columbia University Studies in Comparative Literature, 1912, p. 331.
2. *Works*, III, 41.
3. Page 40.
4. I, 21.
5. Page 179.
6. Cf. III, 41.
7. Page 40.

Old Arcadia than in the *New*. Originally the lion "gave a sore wounde to the lefte shoulder of *Cleophila* [Pyrocles]: And mortall yt woulde have bene, had not the Deathe wounde hee receyved, allredy, taken away the greatest effect of his force." [1] Quite naturally, Gynecia and her daughter applied to the wound "so precyous a balme, as all the heate and payne was asswaged with aparant hope of some amendement." [1] In the new version, "al the Liõ could do, was with his paw to teare of the mantle and sleeve of *Zelmane*, with a little scratch, rather then a wound"; [2] and though Queen Gynecia "found it was indeed of no great importance: yet applied she a pretious baulme unto it, of power to heale a greater griefe." [3]

By these changes the tone of the whole passage has been made both lighter and more consistent. In the *Old Arcadia* the wound was severe, "but yt was sporte to see howe in one instant bothe *Basilius* & *Ginecia* (like a Father and Mother to a beloved Chylde) came ronning to see the wounde of *Cleophila*, into what rages *Basilius* grewe, and what teares *Ginecia* spent." [4] There are many passages, too, of coarser humor, and the whole tone of the scene is hardly consistent with the severity of Pyrocles' injury. In the revision, therefore, Sidney reduces the wound to a mere scratch, mindful perhaps of those "mongrell Tragicomedies" which so unskilfully "matche horne Pipes and Funeralls." [5] The whole incident is now but a sudden scare, to be treated with courtly irony. It is all very well to have a few romantic exploits for our heroes, and lions and bears will serve the purpose. But meanwhile Pyrocles and Musidorus, like Englishmen who encountered Spain, have soon to face realities — war, tyranny, or imprisonment — and their ladies are to endure tortures worthy of the Inquisition.

---

1. IV, 43.   2. I, 120.
3. Page 121.   4. IV, 45.
5. III, 39–40.

In this sophisticated temper Sidney describes the lovers' quarrel between Pamela and Musidorus. The mock-heroic tone is apparent to anyone with a sense of humor.

It was not an amazement, it was not a sorrow, but it was even a death, which then laid hold of *Dorus*: which certainly at that instant would have killed him, but that the feare to tary longer in her presence (contrary to her cōmandement) gave him life to cary himselfe away frō her sight, and to run into the woods, where, throwing himselfe downe at the foot of a tree, he did not fall to lamentation (for that proceeded of pitying) or grieving for himselfe (which he did no way) but to curses of his life, as one that detested himselfe. . . . And so remained he two dayes in the woods, disdaining to give his bodie food, or his mind comfort, loving in himselfe nothing, but the love of her. And indeed that love onely strave with the fury of his anguish, telling it, that if it destroyed *Dorus*, it should also destroy the image of her that lived in *Dorus*: and when the thought of that was crept in unto him, it begā to win of him some cōpassion to the shrine of the image, & to bewaile not for himselfe (whō he hated) but that so notable a love should perish. Thē began he onely so farre to wish his owne good, as that *Pamela* might pardon him the fault, though not the punishment: & the uttermost height he aspired unto, was, that after his death, she might yet pittie his error, and know that it proceeded of love, and not of boldnesse.[1]

The error which inspired a prince with such remorse as to drive him to despair and almost to madness, like Orlando and Tristram before him, is described in language suitably impressive: "The sudden occasion called Love . . . made the too-much loving *Dorus* take her in his armes, offering to kisse her, and, as it were, to establish a trophee of his victorie."[2] Never did Astrophel,

> Biting his truant pen, beating himself for spite,

suffer more torments for Stella than Musidorus when he composed his letter of apology. "Pen did never more

1. I, 355–356.   2. Page 355.

quakingly performe his office; never was paper more double moistned with inke & teares; never words more slowly maried together, & never the *Muses* more tired." [1] One wonders if Stella ever faced a more tragic dilemma than Pamela.

When she saw the letter, her hart gave her from whence it came. And therefore . . . she went away from it, as if it had bin a contagious garment of an infected person: and yet was not long away, but that she wished she had read it, though she were loth to reade it. Shall I (said she) second his boldnesse so farre, as to reade his presumptuous letters? And yet (said she) he sees me not[,] to growe the bolder thereby: And how can I tell, whether they be presumptuous? [2]

The chivalrous author, one fears, is laughing at the lady.

Finespun reasoning, mad despair, exploits against wild beasts — these themes of romantic love stories Sidney admits to his heroic poem when he excludes the enchanters, flying horses, dragons, and yet greater marvels. But the charming absurdity is not lost upon him. Solemn romanticists have claimed him for their own, partly on the ground that he knew men whose hearts were "moved to the exercise of courtesie, liberalitie, and especially courage," "even with reading *Amadis de gaule*, which God knoweth, wanteth much of a perfect *Poesie*." [3] Earnest folk can overlook urbane condescension.

Sidney's best comedy, giving delight without always provoking laughter, is particularly suited to the courtly mood. In Pamela's noble indignation at a proffered kiss, in Musidorus' agony of contrition, in the lovesick queen's lavishing a precious ointment on a dear youth's scratched shoulder, in the airs which Basilius assumes before his Amazon, is there not abundant occasion of delight for those ladies and gentlemen who are visited by the comic spirit? Laughter may come, "but it will be of the order of the smile, finely tempered, showing sunlight of the mind, mental richness rather than noisy enormity." [1] Whenever royal lovers "wax out of proportion, overblown, affected, pretentious, bombastical, . . . self-deceived or hoodwinked, . . . drifting into vanities, congregating in absurdities, planning shortsightedly, plotting dementedly," the author of the *Arcadia* "will look humanely malign," [2] and shower them with his ridicule.

His humor then, if rarely subtle, and frequently quite obvious, is not always the "*macabre* fun" which Mr. Mario Praz [3] finds so little to his taste. The mocking irony is not the prevailing mood, to be sure, and appears but occasionally in scenes or scattered phrases, to lighten the general tone of earnestness. In the *Old Arcadia* the author has not always a sure and fine touch. In the new version, however, he has become the master of an urbane art, conceived with critical insight, for which the name of high comedy may not be too pretentious. It is *par excellence* the art of a well-bred society. Without it the *Arcadia*, for all its heroism, tragedy, and sober morality, its love stories, and its lyric exuberance, would be no adequate reflection of the courtly spirit. Chiefly in the passages of comic irony does Sidney show the light touch of the skilled artist and the perfect courtier.

In *Astrophel and Stella*, as in the *Arcadia*, he reveals a temper at once serious and urbane.

The vexed problem of the biographical value of the sonnets is far too complex for me to enter into. Perhaps they are not to be taken too literally, for, as the author warns us, "the *Poet* never maketh any Circles about your imaginatiõ, to conjure you to beleeve for true, what he writeth." [4] Or perhaps the sonnets relate the story of a

1. George Meredith, "Essay on Comedy," *Works*, XXIII (1910), 46.
2. Page 47.
3. "Sidney's Original *Arcadia*," *The London Mercury*, XV (March, 1927), 512 f.   4. *Works*, III, 29.

real tragedy, "a profoundly moving tale, . . . adorned and
heightened as it is by every consideration of love and passion, of virtue, and frailty, and heart-breaking sympathy,
of honour, and man's divine destiny." [1] What I would
emphasize in *Astrophel and Stella* is that the somberness of
the tone is lightened here and there with banter and
courtly compliment. Whatever view we take of the work
as a whole, these qualities compel us to modify the usual
interpretation of several particular sonnets.

The forty-eighth, for example, begins in the language of
reverent devotion which appears to justify John Addington
Symonds [2] in taking it seriously:

> Soules joy, bend not those morning starres from me,
> Where vertue is made strong by beauties might.

The passion would seem real enough were it not for the
three concluding lines.

> Yet since my death-wound is already got,
> Deere killer, spare not *thy* sweete cruell shot,
> A kind of grace it is to slaye with speede. [3]

Sidney or Lady Rich must have been wonderfully lacking
in humor to take this courtly speech for the language of the
heart. I suspect it is the modern critics who lack humor.
By taking the sonnet too seriously, moreover, they have
missed the finish and deftness of Sidney's art. How could
one beg more gracefully for a glance from a lady's eyes?

Equally light in touch is the sixty-third sonnet. Stella,

> Least once should not be heard, twise said, "No, no."

Hence the triumphant cry of Astrophel:

1. *The Lyric Poems of Sir Philip Sidney*, ed. Ernest Rhys, 1895, pp. xxii-
xxiii.

2. *Sir Philip Sidney*, English Men of Letters, 1886, p. 133.

3. *Works*, II, 261. Here and in all my quotations from *Astrophel*, I correct
the text of the first quarto from M. Feuillerat's list of variant readings, pp. 372 ff.

Sing then, my Muse, now *Io Pean* sing,

.   .   .   .

For Grammer sayes (to Grammer who sayes nay)
That in one speech, two negatives affirme.[1]

No wonder he shifts his measure and breaks into song.[2]
Still clearer is the tone of banter in the group of sonnets
which begins with the seventy-third. Stella is angry

because a sugred kisse
In sport I suckt, while she a sleepe did lye.

.   .   .   .

O heavenly Foole, thy most kisse worthy face
Anger invests with such a lovely grace,
That Angers selfe I needes must kisse againe.[3]

Of this teasing, playful speech, Sidney's latest biographer
can remark, "Desire is recalled by a kiss, stolen while
Stella was sleeping, but repeated when she woke."[4]
The theme introduced in the seventy-third sonnet is
continued through a number of others, and is handled in
the same spirit. Sidney is puzzled to see why he is able to
write verse which "best wittes doth please."

Gesse we the cause. What is it thus? fie no.
Or so? much lesse. How then? sure thus it is;
My lips are sweet inspir'd with *Stellas* kisse.[5]

In one octave, Astrophel sings the praises of Stella's
"sweet swelling lip," then breaks off, for

my mouth will stay,
Loathing all lyes, doubting this flattrie is;
And no spurre can his restie race renewe,
Without how farre this praise is short of you,
Sweete lipp, you teach my mouth with one sweete kisse.[6]

---

1. Pages 267, 377. The punctuation is mine.
2. Cf. pp. 286, 377.
3. Pages 271, 378.
4. Mona Wilson, *Sir Philip Sidney*, 1931, p. 190.
5. *Works*, II, 272, 378.
6. Pages 274, 379. The punctuation is mine.

Stella thinks her kiss has been sufficiently celebrated, and imposes silence.

> But my heart burnes, I cannot silent be;
> Then since, deare life, you faine would have me peace,
>   And I (mad with delight) want wit to cease,
>   Stop you my mouth with still, still kissing me.[1]

So clear is the sportive mood in these clever sonnets that one suspects its presence in others of the sequence. Stella can pity the lovers in fiction.

> Than thinke my *Deere*, that you in me do reed
>   Of Lovers ruine some sad Tragædie:
>   I am not I, pittie the tale of me.[2]

Is this a cry from the heart? In the well-known forty-first sonnet Sidney finds the true cause for his victory in the tiltyard is that

> *Stella* lookt on, and from her heavenly face,
> Sent forth her beames.[3]

If Sidney loved her as Launcelot loved Guinevere, doubtless he meant this chivalric language to be taken literally. To me it seems but a graceful compliment. Consider, too, the beautiful sonnet which in the view of John Addington Symonds, "preludes, with splendid melancholy, to a new and deeper phase of passion." [4]

> With how sad steps, ô Moone, thou clim'st the skyes,
> How silently, and with how wanne a face.
> What, may it be that even in heavenly place,
> That busie Archer his sharpe Arrowes tryes?
> Sure if that long-with-love-acquainted eyes
>   Can judge of love, thou feelst a Lovers case,
>   I reade it in thy lookes; thy languisht grace,

---

1. Pages 275, 379. The punctuation is mine.
2. Pages 260, 376. Cf. Symonds, p. 133.
3. *Works*, II, 259.
4. Page 131.

To mee that feele the like, thy state discries.
Then even of fellowship, ô Moone, tell me,
Is constant love deemde there but want of wit?
Are beauties there, as proude as heere they be?
Doe they above, love to be lov'd, and yet
    Those Lovers scorne, whom that love doth possesse?
Doe they call vertue there ungratefulnesse? [1]

Symonds' interpretation is no doubt a possible one, and
if in reading these haunting lines we imagine Sidney consumed with a hopeless passion, we do indeed find here his
characteristic earnestness. But we miss the polite ridicule
of ladies' foibles, the habit of smiling at lovers' ways, the
playful fancy; we miss, in short, the touch of irony so apparent in the *Arcadia*, the consummate grace of the artist.
To me this quality is one of the greatest beauties in Sidney's poetry, and its loss can hardly be compensated for
by the romantic legend of an enthralling passion.

Some of the sonnets, I confess, seem to me very hard to
interpret except as a plain utterance of personal feeling.
A notable example is the thirty-third. A number of others
strike a note at least of somber eloquence, and some are
set to martial music. It may not be too much to say, with
Miss Wilson, "The whole nature of the lover, by turns
tender, sensual, chivalrous, contemplative, passionate, and
playful, is laid bare." [2] Sidney may have loved Penelope
Rich. But if so, he preserved a sense of proportion somewhat better than lovers are reputed to do. The neatly
turned compliments, the clever twists of reasoning, the
teasing playfulness, the occasional touches of urbane irony,
all reveal the courtly temper which we have learned to
recognize in the *Arcadia*.

The same mood, as we have seen, characterizes the *Defence of Poesie*, where the expression of ardent conviction
is saved from bombast by a sense of humor and an instinct

1. *Works*, II, 255, 375. The punctuation is mine.
2. *Sir Philip Sidney*, p. 203.

for what is fit. Sidney's career shows a like union of courtly qualities. He sets out on a voyage to the New World with Sir Francis Drake, audaciously flouts the queen's messengers, but yields at last without awkwardness, and gracefully ends the incident with a speech to Drake's companions, strengthening them in devotion to their enterprise. Ardor and self-control, the spirit of adventure and the worldly wisdom of the Renaissance, earnest conviction and high endeavor concealed in an air of nonchalance, this courtly ideal was realized by no one in the sixteenth century more fully than by Sir Philip Sidney.

To describe him as wholly a romanticist is absurd, though with his urbanity he has the generous excess of youth and of the Elizabethan era. It is equally absurd to regard him as a would-be man of action who whiled away his leisure hours by merely dabbling in literature. Nor was he chiefly a philosopher. He was a man of his own times, responsive to great political and moral issues, and yet alive to beauty; a man of the world whose enthusiasm and fine tact made him a poet to the depths of his nature. His literary work has not the moral passion of Donne's religious poetry. He was no Milton, dreaming of an heroic poem which his "countrymen would not willingly let die." He was not a seer, but a "maker," a poet of this world, though mindful of another. His most ambitious work is an experiment, and later times have found its form unsatisfactory. Yet an effort so eager, an art so consciously guided by critical law, possessing so often grace and finality, and an achievement which after all has been so enduring, show Sidney to have been a craftsman as devoted as almost any in English literature.

His chief occupation being statesmanship and soldiery, we of today instinctively feel that in other kinds of endeavor he must have been somewhat of a dilettante. We forget the times in which he lived, when one man could be great in many endeavors. Sidney's activities were so

varied that he could look at his writings more objectively
and could attach less value to them than can a professional
poet like Wordsworth. But he was conscious of high literary endowment, and sought like every gifted person to
exercise his powers; like every courtier he wished to excel
the "makers" in their own art. And if fashion, prompted
by the danger of merciless ridicule, ordained that Sidney
should not appear too seriously occupied with literature,
yet he would have agreed with a greater poet who lived in
the expansive Elizabethan times and who, like him, looked
for guidance to the traditions of human culture:

> Although to write be lesser than to do,
> It is the next deed, and a great one too.[1]

1. Ben Jonson, "Epigram XCV, To Sir Henry Savile," *Works*, ed. Gifford
and Cunningham, 1875, VIII, 199.

APPENDIX

Summary of the Plot of the *Arcadia*

THE FIRST BOOK

Ch. 1   The shepherds Strephon and Claius, warm friends though each is devoted to the shepherdess Urania, suddenly cut off their talk of her to rescue a young man (Musidorus) from the sea. Together with him they set out to find his cousin Pyrocles. The sudden appearance of a pirate ship prevents their rescuing him.

Ch. 2   The shepherds befriend Musidorus and take him out of Laconia (where there is civil war between the Helots and the gentlemen) into Arcadia, to the hospitable gentleman Kalander, who develops a fatherly love toward him during Musidorus' six weeks' illness. Musidorus goes by the assumed name of Palladius.

Ch. 3   After his recovery Kalander gives him an account of Arcadia. "The sweetness of the air" and the "well-tempered minds of the people" would remind Sidney's first readers of England under Elizabeth. The elderly king Basilius is remarkably beloved by his subjects. He and his queen Gynecia, a forceful woman much younger than he, have two beautiful daughters. Pamela, the elder, has her mother's wisdom and force without her violent temperament. Her sister Philoclea is beloved for a disarming lack of haughtiness and for the sweetness of her nature.

Ch. 4   Recently Basilius has taken a strange fancy to Dametas, a doltish country fellow whom he admires for his blunt ways. He has actually placed the princesses under the care of this ignorant boor. The king himself has gone into temporary retirement, placing the government in the hands of a regent, the able and loyal Philanax. This nobleman has protested with deference but great frankness against both the king's decision to go into retirement and to make Dametas a man of influence. Basilius' actions have bewildered his subjects and have given rise to rumors of danger from his able and valiant nephew Amphialus. Changing the subject, Kalander observes that everyone in Arcadia, from the highest to the lowest, is given to making songs and dialogues in metre.

Ch. 5   Kalander, on receiving bad news, excuses himself. His steward tells Musidorus that Kalander's son Clitophon has been captured in Lacedemon by the Helots in their war against the gentlemen. Musidorus is alarmed for Pyrocles (who has assumed the name Daiphantus). Clitophon, going to the aid of his friend Argalus, has been captured by the Helots.

     Argalus, Queen Gynecia's cousin, met Parthenia and both fell in love. Her mother preferred the proud, stubbornly stout Demagoras of Laconia. After the mother's death, Demagoras rubbed horrible poison on Parthenia's face, to destroy her beauty. Argalus desires still to marry her, but she refuses and has hidden herself. Demagoras became the leader of the Helots. Argalus killed him to avenge Parthenia, and has been captured by the Helots. Clitophon, seeking to rescue him, has also been captured.

Ch. 6   Musidorus encourages Kalander to rescue Clitophon by force. Since the death of Demagoras, the Helots have gained a new and valiant young leader. Kalander's followers, at Musidorus' suggestion, disguise themselves as rebellious peasants going to the aid of the Helots, and thus gain the advantage in the battle. The Helot's young leader, "Daiphantus" returns. His single combat with Musidorus ends in their mutual recognition and the reunion of Clitophon and Kalander.

Ch. 7   "Daiphantus" (Pyrocles) establishes freedom for the Helots and a secure peace with their former masters. Kalander
and Clitophon return home, taking with them Argalus,
"Daiphantus," and "Palladius" (Musidorus). At Kalander's
house a message is brought to him from Queen Helen of
Corinth about a young noblewoman, a "cousin" of Parthenia,
whose death she reports. Parthenia had told her to offer herself in marriage to Argalus. With great courtesy he refuses.
Parthenia then reveals herself, her beauty almost wholly
restored by Queen Helen's physician.

Ch. 8   Musidorus and Pyrocles recount to one another their adventures since their shipwreck. Argalus and Parthenia are
married.

Ch. 9   Musidorus finds a strange alteration in Pyrocles, and urges
the life of honorable action. To his dismay, he finds his
cousin is in love. Kalander invites them to a stag hunt.

Ch. 10   During the hunt, Pyrocles disappears. "Palladius" and
Clitophon set out to find him. As they pause to rest, Clitophon
discovers scattered pieces of armor which he recognizes as
belonging to his cousin Amphialus. "Palladius" gathers the
pieces and puts them on, hoping in that way to learn news of
the famous Amphialus. They are attacked by horsemen whom
they kill or incapacitate. They encounter Queen Helen who
takes "Palladius" for Amphialus.

Ch. 11   At "Palladius'" request, Helen tells how she was wooed
by Philoxenus. His friend Amphialus had been brought up
with Philoxenus by the latter's virtuous father, Timotheus.
Philoxenus fell in love with Helen, who did not reciprocate.
He brought with him Amphialus, with whom she fell
desperately in love, and revealed her passion to him. He
pleaded eagerly for his friend. She revealed her love for
Amphialus to Philopenus. He in bitter jealousy forced Amphialus to fight. Amphialus defended himself, killed his

lifelong friend, and was overcome with grief and despair. "Palladius" sends Amphialus' armor to him.

Ch. 12 "Palladius," after a long search, encounters an Amazon lady, whose song and voice almost assure him it is Pyrocles. He rebukes him vehemently for his transformation. Pyrocles tells him how he had fallen in love with Philoclea's picture, had disguised himself and sought her out. Musidorus threatens to abandon him, but then renews their friendship.

Ch. 13 Pyrocles tells of his struggle against love, his search for Philoclea, and his disguising himself as the Amazon "Zelmane." He describes Dametas, Basilius, and his first meeting with the Queen, with Pamela, and especially with Philoclea, whom he describes with rapture.

Ch. 14 "Zelmane" tells how both the old king and the much younger queen have fallen in love with him, so that after almost eight weeks he has never been able to have a private talk with Philoclea. Musidorus is now eager to help his friend.

Ch. 15 Phalantus of Corinth (bastard brother of Queen Helen) issues defiance to the Arcadian knights in behalf of Artesia's beauty. He possesses all knightly virtues—such as courtesy, valor, and fidelity, as well as personal charm. Artesia was brought up by Basilius' sister-in-law Cecropia, and there has been talk of her marrying Amphialus.

Ch. 16 Phalantus and Artesia enter in pomp, followed by eleven ladies: Andromana, Queen of Iberia; the princess of Elis; Artaxia, great Queen of Armenia; Erona, Queen of Lycia; Baccha; Leucippe; the Queen of Laconia; Queen Helen; Parthenia; Urania, the shepherdess; and Zelmane, daughter to King Plexirtus. (Nearly all these ladies play important rôles in later chapters.)

Ch. 17 Phalantus overthrows five Arcadian knights and is later overthrown by an "ill appareled knight," Pyrocles in disguise, to the discomfiture of "the Black Knight."

Ch. 18   "Zelmane" (Pyrocles) finds Musidorus disguised as a shepherd, and in love. "Zelmane" teases him for his earlier heresies against love. Musidorus fell in love with Pamela at first sight. He was "the Black Knight" at the tournament. "Zelmane" suggests that "the best way of dealing is by Dametas."

Ch. 19   Dametas enters at this point. Musidorus pretends to be "Dorus," a younger brother of the shepherd Menalcas, who, dying, gave him money for Dametas to take "Dorus" into his service. A monstrous lion and a fierce she-bear suddenly appear. "Dorus" draws Pamela behind a tree. Philoclea is pursued by the lion whom "Zelmane" pursues and kills. Pamela, walking between "Dorus" and Dametas, now joins them, having in her hand the paw of the bear that "Dorus" has killed. She shows graciousness to "Dorus," and with skillful irony exposes the cowardice of Dametas. A messenger from Cecropia carries her apology to the King for the escape of the lion and the bear. Gynecia is suspicious.

The First Book ends with the first Eclogues.

THE SECOND BOOK

Ch. 1   Gynecia, conscious of her guilty love for "Zelmane" and jealous of Philoclea, meets "Zelmane" and pours out her uncontrollable passion. Old Basilius appears, singing a love-song of his own inditing, and examining himself to see if he is still vigorous. "Zelmane" pretends not to understand the Queen. Basilius asks her to return to the lodge, and then makes love to "Zelmane," who counterfeits scorn and departs to consider "her" dilemma.

Ch. 2   "Zelmane" seeks out "Dorus" and describes "her" sufferings. "Dorus" describes how Pamela treated him at first as a mere shepherd. He began to counterfeit the extremest love toward the dull Mopsa, much to Pamela's amusement. He asked leave of Pamela to tell a story showing how a prince disguised his rank to gain a princess.

Ch. 3   "Dorus" told his own story, in the third person—how a prince, Musidorus, besought a princess to send to Thessalia to find if a red mark on his neck did not confirm his identity. Pamela replied with queenly reserve, and warned Mopsa against the well-spoken shepherd. "All I do," says "Dorus," "is but to beat a rock and get foam."

Ch. 4   Basilius spends a day hawking. "Zelmane" and Philoclea ride close together in the coach. Dametas, driving homeward half asleep, overturns the coach. Philoclea falls on "Zelmane"; Gynecia's shoulder is put out of joint. Jealous of her daughter, she separates her and "Zelmane" for the night. The progress of Philoclea's passion is described. She now disowns verses she wrote in praise of Chastity, and says to herself, "O my Zelmane, govern and direct me: for I am wholly given over to thee."

Ch. 5   Philoclea, spending the night with her sister on her mother's orders, discovers Pamela is in love, but she keeps her own love secret. Pamela is delighted with the skill with which "Dorus" has revealed his identity to her without Mopsa's learning it. She loves him for his sincerity of feeling and admires him for his famous deeds, and scarcely less for his wonderful horsemanship. This day he gave her a letter "with trembling hand." Pamela, though deeply in love, has shown him no favor yet. Philoclea lies awake weeping at the contrast between Pamela's happy prospects, and her own strange love for a woman.

Ch. 6   Pamela calls for the shepherd "Dorus," and inquires about Pyrocles (whom she supposes dead) and about Euarchus. "Dorus" describes the justice and efficiency of Euarchus, his love for his subjects and their great love for him, and his warm friendship for the noble Dorilaus. Each married the other's sister. Musidorus is the son of Dorilaus, Pyrocles of Euarchus. Dorilaus died in battle. Soothsayers prophesied wonderful things of Musidorus and Pyrocles.

Ch. 7   Pyrocles' mother dying soon after childbirth, King Euarchus gave Pyrocles to his sister to be brought up with Musidorus. The latter tells Pamela of his and Pyrocles' friendship and of their early training for a life of honorable action; of their first shipwreck and of how two gentleman servants— brothers whom the princes had ransomed from captivity— preserved the princes' lives by giving up to them the plank on which they themselves had found safety.

Ch. 8   The storm separated the two princes. Pyrocles was cast on the shore of Phrygia, was captured, and was sent to the King, who ordered his execution. Musidorus, whom the tyrant hated even more, arranged to die in his stead. Pyrocles, by a stratagem, rescued his cousin. The King's soldiers fled in panic, young patriots cried Liberty, the King escaped but was later slain in battle by Musidorus. The crown was offered him. He declined in favor of an excellent old nobleman of royal blood, but at the same time set up strong safeguards against tyranny.

Ch. 9   The princes' two servants (see above, Ch. 7) escaped to the shore of Pontus and were brought before the Tyrant, an impulsive, easily flattered man, cruel, and full of malignant hate and envy. He quickly made the brothers courtiers, then suddenly threw them into prison. Pyrocles and Musidorus asked the release of their servants. The King had their heads struck off. Gathering forces in Phrygia, the princes defeated the King and slew him on the tomb of their servants. They set up a new king and queen.

In Pontus they slew two huge brothers who had been unjustly treated by the King, but were now taking cruel revenge on the innocent. The princes established a good ruler in Pontus, and pursued new adventures.

Ch. 10   The princes encountered the aged, blind King of Paphlagonia led by his son Leonatus, whom he had disowned through the treachery of his bastard son Plexirtus. The wretched King, in extreme grief, fully confessed his great wrong to Leonatus in ordering his death and in giving power to Plexirtus, who then usurped the throne and put out his father's eyes. Leonatus became his father's guide in his wanderings. Plexirtus, with forty horsemen, arrived to kill his brother. Pyrocles and Musidorus slew many of that company and with the timely aid of the new King of Pontus, they gained the victory. Leonatus was crowned King by his father, who died immediately. On Plexirtus' feigned submission, Leonatus was reconciled to him. Musidorus and Pyrocles went to the aid of Queen Erona of Lycia.

Ch. 11   "Dorus," noticing that Mopsa is asleep, declares his love to Pamela. She awakens Mopsa. Philoclea enters, and "Dorus" departs. Pamela repeats "Dorus'" story to Philoclea. While the princesses bathe naked in a river, "Zelmane" composes and sings a song, "What tongue can her perfections tell?" "Zelmane" discovers a gentleman (Amphialus) in the bushes; she has "never seen a man of more goodly presence." She discovers he is her rival for Philoclea's love. They fight, "Zelmane" wounds him. She is sorry and ashamed, but hopes for a future and more knightly combat. Philoclea binds up Amphialus' wound.

Ch. 12   Philoclea tells "Zelmane" that Plangus visited Basilius and told him of his love for Erona. Basilius was inspired to compose a verse dialogue on this theme.

Ch. 13   Philoclea, with her sister's help, narrates Erona's story. The heiress to the throne of Lycia, she caused Cupid's many naked statues and pictures to be pulled down and defaced. In revenge, Cupid caused her to fall in love with Antiphilus, a young man at court, of low birth. The King offered as her husband, Tiridates, King of Armenia. She refused him with vehemence, thus hastening her father's death. As Queen, she betrothed herself to Antiphilus. Tiridates made war to gain her by force. Pyrocles and Musidorus came to her aid. The princes captured the city, defeating Plangus, Tiridates' general. The war was settled by three single combats. Pyrocles and Musidorus won, but Antiphilus was captured by Plangus. Tiridates threatened that unless Erona married him, he would execute Antiphilus. In great mental agony she yielded, but changed her mind. Pyrocles and Musidorus rescued Antiphilus, and slew Tiridates.

Ch. 14   Miso, to whom Basilius gave authority over Pamela, provides crude comic relief when she interrupts Philoclea's narration, recalls when she herself was "a young girl of seven and twenty year," recites a ballad against Cupid, and tells a pointless tale of a king's daughter and a knight.

Ch. 15   Pamela tells the story of Prince Plangus of Iberia. His mother died shortly after his birth. His father is still King. In youth he had an affair with a private man's wife, Andromana. Rebuked by his father, he praised her lavishly. While he was away at war, his father supplanted him and married her. She plotted against Plangus, and turned his father against him. For harboring Plangus, the King developed a hatred of his nephew Tiridates, King of Armenia, and of Tiridates' sister Artaxia. Plangus' father excluded him from the succession to the throne, in favor of Palladius, his son by Andromana. The story is broken off by the arrival of Basilius.

Ch. 16   Gynecia struggles fruitlessly against her passion for "Zelmane." Basilius makes passionate love to "Zelmane" and is appalled by the harshness of her rebuke. She suggests that the same words from Philoclea might move her, thus gaining an opportunity to speak with her alone. Basilius entreats Philoclea's assistance.

Ch. 17   Philoclea finds "Zelmane" alone and in tears, soliloquizing and writing verses in the sand. "Zelmane" reveals that he is Pyrocles, to Philoclea's measureless joy. They pass the promise of marriage.

Ch. 18   Pyrocles tells how he left Musidorus for a time and sought adventures alone. Anaxius, the eldest nephew of Euardes, whom Pyrocles slew in the combat for Erona, was esteemed the equal even of Amphialus, except in courtesy. Anaxius sent a challenge to Pyrocles, who journeying to meet him, encountered Pamphilus, a gentleman bound with garters, whom nine gentlewomen were pricking with bodkins. Before he could intervene, six or seven knights arrived. Their leader's arrogance precipitated a battle, in which Pyrocles slew all the knights. Dido, one of the ladies, told how Pamphilus by flattery, tears, and vows, had betrayed many women and had got hold of all their property. Hence the women united against him. Dido's attempt to blind Pamphilus was prevented by Pyrocles, who then saved her from Pamphilus' friends.

Ch. 19   Pyrocles encountered Anaxius in single combat. Pamphilus appeared, cruelly whipping Dido. Pyrocles left Anaxius (who called him coward), pursued Pamphilus and rescued Dido. Pamphilus escaped. Dido reluctantly took Pyrocles to the home of her father Chremes, a stingy, treacherous miser, who knew that Queen Artaxia had set Pyrocles' head to sale, for slaying her bother Tiridates. Traveling with Chremes, Pyrocles was suddenly attacked by the Queen's forces. Musidorus appeared and saved him. They won with the aid of Plangus' father, who hanged Chremes.

Ch. 20   Plangus' father entertained Pyrocles and Musidorus royally. The bad Queen Andromana ruled the King. She made love to both Musidorus and Pyrocles. When they denied her, she accused them to the King and had them thrown into a luxurious prison. Her son, Prince Palladius, loved Zelmane, daughter to Prince Plexirtus, but Zelmane fell in love with Pyrocles. Plexirtus is half-brother to Andromana. Zelmane asked Prince

Palladius to procure the liberation of Pyrocles and Musidorus. Queen Andromana prevented it.

Ch. 21   The yearly jousts in Iberia attracted many foreign knights. Those from the court of Queen Helen of Corinth were victorious for the first three days. On the fourth, Prince Palladius, Musidorus, and Pyrocles defeated them. Palladius then attempted their escape from Iberia. Andromana ordered a pursuit. Palladius was killed by one of the Queen's own soldiers. Pyrocles and Musidorus avenged him. Andromana, cursing Pyrocles, committed suicide.

Ch. 22   Musidorus and Pyrocles encountered Leucippe, who lamented her desertion by Pamphilus (see II. 18, 19) for the courtesan Baccha, whom he had married. Next day they were overtaken by Plexirtus' gentle daughter Zelmane, who for love of Pyrocles disguised herself and called herself Daiphantus. Pyrocles, supposing her a youth, made her his servant. He and Musidorus established peace between the King of Bithynia and his brother. Continuing their journey, they stopped a cruel fight between two knights, who to their own great surprise discover that they are brothers (Tydeus and Telenor). Leonatus, after succeeding his father as King of Galacia, had accepted his evil brother Plexirtus into favor. Plexirtus tried to poison him. To keep him out of the way, Leonatus sent him to regain the city of Trebisonde. Tydeus and Telenor gave him great help. Because of their power and fame, Plexirtus distrusted them, and tricked them into fighting a deadly duel. They mortally wounded each other and died in each other's arms.

Ch. 23   Plexirtus' daughter, Zelmane, disguised as Daiphantus, grieved for her father's evil actions. She fell extremely sick. Before her death she revealed herself to the two princes, told her love for Pyrocles, who felt deep grief for her, and asked them to aid Plexirtus out of his present danger. She also asked Pyrocles to take the name Daiphantus when he came to

Greece, and Musidorus the name Palladius. They promised
to do so. She died, and was buried privately. Pyrocles went
to aid Plexirtus, and Musidorus to aid the new King of
Pontus, whom he and Pyrocles had set on the throne. To save
Plexirtus, Pyrocles had to fight a strange beast with the fierce-
ness and strength of six savage animals. He killed the beast.
Plexirtus was set free. Musidorus killed two giants, defeated
Otaves, and made a friend of him.

Ch. 24   The two cousins now hastened toward Greece, because
Anaxius (cf. II, 18, 19) was defaming Pyrocles at Pelopon-
nesus, and because they were eager to meet the famous
knights, Argalus and Amphialus. Plexirtus had pretended
repentance and friendship. On the voyage his counselor
revealed to the princes his order to murder them near
Greece. The captain ordered their murder. There was a confused battle. The ship caught fire and was abandoned. Pyrocles, who had been wounded, got astride the mast, where he
regained his sword, which he had flung into the canvas. Finding the captain also on the mast, Pyrocles killed him. He was
rescued by pirates and taken to Laconia.

Philoclea asks about the fate of Musidorus. "Lost," says
Pyrocles. Philoclea, knowing the truth, teases him for the
falsehood. Pyrocles replies, "What is mine, even to my soul,
is yours; but the secret of my friend is not mine." Philoclea
begins to tell how Queen Erona was betrayed into danger
and why Plangus sought Pyrocles. They are interrupted by
Miso.

Ch. 25   Gynecia has a divining dream of "Zelmane" and of her
husband's apparent death, and his revival. Learning of "Zelmane's" long tête-à-tête with Philoclea, she is consumed with
jealousy. Finding them together, she sends Philoclea to Basilius. Beginning to reveal to "Zelmane" her deadly desires, she
is interrupted by a wild mob of peasants and other rebels.
There is a wild battle. "Zelmane" keeps the mob at bay until

the Queen and her daughters take refuge in the royal lodge. Basilius tries to assert his authority. "Dorus" arrives, and joins "Zelmane," but the multitude grows.

Ch. 26   The King and the two princes regain the lodge. "Zelmane" goes out to address the mob, and asks them to set down their demands. These prove to be violently contradictory. Her pleasing personality, voice, good sense, and valor prevail.

Ch. 27   The crafty coward Clinias, of near trust to Cecropia and privy to her plots against her dead husband's brother Basilius and his family, is one of the first in the mob to shout his loyalty to Basilius. A farmer who loves "Zelmane" is disgusted at his hypocrisy, and strikes Clinias. There is a wild melèe. Basilius asks Clinias to tell how the frenzy began. Clinias replies with flattery and lies.

Ch. 28   Clinias hastens to Cecropia to warn her to act at once before her plots can be discovered. Basilius and the royal party lavish praises on "Zelmane's" handling of the mob. Dametas sings a song praising his own cowardly discretion. The regent Philanax arrives with a hundred horsemen. Basilius now reveals the words of the oracle which caused his retirement. He thinks it is partly fulfilled by "Zelmane" (a foreign "state") sitting in his throne. "Zelmane" asks him to tell what he knows of Plangus and Erona's later story.

Ch. 29   Basilius relates to "Zelmane" how the commoner Antiphilus, whom Queen Erona married, showed his unfitness to govern soon after his coronation. He was in subjection to flatterers, some fawning on him, others secretly hating him. He claimed that his ancestors had been royal before Erona's. After half a year of marriage, he sought a second wife, Artaxia, Queen of Bohemia, who hated him and loved the wicked Plexirtus. To these indignities Erona submitted either from vehemency of affection, or because she was too stunned to protest. Artaxia mortally hated both Erona and Antiphilus.

By treachery she captured and imprisoned both of them and planned their death. While Antiphilus begged contemptibly, Erona showed her strength of spirit.

Plangus showed faithful love to her. She asked him to save Antiphilus. Plangus sought out Artaxia, and devised a plan for Erona's escape, which Antiphilus betrayed to Artaxia. Plangus endeavored to rescue Antiphilus, but all hated him. After being tortured he was forced to throw himself from a high Pyramid.

Artaxia planned to burn Erona alive. Plangus overthrew her military power, took her nephew prisoner, and held him as hostage for Erona. The noblemen of her country pardoned all prisoners except Erona, who was to be burned unless Pyramus and Musidorus rescued her within two years of Tiridates' death. Artaxia heard a report of the deaths of both princes. Plangus, after visiting the despairing Erona, set out for Greece to find them. Artaxia then besieged the castle where Erona was imprisoned, demanding instant delivery of her. She gained more power by marrying Plexirtus. Plangus determined to appeal to Euarchus.

The Second Book ends with the second Eclogues.

THE THIRD BOOK

Ch. 1   "Dorus" takes Pamela in his arms and kisses her. In great indignation, she denounces him. He flees to the woods in agony, and sends her a long letter in verse.

Ch. 2   On the fourth day after the mob attacked the royal lodge, Pamela, Philoclea, and "Zelmane" are invited to rural sports by six maids. They are captured by twenty armed men and taken to Cecropia's castle. Her son Amphialus is partly displeased. She urges him to woo Philoclea.

Ch. 3   He appeals to Philoclea. She replies that he asks pity, but uses cruelty himself; she asks freedom for "Zelmane," Pamela, and herself. The tyrant love compels him to disobey her.

Ch. 4   Amphialus prepares for war. He appeals to his friends and to discontented persons, and prepares his castle for a two years' siege. He chooses his men skillfully. He shrewdly spreads libels against himself, so that no one would know whether they were true or of his own invention. Absent from Philoclea he frames passionate appeals, but in her presence he is "dumb-stricken."

Ch. 5   The wicked Cecropia visits Philoclea and urges her to marry Amphialus. Philoclea says she has vowed a virgin's life. The aunt uses shameless temptations. The niece remains resolute.

Ch. 6   Cecropia now tries to please her with music and daily presents, but still with no success. She then attempts her sister, whom she finds "full of deep (though patient) thoughts." Pamela utters a beautiful prayer that she may always depend confidently on God, concluding with a silent prayer for Musidorus. As Cecropia listens, she realizes her own wickedness. She perjures herself by saying how extremely her son loves Pamela. Pamela beats off all her assaults with the majesty of virtue.

Ch. 7   On the same day, Basilius' loyal army attacks the forces of Amphialus. Clinias shows his base cowardice, Amphialus his splendid skill, courage, and prowess, and sometimes a generous mercy.

Ch. 8   Basilius' forces are rallied first by the Regent Philanax, and then by the Black Knight. Philanax is taken prisoner by Amphialus. The Black Knight performs many exploits, and engages Amphialus in a fierce single combat. Amphialus retreats when Basilius and all his army threaten to cut him off from his town.

Ch. 9   Philoclea is visited by Amphialus, whose love-song is sung by a boy, without effect. Amphialus plans to execute Philanax, whom he has long hated, but at Philoclea's entreaty he not only spares his life but sets him free. Philanax expresses warm gratitude, and urges him to reconcile himself to the King. Cecropia still tries to win Philoclea for Amphialus, but entirely fails.

Ch. 10   Cecropia then goes to Pamela, whom she finds "working upon a purse . . . roses and lilies. . . . The cunningest painter might have learned of her needle." She praises her niece's beauty, "the crown of the feminine greatness," by which women conquer men. Pamela sees through her flattery, and declares she will marry only with her father's consent. The atheistic aunt then tries to remove her conscientious scruples by persuading her that religion is merely the product of ignorance and fear. Pamela, roused to great indignation, interrrupts her, with, "Peace, wicked woman!" and declares that the order, beauty, and constancy in the universe reveal the goodness, the wisdom, and the providence of a God who created and governs all things.

Ch. 11   Cecropia realizes her defeat, but continues her plots. The war is at a standstill, while the besiegers build forts from which to attack the castle. Phalantus, half-brother to Helen of Corinth, challenges Amphialus to single combat. He accepts, but conceals his identity. In spite of Phalantus' very great skill, Amphialus defeats him, and then gives his name. Both men conduct themselves with courtesy and knightly honor. Phalantus goes to seek adventures elsewhere.

Ch. 12   Amphialus continues to defeat all challengers. Basilius summons the famous Argalus. The messenger finds Argalus and Parthenia a picture of domestic happiness. She, greatly alarmed, faints at Argalus' departure. His long combat with Amphialus is bloody to both, fatal to Argalus. At the end Parthenia rushes between them. Argalus takes a loving farewell of her. She is inconsolable in her wild grief, though Basilius himself tries to comfort her.

Ch. 13   This tragedy is followed by a comic episode. The peasant Dametas challenges the clever Clinias to single combat. Both are cowards, but Clinias somewhat the greater. Their combat provides hilarious amusement. "Dametas was with much mirth and melody received into the camp as victorious."

Ch. 14   Clinias' and Artesia's plot to poison Amphialus is revealed to the princesses. Pamela reveals it to Cecropia. Clinias is executed, Artesia is locked up.

Ch. 15   The boastful Anaxius, formerly Amphialus' enemy, is now his friend for the unusual reason that Anaxius saved his life. He and his two brothers battle their way through Basilius' forces and join Amphialus. Next day he and his brothers attack Basilius' camp. Their near victory is turned into defeat by the Black Knight and two others.

Ch. 16   Amphialus, challenged by the Knight of the Tomb, mortally wounds him and finds him to be the Lady Parthenia. She welcomes death, to be with Argalus. Friend and foe regard her with wonder and compassion.

Ch. 17   The deeply remorseful Amphialus breaks his excellent sword in many pieces. He goes to bed to avoid company, is wakeful all night, and at dawn shuts out the morning light. He dwells bitterly on his having killed his close friend Philoxenes and the virtuous Parthenia. He thinks he is "hated of the ever-ruling powers," especially in "his fatal love to Philoclea." When his mother cynically advises a rape, he tells her, "True love is a servant."

Ch. 18   There is a long, fierce single combat between "the forsaken knight" (Musidorus) and Amphialus. Amphialus is defeated and gravely wounded, but is rescued by Anaxius' brothers, after they have fought with two knights, friends of the Black Knight. These three unknown warriors then leave Basilius' camp.

Ch. 19   Amphialus feels bitter shame and grief for his defeat. His mother takes command and threatens death to "Zelmane" and the princesses if the siege is not raised. Kalander recommends raising it. Philanax argues it is bad policy, since even if the siege is raised the ladies may still be murdered. Basilius raises the siege.

Ch. 20   Cecropia still hopes to win one princess for Amphialus, and then poison the other. Both resolutely refuse. She persecutes them with bad diet and lodging, and horrible noises, and furiously scourages them both. Philoclea asks death. Pamela scorns all that her aunt can do. Thinking of Musidorus, she weeps not for herself, but for his grief for her. Fortifying her resolution, she takes "counsel of virtue, and comfort of love."

Ch. 21   Cecropia has Philoclea and "Zelmane" witness the execution of a lady who, because of her garments, they are well assured is Pamela. Philoclea bitterly laments her death.

Ch. 22   "Zelmane" is brought in to influence Philoclea to yield. She prefers death. After some days, "Zelmane" sees Philoclea's head in a gold basin filled with blood. "Zelmane," in despair, cries out against blind providence, and desires only revenge and death.

Ch. 23   Toward dawn he is visited by a gentlewoman who says she has heard nothing from him but weak wailings. He angrily rushes at her and discovers Philoclea. Both she and Pamela are alive. Artesia was executed, not Pamela. Philoclea's head in a dish of blood was a device to influence Pamela. Philoclea expects more torments, but Amphialus has ordered Cecropia to use the princesses with all kindness.

Ch. 24   Amphialus has misgivings about them, goes to them and begins to excuse certain small matters. Pamela denounces him, seconded gently by Philoclea. From a woman servant he learns how Cecropia has treated them. Finding her on the castle roof, he denounces her. Frightened, she misses her footing and falls from the roof. [Presumably the roof sloped gently.] He wounds himself almost mortally with Philoclea's knives.

Ch. 25   The haughty Anaxius takes command, and exacts the oath of obedience from all soldiers and citizens. Though the surgeons assure him that Amphialus' wounds are mortal, he threatens to hang them if they do not save his life. Queen Helen of Corinth comes to take Amphialus to her country, "to the excellentest surgeon . . . known," who has given her sovereign anointments for Amphialus' wounds. She takes him away amid the lamentations of all his people.

Ch. 26   Anaxius goes with Amphialus, first sending a message to the princesses that on his return he will cut off their heads. The princesses accept the prospect calmly. The Black Knight is bringing armed forces to their aid.

Anaxius returns, goes to the ladies, and is awed by Pamela. "Zelmane" challenges him to single combat, assuring him that her skill in arms equals that of the famed Pyrocles. Anaxius promises life to the princesses. He makes advances to Pamela, his brothers to Philoclea and "Zelmane."

Ch. 27   Anaxius sends to Basilius to get his consent to marry Pamela, and implies that if denied he will use force. Philanax vehemently urges Basilius to use force. Basilius sends him to the oracle of Delphos, which unambiguously declares he should deny Anaxius and his brothers, since his daughters are reserved for men dearer to the gods. Philanax denies Anaxius' demand.

Ch. 28   Anaxius' youngest brother Zoilus makes advances to "Zelmane," who pursues him and gives him a blow that almost cuts him in two. Anaxius tells his brother Lycurgus to chastise this vile creature, and goes to see the princesses. "Zelmane" attacks Lycurgus and disarms him. He begs mercy. "Zelmane" begins to relent, but seeing one of his arms tied with a jewel

she gave to Philoclea, she runs her sword through his heart.
Anaxius returns only to beg mercy and see his brother die.
He attacks "Zelmane." Both are so skillful that neither draws
blood for some time.

Ch. 29   After a brief rest, and an exchange of scornful words, they
resume the combat. Anaxius, because of his huge strength,
oftener uses blows. Pyrocles watches "his time to give fit
thrusts." Warding off a blow, he would have wounded him
in his right side, if Anaxius had not leaped away. "Whereat
ashamed (as having never done so before in his life)"

Here, in the middle of a sentence, Sidney's revision of the *Arcadia*
breaks off. In the Dublin 1621 edition of the work, Sir William Alexander ventured to finish the story of Amphialus' war. His contribution testifies to the lively interest in the *Arcadia* long after Sidney's
tragic death. In characters and plot, if not in style, Alexander's passage
seems to harmonize well with the author's own work. Because of its
interest, I have summarized the passage, marking it off by square
brackets.

[The castle is attacked. Anaxius, rushing out, finds three knights,
including the Black Knight, on whom the warriors of the castle are
trying to avenge Amphialus. Anaxius attacks the Black Knight, but
is interrupted by "Zelmane." Anaxius and "Zelmane" fight in single
combat, the former "rioting in rage" at first. "Zelmane," a sword in
each hand, fights with marvelous skill. Finally, as Anaxius rushes forward, "Zelmane's" sword passes through his heart, as his own passes
through her body. The gravely wounded Pyrocles is re-united with
his friend and with Philoclea, who thought she had seen him die.
[Musidorus humbly acknowledges to Pamela the fault for which
she banished him, and receives her queenly pardon. Examining
"Zelmane's" wounds he finds only one dangerous, though not mortal.
He takes command of the castle. He weeps at the death of Philisides,

the white knight—"the knight of the sheep"—his comrade in arms in his encounter with Amphialus. (See III, 15.) In the morning a messenger arrives from Basilius to thank the Black Knight for his victories and his rescue of the princesses. As Pamela looks at Musidorus, he blushes. Basilius was prostrated with grief at a report of "Zelmane's" death, and Gynecia's grief was even more violent. A later messenger has changed their sorrow to joy.

[Musidorus goes reverently to Pamela. With queenly austerity, she says that if he returns to his old master Dametas, he will be restored to his former "estate." He feels he has received a royal pardon for his grave offense in kissing her. He departs, "leaving his heart with her and taking hers with him."

[The regent Philanax arrives, takes over the castle in the King's name, and departs.

[Pamela reminds Philoclea that their troubles are not over, since they shall be watched by one (Gynecia) more jealous than Juno. Next day they return with "Zelmane" to their parents. Gynecia kisses Pamela carelessly, Philoclea disdainfully, and "Zelmane" vehemently. Dametas, boasting his victory over Clinias, is filled with contempt for his man "Dorus." He may chide him, but will not beat him.]

Here Alexander's contribution ends. The *Old Arcadia*, from which the Countess of Pembroke and her assistants filled out the story, is not divided into chapters.

"Dorus" confides in "Zelmane" that he and Pamela intend to go secretly to Thessalia, but offers to remain with Pyrocles, if that is his command. Though stunned at the thought of facing Basilius' folly and Gynecia's jealousy, without his friend, he urges Musidorus to carry out his plans. Musidorus sheds a flood of tears as he takes leave of his friend. When Basilius joins "Zelmane" she rejects his love songs and follows Musidorus. Stopping at a cave, she sings mournful songs until Gynecia arrives and threatens to wreak vengeance on Philoclea for "Zelmane's" scorn. "Zelmane" then decides to appear to yield to both the Queen's desires and the King's.

"Dorus," having found an "unknown way" to the nearest seaport, devises plans to keep Dametas, Miso, and Mopsa from their home all day. Knowing Dametas' covetousness, he tells him that there is a great treasure under a tree ten miles away. Knowing Miso's jealousy, he tells her of seeing her husband making love to a beautiful shepherdess near Mantinea. Knowing Mopsa's envy and curiosity, he remains strangely mute until she asks the reason. Then he tells her a fantastic yarn about Jupiter and Apollo, and a marvelous tree—adding that if anyone sat in it, he would obtain whatsoever he desired. By these devices Musidorus removes Dametas and his wife and daughter for many hours, during which he steals Pamela away. During their journey, Pamela, for the first time and to Musidorus' great delight, declares her ardent love for him.

Stopping for a mid-day meal, he sings songs until she falls asleep. He is then attacked by "a company of clownish villains."

Meanwhile "Zelmane," alone in a cave with Gynecia, tries to qualify her passion with hope. Gynecia feels that her reason has vanished. "Zelmane" somewhat mollifies her passion, and reveals herself as a man and prince. She makes love to him. He promises satisfaction in a few days. Leaving the cave, they encounter the King and Philoclea. Pyrocles appears to neglect her and devote himself only to the Queen. Philoclea is greatly grieved, and wonders if her mother has robbed her daughter to ruin herself. Pyrocles feels like "a soft-hearted mother forced to beat her child." In the morning "Zelmane" desires leave of the King and Queen to remain in the cave a few days to perform certain devotions. They agree readily, each thinking "Zelmane" is arranging an assignation. While Philoclea is a prey to sorrow, "Zelmane" devises a plan to carry her away by night. When alone with Basilius, he urges "Zelmane" to yield to his passion. She demurs at first, but invites him to visit her in the cave. Then, still pretending coolness to Philoclea, she goes to Gynecia and arranges to meet her in the cave at the time appointed also for Basilius. In the cave the King takes the Queen for "Zelmane," while the Queen recognizes that she has been tricked.

Meanwhile Pyrocles goes to Philoclea's chamber, and overhears her soliloquy in which she accuses him of deserting her. When he reveals himself, she continues to accuse. "Every syllable . . . was a thunderbolt to his heart." Philoclea is slow to believe his protestations. At last he faints at her bedside. She thinks him dead, but he soon recovers, and persuades her to flee with him to his father, the noble King of Macedon. Comforted by his words, she falls asleep. Pyrocles accuses himself for his rash attempt. Then he, too, falls asleep.

End of Book III

BOOK IV

Dametas, after a day of hard labor, discovers under a huge stone merely a piece of vellum, containing two derisive verses. He returns home "looking like a she goat when she casts her kid." He discovers Mopsa high in an ash tree, where she has been all day. He calls her to come down, first kindly, then roughly, then with a curse. On what she thinks is the magical third call, she jumps, and is saved from death only by the boughs. Miso returns from Mantinea, where she publicly proclaimed her husband had gone to commit adultery in a certain house. She returns bitterly jealous, mistakes her daughter for a drab, and cudgels her husband. All three are still cherishing the illusions implanted in their dull brains by Musidorus. When Dametas discovers Pamela's flight, he is terrified that he will surely be hanged. Searching the lodge where Philoclea and "Zelmane" are sleeping, he discovers "Zelmane's" sex. He carries off the Prince's sword, and goes around bawling out the news to the Arcadians. Providence has given the fool a part to play in a royal pageant.

Basilius leaves the cave before Gynecia, whom the darkness still conceals from his sight. As he rejoices over the "blessed" night he has passed, the Queen hears all he says. When she joins him and plays the part of a deeply wronged wife, he is astonished to find his mistake, and can make only "a stammering defense." Observing the liquor in her gold cup (supposedly a love potion) he, in spite of her earnest warning, drinks nearly all of it. Then murmuring, "O Gynecia, I die," he drops unconscious. The Queen, suddenly horrified at her sins, realizes that she will be accused of regicide. Shepherds call in Dametas, and she, in her frenzied grief, declares that she caused the King's death, and asks only to be punished. The shepherds mourn their master and recite his kindly and royal virtues.

Philanax arrives, hears her accuse herself of murder, and laments the master he deeply loved. He shows a deadly hatred to the Queen, promises her execution, and urges her to repent. He removes Dametas from his post, places him, Miso, and Mopsa in fetters, and orders them to be whipped every three hours.

When Pyrocles awakes, he misses his sword, and hears Dametas proclaim the scandalous situation in Philoclea's chamber. Thinking his death will preserve her, he utters a prayer, and missing his sword, attempts suicide with an iron bar, but fails. Philoclea is awakened, and after a long debate over whether suicide is forbidden by God's law, she persuades him to give up his purpose. Philanax comes in with twenty nobles, seeking to avenge his master, whom he loved with an extraordinary devotion. He hears Pyrocles declare Philoclea's inviolate chastity. Then he sends him off to prison, and remains to see what he can learn from Philoclea.

On the previous day, Pamela was awakened from her mid-day sleep by "a rascal company, . . . the summy remnant of those rebels" who had attacked Basilius' royal lodge just before Amphialus' rebellion. Musidorus slew two of the ruffians, mortally wounded another, and then returned to protect Pamela. The rebels resolved to kill him. Pamela, in a powerful speech mingling promises and threats, induced them to give up their purpose. The rebels, counting on a handsome reward, took them back to Basilius' lodge. When Musidorus bitterly accused himself for Pamela's bad fortune, she told him she had the comfort of his unblemished virtue. He, thinking it more to her honor that she had gone off with a prince than with a shepherd, proposed that he call himself the prince Palladius, the name he had used when he first came to Arcadia. Arriving at the lodges, the rebels bring Pamela and Musidorus to the authorities. For their pains they are cut to pieces by the Arcadian cavalry, who then conduct the prince and princess to Philanax. Pyrocles is shocked to see them, and presses through the crowd to greet them. Philanax places the two friends in prison together. Pamela, hearing of her father's death, demands to be treated as a queen. Philanax, who scents a great conspiracy involving the Queen, her daughters, and their lovers, confines Pamela in the lodge with her sister.

Basilius' sudden death has produced immense confusion. Some Arcadians wish to crown Pamela, which the law forbids until she is twenty-one or married. Some incline to her younger sister. Some desire Gynecia to be made regent. Timantus, a nobleman of extreme ambition, stirs up trouble among the Arcadian lords, most of whom are very jealous of Philanax. Philanax, in a calm speech, asks them first to punish the King's murderers, and then to establish a sound government. As he ends his speech, a messenger rushes in with news that a crowd is bent on rescuing Pyrocles and Musidorus from prison and proclaiming them princes.

What has happened is that Kalander, calling together his neighbors, the citizens of Mantinea, has declared that Basilius' daughters are of an age to choose their own husbands, and that the Arcadians will never find young men of more heroic qualities than the princes they have chosen. The nobleman Sympathus, who is in charge of their prison, esteems them so highly that he has refused to surrender them to the Regent Philanax.

End of Book IV

BOOK V

A Macedonian gentleman comes to Philanax to say that the renowned King Euarchus is at hand with a very small retinue, and wishes to attend the funeral of his friend Basilius. To end the confusion of counsels, Philanax persuades the multitude to make Euarchus the judge at the next day's trials. Euarchus has been much concerned with two problems—how to assist Erona and Plangus, and how to meet the threat of war from the Latins in Italy. He has come to Arcadia in the hope of uniting the Greek states against the common enemy. Philanax greets Euarchus and persuades him to accept the position of judge on the next day. Euarchus, reminding the

Arcadians that he is fallible, asks them to keep open minds and to put an end to all dissensions.

Meanwhile Gynecia spends the night crucifying her own soul. Pamela and Philoclea spend it in suffering and in prayer. Musidorus and Pyrocles fortify their courage with patience and with discussing God's ways to men. To spare their parents shame if they are condemned, they continue to use the names Palladius and Daiphantus, which they have recently resumed.

Next day the trial begins with King Euarchus, dressed all in black, in the seat of judgement. Philanax, the prosecutor, is convinced that there has been a conspiracy to murder the King he loved, a conspiracy in which Gynecia was the leader, and her daughters and the princes her accomplices. Gynecia is brought in, then Pyrocles is led in by Sympathus, and Musidorus by another nobleman. Musidorus addresses the multitude, ardently defending Pamela as the just inheritrix of Arcadia. Sympathus assures him that the Arcadians all acknowledge her as their sovereign lady. Pyrocles addresses the judge, defending Philoclea's chastity and winning the warm support of the people. Disregarding the crowd, and regarding only exact justice, Euarchus finds Philoclea not altogether faultless, and condemns the eighteen-year-old princess to spend the rest of her life among the Vestal Nuns.

Philanax then begins a bitter invective against Queen Gynecia. She stops him and accuses herself of the sole guilt of Basilius' murder. Euarchus condemns her to be buried alive in the same tomb with her husband.

The two princes question the authority of the court to judge men of princely rank, but are told that they can claim royal immunity only in their own countries.

Philanax, in his love and bitter grief for his King, expresses "the uttermost of his malice" against Pyrocles, accusing him of being a degenerate "mankind strumpet" who has nursed a wicked ambition. Pyrocles defends himself with great vigor. While he is speaking, letters defending their lovers are brought from Philoclea and Pamela. They are delivered to Philanax, who keeps the letters secret lest by

Euarchus' severely just mind the princesses might be endangered or the prisoners preserved. Philanax's indictment of Musidorus is even more bitter and unjust than his indictment of Pyrocles.

Euarchus, after weighing all the evidence, sentences Pyrocles to be thrown out of a high tower, and Musidorus to be beheaded by Dametas. No state can tolerate a conspiracy to murder its King.

Suddenly Kalander cries out to Euarchus and brings in Musidorus' servant Kalodulus, who reveals to Euarchus that he has just imposed the death penalty on his son and nephew. Euarchus, "vehemently stricken with the love of so excellent children," is stunned; but in fidelity to the law he can only re-affirm the sentence, to the sorrow even of Philanax. Musidorus, bitterly denouncing his uncle as a murderer, asks him to let Musidorus alone pay the penalty for Pyrocles as well as himself. Pyrocles, on his part, speaking to his father in all humbleness, asks to die for Musidorus. Euarchus, though suffering more intensely than the young princes, again commands that they be taken off to execution.

At this point, "a great voice of groaning" comes suddenly from the body of Basilius, proving that he is alive. The drink he took was actually only a strong sleeping potion. The King's first act is to send for Gynecia. He tells the assembly how she warned him earnestly against the drink.

With a princely entertainment to Euarchus, the marriages of his son and nephew with the Arcadian princesses are concluded, "to the inestimable joy of Euarchus."

In time, Musidorus, who is to inherit the kingdom, develops a warm friendship with Philanax. The author cannot tell the story of Pyrocles' son and Musidorus' daughter; or of Artaxia and Plexirtus, Erona and Plangus, Helen and Amphialus. But since poetic justice will doubtless continue to rule events, we can infer that Artaxia and Plexirtus will pay the penalty for their crimes, and the noble though faulty lovers will gain their due reward. In particular, we may hope that Amphialus, after being cured by Helen's famous physician, will to her great joy marry her, and gain a deeper happiness and a more selfless virtue than he has known in the tragic past.

List of Characters in the *Arcadia*

Based on the List in the (New) *Arcadia*, ed. Albert Feuillerat, 1922, pp. 568-571. Very minor characters are omitted. Roman numerals signify Books; Arabic signify chapters.

From the point where the *New Arcadia* breaks off, the references are to the 1953 edition of the *Arcadia*, (*Works*, ed. Feuillerat, II, 1-207). Since in this part of the *Arcadia* there are no chapter divisions, the references to different sections are to pages as indicated on the Summary of the plot. Here Roman numerals signify books; Arabic signify pages.

Agenor: younger brother of the Arcadian regent Philanax. III, 7, 8.

Amiclas: King of Lacedemon. I, 5, 7, 8.

Amphialus: son of Cecropia, nephew of Basilius. I, 10, 11, 15; II, 11, 15, 18, 27; III, 2-9, 11-18, 23-25.

Anaxius: nephew of the gigantic Prince Euardes. II, 18, 19, 24; III, 15, 19, 25-29.

Andromana: wicked Queen of Iberia. While a private citizen's wife she had an affair with Prince Plangus, and later married his father. Mother of Palladius. I, 16; II, 15, 20, 21.

Antiphilus: treacherous and cowardly commoner, who married Queen Erona, and promptly took another wife, Artaxia. II, 13, 14, 23, 24, 29.

Argalus: famous and noble knight, husband of Parthenia, slain by Amphialus. I, 5-8, 16; III, 12, 16.

Argus, King of: III, 4.

Artaxia: sister of Tiridates, Queen of Armenia after his death. I, 16; II, 13, 15, 19, 23, 29.

Artesia: wicked sister of Ismenus. Executed by Cecropia. I, 15-17; III, 2, 14, 21, 23.

Baccha: She entered a beauty contest. I, 16; II, 22.

Barzanes: King of Hyrcania. II, 10, 13.

Basilius: King of Arcadia; husband of Gynecia, father of Pamela and Philoclea. I, 3, 4, 13-17, 19; II, 1, 4, 11, 12, 15, 16, 25-28; III, 2, 4, 8, 9, 11-13, 15, 16, 18-20, 25, 27; III, IV, V, *passim*.

Bithynia, King of: II, 22, 23.

Cecropia: sister-in-law of Basilius, mother of Amphialus. I, 11, 15, 19; II, 27, 28; III, 2-6, 9-12, 14, 17-24.

Chremes: a miser, the father of Dido, II, 19.

Claius: a shepherd devoted to Urania, warm friend of his rival Strephon. I, 1, 2.

Clinias: a cowardly scoundrel and hypocrite. II, 26-28; III, 2, 4, 7, 11, 13, 14.

Clitophon: son of Kalander, I, 4-6, 8, 10, 11, 17.

Crete, King of: II, 6.

Daiphantus: the name that Plexirtus' daughter, Zelmane, assumed when disguised as a youth.

Daiphantus: the name that Pyrocles assumed in memory of Zelmane when he arrived in Greece.

Dametas: the crude and naive peasant whom Basilius regarded as wise enough to have important authority. A comic figure. I, 3, 4, 13, 19; II, 2-5, 25, 28; III, 13; III, IV.

Demagoras: Parthenia's wicked suitor who temporarily destroyed her beauty by rubbing poison on her face. First captain of the Helots. Argalus slew him to avenge Parthenia. I, 5.

Dorilaus: Prince of Thessalia, father of Musidorus, brother-in-law of King Euardes. He died soon after his son's birth. II, 6.

Erona: Queen of Lycia; though beloved of Prince Plangus of Iberia, she married the base-born Antiphilus, who treated her outrageously. I, 16; II, 10, 12, 13, 18, 29.

Euarchus: King of Macedonia, father of Pyrocles; a type of the ideal ruler. Judge at the trial of the supposed murderers of Basilius. II, 3, 6, 7, 9, 29; V.

Euardes: King of Bithynia. II, 10, 13, 18.

Eurileon: nephew of Amiclas (King of Lacedemon). I, 5, 7, 8.

Giants: two, and their sons. II, 9, 23.

Gynecia: Basilius' Queen. I, 3, 13-15, 17-19; II, 1, 4, 16, 25; III, 2, 9, 16, 19; III, IV, V, *passim.*

Helen: Queen of Corinth. She loved Amphialus, who did not return her love. Her wonderful physician restored Parthenia's beauty. I, 7, 10, 11, 16, 17; II, 21; III, 25, 26.

Helots: the rebel peasants in Lacedemon. I, 2, 5-7.

Iberia, King of: Father of Plangus. II, 15, 19, 20.

Iberia, Queen of: See Andromana, Plangus' wicked step-mother.

Ismenus: Artesia's brother, slain by Philanax. I, 11, 15; III, 8.

Kalander: the Arcadian gentleman who extended hospitality to Musidorus and Pyrocles. Father of Clitophon. I, 2-10; III, 19; IV, V.

Kalodulus: servant to Musidorus.

Knight, the Black ⎫ names by which Musidorus was known in
Knight, the Forsaken ⎭ the war with Amphialus. III, 8, 15, 18, 26.

Knight, the Green: III, 15, 18.

Knight, the Ill appareled: See Pyrocles.

Knight, the White: III, 15, 18.

Lelius: friend to Philisides. They were rivals in the Iberian Jousts. III, 21.

Leonatus: son and successor to the old King of Paphlagonia (Galatia), half-brother of Plexirtus. II, 10, 22-24.

Leucippe: lady betrayed by Pamphilus. I, 16; II, 22.

Leucippus and Nelsus: Gentlemen servants of Pyrocles and Musidorus. They gave their plank to the princes after their shipwreck. II, 7, 9.

Lycurgus: younger brother of Anaxius. III, 15, 18-20, 25-28.

Megalus: a warrior slain by the Black Knight. III, 8.

Menalcas: a shepherd friend of Musidorus. I, 18, 19.

Miso: wife of Dametas. I, 3; II, 2, 5, 6, 11, 14-16, 24, 25; III, 2, 9; III, IV.

Mopsa: daughter of Dametas. I, 3; II, 2, 5, 6, 11, 14, 25; III, 1, 2; III, IV.

Musidorus: Prince of Thessalia, nephew of Euarchus. Called also Palladius, Dorus, the Black Knight, the Forsaken Knight. In love with Pamela. I, 1-6, 8-12, 14, 15, 17-19; II, 2, 3, 5-11, 18-27, 29; III, 1, 8, 15, 18, 26; III, IV, V, *passim*.

Nelsus: II, 7, 9. See Leucippus and Nelsus.

Otaves: a mighty warrior, brother of King Barzanes. He brought with him two giants. Musidorus captured him and slew the giants. II, 23.

Palemon: a warrior slain by the Black Knight. III, 8.

Palladius: son of the evil Queen Andromana of Iberia, half-brother of Plangus, friend of Musidorus and Pyrocles. Lover of Zelmane, Plexirtus' daughter. Slain by a minion of Andromana's. In his memory, Musidorus took his name during much of his time in Greece. II, 15, 20, 21.

Pamela: eldest daughter of Basilius, beloved of Musidorus. I, 3, 13, 15, 17-19; II, 2, 3, 5, 6, 11, 12, 14, 25, 28; III, 1, 2, 6, 9-11, 14, 19-21, 23, 24, 26-28; III, IV, V, *passim.*

Pamphilus: a man of noble birth, whom Pyrocles found being continually pricked by nine gentlewomen he had betrayed; a man constant only to inconstancy. II, 18, 19, 22.

Paphlagonia, King of: Father of Leonatus and the bastard Plexirtus. The latter usurped the throne and blinded his father. Pyrocles and Musidorus defeated Plexirtus. The King crowned his loyal son Leonatus, and dropped dead. II, 10. (Cf. *King Lear*, Gloucester and his sons.)

Parthenia, wife of Argalus: Her beauty, destroyed by Demagoras, was restored by Queen Helen's physician. She was tragically slain by Amphialus. I, 5, 7, 8, 16; III, 12, 16.

Phalantus: bastard-brother to Queen Helen of Corinth, an admirable knight. I, 15-17; III, 11.

Phebilus: a young knight who has loved Philoclea from infancy; he fights Amphialus, who hearing him name Philoclea, spares his life. I, 17; III, 7.

Philanax: regent during Basilius' retirement. He prosecuted the King's supposed murderers. I, 4; II, 28; III, 2, 4, 8, 9, 13, 15, 16, 18, 19, 26, 27; IV and V, *passim.*

Philisides: a knightly poet who did well in the Iberian jousts. His name suggests some reference to Philip Sidney. II, 21.

Philoclea: younger daughter of Basilius and Gynecia, in love with Pyrocles. I, 3, 13, 14, 17, 19; II, 4, 5, 11, 12, 14, 16, 17, 21, 24-26, 28; III, 2, 3, 5, 6, 9, 11, 12, 14, 19-24, 26-28; III, IV and V, *passim.*

Philoxenus: in love with Helen of Corinth, foster-brother of Amphialus. Philoxenus, jealous of him, forced a quarrel on him and was killed, to the bitter grief of Amphialus. I, 11.

Phrygia, King of: a suspicious and bloody tyrant encountered by Musidorus and Pyrocles. II, 7, 8.

Phrygia, the new King of: II, 8, 23.

Plangus: eldest son of the King of Iberia, in love with Queen Erona. In youth he had an affair with a private man's wife (Andromana). His father supplanted him, married her, and disinherited him. II, 10, 12, 13, 15, 29.

Plexirtus: bastard son of the King of Paphlagonia, and half-brother of Leonatus. II, 10, 22-24, 29. See King of Paphlagonia.

Polycrates: a famous Arcadian knight, who bore an honorable love to Gynecia. I, 17.

Pontus, King of: a vicious tyrant who beheaded Musidorus' and Pyrocles' devoted servants. (See Leucippus and Nelsus). By command of Musidorus this King was slain on the tomb of the two servants. II, 9.

Pontus, the new King of: A nobleman who married the tyrant's virtuous sister, and was placed on the throne by Musidorus and Pyrocles. II, 9, 10, 22-24, 29.

Pyrocles: Prince of Macedonia, son of King Euarchus. In Arcadia he took the name Daiphantus until he fell in love with Philoclea, when he disguised himself as the Amazon Zelmane; in the war with Amphialus, sometimes called the Ill appareled Knight. I, 1, 5-10, 12-19; II, 1-4, 6-29; III, 2, 14, 19-24, 26-29; III, IV, V, *passim.*

Strephon: a shepherd devoted to the shepherdess Urania, warm friend of his rival Claius. I, 1, 2.

Sympathus: an honorable Arcadian lord, keeper of Musidorus and Pyrocles when charged with murder. IV, V.

Thessalia, King of: See Dorilaus.

Timotheus: father of Philoxenus, and foster-father of Amphialus. I, 11.

Timantus: an unscrupulous Arcadian noble, envious, revengeful, and shameless, who opposes Philanax after Basilius' apparent death. V.

Tiridates: King of Armenia. A suitor offered to Erona of Lycia, by her father. After the latter's death, he made war to compel her to accept him, and was slain by Musidorus and Pyrocles. II, 10, 13, 15.

Tressenius: a valiant warrior who fought against Anaxius in Amphialus' war. III, 15.

Tydeus and Telenor: brothers, valiant nobles brought up with Plexirtus, and loyal to him. Plexirtus, distrusting them, trapped them into a duel where each killed the other. II, 10, 22, 23.

Zelmane: See Pyrocles.

Zelmane: Plexirtus' virtuous daughter, in love with Pyrocles. Disguising herself as a young gentleman, Daiphantus, she followed him through many dangers. Sickened by hardships and by her father's treachery, she died, first revealing herself to Pyrocles. In her honor, Pyrocles, on reaching Greece, took the name Daiphantus, and when disguised as an Amazon warrior, the name Zelmane. I, 16; II, 20-23.

Zoilus: youngest brother of Anaxius. With his brothers, he took part in battles in support of Amphialus. Trying to force his love on "Zelmane," he was quickly slain. III, 15, 18-20, 25-28.

NOTES

p. 123, l. 17   Among Catholics, of course, the religious sense was being quickened by the Counter Reformation.

p. 168, l. 21   This is because when the book was read aloud, the details that some of the listeners had forgotten could often be supplied by others.

p. 171, l. 14   It is perhaps an overstatement to say that Minturno was more classical than Scaliger. Each was deeply influenced by Aristotle, but neither had the equipment to interpret him as Butcher could at the end of the Nineteenth Century.

p. 183, l. 30   That is, ought necessarily to write in verse.

p. 203, l. 30   I remind the reader that in spite of taking issue with Greenlaw at this point, my indebtedness to him is very great. Without his work, I probably could never have written this book.

p. 207, ll. 23 f.   Those of Sidney's countrymen who would have been interested in his ideas were far more than half-civilized. As Matthew Arnold observed, "in the England of Shakspeare, the poet lived in a current of ideas in the highest degree animating and nourishing to the creative power; society was, in the fullest measure, permeated by fresh thought, intelligent and alive." ["The Function of Criticism at the Present Time," *The Complete Prose Works of Matthew Arnold*, University of Michigan Press, Ann Arbor, III (1962), 262 f.]

p. 216, ll. 3 f.   These passages are overstated. As compared with great seminal minds like Plato and Aristotle, Sidney is not an original thinker. But he can hold his own with any Italian critic of the Renaissance. Like them, he draws his ideas from many sources, but puts on them the stamp of his own thinking. As Professor John W. Bate has remarked, "apart from its special importance for English literature, the *Apology for Poetry* clearly stands out as the greatest of all Renaissance critical writing."

[*Criticism: The Major Texts*, Harcourt, Brace & World, Inc., New York and Burlingame, 1952, p. 77.]

p. 225, l. 24   That is, it reigns in general, in spite of several deeply tragic episodes.

p. 226, l. 28   That is, a philosophical pagan.

p. 242, l. 20   The last two sentences now seem to me mistaken. In the devotion of Strephon and Claius to Urania, A. G. D. Wiles has recognized "an extravagant compliment to Queen Elizabeth." ["Parallel Analyses of the Two Versions of Sidney's 'Arcadia,'" *Studies in Philology*, XXXIX (April, 1962), 168.] I now believe that Urania was clearly intended also as a symbolic figure. She never has a speaking part. Her name suggests the Platonic contemplation of perfection. The devotion of Strephon and Claius to her is not like that given to the mortal shepherdess, but to an ideal. Only in her has "love-fellowship been maintained between rivals, and beautie taught the beholders chastitie." [*Arcadia, Complete Works of Sidney*, ed. Feuillerat, 1922, I, 8.] The Platonic relation of Strephon and Claius to Urania at once foreshadows, and contrasts with, the idealized but very human love of Musidorus for Pamela, and of Pyrocles for Philoclea.

p. 249, l. 20   This word has here the Latin meaning of "wonder and awe."

p. 250, l. 17   Except to the eyes of faith, the plan is of course obscured in the apparently helter-skelter events of the everyday world.

p. 302, l. 28   I do not now regard the *Arcadia* as an artistic failure. It is not an unqualified success, but it is touched with real genius.

352

BIBLIOGRAPHY OF SIDNEY STUDIES
SINCE 1935

Prepared by William L. Godschalk, Ph.D.

*All chapter references in the commentary are to
the present study,* Sidney as a Literary Craftsman.

Anderson, D. M., "The Trial of the Princes in the *Arcadia*, Book V,"
Review of English Studies, VIII (1957), 409-412. Citing Mornay
to illustrate Sidney's concept of justice, Anderson claims that "the
exemplary value of the heroes belongs to the *New Arcadia*; the
trial belongs substantially to the *Old*."

Baughan, Denver Ewing, "Sidney's *Defence of the Earl of Leicester*
and the Revised *Arcadia*," *Journal of English and Germanic Philology*, LI (1952), 34-41. Baughan tries "to show that Sidney's
Defence of the Earl of Leicester, written in 1584, provided the
occasion for, at least, the genealogical emphasis in the revision [of
the *Arcadia*], if not the whole task."

Boas, Frederick S., *Sir Philip Sidney, Representative Elizabethan: His
Life and Writings*, London, 1955. A general introductory survey.

Buxton, John, *Sir Philip Sidney and the English Renaissance*, London,
1954. Although Buxton's general theme is Sidney as literary patron, he does discuss Sidney's artistic achievement. Most valuable
(though sometimes mistaken in detail) is his account of Sidney's
contact with and influence upon literary figures throughout
Europe.

Danby, John F., *Poets on Fortune's Hill: Studies in Sidney, Shakespeare, Beaumont & Fletcher*, London, [1952], pp. 46-107. Placing
Sidney in his social milieu, Danby discusses the underlying concepts of patience and magnanimity in the *Arcadia*, their relation
to the heroes and heroines, and the relation of the *Arcadia* to
Shakespeare's later plays.

Davis, Walter R., "Actæon in Arcadia," *Studies in English Literature*,
II (1962), 95-110. This ingenious interpretation of Sidney's use of

Ovid's myth points an analogy "between the myth of Actæon and the events in Sidney's cave" (*Arcadia*, Book IV).

——, "Thematic Unity in the *New Arcadia*," *Studies in Philology*, LVII (1960), 123-143. By elaborating ideas in Myrick (Chapters IV and V) and Danby, Davis's analysis of the material added to the *New Arcadia* (1590) makes clear its relevance to the theme.

Dowlin, Cornell March, "Sidney and Other Men's Thought," *Review of English Studies*, XX (1944), 257-271. Using as a point of attack Myrick's idea that the *Defence* is an artistic re-creation of traditional material, and substituting Robortelli for Myrick's Minturno (Chapter IV), Dowlin attempts to "refurbish Sidney's reputation as a thinker," reconsidering his use of Italian criticism.

——, "Sidney's Two Definitions of Poetry," *Modern Language Quarterly*, III (1942), 573-581. Dowlin agrees with Samuel (below) that Sidney used platonic "arguments" in his *Defence*.

Duhamel, P. Albert, "Sidney's *Arcadia* and Elizabethan Rhetoric," *Studies in Philology*, XLV (1948), 134-150. Rhetorically comparing Lyly's prose with Sidney's, Duhamel shows that Lyly is decorative where Sidney is meaningful, using logic as a basis for *dispositio*. Cf. Chapters II, V, *et passim*.

Hamilton, A. C., "Sidney and Agrippa," *Review of English Studies*, VII (1956), 151-157. Hamilton believes that "Agrippa's argument in the *De vanitate* provides a framework within which Sidney attacks the vanity of the arts and sciences and defends the art of poetry."

——, "Sidney's Idea of the 'Right Poet,'" *Comparative Literature*, IX (1957), 51-59. Hamilton analyzes Sidney's neoplatonic idea of the "right poet" and emphasizes his originality stemming from a recreation and integration of major literary and philosophical traditions: Platonic, Aristotelian, and Renaissance Italian. Cf. Chapter VI.

Heltzel, Virgil B., "The Arcadian Hero," *Philological Quarterly*, XLI (1962), 173-180. Making no distinction between the *Old* and *New Arcadia*, Heltzel outlines the qualities of a composite Sidneian hero, which "derives its chief features from the ideal which Sidney himself was thought to exemplify so completely."

Juel-Jensen, Bent, "Sir Philip Sidney, 1554-1586," *Book Collector*, XI (1962), 468-479, and XII (1963), 196-201. An excellent descriptive primary bibliography of Sidney's works.

Kalstone, David, *Sidney's Poetry: Contexts and Interpretations*, Cambridge, Massachusetts, 1965. This study, which promises to be a notable contribution, is slated to appear during the summer of 1965. "The focus of this study is on Sidney's conception of Italian genres . . . and his energetic and complex re-creations and repudiations of the old conventions."

————, "Sir Philip Sidney and 'Poore *Petrarchs* Long Deceased Woes,'" *Journal of English and Germanic Philology*, LXIII (1964), 21-32. Kalstone believes *Astrophil and Stella* reveals a discontent with the Petrarchan tradition and thus looks forward to Shakespeare and Donne. Cf. Chapter VIII.

————, "The Transformation of Arcadia: Sannazaro and Sir Philip Sidney," *Comparative Literature*, XV (1963), 234-249. Kalstone examines Sannazaro's use of the Petrarchan lover and Sidney's use of Sannazaro. "Sidney's poem ['Ye goatherd gods'] must be taken . . . as a criticism of the uncomplicated happiness of Sannazaro's *Arcadia*."

Krouse, Michael F., "Plato and Sidney's *Defence of Poesie*," *Comparative Literature*, VI (1954), 138-147. As does Myrick, Krouse emphasizes the idea of eclectic harmony, but he also suggests that the *Defence* relies on Plato for fundamental concepts of poetry and, secondarily, on Aristotle for matters of external form. Cf. Chapter VI.

Malloch, Archibald E., "'Architectonic' Knowledge and Sidney's *Apologie*," *Journal of English Literary History*, XX (1953), 181-185. Beginning with Myrick's rhetorical analysis (Chapter II), Malloch suggests that the doctrine of self-knowledge underlies the arguments of Sidney's *Defence*.

Montgomery, Robert L., Jr., *Symmetry and Sense: The Poetry of Sir Philip Sidney*, Austin, Texas, 1961. In the first full-length study of Sidney's poetry Montgomery's aim is "to locate and describe the ornate and plain styles." His analysis of *Astrophil and Stella* as a conflict between passion and reason is excellent.

Muir, Kenneth, and John F. Danby, " 'Arcadia' and 'King Lear,' " *Notes and Queries*, CXCV (1950), 49-51. The fullest account of *Lear*'s debt to the *Arcadia*.

——, *Sir Philip Sidney*, Writers and Their Work, London, 1960. A brief survey.

Poirier, Michel, *Sir Philip Sidney: Le Chevalier Poète Élizabéthain*, Travaux et Mémoires de L'Université de Lille, Lille, 1948. Book I deals with Sidney's life; Book II with his works; Book III with his patronage of arts and the rise of his fame. This thorough general study has an excellent bibliography.

Ribner, Irving, "Machiavelli and Sidney's *Discourse to the Queenes Majesty*," *Italica*, XXVI (1949), 177-187. Ribner finds a similarity in spirit in Machiavelli's political writing and Sidney's.

——, "Machiavelli and Sidney: The *Arcadia* of 1590," *Studies in Philology*, XLVII (1950), 152-172. Though suggesting no direct influence, Ribner shows Sidney's political ideas are close to Machiavelli's because both men deal with the same Renaissance problems: absolutism, nationalism, and international rivalry.

——, "Sidney's 'Arcadia' and the Machiavelli Legend," *Italica*, XXVII (1950), 225-235. Ribner states that Sidney agrees with Machiavelli in basic ideas, but nevertheless uses with contempt the traditional Machiavellian tyrant-villain in the *Arcadia*.

——, "Sidney's *Arcadia* and the Structure of *King Lear*," *Studia Neophilologica*, XXIX (1952), 63-68. Ribner shows the over-all structure of *King Lear* to be similar to that of the *Arcadia*: an abdicating king leaving a power vacuum which is filled by evil.

——, "Sir Philip Sidney on Civil Insurrection," *Journal of the History of Ideas*, XIII (1952), 257-265. Discussing both the *New* and *Old Arcadia*, Ribner in contrast to Talbert (below) believes Sidney to be completely conservative in politics. Cf. Chapter VII.

Robertson, Jean, "Sir Philip Sidney and His Poetry," *Elizabethan Poetry*, eds. John Russell Brown and Bernard Harris, Stratford-

Upon-Avon Studies, 2, New York, 1960, pp. 110-129. In a general survey of Sidney's life and art, Robertson (who is now editing the "Old Arcadia") sees the "pull between the active and contemplative life" as his perennial attraction.

Rowe, Kenneth Thorpe, "The Countess of Pembroke's Editorship of the *Arcadia*," *Publications of the Modern Language Association*, LIV (1939), 122-138. Rowe argues from bibliographic and literary evidence that the revisions of Books III-V are Sidney's.

———, "Elizabethan Morality and the Folio Revisions of Sidney's *Arcadia*," *Modern Philology*, XXXVII (1939-40), 151-172. Continuing his investigation of the Arcadian revisions, Rowe questions Myrick's arguments though agreeing with his conclusion (Chapter VII) that Mary Herbert did not bowdlerize the 1593 *Arcadia*. The changes are Sidney's.

———, "Romantic Love and Parental Authority in Sydney's [sic] *Arcadia*," *University of Michigan Contributions in Modern Philology*, IV (1947), 1-58. Rowe, viewing the *Arcadia* from the Elizabethan social background, sees an unresolved conflict between the ideal of romantic love (Pyrocles, Musidorus) and the principle of parental authority embodied in Euarchus, the good ruler. Cf. Chapter VII.

Samuel, Irene, "The Influence of Plato on Sir Philip Sidney's *Defense of Poesy*," *Modern Language Quarterly*, I (1940), 383-391. Samuel argues that the *Defence* tries "to reconcile Platonism, the accuser, with the function and form of poetry, the accused," and that Plato's dialogues are "the main source of Sidney's *Defense*." Contrast Chapter VI.

Scribner, Brother Simon, *Figures of Word-Repetition in the First Book of Sir Philip Sidney's 'Arcadia*,' Washington, D. C., 1948. Brother Simon isolates and classifies the rhetorical figures involving repetition of word or words. As do Myrick and Duhamel, he shows that rhetoric is an organic part of Sidney's style.

Sidney, Philip, *The Poems of Sir Philip Sidney*, ed. William A. Ringler, Jr., Oxford, 1962. This edition contains the best introduction to and text of Sidney's poetry, along with a full textual apparatus and commentary.

———, and Mary Herbert, *The Psalms of Sir Philip Sidney and The Countess of Pembroke*, ed. J. C. A. Rathmell, Garden City, New York, 1963. This is the first edition of *The Psalms* since 1823. It has an excellent introduction by Rathmell who takes exception to Ringler's dating of the translations.

Spencer, Theodore, "The Poetry of Sir Philip Sidney," *Journal of English Literary History*, XII (1945), 251-278. Spencer's short but outstanding survey points out that English poetry needed the experiments of Sidney and his group. Cf. Chapter V on Sidneian experiment.

Stillinger, Jack, "The Biographical Problem of *Astrophel and Stella*," *Journal of English and Germanic Philology*, LIX (1960), 617-639. Stillinger argues that there are no definite autobiographical passages in the sonnets and that Myrick's interpretation (Chapter VIII) is basically correct.

Talbert, Ernest William, *The Problem of Order: Elizabethan Political Commonplaces and an Example of Shakespeare's Art*, Chapel Hill, 1962, pp. 89-117. In the most complete discussion of Sidney's political ideas to date, Talbert places Sidney in the English tradition of constitutional monarchy and reveals his complicated, realistic, and ironic use of political commonplaces. Cf. Chapter VII.

Thaler, Alwin, *Shakespeare and Sir Philip Sidney: The Influence of "The Defense of Poesy,"* Cambridge, Massachusetts, 1947. Thaler investigates the influence of Sidney's *Defence* on Shakespeare's plays.

Thompson, John, *The Founding of English Metre*, New York, 1961, pp. 139-155. Discussing Sidney's meters, Thompson contends that "in Sidney's poetry the metrical system of modern English reaches perfection for the first time."

Tillyard, Eustace M. W., *The English Epic and Its Background*, New York, 1954, pp. 294-319. Acknowledging his debt to Myrick ("I have found some of the best observations on Sidney in this book."), Tillyard suggests that Sidney was turning the *Old Arcadia* into an educational epic of two princes and that the incomplete *New Arcadia* is an "epicising fragment."

Townsend, Freda L., "Sidney and Ariosto," *Publications of the Modern Language Association*, LXI (1946), 97-108. Townsend argues against Myrick's idea that Sidney was following the critical ideals of Minturno, suggesting that Sidney was actually following the practice of Ariosto even though there are no direct parallels.

Tuve, Rosemond, *Elizabethan and Metaphysical Imagery: Renaissance Poetic and Twentieth-Century Critics*, Chicago, 1947. Tuve's study, which frequently uses Sidney for illustration, indirectly suggests certain modifications in Myrick's ideas on "ornament" (Chapter V).

Wiles, A. G. D., "Parallel Analyses of the Two Versions of Sidney's *Arcadia*," *Studies in Philology*, XXXIX (1942), 167-206. Wiles synopsizes both the *Old* and *New Arcadia*, placing the synopses in parallel columns, a method which graphically illustrates the changes made by Sidney. Cf. Chapters IV and V.

Young, Richard B., "English Petrarke: A Study of Sidney's *Astrophel and Stella*," *Three Studies in the Renaissance: Sidney, Jonson, Milton*, New Haven, 1958, pp. 1-88. After an elaborate analysis of Sidney's complex use of the Petrarchan tradition in *Astrophil and Stella*, Young concludes that the arrangement of the sequence significantly exploits the "different modes of the convention." Cf. Chapter VIII.

INDEX

(When numerous references occur under one entry, the more important are indicated by italics.)